MARIA CALLAS

MARIA CALLAS

JÜRGEN KESTING

TRANSLATED BY JOHN HUNT

QUARTET BOOKS

Photographs © by Erio Piccagliani
(Museo Teatrale alla Scala, Milan)

First published in Great Britain by Quartet Books Limited 1992
A member of the Namara Group
27/29 Goodge Street
London W1P 1FD

Originally published in German under the title *Maria Callas*

Copyright © by Claassen Verlag GmbH, Düsseldorf 1990
Translation copyright © by Quartet Books 1992

A catalogue record for this title is available from the
British Library

ISBN 0 7043 7017 4

Phototypeset by Intype, London
Printed and bound in Great Britain by
Bookcraft Ltd., Midsomer Norton, Avon

For Jutta

Contents

A Note on the Illustrations

The photographs included in this book are a visual record of just one of Maria Callas's stage performances, that of Violetta in *La Traviata* from La Scala, 28 May 1955, with Giuseppe di Stefano and Ettore Bastianini. Given the overwhelming number of Callas photographs, the publishers felt that this incomparable record of a legendary production would convey more of her genius than a random and limited selection.

Foreword

'What constitutes the true beauty, true quality and real *raison d'être* of singing is the
combination, mixing and indissoluble unity
of sound and thought. However beautiful
the sound may be, it is nothing if it does not
have something to express. To admit that
one is ravished or transported by the purely
physical or material beauty of a voice is to
be guilty of a weakness, a morbid and inert
state of mind and even inferiority. To find
pleasure in a singer who makes intelligent
utterances but whose voice sounds insignificant or clumsy is proof that one is not
really musical . . . *melody* represents the
supernatural element in singing, which aug-
ments the word – or words – with intensity,
power, refinement, poetry, charm and individuality. It does this in such a way as to
defy analysis and yet allows us to sense its
magic without being able to explain it. On
the other hand it is the words, filled with
feeling and thought, which give melody its
meaning . . .'

Reynaldo Hahn, *Du chant*

Could it be that it is imperfect beauty which turns out to be the most consummate? A beauty that does not attack, but slowly and over a long period infiltrates the senses, that is always with us and fills our hearts with pain – the pain of memory. In the years of my *éducation sentimentale* through the world of opera it was the voice of Renata Tebaldi which first transported me to heaven. The voice of Callas, enthused over by a school friend whom I considered confused and a morbid outsider, seemed to me unsteady, shrill, even ugly – and definitely artificial.

Then came the evening when I was twiddling the knobs of my medium-wave radio and came upon a broadcast of a Callas performance. She was singing *Lucia di Lammermoor* in Berlin and for the first time I sensed a voice both as physical contact and idea: something never to be forgotten. I perceived how the colour of beauty imposes itself on the darkness of pain, as Shelley put it; from that moment this voice was never to leave me. But it took years for me to realise that it was not the voice alone, but much more, it was the singer's ability to give expression to life and emotional intensity; to realise that more important than admiration for *how* she sang was the discernment of *why* she sang: from passion.

The most beautiful words I read about Maria Callas while working on this book were written by Paul Campion, on 16 September 1977, the day of her death: 'On this sad evening, when so many eminent musicians have paid tribute to Callas, I feel the need as a simple lover of opera to write to you and explain my feelings about her and her art [. . .] I never had the luck to hear her in the theatre and yet my admiration has grown continuously. This evening, hearing her sing *La Sonnambula*, I realise more and more what she was expressing [. . .] more than anyone in my lifetime she has been the one who gave opera new meaning and inner sense.'

That is the voice of a seeking listener. Ernst Bloch, in his philosophical fragments on music, asks what it is that he seeks when he listens? He would like to be 'enriched and improved by the content', but he will not achieve that by being carried along, relaxed and comfortable, without striving for something more than enjoyment alone. 'If we do not make the journey, the singing will cease.'

In those words lies perhaps the essence of what has been written on Maria Callas in the past three decades. There are hundreds, indeed many hundreds of articles and certainly more than twenty books – most of which merely paraphrase the *chronique scandaleuse* of this famous woman, at once magnificent, of great simplicity, yet doomed, pitiable. The very attempt to find 'the woman behind the legend' or 'the art behind the legend' has perpetuated that legend.

Each year it becomes more difficult to establish new biographical data. The newspapers recall with more exactitude events that were never actually experienced, repeat inaccurate details from the notebooks of indiscreet journalists. The passing of time does give us the chance to assemble, sort and interpret the facts and fictions. But ultimately the justification for new writing on the great Greek singer cannot be given here; the book must speak for itself.

1

Maria and Megaera
or
Callas as Symbolic Figure

'If one is examining an important person,
one must also have the courage to see everything, to look at everything or at least to
point everything out'

Sainte-Beuve

'Quanto? . . . Il prezzo!'
Tosca, Act 2

Whoever heard her needs only to read these three words and he will hear her again. Not just hear, but see her again. Before our very eyes, trembling, desperate and full of hatred, asking the police chief Scarpia the price of her lover's life. Listening more closely one perceives that she is already aware of the answer in putting the question. Scarpia wants her; he wants that which many men call love: her degradation.

Only 'Quanto?' is sung as a question. 'Il prezzo' is a statement, perhaps even a challenge, and that is how it is in Sardou's text. Only after 'quanto' is there a question mark. After 'il prezzo' there is an exclamation mark. She does not sing it. She speaks it. She transforms a dramatic situation, a torrent of feelings, of anguish, hatred, rage and determination, into gesture. It is no conventional gesture, nor the mechanical depiction from naturalistic or realistic theatre, but a highly artificial one: she forms in sound a sculpture in which the inner nature of human gesture is concentrated.

The secret of this singing is that it is suffered and is vulnerable. It sings of human emotions. The ability to express these emotions is the fulfilment of art. What we experience here is singing of purest pathos, in which a force gives vent to itself, a force in turn entreating, supplicating, cursing, frantic and loving. It is the force of primeval sound. The voice vibrates not only with sadness, melancholy, desperation and aggression, feelings which make it the expressive vehicle of a drama; a drama also unfolds in the voice itself, because a restless, tortured and confused spirit is expressing and purifying itself in sound. And whoever hears this sound is transported to heaven by its power, and thence into a purgatory of conflicting emotions.

Reactions to Maria Callas – to the singer as well as the person – were always different, quite different, from reactions to Marcella Sembrich, Nellie Melba, Rosa Ponselle, Claudia Muzio, Zinka Milanov, Renata Tebaldi and other divas of this century. As a

Greek who was born in New York, Callas did not have the influence on her times which the legendary European prima donnas of the Romantic period had on theirs. And yet like Maria Malibran, Pauline Viardot and above all Giuditta Pasta, the first interpreter of Bellini's Norma, Maria Callas has formed with her dramatic art the way in which we perceive opera of the nineteenth century. For a long time viewed as an artistic anachronism, she restored to opera its original purpose: that is to sing of a beauty fated to be unhappy. She brought to expression the thought that man's most beautiful creations are, in the words of André Gide, 'irrevocably sad' or, in those of Alfred de Musset, 'The most despairing songs are the most beautiful.' If Callas had been merely a technically brilliant singer, endowed with the voice of an angel – 'merely' is perhaps not the right word here – she would take her place in the annals of opera, and only in those of opera, as an interesting and provocative interpreter. As it is she has also aroused imagination, curiosity, love of sensation and affection as well as the hatred of those who did not want their experience of opera influenced, let alone changed. In a deeper sense she has become an artistic figure of quite a different kind, one over which passions did, and continue to, ignite – and she has had no eulogist the like of Heinrich Heine, de Musset or Stendhal.

Her very first appearances in Italy after the war caused irritation and even stirred up violent controversy. Once she had become *assoluta* of Milan's Teatro alla Scala she was admired by critics who understood her technical and historical background, for example Eugenio Gara, Rudolfo Celletti, Fedele d'Amico, Harold Rosenthal, Desmond Shawe-Taylor and Andrew Porter; readers of *Les Temps Modernes*, the periodical edited by Jean-Paul Sartre, could study a thorough and historically comprehensive essay by the composer and Schoenberg pupil René Leibowitz, in which her art and technique were traced to singing *and* composing in the Romantic era. However, reactions from the public and most newspaper critics remained indifferent or opposed, eventually erupting in paroxysms of hatred at an involuntarily isolated figure, whose image was taken up by the tabloids and then distorted into that caricature of the temperamental prima donna, the 'tigress'.

It was only after her retirement from the opera stage on 5 July 1965 – after a performance of Puccini's *Tosca* at the Royal Opera House, Covent Garden in London – and particularly after her death on 16 September 1977, that she became transfigured as the saint of Italian opera; it almost seems as if posterity has wanted to draw a veil over what happened in the lifetime of an artist who, in the words of the writer Ingeborg Bachmann, was an instrument for the world 'to eavesdrop on centuries past; she was the last fairytale'.

A fairytale? Yes, perhaps, but a bitter one, gruesome and strangely archaic: the second act of Offenbach's *Les Contes d'Hoffmann*, known as the Antonia act, is a demonic fantasy about singing, singing which carries the singer to her death. The career of Maria Callas was nothing less than a triumphal procession, but it was also a sacrificial path, like that described in the words of the great dancer Anna Pavlova, where great artists know everything about love but must forget what they know. But that is only the private aspect of a career subject to conditions that might have broken sterner characters – what can be detected as a proud but secretly bitter leitmotif in the singer's remarks about her struggles with impresarios, critics, gossip-mongers and a public eager for sensation, was her pride in triumphs which she had won under duress. Victories like those are never forgiven.

Maria Callas, as magnificent and suffering as the figures she impersonated so brilliantly – Norma, Medea, Anna Bolena, Lucia, Elvira, Amelia, Violetta, Abigaille, Lady Macbeth, Tosca – cannot be comprehended only as a singer or through the analysis of 'that enormous ugly voice', as it was once described by her mentor Tullio Serafin. She was a victim, like the figures she portrayed, and her triumphant suffering became translated over the years into myth. Roland Barthes states that behind the construction of a myth lies 'stolen history'. With the proliferation of legends about Maria Callas, the facts have been obscured. By this I do not mean clumsy attempts in journalistic biographies to deal with private concerns, to define and comprehend an artistic will. The most factual of such life stories, *Maria Callas – the Woman Behind the Legend* by Arianna Stassinopoulos, suffers from its writer's inability to relate to the artistic phenomenon, which should be of prime interest to a biographer of Callas. She allows herself to speculate about the consequences of fame in a society for which opera has long since become a mere diversion. Even if Maria Callas did make some works relevant to the present by dint of her personal aura, this has come to take second place to that 'Callas myth' through which the woman artist is transformed into a strange and remote figurine, an embodiment of long-established fantasies about the feminine ideal. In the most recent biography, by an intimate friend of her later years, Nadia Stancioff, the woman behind the artist becomes helpless, superficial, superstitious, dependent, narrow-minded and amiable, a woman who, once her career was over, lost touch with the world and submitted lamb-like to the ambition and whims of the men in her life.

Even Ingeborg Bachmann, who first experienced Maria Callas at La Scala in 1956 under Carlo Maria Giulini, has not been entirely able to penetrate this projection of masculine desires, this figure who is at once Maria Magdalene and Megaera. 'I have often wondered,' she writes,

> how those who heard Maria Callas never went beyond hearing in her a voice which was both extraordinary and subject to danger. For it was not just the question of the voice, certainly not in a period when so many exceptional voices were to be heard. Maria Callas is not a vocal wonder, she is far more than that – she alone has ever conquered the operatic stage. A creature whom the press are incompetent to judge, so evident are each of her movements, her breathing, her tears, her joy, her precision, her pleasure in making art: she portrays tragedy in a way that is far removed from everyday experience. Not only her coloratura – and it is overwhelming – but also her arias or just her partnership are exceptional, even simply her breathing and articulation. M[aria] C[allas] has such a way of uttering a word that nobody who is not deaf or who for reasons of jaded taste or snobbery has gone in search of fresh sensation [. . .]

Here Bachmann's paean of praise suddenly breaks off, then continues in the same vein:

[. . .] with her one can never forget that there is I and You, that there is pain and joy, she is great in hatred, in love, in tenderness and in brutality, in every expression; and if she misses an expression, which doubtless can be proved on occasion, she is still wise, never insignificant. She can miss an expression because she knows what expression really means. She is ten times bigger or more, in every gesture, in every cry, in every movement, she [reminds] one of Duse : *ecco un artista*. She did not sing roles, ever, but lived them on the razor's edge, she gave new life to a recitative which seemed stale, and more than new life, she was so actual that all those who composed the roles she sang, from Verdi to Bellini, from Rossini to Cherubini, would have recognised in her not only their fulfilment but much more. *Ecco un artista*, she is the only person who was justified in treading the boards in those decades, she made [the audience] shiver, suffer and tremble, she was always art, yes art, and always a human being, always the most pitiable, most haunted Traviata. She was [. . .] the nightingale of these years, of this century, and she was the tears which I shed. I do not need to be ashamed of them. Many foolish tears are shed, but the tears shed for Callas – they were not foolish. She was the last fairytale, the last reality in which a listener could participate. It is both very difficult and very easy to recognise greatness. Callas – when did she live, when will she die? – is great, is a human being, is unfamiliar in a world of mediocrity and 'perfection'.[1]

Ma: quanto? Il prezzo? What must it have cost her, always to be art and to be the most haunted? What Bachmann describes in her state of transport is above all her own deep emotion, her own surprise – but she scarcely describes the role of Callas in reality, in the bustle of musical life in the 1950s. Bachmann has Callas appear as a tragic heroine, who sings 'Vissi d'arte' not as social being or feminine myth, but as a woman with a 'stolen history'.

Callas's image became that of a woman as 'outsider': she was vamp and *femme fatale* on the one hand and idealised woman on the other. At the height of her career, from the early to mid-fifties, she was admired as the portrayer of woman as suffering, vengeful, abused, consumed by passion. She was the singer who, as Verdi said of Gemma Bellincioni, 'breathed new life into an old sinner' (his Traviata); she also gave new life to the nineteenth-century cult of the Virgin.

The opera heroine who was the embodiment of fantasies of power, conquest and subjugation is examined with clarity by Cathérine Clément in *Opera, or the Undoing of Women*. From a feminist viewpoint she explores such fantasies, although she does not acknowledge the desire of man for the suffering beauty, the persecuted innocent woman, or for the Medusa figure marked by pain, corruption and death.

Callas brought these figures to life through her extraordinary expressive ability and superb technique. Thanks to thorough training and an eminent musicality she had command of the entire grammar of Romantic bel canto singing, this being no less than a compendium of the operas composed between 1790 and 1850; expressively, she knew how to illustrate that the feelings and states of mind depicted in nineteenth-century music are relevant and that there may even be a close link between the epoch in which she sang and the epoch from which she sang.

The intensity of her portrayals was, however, projected onto the other Callas, the public figure who hit the headlines as tigress, as *diva furiosa*. For a long time her name was associated with scandal, and whatever she did became fresh material. After the vamp, as conceived by Hollywood, and the wicked temptress had long been reduced to a cheap and domestically acceptable image, the prima donna as imagined by the bourgeois world, and as Maria Callas embodied or was forced to embody her, was born again.

Until the mid–1950s, Maria Callas was at the centre of the artistic world; she was simply the most celebrated singer of her time and in no way the victim of published opinion's sinister imaginings. Certainly she had the reputation of being a woman of violent temperament, ruthless ambition and consequent hardness; she was not and is still not depicted as kind by those who supported, admired, respected and loved her. But when did genius go hand in hand with kindness, strong character with a conciliatory nature, or highest discernment in artistic matters with friendliness? Her image, mistaken by the public for her nature, was moreover moulded by their amazement and shock at the intensity, energy and expressive fury of her interpretations; by the envy of colleagues who declared her a monster so that they themselves would not be judged by the standards she set herself; and ultimately by the power of pictures, of which the most famous and notorious is the photograph from a Chicago newspaper showing Callas as a raging fury, abusing two officials through her grotesque, stage made-up lips. Who now remembers that those two men had burst into her dressing room immediately after a performance of *Madama Butterfly*, to hand her a financial claim from an agent who had done nothing for her?

At the time that snapshot appealed only to the public, probably it was a cause for some amusement. It demonstrated the popular belief that prima donnas are crazy. Yet it was to prove a fatal picture, a wound from which the singer slowly bled to death; for it was this quite arbitrary picture, capturing the justifiable anger of an arbitrary moment, that became her terrible public image: a permanent illustration of that infamous and damaging *chronique scandaleuse*, to which her cancellation in the middle of a performance of Norma in Rome in 1958 belonged as much as her *liaison fatale* with the Greek sybarite Aristotle Onassis. When she entered the '*beau monde*' the demon of public opinion created a new Maria Callas. The prima donna *assoluta* stepped down to become the most famous woman in the world, and this at a time when she could no longer justify her fame through the immense talent which ten years before had been the justification for that fame – now ruinous fame – for the public could not tolerate a woman whose caricature they had drawn or helped to create.

Maria Callas had very early recognised and suffered from the destructive aspect of fame. However she did not want to adapt to social norms, and did not attempt to be nice – can there be a more destructive adjective than 'nice'? She was mistrustful of precisely those who praised her, especially after performances that she herself considered less successful. Above all she never conformed to the Hollywood code of behaviour, in accordance with whose rules every 'star' had to play a role whose scenario had been composed for public opinion.

Susan Sontag observes in her essay 'Notes on Camp' that there have been many histories of ideas and societies but very few of emotions and sensibilities. In the literature on Callas there is no discussion of the type of woman who was acceptable artistically, aesthetically and morally in the 1950s or as to what behaviour was expected of her in individual countries. In the Federal Republic of Germany figures like Brigitte Bardot, Michèle Morgan, Marilyn Monroe, Jane Russell and Anita Ekberg were prime portrayers, to use a film title, of *Forbidden Fruit*. Favourite German stars were Maria Schell, Ruth Leuwerik and other women of the *ingénue* type. Romy Schneider had to go to France in order to escape her ambiguous little-girl image and underwent years of avoiding scandal-mongers. Callas began to experience the consequences of her refusal to conform in 1958, after walking out of *Norma* in Rome. Within a few years she found herself an outcast from the world of opera; she was moreover blacklisted by the media. The will to destroy that was mercilessly directed at Callas was never turned to Liz Taylor, Brigitte Bardot, Jacqueline Kennedy or Monroe. Callas was a 'tigress': the metaphor is that of the hunt of the woman as a beautiful wild animal.

Not only the tabloid press conducted this smear campaign but also magazines which were rated as serious and which pretended to be informed. The prima donna myth thereby gained credibility with the result that its real figure could no longer escape from the prison of that picture. Two front-page features were symptomatic of this, one published in the New York periodical *Time* in the autumn of 1956 and the other in the Hamburg *Der Spiegel* in February 1957. In both reports Maria Callas is celebrated as prima donna incarnate and as musical wonder of the world, but at the same time her character is poisoned by innuendo. The American magazine quoted the Greek's derogatory remarks about her Italian rival Renata Tebaldi and, far more dangerous, the bitter utterances about her own mother which she was supposed to have made to the effect that if her mother could not afford to keep herself, then she should jump out of the window: an unbearable violation of tabu for American matriarchal society. *Der Spiegel* itemised the 'numerous authenticated and non-authenticated scandals' making up the image of Callas as *monstre sacré*. Absurd errors of fact were made, like the report of the baritone Enzo Sordello being sacked after Callas's New York Met début because he held on to a high C longer than the diva: neither in *Lucia di Lammermoor* nor in any other opera do baritones sing high C – the baritone range goes up to A flat, or at the highest to A. Many articles written to satisfy the public need to see Callas as mad appeared in the guise of serious criticism.

For example, *Der Spiegel* reported that the singer had refrained from prima donna behaviour towards a journalist from *Time*, who was writing a front-cover story about her, and that she had asked him, among other things, to bring to her in Milan a miniature poodle from Rome. Anxious about his interview, the *Time* representative – a 1952 Pulitzer prizewinner – had carried out this unusual errand but in the process the animal, not yet quite housetrained, had, as revealed gloatingly by the Italian periodical *Oggi*, messed up his suit so that he had to take it to the drycleaners. Only after this was he in a state to meet Signora Meneghini Callas for a talk in her luxurious Milan palazetto in the Via Buonarotti.

The *Time* feature brought Callas her greatest publicity success to date, for the expensive interview was also obtained by *Life* magazine, with its circulation of millions. This in turn led to *Oggi* publishing the first so-called Callas autobiography, in instalments.

So much glaring publicity irritated even Callas, who was reckoned to have strong nerves. Before her first appearance at the Met she was overcome with a fit of weeping. Apparently 'star grandmother' Marlene Dietrich had sought to comfort her by bringing her chicken broth prepared with her own hands. Husband 'Titta' hurriedly brought in a huge casket of jewellery so that his wife could comfort herself by 'suffering in gold and diamonds'. Meneghini's household remedy was apparently completely successful. The pampered Met audience raved and called for twenty-eight curtain calls.

In his essay 'The Language of *Der Spiegel*'[2] Hans Magnus Enzensberger discusses the workings of innuendo: the whispered suggestions and defamatory rhetoric which indissolubly mix facts and supposition. Typical of the insinuation from which she suffered is this story from *Oggi*. Such reports were the vehicle for nonsensical ideas about a singer's needs before important performances. In any case Dietrich did not prepare mere chicken broth to cure a fit of weeping. The 'star grandmother' made a consommé from eight pounds of beef for an exhausted singer who had worked to her limits at rehearsals. As for the jewels in which she was supposed to have 'suffered', they had come from the jeweller Harry Winston, lent to Callas for the première party at the Ambassador Hotel. The so-called 'autobiography' in *Oggi* turns out to be merely recollections which were taken down and elaborated by Anita Pensotti for the Italian periodical.

It is evident that these recollections were written by a journalist, as in tone and style they bear no resemblance to Callas interviews which were recorded. Yet the piece appeared with her agreement and it fits the picture the singer wanted to paint of herself at that time. Also noteworthy is the fact that in *Time* and *Der Spiegel* Maria Callas is referred to as the diva 'who is hated by her colleagues more than any other living singer'. Yet in contrast with that is the statement by the baritone George London – albeit only published later:

> When I heard upon my arrival in New York, early in the fall, that I was to sing Scarpia to Callas's Tosca, I must admit that I had a few forebodings. So much had been printed about the 'stormy' star that I was prepared for almost anything [. . .] The first rehearsal assured me. Here was a trouper, a fanatical worker and a stickler for detail [. . .] Callas and I sang a scene from the second act of *Tosca* on the first Met broadcast of the *Ed Sullivan Show*. Again she was a most co-operative colleague [. . .] Yet, the day after the broadcast many papers reported that Callas and I had had a tiff during our rehearsal. I tried to tell my friends tht this was just not so, but I finally gave up. I realised that Callas, the prima donna reincarnate, fires not only the imagination of her audiences, but also of the press. They want her to be 'tempestuous' and 'fiery' and that is the way it is going to be [. . .]³

It was exactly this kind of reportage on events in Callas's life that were not easily verifiable, if at all, suggestive remarks made by colleagues and vague aesthetic judgements, that caused a 'type' to replace the real person, making Callas a target for projections and fantasies. At the beginning of the 1960s the picture began to change, increasingly so after her farewell to the stage and completely after her death. The Megaera gradually changed into Madonna and Martyr, the Singer into an Idea and finally, a Saint of Art. Ten years after her death the critic Rupert Christiansen wrote in the English magazine *Opera* that it was impossible simply to hear Maria Callas. Any perspective on her achievement had been lost and even failures acknowledged by her admirers had been assimilated into her myth.

Even in this posthumous transfiguration of the singer lies a specific mode of representing the feminine, in which Cathérine Clément detects a 'longing to desecrate the dead' – that degradation, exploitation, violation and consuming of the woman which is the theme of almost all the operas which Maria Callas sang. She often saw herself as playing this sacrificial role; it was just that such utterances did not fit the picture people had painted of her. Who *was* interested in the real Callas? She became a figure in a 'panopticon of femininity' (Silvia Bovenschein): biographers like Arianna Stassinopoulos and Nadia Stancioff attach as much importance to the slimming cure, the Onassis relationship, the walks with her poodle, the hours spent in front of the television and the fraught relationship with her family as to received aesthetic judgements of her voice and to evaluations of Callas for the history of opera and its interpretation. Once again we experience how she suffers, mourns and dies – both a stage death and her real one. Once again we experience and entertain ourselves with her agonies.

2
The One and Only

'A hand in repose can be more immediate
than a countenance. And the voice can be a
direct physical contact'

Joseph Roth

'The one and only' is the heading for the last chapter of a collection
of conversations which Lanfranco Rasponi conducted with *The
Last Prima Donnas*.[1] An informative and appropriate title, for in
the world of music memory plays a very special role. The past,
and figures from the past, are never dead. They have not really
passed away, a fact which applies to nobody more than the one
and only. To Maria Callas. Naturally, Maria Callas.

However, the Italian-American journalist was never able to
interview the singer at length. At their short meeting, it seemed to
him that she revealed herself as a 'rather ignorant and uninformed
woman' who, if she had been truly intelligent, would have
remained at her peak for a much longer period. Rasponi concluded
that she was purely a creature of instinct. Whatever she had
achieved was not the result of careful thought or profound study
but of her inborn ability to identify with the character she was
portraying.

Such a statement reveals an ignorance on the part of the writer
far greater than that which he was attributing to Maria Callas.
The strength of an assumption and the energy of a portrayal in
no way depends, as Rasponi suggests, on whether the performer
knows how many wives Henry VIII had or from which royal
house Mary Stuart came. Rasponi describes with praise how Beverly Sills studied a small library of historical material before starting to portray the Tudor queens of Donizetti's operas, which
indeed says much for that singer's industry. But can one hear it
in her performances? Decisive for singing and portraying is the
shaping of expressive character and of figures in sound, or to
quote Wagner, the transformation of the essence of human gesture
into sound. It is open to question whether this really has anything
to do with identification. The great artist thinks with his heart

and feels with his mind, and all too often it is approaching a role with feeling that makes for a bad actor and an even worse singer. Singing is not a realistic art but a stylised one; not a direct expression of love and suffering, joy and sadness, but the forming of those things into sound and mime. Our experience of a singer's expression as something immediate has to do with our feelings and the power that singing exercises on our souls.

However, the strength of our feelings which can be triggered off by singing tends to blur our judgement of the singing itself,[2] and Maria Callas is the one and only precisely because she has aroused more violent controversy and fanaticism than any other singer in living memory. Whenever a new recording appeared of *Norma, Tosca,* or *Medea,* the interpreters of the title roles – whether Montserrat Caballé, Beverly Sills, Joan Sutherland, Leontyne Price or Sylvia Sass – were measured against the great Greek singer.

Why great? According to Nietzsche, greatness means 'giving direction'.

Can this definition be applied to an interpreter, to a re-creative artist? When Alfred Einstein wrote his essay 'Greatness in Music' four decades ago, just after Callas's début in Italy, he did not deal with interpreters but with composers. Nor did he investigate how the rediscovery of forgotten music, so much a feature of the modern music business, often depends on the personality of great interpreters; furthermore, he did not look at how music that seems dead can be revived if only the right performers can be found.

I am not referring to those figures who are attributed, in a manner as careless as it is mechanical, with so-called charisma. It is an open question whether the recognition of the world is awarded to the truly great or to those who have been made great. In a society which is culturally at a standstill and does all it can to renounce the *avant-garde,* the role of the genius is attributed, in the ironic assertion of Hans Magnus Enzensberger, to the star. The star, in order to meet the demands of his admirers, must be attributed with genius, especially if he or she is to play the role of cultural high priest. Take as an example the iconography of Herbert von Karajan, deep in meditation, eyes closed. He has to be experienced by his disciples as close to them, even if the proximity is technically engineered. 'In this connection, observing [the star] is curiously ambivalent,' writes Dwight McDonald in his essay 'Masscult and Midcult': 'the masses set great store by personal genius, or the charisma of the re-creative artist; but at the same time they want to participate in it. They have to play a game – their game, a game which distorts the artist's personality in order to please them.' With this 'descent into fame', as Brecht described it in the case of Helene Weigel, there begins a double life for the artist. In public he has to play for his fans a role which is no more than the sum total of the projections of his supporters. If he departs from that role only once, then he is undone. There are few artists in the realm of so-called serious music who have suffered more bitterly than Maria Callas from the consequences of that 'descent into fame'.

In the work of every artist lies the attempt to create himself, to form a new person out of two elements: on the one hand his inheritance and on the other the power of his imagination with which he subtly changes and transforms that inheritance. Each attempt takes as its starting point a new partnership with which the artist wants to enter into a dialogue. The drama in an artist's life sets in at the moment when his imagination and ideals do not conform with, or when they go further than, those of the public. An artist cannot allow the public to be satisfied with things which it has previously accepted. Nor can he be satisfied with being accepted as the image which the public has already formed of him.

Public recognition of the interpreter as a star – or more precisely, blind worship – is the start of his being misunderstood as a musician. The title usurps the action or talent that is the origin of fame, so that eventually the fame is mistaken for the achievement. Theodor W. Adorno analysed this change in a critical essay on Arturo Toscanini, 'The Mastery of the Maestro'. He describes how the power of the star principle derives from the distinction between the star and the popular music which he is playing (or singing). 'The new Toscanini recording,' one reads in a review of his 1939 recording of Beethoven's C minor Symphony, 'unfolds all the blaze of this masterwork. This is no interpretation,

this is the symphony itself.' Such crass manipulation of criticism
into advertising is standard practice in the making of a star. The
result is that an artist can have a double influence: he can operate
both inwards and outwards, can give music new life and at the
same time endanger it, possibly even destroy it.

Adorno absolutely recognised the historical context of criticism
of Toscanini. He viewed him as one of the first representatives
of that new objectivity opposing the distortions of 'Romantic
subjectivity'; he drew a parallel with the structural performances
of music which Arnold Schoenberg was aiming at; and ultimately
saw in his musical objectivity the basis for Toscanini's 'intransi-
gence in the face of fascism'.

What the philosopher did find problematical with Toscanini
was that the idea of perfection became more important than the
question of musical meaning, and he thought it disastrous that
Toscanini's perfection had become rigid ideology. He had learned
to master the orchestral machine at the price of becoming more
like a machine himself. This musical ideal largely moulded by
Toscanini, and characterised by Adorno as 'streamlining', has its
effect on the works themselves, standardising them – this became
all the more true when other conductors who subscribed to Toscanini's outlook began to imitate him. Here again the historical
effect works both inwards and outwards. In the light of this, it
is strange that musicology deals almost exclusively with history
and interpretation. Adorno agrees that 'it has little to do with the
content of the music that Mr X plays the Beethoven G major
concerto better than Mr Y, or that the voice of a particular tenor
is strained,' but the history of interpretation has nothing to do
with musical skill – which may be of concern to the critics – but
rather with the importance of the interpreter for the musical end-
product. This is all the more true since the ideal listener, who is
able to follow the musical structure at every moment and even
hear the music through reading a score, scarcely exists any more.

Whereas the evaluation of musical greatness – musical in Einstein's sense of compositional – has not changed in the course of
an entire century, the judging of interpreters depends on circumstances at the time, or on intellectual currents and even on fashion.
As for Toscanini and Callas, they are considered to be the two

most important interpreters of Italian opera in the twentieth century.

When Toscanini came to the Metropolitan Opera in 1908, William James Henderson wrote that his arrival marked the start of 'a new era in the history of opera'. Fifty years later the director Franco Zeffirelli would speak of the eras BC and AC – 'before Callas' and 'after Callas'.

'È strano' is Violetta's call in *La Traviata*. At the start of the 1950s Maria Callas was to have sung under Toscanini the Lady in Verdi's *Macbeth*. There were simple practical reasons why she never did so. Yet at another level it was no accident that Callas did not sing under Toscanini. As has often been said without full realisation of its importance, the conductor had broken the primacy of the singer and made performance of central importance. There was a price to pay for this: the loss of the singer's spontaneity, that 'compositional originality' which was praised, for example, in a singer like Maria Malibran.

Not that Maria Callas had revived what Verdi described as the 'curse of the prima donna rondo' – that is, self-satisfied bravura – but rather she had restored to singing its old significance without assuming the habitual wilfulness of narcissistic prima donnas. As far as her artistic integrity and musicality were concerned, there burned within her that *fuoco sacro* which had also burned in Toscanini. To put it simply but paradoxically Maria Callas was a singer who sang in Toscanini's spirit but against him. Her service to tradition lay not in bending to (Toscanini's) rules, but in making something new. Unlike Geraldine Farrar, who had to hear Toscanini say about her that 'the only stars are in heaven', Callas was not a prima donna who bestrode the stage with vanity, but a singer dedicated to music. She was – perhaps – the ideal Toscanini singer and yet could not be that.

Could she ever have been the right singer for Toscanini? The question begs the question of interpretational history. Toscanini was not in the least interested in the singers' operas which Maria Callas had revived. He was dedicated to the ideas of Richard Wagner and the late works of Verdi and he advocated new works by contemporary composers, although he could not hide certain reservations (especially as far as Puccini was concerned).

In contrast to the works of the composers just mentioned, those of Handel and even Mozart, of Rossini and the Italian romantics are perfect for singers of both technical and virtuoso ability. By the end of the 1940s people seemed to have forgotten that formal language in the old operas was not just decoration but in itself a means of expression, and that it had inevitably led to quite individual vocal expressiveness. When at the end of the 1940s and at the start of the 1950s Maria Callas sang works like *Armida, Medea, Norma, I Puritani, La Sonnambula*, and *Anna Bolena*, these operas radiated an extraordinary power.

They gave the singer not just the opportunity to find the new in the old; they offered her the chance to show that the relationship between singer and composer in the eighteenth and early nineteenth centuries was quite different from that between, for example, Wagner and Wilhelmine Schröder-Devrient. Formerly the singer served not only as muse or as helper in fulfilling the composer's intention – he or she was shaping and helping with the composition. Handel and Francesca Cuzzoni, Hasse and Faustina Bordoni, Rossini and the castrato Velluti, the tenors of the family of the Davids and Isabella Colbran, Mozart and Lucrezia Agujari, Nancy Storace, Aloysia Weber and Ludwig Fischer, Bellini and Donizetti and Giuditta Pasta, Maria Malibran, Pauline Viardot, Giulia Grisi, Giovanni Battista Rubini and Luigi Lablache all worked together in the compositional sense. Mozart liked to tailor his arias to his singer; from Rossini operas in which his wife Isabella Colbran sang, one can tell precisely what state her voice was in at the time, particularly her top range. Domenico Donzelli wrote to the composer of *Norma* before the first performance, giving the exact range of his voice. Wagner even had to admit that everything he knew about the art of mime he owed to the incomparable Schröder-Devrient. What he meant was portrayal by means of vocal expression. In his theoretical writings Wagner even speaks of 'taking away the power of the eye' when the 'very essence of human gesture' can be evoked in sound.

For the past fifty years we have been in a period of post-history as far as opera is concerned, and as little is being produced that might have a universal appeal, singers are not being stretched – apart from those few who inspire composers to write for them.

This is the case with Dietrich Fischer-Dieskau and Aribert Rei-
mann, and was the case for the English singers around Benjamin
Britten: Sylvia Fisher, April Cantelo, Janet Baker, Peter Pears,
Peter Glossop, John Noble, Owen Brannigan and others. But
those who are in the mainstream of the opera business have little
new to offer.

If greatness consists of giving direction, then who has been
great in recent decades? Great in the sense of historical influence?
Today's singers see a vast repertoire before them which cannot
be ignored nor even less mastered. A solution is to concentrate
on a few well-known roles that are generally in favour. This is
what has been done by established artists like Zinka Milanov,
Renata Tebaldi, Birgit Nilsson, Mario del Monaco, Giuseppe di
Stefano, Luciano Pavarotti, Leonard Warren and Boris Christoff
– to name only a few. Criticism of such a course is understandable
but not relevant for it takes no account of the musical demands
on a singer's career in the modern set-up which the singer cannot
challenge. Others give an impression of diversity by singing roles
in the recording studio which they do not take on stage – to
which one must add they 'could' not sing on stage. Listening to
these hastily assembled recordings one can almost hear the sound
of the knife which Miss Caballé or Mr Domingo cut the pages
of their brand-new scores. Others view themselves as representatives of music and sing everything they can cope with, using
the gramophone record as a kind of *musée imaginaire*: Elisabeth
Schwarzkopf, Janet Baker, Nicolai Gedda, Dietrich Fischer-Dieskau, José van Dam.

What is forbidden all singers is a free handling of the text, a
creative artist's spontaneity. The modern singer must sing precisely what is permitted by the law of fidelity to the work: the
printed text. It has long been recognised that this not only imp-
overishes expression in vocal music of the late seventeenth, eighteenth and early nineteenth centuries but is the exact opposite of
fidelity to the work. Yet this truth is ignored by those very
conductors who rule operatic life: Claudio Abbado, Riccardo
Muti or James Levine, whose music-making, to quote Andrew
Porter, sees no further than the bar lines, and prevents them, say
in the operas of Verdi, from achieving the flow and dramatic

tension of Toscanini. If musical reasons are to be found for the
current crisis of singing, they lie in that Procrustean bed of textual
fidelity which cripples spontaneity. It is striking and curious that
the crisis most severely affects the performance of operas by
Wagner, Verdi, Puccini and Strauss, in which large and generous
voices are called for. The works of these composers are now
scarcely performable to the highest standard.

There seems to be a contradiction here, for the vocal parts of
these composers are written out in detail. Yet even in Wagner
there are many decorations. Brünnhilde has to sing trills at the
beginning of the second act of *Die Walküre* and in *Die Meistersinger*
much is made of the rules of virtuoso singing: David's 'Sing-
schule' for Stolzing is like a lesson. The part of Kothner contains
tricky coloraturas. A command of the language of vocal forms
enables the singer who performs Wagner and Verdi to go back to
Mozart and Donizetti, Weber and Rossini for the regular training
which keeps a voice fresh and agile. To put it another way:
operatic practice today forces many singers to specialise and does
not allow the natural development of their so-called dramatic
voice. The history of singing shows that Lilli Lehmann, Lillian
Nordica, Frida Leider and Kirsten Flagstad did not take on high
dramatic roles until they were forty and even then retained those
parts which helped them to stay technically flexible. Both
Lehmann and Leider viewed this as a requirement for the quality
of their singing – and for a long vocal lifespan.[3]

Things are much better in the older repertoire. Even before the
return to old performance practices made us aware of different
singing styles, Maria Callas had become a decisive influence. She
showed that technical virtuosity is essential if one is to do justice
to the rich formal language of singing, that one's pleasure in a
voice does not ultimately lie in its sweet and delicate sound and
finally, that symbolic or allegorical expression can be more pleas-
ing than verismo with its violence and passion. For many years
there were problems in casting *travesti* roles in older operas
because of the compulsion to cast on the basis of sexual realism
(though with Mozart's Cherubino or Strauss's Oktavian, play
on sexual ambiguity has been accepted). In more recent times
many listeners are discovering the charm, less sensuous than

aesthetically musical, in the voices of countertenors, especially when they sound as spontaneous and lively as that of the phenomenal Jochen Kowalski. And they discover that the effects employed by a veristic singing style – declamatory outbursts, screaming and sobbing – lead ultimately to an impoverishment of musical expression.

Since time immemorial the quality of singing has been linked with composing. The deliberate artlessness of verismo was met in many singers by an artless delivery – an awful misunderstanding, because verismo was intended to be only an *art* of artlessness. And its portrayal is only possible with a singer's technique. But in order to do justice to the poetry of musical realism, singers began by heavily darkening their voices. They wanted to produce a heavier, sensual and sexual sound,[4] but in the process ruined their voices. Celletti writes about this type of vocal production:

> A solution which renders the voice hard therefore has a negative effect on modulation, and in tiring the high notes causes harshness and shrillness. [. . .] the attempt to create a realistic effect by using a 'speaking' or 'screaming' cadence only leads the singer to neglect the rounded full and soft tone which is the result of a voice produced *in maschera* and *sul fiato* and of the change from middle to high register. They do this . . . ignoring the fact that some verismo composers . . . prefer to place the most violent and passionate or strongly declamatory phrases in those areas where a change of register is unavoidable if one wishes to avoid having the voice sound raw, guttural or forced. In the field of verismo this means that the habit of 'open singing', which could be the best means of distinguishing dilettantes from professional singers, defeats itself.[5]

Consequently performers with great dramatic gifts can, without the technical skill, take on (if not actually sing) parts in verismo opera. Even if it was wrong to accuse Toscanini of having caused Verdi's music to be sung with the aesthetics of verismo, yet his recordings prove that he was opposed to singers making vocal nuances – the *tempo rubato*, careful *portamento*, fine colouring (which Verdi called *miniare*), eloquent embellishment and even the interpolation of cadenzas at the end of a second strophe.

Greatness means giving direction. Toscanini's denial of subjectivity – and the distortions – of the late Romantic interpretive style, his insistence on impartiality and denial of expression, all made him a 'Settembri of music' (Adorno), who knew no goal other than the perfect performance, or opera as a festival *en permanence*. Greatness also means giving a *new* direction. Just as there was a sloppy opera tradition *before* Toscanini and *before* Mahler, and just as there were performers of high quality *under* Toscanini, also under Fritz Busch, Bruno Walter, Erich Kleiber and Fritz Reiner, all soul-mates of Toscanini, so there is, as far as singing is concerned, an era before Callas and after Callas.

'It is recognised that good singing (for the Romantic composers) and bel canto (for the pre-Romantics) was not revived as a result of intervention from musicologists, opera historians, critics or conductors,' writes Celletti, 'but thanks to one singer: Maria Callas.' Not only did she revolutionise singing technique (by which we mean turning musical style into theatrical expression), but thereby brought music which seemed dead back to life. Celletti sums this up:

> The starting point was to think back to a pre-verismo state, even in certain respects a pre-Verdian state, which brought four guiding principles: i) the re-introduction of diverse and analytical phrasing which enables one to observe the expression marks of the composer by means of degrees of colour and accent, and which aims to bring out the deeper meaning of the words by means of highly subtle playing with dark and light effects and with gradation of colour; and this applies equally to recitative, aria or duet; ii) a return to genuine virtuosity, which consists of imbuing the coloratura with expressiveness and of making audible what Rossini called 'the hidden accents'; iii) the return of pre-Romantic or Romantic *cantabile* which requires softness of tone, clean *legato*, staying power, concern for pathos or the elegiac, as well as lyrical strength; iv) the return of archetypes from classical and proto-Romantic music theatre, which had been debased by the interpretive practices of late

Romanticism and verismo: the queen, the priestess and the magician.

Maria Callas did not simply sing 'better,' certainly not with a better or more beautiful voice than her rivals (if she really has a rival), but she indicated a new direction, caused the resurrection of the Romantic coloratura soprano with dramatic possibilities of expression – and with this the musico-dramatic *oeuvre* of Rossini, Cherubini, Bellini, Donizetti and the young Verdi.

A re-creative artist always has quite definite characteristics. When Wilfrid Mellers sees in Franz Liszt the 'artist as hero', he is describing a nineteenth-century romantic role, such as Vladimir Horowitz, for example, has carried into the twentieth century, albeit with unintended comic effect. The prima donna and the cult of the deified singer, or diva, was a product of the eighteenth and early nineteenth centuries, but bore no relation to the modern star system, which is merely the boring result of what Thomas Mann aptly if politely called 'humanely democratic levelling-off'. The prima donnas already mentioned, together with those from the second half of the nineteenth century such as Fanny Persiani, Jenny Lind or Adelina Patti, were worshipped by the masses and inflamed the senses and the intellect of great poets – and won the admiration and love of the composers. It is probable that Nellie Melba was the last real prima donna – and Maria Jeritza the first modern star, to whose vocal qualities were also added 'unbelievably beautiful hands and the longest legs ever seen on stage' (Gustl Breuer). The extent of the change is illustrated by the words of Richard Strauss, who said during a *Salome* rehearsal: 'If you don't have to look at the score, you are a true genius.'

Anyone can be a star today – the word is applied, in the grubby accolades of critics, to football players, newsreaders, talk-show hosts, designers and trendsetters. They are all stars, all prominent, without standing out for any special quality. And yet the art form of opera is no longer so popular that its representatives can just play the parts of stars, except for a few who have become travelling salesmen for the so-called beautiful voice – like Placido Domingo and Luciano Pavarotti.

Singers such as Renata Tebaldi, Zinka Milanov, Leonie

Rysanek, Joan Sutherland, Birgit Nilsson and Marilyn Horne certainly are or have been 'famous', yet their fame does not compare with the aura that has surrounded Maria Callas since the mid–1950s. Callas has been the only prima donna in the original sense. Yet what did she do to achieve this title? What is the meaning of prima donna – often used too freely? The requirements and the knowledge needed of the technical, virtuoso and musical abilities of a prima donna are so great that those who take their work seriously can be broken by their own ambition. The prima donna must have not just a beautiful, sensual and distinctive voice; without musicality, technique, strong nerves, an athlete's energy, diplomatic skill, aura, personality and inner fire (not to be confused with glamour) there will be no room for her in the ranks reserved for the prima donna. There are singers who only have to open their mouth to bathe the listener in waves of beautiful sound, blessed as they are with a well-placed voice. Others use their aura and personality to make us forget that they are performing with an only average instrument; they earn recognition and respect. Some are technically so well versed that they can learn a difficult role within a week, others cannot read music and learn by singing along to another singer's recordings.

The way up, barred by the hurdles of envy, jealousy, and resentment is hard; the way to fame is a stony path. There are producers who are interested only in the effect which *their* production makes. The singer becomes a mere requisite, forced into actions and contortions which make singing difficult if not completely impossible. There are conductors who, because everyone is interested in the success of his guest appearance (and who nowadays grants anything other than guest appearances?), prematurely force young singers into roles which are too big and too difficult, and quite frankly they care not a damn if they are ruining a voice. Then, there are conductors who ignore their singers and have the orchestra play too loud (and often pitched too high),[6] compelling the singers to force their voices and to use muscular energy in order to achieve a bigger tone. There are impresarios, according to Lisa della Casa, who press the talents entrusted to them like a lemon, then throw them away. There is a public which is loyal and fair and, above all, grateful, and there are fans with manners that would shock the most boorish football reporter. To sum up, the waters of the opera world are shark-infested – how can an exotic specimen survive in such a place?

Once again: what is a prima donna? She is no mere travelling saleswoman with a beautiful voice. She is never, ever the efficient, reliable, well-prepared singer who steps in when a real prima donna cannot be found. The prima donna has everything: musicality, temperament, charisma and dedication, and she needs, according to Rossini, 'voice, voice and still more voice'. But in whom does one find all these qualities? Perhaps in Rosa Ponselle? She possessed a voluptuous, splendid voice and her musicality was very good, but her technique was only adequate and her temperament too much under control. Or Nellie Melba? She had an incomparably brilliant voice, superb technique, eminent musicality, but the temperament of a marble statue. Or Kirsten Flagstad? She had a wonderful voice but the charisma of a matronly housewife. Typical was her saying of Lotte Lehmann after a performance of *Die Walküre* that only a wife (in the privacy of her bedroom) should behave with her husband in the way that Lotte Lehmann played Sieglinde. And Lotte Lehmann? Excellent musicality, dramatic and poetic imagination, spontaneity, temperament, a splendidly beautiful voice and a technique that was often endangered by her desire for expression. Martha Mödl? Temperament, dedication, strength of expression, but an average voice and a problematic technique. Montserrat Caballé? A beguilingly beautiful voice, secure musicality and the temperament of a marmot.

It is not easy to describe what a prima donna is when voice, musicality and temperament are so different for each singer. The voice of Janet Baker was smaller, more delicate and sensitive than that, for example, of Ottilie Metzger or Ebe Stignani; her temperament was less fiery than that of Conchita Supervia or Astrid Varnay, yet when one hears her in Gluck's *Orfeo* or in the *Lamento di Arianna* by Monteverdi, one notices an inner tension and genuine pathos missing from the singing of others. Voice is something quite different for Birgit Nilsson, Amy Shuard, Renata Tebaldi or Mirella Freni; virtuosity for Joan Sutherland or Marilyn Horne is different from virtuosity for Maria Callas or Magda

Olivero. But only a diva – must it be emphasised that 'diva' translates as 'goddess'? – knows by pure alchemy how to combine all her abilities, virtues, characteristics and qualities and dares, like everyone we consider great, to live dangerously or, in the words of Nietzsche, accepts martyrdom in order to qualify for the loneliness of fame.

The prima donna, summing up with a familiar distinction which may even be a polarisation, becomes incarnate in the vocal/artistic diva. The cliché is of the vocal diva practising her trills and checking her costume before singing Gounod's Marguérite, whereas the artistic diva reads Goethe. Yet there never was a vocal diva without artistic powers of imagination, and never an artistic diva without a stupendous voice. From Callas, in whose voice even her admirers found faults, Tito Gobbi reported having heard sound which one hears once in a lifetime.[7]

The perfect moulding of a voice is itself an artistic task demanding unusual qualities, as the critics of Sutherland and Caballé should note. On the other hand, even where the wish to be expressive gets in the way of performance technique, as it might with Lotte Lehmann, Claudia Muzio, Anja Silja or Magda Olivero, even then the technique and functioning of the voice remain ultimately as the basis of expression. In a nutshell: To abandon either technique or artistic control is to lead to aesthetic disaster.

If not the greatness, then at least the historical influence of an interpreter can be culled from the writings by or about that interpreter. The reminiscences of Bruno Walter, Fritz Busch, Thomas Beecham and Gregor Piatigorsky are important documents. Only seldom would one find in them flights of self glorification or stylisation. And that goes too for Yehudi Menuhin's *Unfinished Journey*.

Most of the Toscanini portrayals, however, are coffee-table books, pretentious stuff written for the fans. Typical is the biography of Toscanini written by someone who never heard him conduct: Harvey Sachs. In most biographies of singers and always in 'autobiographies' by ghost writers the reader enters an aesthetic basement, be it te Kanawa's *Kiri, More Than a Diva* (Renata Scotto), Pavarotti's *My Own Story* or even *Opera People* (portrayed by Christian Steiner in the manner of *Vogue*). There are at least twenty books about Maria Callas, many of which deal with so-called revelations by the indiscreet. Factual portraits have indeed been written, by George Jellinek (as early as 1960!) and Pierre-Jean Rémy (1978). Indispensable are John Ardoin's *The Callas Legacy* and the book of photographs and interviews which Ardoin produced together with Gerald Fitzgerald, containing contributions from almost all the singer's important colleagues. Arianna Stassinopoulos promises a glance *Behind the Legend*, but only weaves around it. Revealing many biographical details, particularly from the shadow side of Callas's life and career, simply cannot excuse the author's incompetence in the face of the artistic phenomenon of Maria Callas.

3

The Paradox of Expression
or
The Beautiful and the Ugly Voice

'. . . For Beauty's nothing
but beginning of Terror we're still
just able to bear,
and why we adore it so is because
it serenely
disdains to destroy us'

Rilke, *First Duino Elegy*

'The performance was not as good as I sang it in my imagination,' said Maria Callas after a much-praised première of *Norma* in 1948.

This self-critical statement, and self-criticism was among the singer's greatest virtues, is worth re-reading. The reason is that one has to become aware of the scruples felt, in the face of the difference between artistic imagination and practical execution, by an interpreter with an absolute artistic will and a precise interpretive conception. Or should one not speak of an act of suffering? Walter Benjamin clarified the difference in a moving simile: 'The work is the death mask of conception.'

As far as the performing arts are concerned, and especially music, the singer, more than any other interpreter, is faced with the impossible task of realising conception in performance. While the instrumentalist has to master his instrument technically, the singer becomes the instrument which he is playing and is therefore exposed to the workings of his body. Unlike a skilled instrumentalist a singer can never turn on to automatic pilot during a performance. Jascha Heifetz said that playing the violin presupposes, beyond a perfect technique, the peace and concentration of a Buddhist monk and the nerve of a matador. The singer may have this peace, this concentration and this nerve, but what if the technique is impaired by the body's weakness? Above all what if a singer does not simply want, as Maria Callas put it, to 'fit the part to her voice' but aspires to perform it as immaculately as Jascha Heifetz does his concertos, sonatas and bravura pieces?

The singer, more than any instrumentalist, requires a body relaxed in feeling and concentrated in mind in order to allow the voice to flow; without this inner feeling the almost animal instinct to produce a sound, which is the characteristic of great singing, cannot come about.

Beauty – used to describe the human voice, the word can be both magical and banal. When Serafin spoke of 'this big, ugly voice' he certainly did not mean it perjoratively even if his description seems to endorse that frequent criticism of Callas, that her voice's natural qualities were less noble than those of Nellie Melba, Rosa Ponselle, Zinka Milanov or Renata Tebaldi. This may be so, but it is only half the truth and artistically speaking, it is a lie.

In another connection Serafin, who acted as repetiteur and conductor for all the great singers of his time, said that he had come across only three vocal wonders in his lifetime: these were Caruso, the Italian-American soprano Rosa Ponselle and the baritone Titta Ruffo. Serafin was referring to the essentially sensuous and direct effect of the sound, delivery and emotional impact of these voices, the seductive beauty of their timbre – which means that the technique is invisible, leaving an impression of absolute spontaneity. This is everything described by Ernst Bloch in *Das Prinzip Hoffnung* as the 'tangible magic of the singing eroticon'. Besides these 'vocal wonders', added Serafin, he had experienced a 'handful of marvellous singers', of whom one can assume that Maria Callas was one.

Serafin put his finger on a distinction recognised from the early days of opera. The seventeenth-century French theoretician Bénigne de Bacilly observed two kinds of voice: the good and the beautiful. The former expressed everything required by the music and the role, with no special natural qualities of their own, whereas the latter, confident of their natural qualities, were incapable of expressing anything.

The word 'beauty' is really only an approximation. The general understanding of a beautiful voice is that of a sensual quality and the emotions which that releases in the listener, and emotions are, according to Hegel, 'the hollow region of the mind'. Dialectically speaking, to use the word 'good voice' just creates an antithesis. But however unsatisfying a beautiful sounding but unexpressive voice may be in the musico-dramatic sense, a 'good' one which has no adequate aural quality or technical discipline is aesthetically just as much of a problem. It is part of the ambivalence, even the parodox, of musical expression in opera that the most violent feelings of anger and hatred express themselves in what Thomas Mann called the 'fullness of euphony'. And to that extent to invoke 'beautiful' and 'good' voices as opposites is just a means of setting out the problem – but only as one of opposites.

This dichotomy has continued in aesthetic discussions throughout the centuries. People particularly like to immortalise composers' comments as if they were strict rules of interpretation. For example, there is the often quoted reply of Richard Wagner when asked about the voice of Wilhelmine Schröder-Devrient, which he valued highly:

> Concerning this artist I have again and again been asked if her *voice* was really so remarkable, since we glorified her as a singer – her voice being all people seem to think about in such a case. It constantly annoyed me to answer this question, for I revolted against the thought of the great *tragédienne* being thrown into one bevy with the female castrati of our Opera. Were it asked once more today, I should answer somewhat as follows: No! She had no 'voice' at all; but she knew how to use her breath so beautifully, and to let a true feminine soul stream forth in such wondrous sounds, that we never thought either of voice or singing!

This too sounds like a vote in favour of the 'good' and against the voice which was just beautiful or virtuoso, and it was grist to the mill of those Wagnerians whose ideal was the singing actor and not the acting singer, and of the aestheticians of expression to whom the word 'technique' was *diabolus in musica*. It would certainly be interesting to know how Schröder-Devrient managed her breathing when singing roles like Pamina, Leonora, Agathe, Norma, Amina and Desdemona (in Rossini's *Otello*). She must also have been a first-class singer technically, even if that became less important to Wagner than her capabilities of dramatic portrayal and gesture-singing.

This old controversy broke out again with extreme animation on Italian radio in 1969, when there was a major debate on Maria Callas with the title *Processo alla Callas*, transcribed and translated as 'The Callas Debate'. Participating were Eugenio Gara, Fedele d'Amico, Rodolfo Celletti, Giorgio Gualerzi, Luchino Visconti and Gianandrea Gavazzeni. Her admirers admitted then, and have

continued to do so, that they shuddered at the jerky attack of
Callas's tremulous high notes, but even her critics could not, and
cannot, resist being enchanted and touched by the *melancolia tinta*
in her timbre and are astonished by her dramatic portrayals.
Wagner's assertion that a singer could have an ugly voice but do
beautiful things with her breathing continues to enjoy as much
currency as the typical criticism that every note has its place in
the dramatic structure of a phrase, recitative or aria and that the
successful entity is of more importance than the single wrong
note.

The question is when and how a harsh, shrill and possibly ugly
sound achieves dramatic validity. Does Tosca have to bark her
'È l'Attavanti'? Should Lady Macbeth have an ugly voice? Maria
Callas's studio and live recordings compel us to face these questions because on many notes and phrases one is aware of the
expressive will giving the singer trouble. However convincing
this may be dramatically – or however effective, because we are
listening sympathetically – it is a problem when judged by strictly
vocal and aesthetic standards, even if one considers the dramatic
conception to be vital. In matters of vocal technique there is none
the less, to take up Ingeborg Bachmann's idea, a miscarriage at
various levels, a miscarriage which many singers avoid because
they do not expose themselves to the problem in the first place.

It is beyond dispute, to start with the negative side, that Callas
certainly did not possess a faultless tone such as that of Adelina
Patti, so highly praised by William James Henderson in *The Art
of Singing*. She was not just the producer of tones of extreme aural
purity and roundness. This in itself is a deficit because the forming
of such tones is not just a technical but also a musical process. A
first-class timbre, refined by technique, is among the most rare
and precious qualities of the voice and of singing. The timbre
of Callas, heard just as sound, was certainly characteristic and
immediately recognisable, but not beautiful and, in the opinion
of Rodolfo Celletti, even 'basically ugly'. Occasionally she produced a thin dry sound which had a certain sharpness, a sound
which had, in the language of singing, nothing of velvet, silk,
lustre or sweetness. What stood out all the more was a metallic

quality in her voice, a hard penetrating core in the tone, which was the prerequisite for its brightness and carrying power.

Can one sing beautifully with a timbre like that? Let us look at the problem by referring again to Adelina Patti, who in old age, as George Bernard Shaw pointed out, transposed everything down by a minor third but to a great extent still retained the quality of her voice. When over sixty years of age the diva produced the most even and rounded trills to be heard on any recording. In her *Memoirs of an American Prima Donna* the American soprano Clara Louise Kellogg attributed the healthy state of Patti's voice to the fact that she 'never allowed herself emotions', because emotions tire and damage a voice. Kellogg went on to say that 'she never acted, and never, never permitted herself to show feeling'.

To observe Patti in that way might seem severe judgement, even if her style of interpretation seems strange to most people nowadays. And yet Giulietta Simionato used the same argument to defend Montserrat Caballé against critics who attacked her for cultivating sound and reproached her for the paucity of her expression; she specifically mentioned emotional surrender to dramatic roles as highly dangerous to the voice. It is an old argument whether an artist should be consumed by the emotions and by the character which he has to portray. Diderot wrote in his *Paradoxe sur le comédien* that an actor's tears should come from his intellect and that it is feelings which characterise the poor actor. The good actor should always be the observer of what he is playing. Even such an expressive singer as Feodor Chaliapin, who rates as one of the first singer-actors in the history of opera, and whose influence is certainly comparable to that of Callas, set great store by acting which is precisely conceived and executed, and which is immutable. It is a matter of finding appropriate gestures and movement, a matter of achieving that naturalness which comes from consciousness.

This can certainly be applied to singing. Singing, according to a definition by Henderson which may at first seem somewhat simplistic, is 'the interpretation of a text through musical sounds which are produced by the human voice'. Henderson defines 'musical sound' as 'beautiful sound', and beauty as roundness, brilliance, intensity at every dynamic shift and the harmonious combination of key and notation. That certain roles call for the *voce soffocata* (stifled voice) – like Verdi's Otello – or for an enormous sound of suffering – like Wagner's Kundry – that verismo gave rise to the *aria d'urlo*, the aria of screaming, does not in any way make the definition relative; they only show that composers at the end of the nineteenth century were employing means of expression which were different from 'tone', that is, the scream, the exclamation and the sob.

It goes without saying that beautiful sound must not be an end in itself; it has to illuminate the word, the phrase and the dramatic coherence. Pier Tosi emphasised in his essay 'Opinioni de'cantori antichi e moderni' that the singer sets himself apart from the instrumentalist by his use of words. And Ernest Newman wrote, after a performance of *La Traviata* with Rosa Ponselle that 'great singing, provided the voice is good, only comes about through the intelligent use which a clever mind makes of the inner meaning of the music'. The meaning, however, is conveyed by words which are the vehicle of musical thoughts. There is no doubt that the more intelligent and conscious the acting, the more risk there is to the technique: to the production of the voice. The ideal sound can only be produced if a slow, gentle, deep intake of breath reaches the vocal chords in a perfectly even flow and if it then causes the vocal chords to vibrate with no clicking of the glottal stop and, finally, if the sound produced by this is then cut off with no release of the breath. Every feeling, every agitation, every emphasis, every attempt to express, in short every form of interpretation designed to convey an 'emotion' must alter or jeopardise the purity of sound.

Yehudi Menuhin summed up this opposition of technique and expression thus: 'Interpretation is the greatest enemy of technique.' Interpreters who come as close to technical perfection as the violinist Jascha Heifetz, the pianist Josef Hofmann, the young Vladimir Horowitz or the soprano Nellie Melba are charged with paucity of feeling or with soulessness precisely because they seldom or rarely reveal the effort behind their interpretation; or they are accused of having problems with their very lack of apparent problems. The cultivation of perfect tone and perfect technique is not external to music and singing but is the essential goal, witness Verdi's admiration of the 'perfect' singer Adelina Patti as a consummate artist.

This perfection was unattainable for Maria Callas. From the first the will to interpret was evident in her singing as a determination to express something, and her technique, in so far as it concerned the formation of her voice, was affected by this. Various observers have referred to the idiosyncrasy of her vocal production, to the effect that her soprano was not completely equalised, not correctly 'masked'. It sounded as if it comprised three voices; in no way did it approach the modern ideal of the 'single register' with an unbroken transition from low to high. The unique qualities of the voice were described by Walter Legge, producer of her most important studio recordings from 1953 onwards:

Callas had that *qua non* for a great career, an immediately recognisable personal timbre. It was a big voice and in her best years had a range of almost three octaves, though the extreme top was sometimes precarious and, as we discovered in trying to record Dalila's 'Mon coeur s'ouvre à ta voix', the lower register needed more consistent power than she could sustain. The basic quality was luxurious, the technical skill phenomenal. Callas possessed in fact three different voices, all of which she coloured for emotional effect at will – high coloratura, ample, brilliant (and when she chose, darkened), admirably agile. Even in the most difficult *fioriture* there were no musical or technical difficulties in the top part of the voice which she could not execute with astonishing, unostentatious ease. Her chromatic runs, particularly downwards, were beautifully smooth and her *staccatos* almost unfailingly accurate, even in the trickiest intervals. There is hardly a bar in the whole range of nineteenth-century music for high soprano that seriously tested her powers, though she sometimes went sharp on sustained high notes or took them by force.

The centre of the voice was basically dark-hued, her most expressive range, where she could pour out her smoothest legato. Here she had a peculiar and highly personal sound, often as if she were singing into a bottle. This came, I believe, from the extraordinary formation of her upper palate, shaped like a Gothic arch, not the Romanesque arch of the normal mouth. Her rib cage was also unusually long for a woman of her height. This, together with what must have been her well-trained inter-costal muscles, gave her unusual ability to sing and shape long phrases in one breath without visible effort. Her chest voice she used mainly for dramatic effects, slipping into it much higher than most singers with similar range when she felt the text or situation would gain by it.[1] Unfortunately it was only in fast music, particularly descending scales, that she completely mastered the art of joining the three almost incompatible voices into one unified whole, but until about 1960 she disguised those audible great changes with cunning skill.

When Callas sang 'into a bottle', as Legge put it, the sound took on a guttural tone, which happened particularly at the point of change from lower to middle range, between G and A. The transition from middle to high range, between F and G, was tricky in another way. At the top, at D and E and above all E flat – often the case in the ending of a Donizetti or Verdi cabaletta – she sometimes had difficulty in keeping the sound concentrated; a wobble would creep in. The total range of the voice extended from low F sharp right up to E *altissimo* or even F, which she sang in Rossini's *Armida*.

Let us return again to Rodolfo Celletti's evaluation of the voice. The critic felt, as did Tullio Serafin, that the sound and timbre were, judged by normal standards, ugly; yet his opinion was that 'a great part of her effect came from the lack of velvet and silk'. One of the most eminent connoisseurs of singing has written about this strange and aesthetically ambivalent phenomenon which he observed in another singer:

[. . .] she possesses the rare ability to be able to sing contralto as easily as she can sing soprano. I would suggest, in spite of my atrocious lack of technical knowledge, that the true designation of her voice is *mezzo-soprano*, and any composer who writes for her should use the *mezzo-soprano* range for the thematic material of his music, while still exploiting, as it were incidentally and from time to time, notes which lie within the more peripheral areas of this remarkably rich voice. Many notes of this last category are not only extremely fine in themselves, but have the ability to produce a kind of resonant and magnetic vibration, which, through some still unexplained combination of physical phenomena, exercises an instantaneous and hypnotic effect upon the soul of the spectator [. . .] it is not all moulded from the same *metallo*, as they would say in Italy (*i.e.*, it possesses more than one *timbre*); and this fundamental variety of tone produced by a single voice affords one of the richest veins of musical expression [. . .] a large number of other outstanding singers of the old school long ago demonstrated how easily an apparent defect might be transformed into a source of infinite beauty [. . .] In fact, the history of the art might tend to suggest that it is *not* the perfectly pure, silvery voice, impeccably accurate in tone throughout every note of its compass, which lends itself to the greatest achievements of impassioned singing. No voice whose *timbre* is completely incapable of variation can ever produce that kind of *opaque*, or as it were, *suffocated* tone, which is at once so moving and so natural in the portrayal of certain instants of violent emotion or passionate anguish.

This could be a description of the voice and the effect of Maria Callas. It comes from an author who never heard her: Stendhal, writing lyrically in *La Vie de Rossini* about Giuditta Pasta, the first singer of Norma. In the literature one reads of Pasta that she formed some notes like a ventriloquist, an observation sometimes also made of Callas. For this reason let us consider another description of Pasta's soprano, a description indicative of the development of the particular type of singer of which Maria Callas was the last great incarnation. Henry Chorley, also a connoisseur of singing and operatic life in the early nineteenth century, wrote of Pasta in 1862, in his memoirs:

. . . she subjected herself to a course of severe and incessant vocal study, to subdue and to utilize her voice. To equalize it was impossible. There was a portion of the scale which differed from the rest in quality and remained to the last 'under a veil', to use the Italian term. There were notes always more or less out of tune, especially at the commencement of her perform- ances. Out of these uncouth materials she had to compose her instrument, and then to give it flexibility. Her studies to acquire execution must have been tremendous; but the volubility and brilliancy, when acquired, gained a character of their own from the resisting peculiarities of the organ. There were a breadth, an expressiveness in her roulades, an evenness and solidity in her shake, which imparted to every passage a significance totally beyond the reach of lighter and more spontaneous singers.

Madame Pasta was understood to be a poor musician, a slow reader; but she had one of the most essential musical qualities in perfection – a sense for the measurement and proportion of time. This is more rare than it should be, and its absence strangely often passes unperceived even by artists and amateurs who are sensitively cultivated in other respects. It is not such mere correctness as is ensured by the metronome, not such artful licence in giving and taking as is apt to become artifice and affectation, but that instructive feeling for propriety which no lessons can teach – that due recognition of accent and phrase – it is that absence of flurry and exaggeration, [. . .] that intelli- gent composure without coldness, which at once impresses and reassures those who see and hear it.

With these descriptions by Stendhal and Chorley, we arrive by means of history at the strange phenomenon of *voci parallele*, of which the highly cultured Italian tenor Giacomo Lauri-Volpi made an absorbing study – he had concerned himself exhaustively with the problems of vocal education and history. That study goes into vocal, and naturally also historical, analogies which extend far beyond obvious similarities of timbre such as exist between Beniamino Gigli and Ferruccio Tagliavini, Tito Schipa and Cesare Valletti or Titta Ruffo and Gino Bechi. By means of individual comparisons Lauri-Volpi demonstrates what nine- teenth-century witnesses reveal: that extraordinary voices become a distillation of the music and roles which they bring to life.

With this in mind let me return to the voice and technique of

Maria Callas. Her voice too had that mezzo sound in the low and middle range which Stendhal noted in Pasta. At the top she reached notes which because of type-casting had been allocated since the end of the nineteenth century to the light, high soprano: the notes between C and F. While the so-called *soprani sfogati* like Malibran and Pasta extended their voices upwards, often with painful exertion and sometimes fatal consequences after only a few years on the stage, the high, light sopranos reached notes in the vocal stratosphere with bell-like and above all gentle attack: Jenny Lind, Henriette Sontag, Fanny Persiani, Adelina Patti and Marcella Sembrich were sopranos of this type, as were more recently Amelita Galli-Curci, Lily Pons, Mado Robin or Erna Sack. Even if the high notes and easy coloratura of these singers delighted a wide public – the top E flats and Es seeming to break the sound barrier – their effect was scarcely dramatic; and when *soprani leggieri* sang parts like Lucia di Lammermoor, Rosina in Rossini's *Il Barbiere di Siviglia*, Gilda in *Rigoletto* or even Leonora in *Il Trovatore* or Violetta in *La Traviata*, they missed that vital expressive dimension: the dramatic.

Maria Callas also was capable of singing notes above C *altissimo* with a gentle attack, but she always sang them with more energy, more volume even in *piano*, and above all with more vocal colouring. What one heard was, according to Celletti, 'more voice and less instrument', all the more so because she could approach the notes with the added vehemence of a full attack, that is with the energy of a dramatic soprano singing with maximum tension; a twentieth-century development leading to the solution of the problem which had arisen in the nineteenth was that this dramatic soprano reached her upper limit with C. After Lilli Lehmann and Lillian Nordica there were very few singers who performed both ornamented music – which can be fully dramatic – and Wagner roles. Both the typical Wagner soprano and the divas of verismo can at best reach C, and it is said that many thank their lucky stars when they do so.

Maria Callas, on the other hand, sang C, D flat, D and E flat without fear or effort, particularly in the early years of her career. One can take it as a natural limitation of the voice that not every note in her wide range – from low A to F *altissimo* – was sung with technical perfection.

In addition to technique in the sense of vocal training there is also musical technique. It is praise indeed when Walter Legge says that in all the music written for the voice in the nineteenth century, there is not a single bar which would have caused her problems. It is an enormous assertion and, if exaggerated, does point to the ambition of the singer who once stated that it was not her intention to make a score fit her voice. She literally formed an individual voice for each role and developed it through the role.

In the *Processo alla Callas* programme Rodolfo Celletti said that in twenty years he had not heard the part of Norma sung with the voice of a Gioconda or a Santuzza. The evidence for his thesis is the complete 1937 recording of *Norma* with Gina Cigna. On the contrary Callas newly learned the role note by note, phrase by phrase 'in order to produce a voice which was consonant with the opera in question'. A significant achievement, innovation even, was 'singing in the mask' which involves projection of the sound in the head cavities without allowing the voice to develop any nasal quality.

This is a completely different vocal and sound projection to that which had dominated the verismo school since 1910, where the middle voice is driven up very high, causing the highest part, which can only be reached by means of extreme tension, to strain and to become limited. This sort of singing is a kind of musical-ised speech in the sense that sound is given to words. The articulation suffers in a curious way, and with it the plasticity of the diction, whereas when singing in the mask the words are bedded in the sound and thereby can be made to stand out much more clearly. With a technique that is artificial through and through Maria Callas sings with far clearer diction than, for example, Renata Tebaldi or Mirella Freni. Over and above that, singing in the mask assured Callas of the agility which was essential for nineteenth-century music and also gave her the flexibility for the endless dynamic shifts which exist between *mezzoforte* and *piano*. To hear Callas as Norma, Elvira, Amina or Lucia is to have veritable lessons in the differentiation of dynamics. This was how she overcame that tradition of the *soprani leggieri* which had reduced the ornamental roles to superficial warbling. Sopranos like Amelita Galli-Curci, Lily Pons, Bidu Sayão, Mado Robin and several singers of the German school sang ornaments as if they were mere arabesques or decorative figures without inner dramatic meaning. A grave musical error. Or perhaps a misunderstanding about *canto fiorito* which had arisen as a result of a fault both in technique and expression.

Ornamented singing had become discredited since Richard Wagner introduced his aesthetic of expression and with it a denial of *solfeggio*. In the work of middle and late Verdi, as in the verismo operas, one can see at any rate the remains of those artistic forms and formulas which were the constituents of grammar of *canto fiorito*. From the beginning of the twentieth century a different aesthetic ruled opera: the aesthetic of expression, the language of emotion, psychological clarity, and there were comparatively few singers of the old school who were able to conserve their singing style on gramophone records: Marcella Sembrich, Adelina Patti, Fernando de Lucia, Mattia Battistini, Pol Plançon. But their recordings were far less popular than those of Caruso, Titta Ruffo, Chaliapin or Rosa Ponselle.

By the thirties one no longer heard anything on the stages of Berlin, New York, Vienna or above all Milan, which even remotely recalled the art of bel canto – this was primarily due to the influence of Toscanini, under whose aegis the operas of the eighteenth and early nineteenth century were rarely played at La Scala. Ornamented singing was considered an anachronism, as purely mechanical and decorative, emotionally empty and extremely virtuoso; singers of ornamented roles like Rossini's Rosina and Almaviva, Armida and Semiramide, Cenerentola and Isabella, Bellini's Amina, Elvira and Norma, Donizetti's Lucia, Verdi's Gilda and Violetta, did not have the means to convert the expressive meaning of those devices into sound and gesture.

In the process all these devices served expressive purposes. Composers like Bach, Handel and Mozart, in whose cantatas, passions, oratorios, masses and operas are found the elements of florid style, scarcely composed any virtuoso vocal music at all. Henry Pleasants explains in *The Great Singers*:

Brilliant roulades or divisions served the expression of rage, anger, revenge, release or, according to the harmonic articulation or figuration, of rejoicing and happiness. Trills or slides were intended to give emphasis to endings or cadences. Appogiaturas lent dignity, weight and tension to a long melodic line. *Portamenti* and rapid scale passages, whether diatonic or chromatic, whether rising or falling, could fill a crowning note with weight and with pathos. Ornaments could be extended according to situation or personality and thus became a constituent element in the characterisation.

The elements of decorative style were mastered by the singers of the eighteenth and early nineteenth centuries as if they were part of the composition and were understood as such by the public – and not just sensed, as may be the case nowadays. Maria Callas therefore, at the end of the forties and the beginning of the fifties had the impact of 'a planet which has strayed into an unfamiliar galaxy' (Teodoro Celli), because she gave back to ornamented singing its original meaning, carrying on where the singing of Pasta and Malibran had left off.

Celletti explains that Rossini needed not a light and flute-like trill but a vehement one. In the live recording of *Armida* one can hear that Callas sings a richly decorated part with positively blazing energy and yet always with the most refined shaping.

Her lines, *fioriture* and divisions have the effect, speaking pictorially, of the finest etching. Even when performing the passage work of Norma, Elvira and Lucia with virtuoso brilliance, she still used the intensity and force of attack and the concentration of her burning tone to give the passage-work an expressive tension which was literally unheard of. And with just as little effort she could sing long lines, passages and embellishments in *mezza voce*, could shade her tone elegiacally, with melancholy or gentleness, and give the impression that the sounds, independent of her body, fell like stars from the heavens of the theatre.

Let us return to the dichotomy of the good and the beautiful voice. Maria Callas was certainly not born with a beautiful voice. She did not have for example the flowing and naturally musical sound of Rosa Ponselle, whose name one learned not to mention in her presence. 'She started out with better material,' she said to Walter Legge. The voice was in all probability incapable of being shaped by training to achieve the faultless tone of Patti or Melba. But what was decisive was that Maria Callas was an interpreter of pathos, an expressive singer – and interpretation and expression are, to quote Yehudi Menuhin again, the enemies of technique. Enemies not of musical technique, for this functioned perfectly throughout the first decade of her great career from 1949 to 1959, but rather of vocal technique. Like Malibran and Pasta, who were described as at once sublime and vocally imperfect, Maria Callas was an imperfect miracle – and in that sense a kind of reincarnation, because she sang her roles like the interpreters of the first performances; not as a stylistic copy but through a composer's and actor's imagination, by means of which her soprano became the voice of music. In that sense Ingeborg Bachmann was correct to imagine that composers would have seen perfect fulfilment in Maria Callas's performances of their music. Yet it was often said too of Giuditta Pasta that her performances were not renderings but 'creations' with an originality and spontaneity like the composer's.

Although harmony and beauty of sound are essential, they are only the means, and not the end, for singing and dramatic expression. Each expression is related in tension to the ideal sound, which can and must be only a technique, whose aim is to preserve the dichotomy between the good and the beautiful voice. Callas may have had faults in her voice, but as a singer she came, despite various vocal weaknesses, as near to perfection as is possible. Her achievement came about from her never being a slave to her means and never presenting her vocal virtuosity as an end in itself. In contrast to certain eminent colleagues she never just sang beautiful passages, phrases or brilliant notes for effect, and only under the greatest duress would she simplify a difficult passage or avoid a vocal hurdle.

It is unthinkable that at the end of the Nile duet in Verdi's *Aida* she would have simply made a rising climactic phrase – 'su noi gli astri brilleranno' – into a vocalise, as Zinka Milanov did. Her portrayals were worked out down to the last detail, even indeed to the extent that, as Fedele d'Amico observed, she gave the impression in individual roles of being physically a different person: that is one of the greatest secrets of the performer's art. Each role that she sang was given its own characteristic sound so that we can see her before our eyes even if are only listening to her. However inimitably she may be Callas in timbre, expression and gesture, yet in every role she is as different as Rosina and Armida, Norma and Amina, Lucia and Anna Bolena, Gilda and Lady Macbeth, Violetta and Amelia, Tosca and Lauretta, Butterfly and Turandot can be.

As we shall show, one of the great aesthetic pleasures of nineteenth-century music is when an imperfect sound becomes part of the harmonic whole, and becomes transformed in the beauty of terror. Most of the figures Maria Callas portrayed come from that world of dark Romanticism, whether they be persecuted innocents or demonic women. In this connection, it is surprising that, apart from four performances of *Die Entführung aus dem Serail*, she never sang parts like Elvira or Donna Anna, the Countess or Fiordiligi on the stage.

'Most of Mozart's music is dull,' she later said at a masterclass in the New York Juilliard School, a remark which caused her biographers some irritation but was probably not to be taken literally. She told her students: 'Mozart is too often sung on tiptoe and with too much fragility. He should be performed with the same directness as *Trovatore*.' As Mozart was an Italian composer, viewed historically as well as aesthetically, this opinion is tenable. However, the question remains unanswered as to why Maria Callas let those vocally grateful roles pass her by.

The reason can only be that she could not identify with the roles, and in two senses. She did not possess, as we explained at the outset, a harmonious voice, but one in which a drama unfolded. From that voice came the emotional sounds of an injured, confused and vulnerable soul. Her temperament did not know moderation, but rather outburst, agitation and exaltation. Even when she was portraying a pastoral figure like Bellini's Amina and singing her cantilenas with infinite delicacy and even sweetness, one could still detect, so to speak, the shadow of the Romantic death-wish. Mozart, on the other hand demands of singers a sense of form which is not merely external – a sound which does know vocal exertion or agitation (without being anae-mic), and which also demands a portrayal without gestures of suffering, sacrifice, lasciviousness, demonism, darkness and mad-ness, which are the gestures of Romantic singers, in the tradition of ancient tragedy.

Maria Callas possessed a voice of suffering and wildness, a voice of the night and one that in going to its limits corresponded to the states of mind which are depicted in nineteenth-century literature (opera belongs undoubtedly to that literature). Particu-larly among its themes were erotic feelings, including pleasure from fear and atrocity, from incestuous and stigmatised relation-ships. Callas had a voice for the beauty of terror, as demanded by Verdi in a letter dated 23 November 1848 to his librettist Salvatore Cammarano:

> I know that you are about to start preparing *Macbeth*, and as this is an opera which interests me above all others, please let me say a few words on the subject. The part of the Lady has been assigned to Tadolini and I am amazed that she has agreed to sing it. You know how much I value Tadolini, as she also knows herself; yet in the interest of all involved I find it neces-sary to give you some suggestions. The talents of Tadolini are much too good for this role! This may strike you as an absurd thing to say!!! Tadolini has a beautiful and attractive presence; and I would prefer it if the Lady does not sing at all. Tadolini has a splendid voice, clear, fluid and powerful; and I would like the Lady to have a harsh, throttled and heavy voice. Tadolini's voice has something angelic about it; and I want the Lady's voice to sound like a devil.

The point could not be made more clearly. This letter has always been quoted when the question of justifying a shrieking singer has arisen. Yet the Verdi studies by Julian Budden, and especially *Verdi's* Macbeth: *A Source Book* edited by Andrew Porter and David Rosen, point to there being no doubt that Verdi's letter is an argument *ad feminam* and that it is a warning for us today against allowing a voice like Mirella Freni's or Kiri te Kanawa's to portray a demonic woman.

In an essay entitled 'Madness, Hallucination and Sleepwalking', contained in the source book, Jonas Barish has explained the composer's need to find a dramatic voice for the part. A similar argument is put forward by Marilyn Feller in her essay 'Vocal Gesture in *Macbeth*': Verdi did not ask for the conventional *buon canto* but for a plastic vocal gesture of dark beauty. Not that his letter should be taken as condoning bad singing or even yelling by means of pushing up the chest register. Julian Budden interprets the letter as a warning against a prima donna's possible 'narcissistic disposition'. A look at the score reveals that the vocal line – in 'Vieni! t'affretta', for example – is ornamented: there are difficult *gruppetti* and, at the ends of phrases, trills. Obviously these passages should not be sung as decorative forms but rather with the violent *espressivo* of dramatic gesture. Verdi describes with profligacy and passion every expression which is spiced with a touch of depravity. According to this the Lady should be sung with a beauty which freezes, with an authority which injects fear and with a temptation which at the same time repels – with vocal gestures of extreme ambivalence, dark and yet glaring.

And yet, the *musical* tone must be preserved. Expression has nothing to do with rhetorical exaltation. Vocal expression rather comes about in three ways: by vocal acting, musical expression and emanation or expression of the soul. The means for musical expression are dynamic shifts, accentuations, emphatic intonation, colorations of brightness or darkness and the tense articulation of musical time. In vocal acting it is solely a matter of giving emphasis to the words and of colouring the vowels. It is difficult, if not impossible, to write in a technical context about emanation or expression of the soul. This is a capability which lies beyond technical dexterity and it is easier to collect examples of such singing than it is to explain it. This mystical quality can be felt in Francesco Tamagno's recordings from *Otello*, in some recordings by Esther Mazzoleni and Maria Farneti, in Caruso's call 'O figli' before the Macduff aria, in Eléazar's aria, in 'Core 'ngrato'; in the sound of the voices of Kathleen Ferrier and Joseph Schmidt; in Magda Olivero's singing of the death scenes from *Fedora* and *Adriana Lecouvreur*: orphic gestures. The voice of Callas could create such gestures – as also gestures of suffering. In his obituary 'Heart's Death of the Prima Donna' the film-maker Werner Schroeter writes that it was their ambition to 'present these few portrayable feelings – life, love, joy, hatred, jealousy and the pain of death – in their totality and immediacy, without analysis'.

Without analysis, certainly, and yet one can detect in that voice something of the emotions which, to use a title by Auden, can only be born in an 'age of anxiety'. The voice itself is a drama, and more so, it is both tragedy and an ancient artefact. As Teodoro Celli wrote, 'It could make a sword of fire out of anger, just as it converted melancholy into an essence capable of breaking one's heart.' And without in any way detracting from the drama it shaped the music anew: each word, each phrase was carefully weighed and measured; the words became the parts of a musical sculpture which it brought to life; it raised vocal fireworks to new levels of expression and never allowed them to sink to being mere ornaments. Technique was subordinate to the musical expression, vocal beauty to the dramatic truth – 'It is not enough to have a beautiful voice,' Callas said. 'What does that mean? When one is interpreting a role, one must have a thousand colours in order to express happiness, joy, sorrow and fear. How can you do that simply with a beautiful voice? Even if at times you sound harsh, as I often have, that is a necessity of expression. One must do it, even if people do not understand!'

Let us go back again into history for an analogy, for the *voce parallele*. The composer Saint-Saëns wrote about Pauline Viardot, (sister of Maria Malibran and daughter of Manuel Garcia):

Her voice was enormously powerful and rich in its range. She could command all the technical difficulties of singing, yet this wonderful voice did not delight all listeners, for it was in no way supple or velvety. In truth it was a little harsh, its taste comparable to that of bitter oranges. But it was a voice for a tragedy or for an epic, because it was a supernatural voice and not just a human one. It lent incomparable grandeur to tragic roles [. . .] and lighter roles were completely transformed, becoming the plaything of an Amazon or a giant.

A voice which is not solely a medium of dramatic portrayal but which is a drama in itself, raises a contradiction which Pier Tosi, in 'Opinioni de'cantori antichi e moderni', considers incapable of being resolved: 'I do not know if a consummate singer can also be a consummate actor; for when the spirit is confronted with two completely different tasks, it will doubtless apply itself more to one than the other. What a joy, if it were to possess both capabilities in equal measure.'

At least in some performances Maria Callas caused the contradiction to disappear. But the effort that she had to summon cannot easily be described. She probably expected more of herself and her voice than her nerves had the strength for, or more than her soprano could physically withstand. Pauline Viardot said to a student at the end of her life, 'Don't do what I have done. I wanted to sing everything and have thereby ruined my voice.' In the view of her teacher Elvira de Hidalgo, Maria Callas 'abused her voice'. Not only at the beginning of her career did she sing in the course of one week both Brünnhilde in *Die Walküre* and Elvira in *I Puritani*, but parts like Abigaille in *Nabucco*. The last is a hybrid part with enormous intervals, which makes great demands on volume and cutting power on the one hand and on *agilità* on the other. She sang Kundry and Turandot, Norma and Medea and then those roles from the verismo repertoire which even dedicated divas of verismo have described as killer parts: Gioconda, Butterfly and Tosca. These parts are so difficult for the very reason that their singers must sing against large orchestras both in their middle and top ranges, and with maximum tension and vehement attack for most of the time.

Above all Callas sang with full commitment. 'She could have sung so many more Normas,' said Franco Zeffirelli, 'if only she could have persuaded herself to cheat; but that was a way out which she could never accept.' It was a constant challenge, perhaps demanding too much from her willpower and ambition, which Walter Legge described as Shakespearean. This ambition did not demand too much of her musical technique, but what it did in the early years of her career was to abandon her voice to the demon which consumed her: ecstasy.

4

Maria Callas
and the
Opera World of the 1950s

'Works of art are destroyed if the understanding of art disappears'

Goethe

'I can only say that Maria is possibly the most disciplined and professional material that I have ever had occasion to handle. Not only does she never ask for rehearsals to be cut down; she actually asks for more, and works at them with the same intensity from beginning to end, giving everything she's got, singing always at full voice – even when the producer himself suggests she shouldn't tire herself out and need only indicate the vocal line. So involved is she in the total outcome of a production that it irritates her when a colleague arrives late. If being a prima donna has some other meaning than this, then Callas is no prima donna'

Luchino Visconti

Early in 1951 Maria Callas had a telephone call from Antonio Ghiringelli, intendant of La Scala. He asked if she would substitute as Aida for the indisposed Renata Tebaldi, as she had already done a year earlier but with only token success. Now, having just enjoyed great success in South America, she was confident enough to give Ghiringelli the cold shoulder. She replied that she would come if La Scala wanted her, but only for her own roles and not to take over parts from other colleagues. Shortly afterwards she did indeed travel to Milan, but the visit had nothing to do with La Scala. Arturo Toscanini was in town and looking for a singer for the role of Lady Macbeth which he intended performing in New York. His friend Vincenzo Tommasini, an established composer, had suggested Maria Callas to him and Toscanini's daughter Wally had arranged the meeting and audition. It is not clear why the plan never materialised, whether it was because of the conductor's declining powers or whether he had some reservation about Callas; at that time Toscanini was considered to be an advocate of Renata Tebaldi. Whatever the reasons, Maria Callas missed out on a production that might have been one of the greatest triumphs of her career and on a recording of unique quality.

A performance with Maria Callas under Arturo Toscanini would have been a union of the two most influential artists in twentieth-century opera. Gianandrea Gavazzeni, an assistant to Toscanini and conductor of many performances with Maria Callas, has written of Toscanini's work at La Scala in the ten years between 1920 and 1930:

> It was a completely new method of working for the Italian opera tradition in that he introduced distinct order and method [. . .] Of course there were great performances, great conductors, great singers before Toscanini but there had not been any system of aesthetic or even moral realisation which embraced all aspects [. . .] in the Toscanini era the public was educated to consider the theatre not as an amusement but as an institution with an aesthetic and moral function, as an organisation which plays a role in social and cultural life.

At the time of Toscanini's birth on 25 March 1867 Verdi and Wagner were both fifty-four years old, *Aida, Otello, Falstaff* and *Parsifal* had not been composed and the Bayreuth Festival was a distant dream. Puccini was still at school. Caruso had not been born, the gramophone not invented and operatic life in Italy was quite haphazard. Established orchestras with musicians engaged on a permanent basis did not yet exist. The manner of working which Gavazzeni described, and which Toscanini had begun to introduce during his first period at La Scala, would not have been possible in the technical and economic conditions of the mid- or late nineteenth century. In small and medium theatres the musicians were engaged from opera to opera and did not even audition. It therefore goes without saying that no basic repertoire could be established. Toscanini in Milan and Mahler in Vienna became key figures in modern operatic theatre because they were rigorously dedicated to their goal of putting on the great masterpieces in an appropriate style.

Masterpiece – that is a concept which presupposes a certain distance in time, just as greatness in any form can only be assessed from the distance of generations. The performance of a masterpiece demands the stance of servitude, the stance of executor for something greater.

It is symptomatic that the young Toscanini, not yet thirty years old, made himself the advocate of Richard Wagner. In 1895 he gave the first Italian performance of *Götterdämmerung* at the Teatro Regio in Turin, he brought out *Tristan und Isolde* there in 1897 and in 1898 made his début as director of La Scala with *Die Meistersinger von Nürnberg*. There is no doubt that Toscanini was as fascinated by Wagner's idea of opera as the aesthetic school of the nation as he was by the idea of the Bayreuth Festival. He had made a radical break with the notorious sloppiness of operatic life, above all after his apprentice years as a conductor. Before being appointed head of La Scala in 1898 he had in twelve years directed 113 productions of fifty-eight operas in a total of 1500 performances, in addition to which he had learned 150 symphonic works in a period of two and a half years. Mussorgsky's *Boris Godunov*, which he brought out in the USA in 1913 with the bass Adamo Didur, had already been familiar to him when the work was still unknown in Western Europe; and it is an indication of how *avant-garde* he was that he had been responsible for the Italian premières of Debussy's *Pelléas et Mélisande* and Tchaikovsky's *Eugene Onegin*.

Principally he placed himself at the service of the two greatest operatic dramatists of the nineteenth century, Verdi and Wagner, both of whom were revolutionaries by virtue of their demands on the theatrical apparatus. For them he had to create a perfect apparatus and moreover break with many traditions – above all with the liberties which singers had been permitted to take. These bore no relation to the concept of *Werktreue* which was then coming in. Toscanini pushed through what Verdi (for many years) had been striving for, he interpreted traditional Italian opera from the perspective of what the composer stood for at that time.

A report by the tenor Giovanni Martinelli of a performance of *Il Trovatore* at the Metropolitan Opera – to be found in *Musical America* 1963 – leads us to the conclusion that Toscanini wanted to rescue 'singers' opera' with the spirit of music drama. When he took over the direction of La Scala for the second time in 1920 his ambition was to create a permanent festival, to which end he demanded of himself herculean strength. Harvey Sachs was clearly impressed by the description of this performance, included in his Toscanini biography, and it is more than probable that none of comparable quality has been heard since.

But revolutions, even aesthetic ones, demand sacrifices, and Toscanini, dedicated as he was to fidelity, sacrificed one decisive element of singing, that of improvisation and embellishment, that art of creating with the composer which had been taken for granted at least until the middle of the nineteenth century. In making this sacrifice Toscanini was misunderstanding Verdi, who admittedly rejected the arbitrary liberties taken by singers but who was no stickler for fidelity to the score; in his old age he said that where there had been the arbitrariness of the prima donna's rondo there was now the 'tyranny of the conductor', which was much worse.

The fact that typical 'singers' opera' from the early nineteenth century scarcely appeared on the programme of La Scala between 1920 and 1930 speaks for itself. That included the works of Rossini, Bellini and Donizetti, but it notably excluded Rossini's *Barbiere* and Donizetti's *Lucia di Lammermoor*.

It is particularly instructive to look at the repertoire conducted by Toscanini at La Scala. In his first season, 1921–2, there was *Falstaff*, *Rigoletto*, *Boris Godunov*, *Mefistofele* and *Die Meistersinger von Nürnberg*. A year later followed Pizzetti's *Debora e Jaele* (first performance), *Manon Lescaut*, Charpentier's *Louise*, *Lucia di Lammermoor*, Giordano's *Madame Sans-Gêne* (which had been given its first performance under Toscanini at the Met in 1915) and Mozart's *Die Zauberflöte*. 1923–4 brought *Aida*, *La Traviata*, *Tristan und Isolde*, Mascagni's *Iris*, Gluck's *Orfeo* and the first performance of Boito's *Nerone*. In 1924–5 Toscanini premiered Giordano's *La Cena delle Beffe* and then Zandonai's *I Cavalieri d'Ekebu*, and he concluded the season with Debussy's *Pelléas et Mélisande*. New works for 1925–6 included *Un Ballo in Maschera*, Gounod's *Faust*, Puccini's *Madama Butterfly*, Debussy's *Le Martyre de Saint Sébastien*, and the first performance of *Turandot*. The other operas which Toscanini conducted up to the end of the decade were *Fidelio, Tosca,* Dukas' *Ariane et Barbe-Bleue, Otello, Don Carlo,* the first performance of Pizzetti's *Fra Gherardo, La Forza del Destino, Parsifal* and the first performance of Giordano's *Il Rè.* With the exception of *Lucia di Lammermoor,* Toscanini conducted not one Italian opera from the first half of the nineteenth century; he concentrated on Verdi and Wagner, and gave his support to works by Mussorgsky and Debussy (which were, by Italian standards, peripheral), and above all to the presentation of new pieces.

It cannot have escaped Toscanini's attention that new music was in a state of crisis. Yet it was a matter of course for him that he should première contemporary operas, while for Verdi and Wagner, whose contemporary and active interpreter he had been for more than a decade, he was continuing the fight which the composers themselves had initiated. It was the fight for opera as *Gesamtkunstwerk* (the total work of art), as seen from the interpreter's perspective. Toscanini attempted to fulfil the idea of a festival with each performance. The pedantic exactitude with which he sought to form a unity out of the musical and scenic action has no parallel in operatic history.

Characteristic and typical was the conductor's decision to cancel a production of *Norma* in 1899 after the dress rehearsal and after weeks of preparation. The reason he gave was: 'Have you ever heard this opera? I have never heard it as it should really be performed. I have tried to produce it. I have not succeeded.' One cannot imagine that he viewed this failure as *his* failure, because problems in the orchestra never really existed for him. The cause of the cancellation must surely have been the singer of the title role: Ines de Frate, difficult to imagine as a mistress of expressive florid singing.

Or was there a deeper reason, of which the conductor was possibly unaware – his lack of relation to the formal language of romantic bel canto opera? It was certainly obvious how angrily or violently he would react when a singer took the slightest liberty with the printed score, which in bel canto was the usual practice and was even requested by the composer. Toti dal Monte told how she once enraged Toscanini with a lightly ornamented rendition of Gilda's aria. And how conspicuously, in his recording

of Verdi's *La Traviata* with Licia Albanese, has every trace of
ornamentation been radically expunged from the *brindisi*, from
Violetta's 'È strano', from Alfredo's 'De'miei bollenti spiriti' and
from Germont's 'Di provenza'. This has the effect of making the
vocal parts sound less cleaned up than skeletal, robbed as they are
of their variety of form and charm. This is a fidelity to the text
which has nothing to do with fidelity to the work. That Toscanini
replaced a mannerism of style which he considered antiquated
with his own mannerism is illustrated by how ruthlessly he allows
Jan Peerce and Robert Merrill to sing their way over the subtle
nuances of Verdi's dynamics. The undeniable quality of this
recording lies solely in an orchestral tension which is febrile in its
wild and violent rhetoric.

The *espressivo* style, which aimed at realism and immediacy,
can be traced back to compositional developments in Toscanini's
lifetime, to the music of the verismo school. For all their differences, composers like Ponchielli, Puccini, Mascagni, Leoncavallo,
Zandonai and Cilea renounced to a far-reaching extent the formal
language of classical singing. Admittedly one still finds some
ornaments in their operas but mostly only in the form of simple
joins or downbeats, rarely elaborate *fioriture* or extended trills. In
works like *Pagliacci* which are concerned with the bitter truth of
real life or disturbed states of mind, virtuoso devices had lost
their meaning; they were replaced by expressive effects that were
naturalistic. One symptom of this is the emergence of the *aria
d'urlo*, the aria with a scream. Within a few decades, roughly
between 1890 and 1910, the aesthetics of singing changed: there
developed, out of an art with artificial forms which demanded
the techniques of differentiation, a new language of naturalistic
expression which reached its culmination in figures of violent
affect. It was the same development that was taking place in
drama: for example, in moments of violent emotion the characters
in the plays of Gerhart Hauptmann express themselves less
through the logic of their language than with violent gesture.
This was alien to those prima donnas from the decade immediately before the turn of the century – for example Adelina Patti,
Marcella Sembrich or Nellie Melba. And it was in the first ten
years of this century that the prima donna was to lose her central

position in the operatic hierarchy. With Caruso, the tenor became the star of the footlights. By 1904 the Neapolitan's fame overshadowed that of all his soprano partners.

The reasons for this are not entirely musical ones. Born in 1873, Caruso was the first to reach his public via the new medium of the gramophone record; this was partly because his dark-toned tenor voice fitted perfectly into the frequency spectrum which the acoustic recording method could achieve at that time, and could be reproduced better than female voices demanding higher frequencies, which often sound disembodied, stiff and lacking in vibration; in contrast to the divas and his tenor and baritone colleagues, he placed his bel canto technique at the service of verismo music with a verve bordering on aesthetic impudence. Even though Caruso did not lose his vocal flexibility in the course of his career, from 1906 onwards he did never the less almost always sing with full tone: at *mezzoforte* and *forte*. That his wonderful early recordings were for a long while scarcely acknowledged and later acknowledged only by connoisseurs who then partially dismissed them again, cannot be put down simply to inferior recording techniques or to the piano accompaniments; rather it was that, viewed in the light of the later recordings, they were felt to be anachronistic because they contain clear references to *canto fiorito*: extended spinning out of the tone, more *rubato* and chiselled decoration. Wolf Rosenberg, author of the diatribe *Die Krise der Gesangskunst*, took as an example Caruso's 1911 interpretation of 'Una furtiva lagrima' and compared it to the 1904 version, finding the earlier one mannered, artificial and stylistically out of date. In doing so he places the dramatic *espressivo* singer above the vocal artist.

One cannot say that this is not a tenable view; it fits the current fashion. But the crisis in singing, which Rosenberg does not fully explain, can be substantially attributed to the decline of vocal art, attributed moreover to the *espressivo* singing which Caruso initiated.[1] One of the most celebrated and greatest recordings of Caruso shows that the writing was on the wall: the lament 'Recitar' from Leoncavallo's *Pagliacci*. He bursts into loud sobs, which sound not artificial, but spontaneous and genuine, and he follows the phrase 'bah, sì tu forse un uom' with a laugh of desperation, as marked by Leoncavallo in the score. The climactic phrase 'sul tuo amore infranto' is formed in one sustained breath, sung with an almost endless elasticity on 'infranto' and with a thrilling vocal emphasis. The vocal gesture at 'il cor' indeed touches the heart; it is above all inimitable.

Unfortunately these affective gestures were imitated to excess. Beniamino Gigli, Miguel Fleta, Mario del Monaco and most recently Placido Domingo fill even the extended postlude with sobs and clearly audible weeping. What was spontaneous with Caruso, singing with blazing affect, degenerated into a histrionic sham. Singing *con forza* with tonal production at maximum tension, the middle range forced upwards in a coarse manner, spawned many imitations. In a Caruso aria the transitional F was treated as a high note, so that the high A remained within his range with no effort. Many successors treated these *passaggio* notes as if they were from the middle range and forced their voices into the chest register with too much tension. This resulted in a darkening sound, with all vowels approaching in colour a mixture of 'o' and 'a', as pronounced in the English sound 'aw'.

In its combination of classical technique and modern expression Caruso's singing can be seen as the consummation of bel canto – and also its end. He was one of the last singers to learn at the highest level the grammar of the old style and who was then able to reconcile this with the gestures and the behaviour of verismo. He was able to convince through the strength of his personality and the truth of his acting.

His death in 1921 also marked the end of traditional opera. Puccini's *Turandot*, first performed by Toscanini at La Scala in 1926 in the incomplete version left behind by the composer, was the last grand opera. At that time conductors like Toscanini and Fritz Busch were starting to serve the great masterpieces by cultivating a repertoire which had become part of a musical history. It was a heroic struggle: the attempt to historicise in the grand manner and at the same time to transfer opera into the museum. Repertoire: those are the exhibits of a museum. But it was the gramophone record that made opera widely available in the museum of the imagination. It was Caruso's records that made an instrument out of a cultural pariah. His recordings capture the end of grand opera in a double sense.

Heritage cannot simply be passed on as a concrete possession. 'What you inherit from your fathers,' as it says in Goethe's *Faust*, 'acquire, in order to possess it.' Inheritance requires the recognition of constant change and, even more important, reconciliation with the new. This reconciliation, which was still possible for Caruso, was scarcely to be possible for his successors.

Adorno's opinion was that opera had lost its universal significance. Works like Berg's *Wozzeck* and *Lulu* made a radical break with grand opera and the products of late Strauss can be mildly characterised as 'masterly confections'.

A second reason for the change in the traditional art of singing was the gramophone record. It was responsible for changing our hearing and, in a quite specific way, our relation to time; it also changed our aesthetic sense. In a musical performance there exist both real time and the time of our experience – a phenomenon which is thematic in literature at the turn of the century, as in Marcel Proust's *A la recherche du temps perdu*. Both in the theatre and the opera house we can completely forget real time, and enjoy the moment with that pleasure which yearns for eternity, according to Friedrich Nietzsche. We can sense that this time that stands still is composed into both the *fioriture* of Bellini and the arabesques of Chopin.

The sense of time being suspended is not present when music is reproduced mechanically. A *rubato, fermata* or a gesture of sentiment which might move us in performance can be problematical, even disturbing on record, precisely because of the phenomenon of reproduction. It is striking how on recordings from the 1930s romantic music-making with its *rubato* is replaced by performances which are metrically strict and accord with the 'chronos of the present day', as Igor Stravinsky put it in his musical poetics. It was Toscanini who made a fetish of almost mechanical precision, and who placed perfection above musical meaning.

In an article on Furtwängler entitled 'Guardian of Music' Adorno wrote:

The relevance of Wilhelm Furtwängler today seems to me to

be indicated by the fact that in musical interpretation overall there is something missing which Furtwängler possessed in the highest measure: the organisation of the musical meaning, as opposed to the pure functioning which became an ideal for the musical world in following Toscanini. One could say that Furtwängler was a sort of corrective for a certain type of music-making which aimed solely at the perfection of the apparatus.

The perfection of the apparatus, in the sense of an orchestra which functions without mishap, seems indispensable to the aesthetic of the gramophone record. Its ideal is a reproduction perfectly tuned in every detail and free of error, in contrast to the performance which is weighed down by the risk of making mistakes. Adorno's assertion could be supplemented to the extent that pure functioning did not only come into the world of music with Toscanini, but above all with the development of technical reproduction.

It was more than just rancour against things technical that led Toscanini's great rival Furtwängler, prototype of the Romantic conductor, to be sceptical about recording in a studio, indeed to reject it. Furtwängler was aware of the incompatibility of his musical sensibility (and his sense of time) with technical recording (and its quite different rules of timing).

The history of interpretation as documented by the gramophone record illustrates that nothing is more difficult to incorporate into the chronos of the present day, which dictates the length of the record, than the way in which time is made to stand still by the artist. The *rubato* playing of performers such as Paderewski, Thibaud, Mengelberg, Barbirolli and the singing of Fernando de Lucia sound curious and old-fashioned to a listener who is not familiar with the performance practices of earlier times; the recordings of those artists seem to confirm the prejudices of those who accuse them of romantic arbitrariness and self-indulgent mannerism. To that extent they fall outside of time in two senses: outside of the real time which the record demands, and outside the taste of our own time.

After Caruso's death it was the tenor voice which remained the public's favourite for another three decades. The virtuosa, the dramatic *soprano d'agilità*, disappeared more and more from the stage. The florid roles went to coloratura singers with voices which were often too light, while lyric and dramatic parts went to the *soprano spinto*. No soprano after Caruso, not even Rosa Ponselle, achieved the popular fame of Beniamino Gigli, Richard Tauber or Joseph Schmidt who, courted by film-makers and the public, gave the masses what they wanted: music of the 'soul' and plenty of hype complete with sobs and sighs and a mixture of emphasis and vibrato which later infiltrated its way into pop music.

Vocal art in its strictest sense, the creation of a form with its own complex grammatical rules, began to decline. Even the lyric tenors who followed Fernando de Lucia, Alessandro Bonci and Giuseppe Anselmi, that is Tito Schipa, Cesare Valletti, Luigi Infantino, Ferruccio Tagliavini and Luigi Alva, were no longer virtuosi and were often out of their depth in florid music. The dramatic tenors took up the *cantare con forza* which we have already mentioned and which reached its culmination in the 1950s in the singing of Mario del Monaco. Even a lyric tenor like Giuseppe di Stefano, who possessed one of the most beautiful sounding voices ever, overtaxed himself by singing which was too open and which put too much upward pressure on the middle voice. Caruso had assured the tenor his central position on the stage, and his influence created a style. It is on Caruso, as Michael Scott writes in his biography, that all tenors have modelled themselves, from Martinelli, Gigli and Pertile to del Monaco, di Stefano and Domingo. Sopranos have not had a similar model. The tradition of classical and romantic singing had already ceased with Patti, Sembrich and Melba, or with Rosa Ponselle at the latest. Most of the sopranos heard under Toscanini belonged to the verismo school. Often they were very expressive singers, but no longer virtuosi. All the more disturbing, then, must have been the effect made at the beginning of the 1950s by a singer like Maria Callas.

For the operas of Verdi, Puccini and the verismo composers, Callas found in Giuseppe di Stefano and Mario del Monaco, Richard Tucker and Eugenio Fernandi partners who were stylistically far from her equal (they all sang without differentiation), but who were at least fully competent and fitting to the taste of the time. However, when Callas performed bel canto parts like those of Rossini, Bellini and Donizetti or even early Verdi, she was far superior to her partners in her mastery of the music's formal language. What was decisive was that she carried on the tradition not of the *soprani leggieri* but of the *soprani sfogati* of the nineteenth century. And it was in that respect that she succeeded, with great emphasis, in making a relevant contribution.

Whereas Toscanini at La Scala and the Met had been a contemporary of Verdi and Wagner and, within limits, also of the verismo composers, Callas was only able to find the new in the old. It is not sufficient to attribute her success only to heroic efforts and the attempt to do what all great artists do, namely to make time stand still. She could only make time stand still thanks to her mysterious ability to transform even the most familiar formulas or set phrases into musical architecture: and this was through her quite specific sense of measure and proportion in time.

Werner Schroeter wrote in his obituary of Callas that she had made use of an archaic art form, Italian bel canto opera, that she had thereby penetrated an artistic and social world which was lacking in vitality, and that she had to present herself to a society whose decadent upper classes looked on her greatest performances as prestigious social events.

Notwithstanding Schroeter's passionate support of Callas, to see her as victim of a decadent class is a misrepresentation. She also became the victim of a democratic system with an aesthetic inferiority complex and a tendency to level things out. What she had to fight against was mediocrity, the routine of theatrical business and the slovenliness of repertoire performances.

For some years she achieved triumphant successes against all imaginable odds. If one listens to the live recordings of *Nabucco* under Vittorio Gui in Naples, *Aida* and *Il Trovatore* from Mexico City, Bellini's *La Sonnambula* and Verdi's *La Traviata* or *Un Ballo in Maschera* from La Scala; if one listens carefully to the reactions of the audience in the performance of Donizetti's *Anna Bolena*; and if one experiences how Callas, opening the La Scala season as Norma on 7 December 1955, makes the phrase 'Ah, sì, fa core, abbracciami' soar through the air on one thread of breath, causing the audience to sigh audibly with admiration, pleasure and pain; if you hear all these things, then you must acknowledge that at least in the theatre she had real listeners – listeners who let themselves be transported and who were aware of the extraordinary quality of her singing. Even applause has its own quality: during and after Callas performances the applause is of stunned amazement and inspiration.

No, Maria Callas did not sing in a period that was unresponsive to opera; this set in after she had left the stage and both the new and the old worlds became sated with 'special festival occasions' (Adorno). The reminiscences of Luchino Visconti show, as do those of Franco Zeffirelli and Walter Legge, that she sang for a time which had a sense of time. Admittedly as a young singer she had had to study the role of Elvira in Bellini's *I Puritani*, bearing in mind its very different stylistic and technical demands, in the very same week that she was performing Brünnhilde in Wagner's *Die Walküre*; and for Rossini's *Armida* the maximum time she had was five days; but the fact that she could take on and meet these challenges reveals the store of technical training with which she could master even the most intricate problems of florid singing.

Once she had arrived, she could, at least in Milan, Florence, Venice, London and Chicago, work on productions and sing in performances which radiated what a festival performance must radiate: the ambition to achieve perfection, which was shared by at least some of her colleagues and partners. Perfection – what an imperfect and abstract concept. We are talking about expression, about the painful pleasure of making art and of making 'a tragedy, which in the normal way of things we do not seek to experience' (Ingeborg Bachmann), transforming it into one of those events which unites the special awareness of the participants with the special awareness of the observers.

On the evening of 28 May 1955 . . . no, it is happening even now, we can hear it, because time can be recalled in order to hold dialogue with eternity. Then, yesterday, now, tomorrow or in ten years' time we could or can experience what Carlo Maria Giulini, who conducted then and will conduct tomorrow, described as the moment when he was bringing the *Traviata*

prelude to a close and the curtain was rising on the *allegro* which
describes the ballroom scene:

> My heart skipped a beat. I was overwhelmed by the beauty of
> what stood before me. The most moving, most exquisite décor
> I have ever seen in my entire life. Every detail of Lila de Nobili's
> extraordinary sets and costumes made me feel I was actually
> entering another world, a world of incredible immediacy. The
> illusion of art – or should I say artifice – vanished. I had the
> same sensation every time I conducted this production – over
> twenty times in two seasons. For me, reality was onstage. What
> stood before me, the audience, auditorium, La Scala itself,
> seemed artifice. Only that which transpired on stage was truth,
> life itself.[2]

That was the very performance which inspired Ingeborg Bachmann. '*Ecco un artista* – she is the only person who was worthy
to be on the stage in these years, who has made the audience
below freeze, suffer and tremble, she was always art, yes art . . .'
That was also the performance with which Luchino Visconti
created an idea, that of consummate theatre:

> I staged *Traviata* for her alone, not for myself. I did it to serve
> Callas, for one *must* serve a Callas. Lila de Nobili and I changed
> the period of the story to the *fin de siècle*, about 1875.[3] Why?
> Because Maria would look wonderful in costumes of that era.
> She was tall and slender, and in a gown with a tight bodice, a
> bustle, a long train, she would be a vision. [. . .] I sought to
> make her a little of Duse, a little of Rachel, a little of Bernhardt.
> But more than anyone, I thought of Duse.

That was also the evocation of which the set designer Sandro
Sequi said:

> Visconti taught us to believe what we see but that truth must
> be filtered through art. And although everything in his *Traviata*
> was completely realistic, it was not realistic at all. For most
> theatrical people in Italy Lila de Nobili is the greatest set

designer in the world because of her wonderful ability to crys-tallise a mood. Her work creates the illusion of truth, yet with the impression of a painting, with a sense of poetic distance. She can awake a mood which reaches out beyond reality. I recall the huge chandelier in the first act, which was not really there but was painted, framed in silk, gauze and tulle. When lighted up it was transformed into a living picture. The same went for the large oriental vases and curtains which she designed for this scene – there was not a single authentic detail of oriental art about these objects. Yet one saw them and believed in their authenticity. The entire production had a trace of *décadence*, and it was right. Visconti and de Nobili produced an unforgettable dream of the *belle époque*.

That was also the performance in which the fruits of scrupulous and inspired work became an artistic reality. Carlo Maria Giulini:

In performance, she sang and acted with an ease as though she were in her own home, not in the theatre. And this was vital for our vision of Violetta, for the audience had to believe everything she did. In the first act, Callas was dressed and moved very much like the other courtesans, except she had this mysterious aura that made her different from all the others. It was not that she was better lighted or had more to do, she simply possessed this unique magnetism. Long before I began musical rehearsals with the soloists, chorus and orchestra, before Visconti began his staging with the cast, we worked with Maria alone over an extended period. We three arrived at her characterisation, with a complete synthesis of words, music, and action. Visconti – apart from the fact he is a genius of the theatre – has incredible sensitivity to romantic Italian opera. Each of Maria's gestures he determined solely on musical values. We concentrated much attention on Violetta's state of mind, trying to penetrate the psyche of this fragile feminine creature. In doing this, we discovered a thousand delicate nuances. I'm sure that anyone who saw Maria in this *Traviata* could no more forget her than forget the beauty of Greta Garbo in *Camille*. One was upset, moved [. . .] As for Callas's singing, I had conducted a single *Traviata* with her four years before at Bergamo – my first experience in the theatre. She came at the last minute as a replacement for Renata Tebaldi, who had sung the première. We scarcely had time to go over the score with the piano before the performance. Of course, Maria sang magnificently – she was immense then – but her Violetta at La Scala was something else. Very interior, so tender. As she, Visconti, and I went step by step through our preparations, she found new colours in her voice, new values in her musical expression, all through a new understanding of Violetta's innermost being. Everything came into rapport. Let me assure you, it was slow, fatiguing, meticulous work, done not to win popular success but for theatre in its deepest expression.

It was and still is there, this pleasure – and all pleasure wants eternity, deep, deep eternity – the painful pleasure of making art. Giulini:

Maria did not know the meaning of caprice or routine, even if she had to repeat a thing a hundred times. She was one of the few performers I have known – singers, instrumentalists, conductors – for whom the last performance was as important, as fresh, as exciting as the first. With others, and this is the woe of the theatre, after the opening night and a few performances, everything starts to go down in quality, to get stale. But with Maria, I assure you the eighteenth *Traviata* was as engrossing and intense as the première. Some nights, of course, were better than others. No singer is a machine. But one thing remained constant, Maria had a dedication to her work and to the theatre, and she had the desire to give to the public. You felt her inspiration not only in the big moments, the famous arias and duets, but also when you heard her call the name of her maid in a recitative. It could break your heart.

She was there and is there, the only artist who ever deserved to be on the stage, whereas her partner Giuseppe di Stefano began rehearsals for the first tender approaches in a state of boredom

and then came to rehearsals either late or not at all. Visconti:
'Maria became angry at this behaviour. "It shows lack of respect
for me, lack of dignity – and to you as well." ' There she was
and still is, the lever who turned a world for those who could see
and hear.

Piero Tosi, who two months earlier had designed the performance of Bellini's *La Sonnambula*:

De Nobili's first set, with its funereal colours of black, gold,
and deep red, filled the air with a premonition of Violetta's
death. Visconti gave each member of the chorus a sharply
defined character, each courtesan an individual personality.
Gastone he made a mincing homosexual. The disorder and
confusion of the stage action was that of a real party, a rowdy
one. Since the set had an offstage pavilion, Violetta's guests
could exit for dinner and return naturally. During the duet 'Un
di, felice', the lovers were alone. Callas in a black satin gown
and long white gloves, a bouquet of violets in one hand. As
Alfredo declared his love, she slowly backed away from him
towards the proscenium [. . .] Her white-gloved arms were
stretched out behind her, in caution. Finally, standing like this,
she was embraced by Alfredo. In surrender, the bouquet fell to
the floor, chairs in disorder. Then the maid Annina entered to
extinguish the chandelier and candles as Callas huddled by the
fireplace, wrapped in a shawl and lit only by the flames. Remov-
ing her jewels and the pins from her long hair, which fell to
her shoulders, she sang 'Ah, fors è lui'. Rising for the cabaletta
finale, 'Folliè! Folliè!', she moved to the table, sat, threw back
her head, and kicked off her shoes – the image of Zola's Nana.
Then the voice of Alfredo interrupts her song. It is a sound she
doesn't understand. Is it in her heart, her mind? Or is it real?
Vainly she searches for the voice, running toward the verandah.
You could feel her heartbeat at that moment.

There she was and is still, she who did not sing roles but who
lived on the razor's edge and who made the audience below
freeze, suffer and tremble. Giulini:

The brilliance with which Callas had depicted the courtesan's selfish desire for pleasure in the first act made all the more moving her transformation into a woman consumed by love in the second. This contrast in emotions is what Maria, Luchino, and I had sought during our long rehearsals. Callas, using every vocal, musical, and dramatic device at her command, fully revealed Violetta's capacity to give, her infinite ability to dedicate herself to another – even to the point of making a complete sacrifice of herself, of leaving the only true love she has ever known. It was incredible how, during this long duet, Callas drew an unending line of differing moods and feelings.

One heard it and we hear it again, how she sings 'Ah! Dite alle giovine'; no, she does not sing it but whispers, and how the voice dies away, suffers and turns in on itself, yet filling the entire theatre. And before us we see her as the picture of sadness and desperation. Visconti:

> At this moment, Violetta is all but dead. While Maria sat at the table, she made not one move we had not prepared in rehearsal – how she cried, how she grasped her brow, how she put the pen in the inkwell, how she held her hand as she wrote, everything. No singing, only acting as the orchestra accompanied. Some members of the audience wept as they watched Callas in this scene.

And only she was still there, she alone; the scenery disappeared, and was only materialised in her expression, as Piero Tosi describes. And we see her as the afflicted woman who is destined to die in the last act, when the curtain rises and men are carrying Violetta's furniture off to sell it; then we see her rise from the bed and she looks, in Tosi's words,

> like a cadaver, a figure from a wax museum – no longer a human being but a living corpse. And she sang with a thread of a voice, so weak, so ill, so touching. With great effort she reached the dressing table, where she read Germont's letter and sang 'Addio, del passato'. Then you saw the lights of the

carnival crowd passing outside the windows. On the wall were shadows of the celebrants at play. For Violetta, the world had become nothing but shadows. In Callas's every gesture, death seemed imminent. Even during the joyful reunion with Alfredo, she was so wan and frail that she scarcely moved. After the lovers sang of their dream of living together in happiness far from the city – 'Parigi, O cara' – Violetta was seized by a desperate need to escape the deathtrap in which she found herself. She called her maid to bring some clothes and began a terrible struggle to dress. Then came the moment when she tried to put on her gloves, but could not because her fingers had already grown rigid with approaching death. Only then did Violetta realise there was no escape, and in this awareness Callas let forth with overwhelming intensity the outcry 'Gran Dio! Morir sì giovine'. For the moment of death, Visconti called upon all Callas's genius as an actress. After accepting her fate and giving Alfredo a locket containing her portrait, Violetta spoke the famous concluding lines. Radiantly, she told Alfredo that her pains had ceased, that her old strength had returned, that new life was being born and, on the words 'O gioia!' she died, her great eyes wide open, fixed in a senseless stare into the audience. As the curtains fell, her dead eyes continued to stare blankly into space. For once, an entire audience shared Alfredo's shock and grief. They too had felt death.

Such performances were still possible in the 1950s, primarily at La Scala when Callas sang the most unforgettable of all *Norma* performances on 7 December 1955, Donizetti's *Anna Bolena* under dramatic circumstances on 14 April 1957, Verdi's *Un Ballo in Maschera* on 7 December 1957 and Donizetti's *Poliuto* on 7 December 1960. And such performances were no longer possible when at last, in 1956, she arrived at the Metropolitan Opera and then had to sing her meticulously honed portrayals on poorly contrived sets. According to the description of Irving Kolodin in *The Story of the Metropolitan Opera*, Callas brought dramatically convincing portrayals but 'what remained, and it was all the more irritating, were slovenly sets'. Nor did Callas receive what was taken for granted in Milan: a sufficient number of rehearsals.

Developments in the recording studio were no different. After
Walter Legge, following months of difficult negotiations, finally
sighed, 'Callas – finalmente mia' over the singer's contract which
was signed on 21 July 1952, he could start the first recordings in
1953. He reported:

Our first recordings together were made in Florence after a
series of performances of *Lucia* there with Serafin. The acoustics
of the hall our Italian branch had chosen were antimusical and
inimical. I decided to make a series of tests of 'Non mì dir'[4]
with Callas for two purposes – to get the psychological feel of
working with her, sensing how receptive she would be to
criticism, and to find placings to give at least a decent sound.
It was soon clear that she would take suggestions without a
murmur. I had found a fellow perfectionist as avid to prove
and improve herself as any great artist I have ever worked with.
(Ten years later we were to spend the best part of three hours
just repeating the last dozen bars of the *Faust* Jewel Song to get
a passable end to it.) We delayed publication of this *Lucia* until
after *I Puritani*, made a few weeks later. Angel's first Callas
recording had to be a revelation, for her sake and for Angel's
reputation for quality, which we had yet to establish. Also, *I
Puritani* was the first-fruit of EMI's contractual collaboration
with La Scala – a double coup – though it was recorded in a
Milan basilica.[5]

What the producer describes here is the making of Callas's
career, but by artistic means and not those of publicity and mar-
keting. His report of the production of Puccini's *Tosca* between
10 and 21 August 1953 shows how all the participants were
working towards the ideal of a performance which was sonically
perfect. Legge writes:

The supreme Callas recording was her first *Tosca*, after nearly
twenty-five years still unique in the history of recorded Italian
opera. De Sabata and I had been friends since 1946 but never
recorded together. In those pre-stereo days, effects of distance
were more difficult than now. To achieve Tosca's convincing

entry, her three calls of 'Mario' were done separately – all from the wings, each one nearer the microphones – and spliced together later. The 'Te Deum' took the greater part of two sessions. Tito Gobbi recently reminded me that we had made him sing all his first-act music thirty times, changing the inflections and colours even on individual syllables, before we were satisfied. Callas had arrived in superb voice and, as always in those days, properly prepared. Only for 'E avanti a lui tremava tutta Roma' was she put through de Sabata's grinding mill for half an hour – time well spent. We used miles of tape.

Legge's recollections show, like those of Giulini or Visconti, that Maria Callas was first able to sing in a period which possessed a sense of time. That was no longer possible when, having become a world star, she was freed from the exacting artistic world of congenial directors and producers who had enabled her to unfold her ability and her expressive powers. As she began her descent to become the most famous woman in the world, the first signs of her artistic decline appeared. It was like an incubation. There followed periods of exhaustion and nervous crisis. The first symptom was her cancellation of a performance of *La Sonnambula* when La Scala was giving guest performances in Edinburgh in August 1957, and a greater one after a performance of *Norma* was interrupted in Rome in January 1958, leading to an incredible scandal which was as great as her fame itself. The decline then manifested itself further when, at the end of the 1950s, Callas appeared everywhere in concerts which had a luxurious circus atmosphere, in Hamburg and Munich, Barcelona and Athens, London and Amsterdam, in circumstances where she could not develop her best talents, those of dramatic portrayal. The jubilation on these occasions was mere hysteria resulting from the sensation which her appearance caused. It must have resounded painfully in her ears as well as those of critics who sensed that her triumphs had become Pyrrhic victories (not that there is anything against an artist making hay in the late summer of her career – it is her right). This was the time when operatic life began to change and decline into an opera business: with galas and ubiquitous stars who were only available for short rehearsal periods and that at the expense of the entire world. Stars who dictated, as is now normal practice, which works a theatre should perform, works which the singers had recently taken into their repertoire and which they had prepared badly in other theatres, rather than works chosen with any sense of appropriateness. There is no logical connection between the way in which musical life developed into a festival market and the extinguishing of that great comet which had illuminated the operatic firmament for almost a decade. Maria Callas had consumed herself: 'Everything I touch turns to light, everything I leave behind turns to ashes, I am surely a flame.'

But her end was a symbolic end, a mystery for her contemporaries. How could she have lived on or sung on in this sinking world?

5

Apprenticeship

'A singing teacher must have perfect command of three things and of three ways of listening to his pupils – he must be able to hear them as they are, as they could be and how they should be [. . .] He must develop their understanding as well as their body. He must help them to unfold their character. He must awaken in them the desire for beauty'

Giovanni Battista Lamperti

A Stolen Childhood?

'Old newspapers are a first-class education
about transitoriness'
Robert Musil

'Ultimately it is a question of how much
truth there is in a lie'
Thomas Bernhard

It was the opinion of Thomas Carlyle that it was the duty of
biographical writing to teach hero-worship – admiration of
geniuses, of the great and the immortal. Private matters – they
were irrelevant. In some Callas biographies the artist's stature is
used to make the most intimate details of her private affairs the
basis for psychometry. Her liaison with the Greek entrepreneur
Aristotle Onassis has been the subject of more writing than her
full 600 performances, the scandals the subject of more writing
than her achievements and triumphs. It is not possible to reveal
new details, but it is very important to discard the irrelevant ones.
And this should be done not in order to transfigure the singer
and to stylise her as a person, but rather because the historical
phenomenon of Callas must be understood and placed in its historical context. Walter Legge was able to do this, with a mixture
of admiration and coldness, in his essay 'La Divina':

> More than enough has been published about her unhappy child-
> hood, quarrelling parents, myopia, avoirdupois and depri-
> vations, but no one has assessed the effects of these disadvan-
> tages on her career and character. Callas suffered from a
> superhuman inferiority complex. This was the driving force
> behind her relentless, ruthless ambition, her fierce will, her
> monomaniacal egocentricity and insatiable appetite for

celebrity. Self-improvement, in every facet of her life and work, was her obsession. When she was first pointed out to me, a year or two before we met, she was massive, shabbily dressed in a nondescript tweed coat, and her walk had the ungainly lurch of a sailor who, after months of rough seas, was trying to adjust himself to terra firma. At our first meeting I was taken aback by her rather fearsome New York accent, which may have had a booster from GIs when she worked as interpreter for the American forces in Athens. Within months Callas was speaking what the English called the King's English until the BBC murdered it. A gifted linguist, she soon learned good Italian and French. When she had slimmed down from over 200 pounds to less than 140, she became one of the best-dressed women in Milan. Her homes in Verona, Milan and Paris paid silent tribute to her taste and love of order. Attached to every garment in her wardrobe in Milan was a list giving the date she had bought it, what it cost, where, when and in whose company she had worn it. Gloves – each pair in a transparent plastic envelope – and handbags were similarly documented, and every object had its place. These were private reflections of the meticulous care she put into her work.

How this elegant tribute contrasts with the psychological speculation indulged in by the trivialising biographers of Callas. To refrain from gossip is not the same as examining the singer's development and, according to the maxim of Sainte-Beuve, 'from seeing everything, looking at everything or at least pointing everything out'. It must be admitted that she was not a particularly kind person but again quoting Walter Legge, who was not a kind person either: 'She could be vengeful, vindictive, malicious in running down people she was jealous of or had taken a dislike to, often without reason. She was ungrateful; for years she refused to work with or even talk to Serafin, who had been her invaluable help and guide since her Italian début, after he recorded *La Traviata* with Antonietta Stella.'

Such behaviour can be explained in the light of the shyness and insecurity of a career woman who had had an unhappy childhood. She was born on 3 December 1923 as the third child of Evangelia and George Kalogeropoulos in New York's Fifth Avenue Hospital and christened Cecilia Sophia Anna Maria. Arianna Stassinopoulos writes that Maria Callas always celebrated her birthday on 2 December. Dr. Lantzounis, who was present at the birth in the hospital, confirms this date. Her mother says it was 4 December. At her school the date is registered as 3 December.

Her parents had emigrated from Athens to the United States on 21 August of that same year after the death of their three-year-old son. Her mother reports in *My Daughter, Maria Callas* that after the death of Vassily she had constantly 'prayed for another son to fill the empty place in my heart'. After the birth of her daughter she was bitterly disappointed and 'it was four days before I looked at the child'. But when the child's dark eyes seemed to ask, 'Mother, why don't you love me?' she suddenly began to feel maternal love.

The family's financial position had worsened. George Kalogeropoulos, who in Athens had been a quite successful chemist, had to support his wife and two daughters with work as a travelling salesman for pharmaceuticals. When his wife insisted on giving their daughters training in music, he felt it to be a senseless extravagance, considering the economic depression. Evangelia reports that at the age of four Maria was already listening with enthusiasm to the family pianola. She tells us also that she bought records of excerpts from *Faust, Mignon* and *Lucia di Lammermoor* and that the two girls admired the voice of Rosa Ponselle and sang along with it. Another legend which the mother propagates is that one afternoon the family heard a Met broadcast of *Lucia di Lammermoor*. The singer of the title role is supposed to have botched the Mad Scene, which Maria found lamentable, saying that she could sing it better.

Maria received her first piano lessons at the age of eight. Later she was able to play all her parts at the piano without the help of a repetiteur. At ten she was singing arias from *Carmen* and the story goes that people passing by stopped to listen under her window when she sang 'La Paloma' and other songs. In a competition organised by the Mutual Radio network she won a prize, a Bulova watch. This was the beginning of her participation in numerous other competitions which she was pushed into by the

ambition of her mother, who saw both her daughters as prodigies.
Maria Callas later complained bitterly that 'there should be a law
against it' – that her mother had stolen her childhood from her.
'I only felt loved when I was singing.' She suffered even more
from the fact that she was plump and extremely shortsighted.
'My sister Jackie was a beautiful girl,' she said later, 'but I
was fat and covered with pimples. I was much too mature for
my age and was anything but happy. I was very much the ugly
duckling.'

In the last weeks of 1937 the mother decided to return to Greece
with her two daughters. She was convinced that Maria would
only be able to get the most suitable vocal training in Athens.
George Callas – the Greek had changed his name in New York
– agreed. A few days after finishing her eighth school year she
boarded the ship *Saturnia* with her mother. During the crossing
she sang, to entertain the captain and passengers, songs like 'La
Paloma' and 'Ave Maria', finishing with the Habañera from
Bizet's *Carmen*. On the final phrase 'Prends garde à toi' she is
supposed to have plucked a carnation from a vase and thrown it
to the captain.

More Than a Teacher: Elvira de Hidalgo

'The technique of singing is simple and
always the same. The only difficult part is
teaching a person to do the right thing technically. Only a good teacher can do that'

Luciano Pavarotti

On the day following her return to Athens the girl's life was
transformed into an 'audition machine'. She had to sing for everybody. In September 1937 her uncle Efthimios succeeded in arranging an audition with Maria Trivella, who was teaching at the
Athens National Conservatory. Immediately before this test she

was filled, as at many later performances, with anxiety and panic. 'Before I start singing I forget everything, can no longer remember my part and do not know where to begin.' Trivella, who had had no great success as a singer but was experienced as a teacher, immediately accepted Maria Callas as a pupil and took the step of falsifying the girl's age: Maria was thirteen – but admission to the conservatory was allowed only at the age of sixteen.

Maria sang music from *Carmen, Lucia di Lammermoor* and *Cavalleria Rusticana*. It was in Mascagni's opera that she made her début in a student performance in November 1938, shortly before her fifteenth birthday. This won her the conservatory's first prize. Pierre-Jean Rémy sees it as symbolic that that very first role portrayed a suffering and victimised woman. 'Throughout her life she moved between these two extremes, from victim to tigress. But even the tigress, be it Santuzza or Medea, is a victim.' After two years' work with Maria Trivella she made a renewed attempt to be accepted at the Athens Conservatory. She sang for the Spanish soprano Elvira de Hidalgo who insisted that the girl should be admitted regardless of her young age.

Elvira de Hidalgo, born in 1892, was a pupil of Paul-Antoine Vidal. She had made her début at the age of sixteen at the San Carlo in Naples with the role of Rosina in Rossini's *Il Barbiere di Siviglia*. The legendary impresario Raoul Ginsbourg engaged her for the Monte Carlo Theatre where she once again sang the role of Rosina in the company of Dimitri Smirnov as Almaviva and Feodor Chaliapin as Basilio. Giulio Gatti-Casazza brought her to the Met because he needed a counter-attraction for Luisa Tetrazzini, who was singing at Oscar Hammerstein's opera house. De Hidalgo was no competitor for the Italian virtuosa. After hearing the Spanish soprano William James Henderson wrote that the Met was 'no place for pampering little girls'. She returned to Europe, made her début at La Scala in 1916 as Rosina (alongside the Figaro of Riccardo Stracciari) and from then on sang in middle-ranking Italian theatres and above all in South America. She had come to Athens in the 1930s with a travelling opera company, and when the outbreak of war made further tours difficult she accepted a professorship at the conservatory. She only wanted to work there for a year; but this turned into years.

The Spanish singer recalled her first meeting with the ugly and inhibited girl:

It was simply laughable that she even entertained the idea of becoming a singer. She was tall, very stout and wore thick spectacles. When she took them off she gazed at one with large but vague eyes which saw nothing. Everything about her was gauche. She wore a dress that was much too large. It was buttoned at the front and rather shapeless. Not knowing what to do, she sat quietly in the corner biting her nails and waiting for her turn to sing.

Maria sang Rezia's 'Ocean, thou mighty monster!' from Weber's *Oberon* and the teacher was fascinated by the 'violent cascades of sound which were not yet perfectly controlled but were full of drama and emotion. I listened with my eyes closed and imagined what a joy it would be to work with such material and to mould it to perfection.' Maria was accepted at the conservatory as a private pupil of de Hidalgo without payment, the reason for this being that the teacher, whom Rémy describes as 'a female Pygmalion', pinned all her hopes on making her pupil into a singer of a stature she herself had never achieved. 'I began lessons with her at ten in the morning', Maria Callas related in 1970, 'then we took a break at midday to eat a sandwich and then carried on our lessons into the evening. I never thought of going home earlier simply because I would not have known what to do with myself at home.'

At that time the Callas voice had such a limited range that some teachers took her for a mezzo, a more limited voice. The cautious work of extending it both upwards and downwards became for her a sort of athletic training. 'I was like a sportsman', she said, 'who takes pleasure from using and developing his muscles.' Elvira de Hidalgo became more than a teacher. She also became her pupil's closest confidante emotionally.

The closer the relationship became with the teacher, so Callas became all the more critical of her mother, who would later take revenge when she wrote a book about her daughter. De Hidalgo, on the other hand, remained one of the few people, perhaps the only one, who never lost the singer's affection. When Callas died the only portrait found in her flat besides that of the legendary Maria Malibran was the one of de Hidalgo. It was she who had started to transform the 'ugly duckling', not only through musical training but also with practical help in other matters. She showed her how to move on the stage, how to dress and how to hold herself.

The mother had wished only for the fame of her daughter. 'All that I wanted for her was fame.' In that wish she had robbed her daughter, as Callas later saw it, of her childhood. Elvira de Hidalgo had, on the other hand, set her on the path to fame and thereby given her a sense of her own worth that Maria Callas had never received as a child. Yet the influence of both women doubtless left its mark on the singer's disposition and reactions.

As part of her vocal education de Hidalgo advised her pupil to concentrate on the lighter coloratura parts, on *canto fiorito*. Only after finishing her technical development would she attempt heavier, more dramatic roles. Nevertheless, it was clear from the start that Maria Callas would not become a *soprano leggiero* but rather a *soprano sfogato* like Giuditta Pasta, for whom Bellini composed the roles of Norma and Amina in *La Sonnambula*, a soprano extended to encompass both coloratura agility and dramatic verve. 'I resembled a sponge,' Callas said later, 'ready to absorb everything.'

Her teacher brought her a thorough and all-embracing technique. She lent her scores which she then learned by heart, often working long into the night. She studied *Lieder* by Schubert and Brahms, Pergolesi's *Stabat Mater* and Purcell's *Dido and Aeneas*, even Bach's *St Matthew Passion*. Without this systematic and comprehensive training, comparable to the *études* essential for pianists and violinists, Maria Callas would never later have been able to learn and master the most difficult roles within a few days. The training in that art which is casually defined as bel canto was for her 'the specific training of the voice and the development of a technique for her use, in the way that a violinist or a flautist trained, in order to master their instrument completely'. De Hidalgo enabled her pupil to participate in a student performance of Act III from Verdi's *Un Ballo in Maschera* and in Puccini's *Suor*

Angelica. In that same year, 1940, de Hidalgo also obtained for her her first engagement at the Athens Royal Opera; on 27 November she sang the small part of Beatrice in Suppé's operetta *Boccaccio*. Two years later she would replace an indisposed colleague at the Royal Opera when she sang thirteen open-air performances of Puccini's *Tosca* at the Thellentas Theatre.

Around these performances rumours circulated, like premonitions of those scandals which overshadowed her later career. Apparently the sick diva was manipulated by a group of Callas opponents. When she heard that the hated competitor was going to sing Tosca, she is supposed to have sent her husband to the opera in order to prevent her rival from appearing. Full of anger, Maria Callas apparently scratched him in the face.

This incident was put forward as the reason why Callas did not like the work. In interviews she often expressed the opinion that she did not like the part of Tosca nor indeed any of Puccini's music. The most plausible explanation for this is that the role of Tosca, which is one of her most sublime portrayals, was not one that she could sing with that vocal ease or achieve with the balance that she found in the great bel canto parts. This would explain why, apart from her forty-six performances of Tosca and twenty-three of Turandot (all of these in the years 1948 and 1949, when she was still fighting her way to the top), she sang roles like Cio-Cio-San on the stage three times, but never Mimì in La Bohème, or Manon Lescaut. In her great years between 1953 and 1958 Puccini's heroines played no part in her career or in her rise to the position of greatest prima donna of the age. And yet she enjoyed success with Tosca right from the first performances, even if it was a part she did not like. Alexandra Lalaouni wrote in *Vradyni* after performances in August and September 1942:

All the mistakes, all the weaknesses in the production are forgotten as soon as Maria Kalogeropoulos appears, a young girl, still almost a child [. . .] Not only does she get through the role without error, not only does she sing correctly, but she also knows how to present it with a strength of conviction which often overwhelms the audience. The voice has a fullness over the entire range of her extended register. Quite apart from

how good her training has been, it seems to me that she possesses something which goes far beyond that. Musical instinct
of this high quality and a dramatic sense are both gifts that she
cannot have obtained from her training and that one certainly
cannot have acquired by her age. She was born with them.

The fact that she sang Tosca more frequently at the end of her
career proves the thesis that roles from the verismo repertoire can
be mastered by the art of acting and with only the remnants of a
voice.

After 1940, during the German and Italian occupations of
Greece, the standard of living deteriorated for Evangelia Callas
and her daughters. Food was so short that the seventeen-year-old
girl had to give concerts in Athens and Saloniki. As a fee she
was given spaghetti and vegetables. Eventually the Athens Opera
engaged the young singer for a fee of 3000 drachmas. She was
not yet allowed to choose her own repertoire; she had to sing
what was announced on the programme. In April and May 1944
it was six performances of d'Albert's *Tiefland*. In the *Deutsche
Nachrichten in Griechenland* the critic Friedrich W. Herzog wrote
that she already possessed everything that other singers had to
learn: dramatic instinct, intensity of acting, interpretive imagination. It also strikes one that he mentioned the 'penetrating, metallic strength' of her voice in its upper range. On 14 August 1944
there followed two performances of Beethoven's *Fidelio* in the
Herodes Atticus Theatre in Athens under the German conductor
Hans Hörner. Two months later the occupying powers lost control of Athens and Greece. Then the British fleet landed in Piraeus.
Maria Callas decided to return to the USA and to her father. On
3 August 1945 she gave a concert in Athens in order to pay for
the journey and in which she sang 'Bel raggio' from Rossini's
Semiramide and arias from *Don Giovanni, Aida, Il Trovatore* and
Oberon. The programme indicated that she possessed the potential
of a dramatic *soprano d'agilità*. A performance of Millöcker's *Der
Bettelstudent* followed on 5 September. A few days later she
boarded the *Stockholm* and travelled to New York, having said
farewell to Elvira de Hidalgo.

Entr'acte in New York

'I prefer to rely on myself and myself alone'
Maria Callas, 1970

She was met by her father, who was living in modest circumstances. Arianna Stassinopoulos reports that the singer yielded to the temptations of incessant eating and got fatter and fatter ('I was as hungry as one can be after having not eaten any proper food for a long time'). Attempts to get engagements failed. She sought assistance from the Greek bass Nicola Moscona, who was well known for his various Verdi performances under Toscanini and who had been much impressed by his young colleague's performances in Athens. After she had managed to reach him and asked him to introduce her to Toscanini, he categorically refused to recommend an ambitious young singer to the old maestro. However she did get the chance to audition for the tenor Giovanni Martinelli.

Martinelli, born in 1885 in Montagnana (like his colleague Aureliano Pertile), had come to the Metropolitan Opera in November 1913, had made his début there as Rodolfo in *La Bohème* and in the 1920s after Caruso's death, had taken over that tenor's dramatic roles like Radames, Canio, Alvaro, Dick Johnson and Andrea Chénier. Up to 1946 he had sung in every season at the Met: altogether more than 650 performances in thirty-six roles and 300 further performances on the Met tours. He was a highly dramatic singer with fantastic breath control and a majestic line; yet his vocal production was not altogether free-flowing. Stylistically he had moulded himself to the dramatic *espressivo* style of Arturo Toscanini: few tenors this century have sung with more fire, pathos, and rhetoric. Martinelli was sympathetic in his assessment of the voice of Maria Callas but advised her to seek more tuition. It can only be assumed that he may have been irritated by the voice's imbalance with its audible 'gear changes'.

On the other hand Edward Johnson, who after his own tenor

career at the Met had taken over its directorship from Giulio Gatti-Casazza, found the Callas voice 'impressive'. He offered the twenty-two-year-old singer two productions for the 1946–7 season: Leonore in Beethoven's *Fidelio* and Cio-Cio-San in Puccini's *Madama Butterfly*. Her refusal, and especially the reason for her refusal, has become part of the Callas legend. Rémy reports that she had suggested Aida or Tosca and that Johnson's angry reaction was to put the contract back into his pocket.

John Ardoin's version is more plausible. Maria Callas could not, with her generous figure, see herself as the Japanese geisha, and as she did not want to sing Leonore in English, the Beethoven part eventually went to Regina Resnik. Callas's behaviour shows, however, how aware she was of her capabilities and her value, but above all how uncompromising she was. Nadia Stancioff appears to have heard quite a different version to John Ardoin. Johnson had offered the singer an engagement on condition that she could improve the top and bottom of her voice, precisely the advice which Giovanni Martinelli had offered. She did not want to confront her father with this rejection as she had already enthused to him about her successes back in Greece. In order to save her face, she then invented the heroic legend which she was later to relate with such frequency that she came to believe it herself.

The truth may even be that she made Johnson an offer to sing Tosca and Aida without a fee. Arianna Stassinopoulos dates the singer's hatred for the Met from this period. She is quoted as saying, 'I shall be back; you will beg me, on bended knee, to come back.' The sort of thing one finds in the fiction on every artist's career which monotonously recurs whenever the difficult early years are discussed. Another anecdote which fits the legend just as well is the one about an audition at the San Francisco Opera for the director Gaetano Merola. He is supposed to have told Callas that she was too young and should go to Italy to establish herself; then he would engage her. 'Thank you, but when I have made my career in Italy, I will not need you.'

In January 1946 came a meeting which was to have momentous repercussions. Callas met Eddie Bagarozy, an opera-crazy lawyer, who was married to the singer and teacher Louise Caselotti. The couple immediately showed great hope in the young soprano, although they found her voice coarse at the top and uneven. Caselotti offered further tuition and there again followed weeks of intensive study. In his enthusiasm for his wife's pupil Bagarozy had the idea of forming an opera company. With the United States Opera Company he wanted to bring the Chicago Lyric Opera back to life. As there were many artists in Europe waiting for engagements, it was easy to secure stars with big reputations: the Wagner tenor Max Lorenz, the sisters Anny and Hilde Konetzni, the young soprano Mafalda Favero and the well-known bass Nicola Rossi-Lemeni, son-in-law of Serafin, who later was often to sing alongside Callas. Puccini's *Turandot* was planned for the opening performance in Chicago. For the title role a sensational new soprano was announced: Maria Callas. But the opening, planned for 27 January 1947, never took place. The union representing American chorus singers demanded a financial guarantee which Bagarozy and his partner, the Italian agent Ottavio Scotto, could not meet. Bagarozy had to sell his car and even his wife's jewellery in order to settle some of the debts. On 6 February 1947 Maria Callas returned, disappointed and poorer by one hope, to New York. The United States Opera Company had foundered and was apparently a write-off.

Nicola Rossi-Lemeni was convinced of his young colleague's talent and introduced her to Giovanni Zenatello. This veteran tenor, for many years Francesco Tamagno's successor and the most important interpreter of Verdi's *Otello*, was artistic director of the Verona Opera Festival. He had come to New York in search of a singer for Ponchielli's *La Gioconda* to open the 1947 season. He had a choice of two well-known and esteemed sopranos: Zinka Milanov and Herva Nelli, the latter Toscanini's favourite. On Rossi-Lemeni's advice Zenatello invited Maria Callas for an audition. He was so inspired by her singing that he joined in the Act 4 duet 'Enzo! . . . sei tu!' Zenatello engaged the unknown Greek girl as well as a young American tenor who was then at the beginning of his big career: Richard Tucker. Tucker had already sung the role of Enzo at the Met alongside Milanov. Zenatello described the meeting as 'a revelation, not just an audition'.

On 27 June 1947 Maria Callas left the United States on the ship *Rossia*. On the same day she had signed a contract with Edward Richard Bagarozy, in accordance with which the lawyer would be her sole agent for a period of ten years. For his work he would receive ten per cent of her fees for 'all appearances in opera, concerts, radio, recording studios and television'. Bagarozy contracted himself to make 'every possible effort to promote the artist's career'. As Stassinopoulos reports, Maria Callas hesitated a long time before signing the contract; that she did so, on the very day of her departure, was a decision made on the spur of the moment, a decision in making which her usually so reliable instincts appear to have deserted her.

Elvira de Hidalgo had advised her pupil to start her career in Italy – which she now did after an eighteen-month intermezzo in New York. The first nine years of her career, from the début as Santuzza at the Athens Opera until her first appearance in the Verona Arena on 3 August 1947, are a twilight period, only sporadically illuminated by anecdotes and incidents. Nine years without any significant development, nine years of fanatical learning with no real recognition, nine years of struggle without real success, nine years of hunger and longing for fame.

Whatever is known about the 'ugly duckling' of the decade 1937–47 is fragmentary. The conductor Nicola Rescigno said: 'It is a great mystery how a girl from the Bronx, born into an unmusical family and growing up in circumstances without any connection with opera, could have been blessed with the ability to sing the perfect recitative. She possessed an architectural sense of which word in a musical sentence had to be emphasised and of which syllable in that word had to be stressed.' That is a description of her ability, not an explanation. This ability is just as inadequately explained by the often quoted advice given to her by Tullio Serafin, that she needed only to speak the words of a recitative slowly in order to find their dramatic meaning. It is advice which Serafin may have given hundreds of singers; only a few knew how to take it with imagination. Maria Callas possessed not only a dramatic sense but also a composer's sense of how to shape words, which were articulated in a plastic and expressive way into a suggestive sound; and she was trained in the technique in such an exemplary way that she always fitted the words to the sound and thus made the words musical.

It is insufficient to trace her ability to the ambitions of a frustrated child, to the inferiority complex of an unattractive girl, to the enormous and one-dimensional passion of a woman eager for fame or to the ruthlessness of a career person; such explanations are mere popular psychology. Like for example Feodor Chaliapin or even Charlie Chaplin, Maria Callas had at her disposal the most highly developed imagination and mimetic strength, plus a technique which had become second nature. Her unhappy youth may have driven her to unusual exertion. But genius lies not only in bearing inordinate pain, but also in setting one's aims high and in endless effort to acquire the means of fulfilling those aims.

6

The Years of Travel

Meneghini

'I want to tell you one thing, my beloved:
that I love you and that I venerate and
respect you. I am so proud of my Battista!
There is no other woman as happy as I am.
Even if I am famous as a singer, it is much
more important that I have found the man
of my dreams!'

Maria Callas, letter dated 2 May 1949

A marriage based on reason, affection and security did not fit
well into the fantasy world of the 1950s. That a woman who was
admired as 'divine' and hated as a 'tigress', and whose career
furnished material for hundreds of scandalous stories, should have
married a man viewed in the press as 'bachelor' and 'old opera
roué', as 'penny pincher' and 'provincial Casanova', fitted badly
into the fairytale which dream manufacturers had invented of
the ideal couple with its consuming passion and its marriage of
love. Still less so when Maria Callas was on stage the most
consummate portrayer of those passionate, suffering, dangerous
and endangered females which the nineteenth century had con-
jured up. To repeat: after the *femme fatale* had long been domesticated, the *mystery* of the feminine principle had survived in the
myth of the prima donna as resurrected by Maria Callas; it was
certainly not matched by the figure which the industrialist
Meneghini embodied, a successful and average middle-class man
who was not even particularly attractive. The story which is
handed down in the book by Stassinopoulos as well as in many
newspaper articles, and which describes the marriage between
Maria Callas and Giovanni Battista Meneghini as never having
existed on an erotic level, infers that a web of erotic tension
was the source of the singer's artistic expression; this supposedly
explains the effect which the 'tank-owner Onassis' was to have
in the late 1950s when he crossed her path.

It is scarcely to be conceived that marriage with an ageing
Veronese would have taken place if it had not served a practical
purpose. Friedrich Nietzsche has described how a marriage can
only last 'if the wife wants to achieve fame through her husband
and if the husband wants to become popular through his wife'.
This is not a 'romantic' but a thoroughly realistic definition of
the relationship between Callas and Meneghini. Walter Legge,
who knew the couple closely, saw it no differently and considered
that close friendship was its real basis. It is also possible that Maria
Callas became what Meneghini saw in her as a result of the
affection and trust which he placed in her, and what he saw was
the great and unique singer.

Maria Callas in Verona: another piece in the mosaic of her
legend. After landing in Naples on 27 June 1947 from the SS
Rossia, Maria Callas travelled to Verona with Louise Caselotti and
the bass Nicola Rossi-Lemeni. Gaetono Pomari, a representative
for the Verona Festival, had arranged a supper with the industrialist, who shared with most prominent bourgeois Italians a passion
for opera and the festival. George Jellinek describes Meneghini as
a short, compact man with grey and thinning hair but at the same
time 'shrewd, alert and dynamic'. He was immediately interested
in the singer and fascinated by her. Later on she is supposed to
have declared: 'I knew in five minutes that he was the one.' The
next day he accompanied her on an excursion to Venice and from
then on they were inseparable. She had a feeling of well-being and
of being protected in the company of this quiet and self-confident
man, who was politely courting her, even if it was not, according
to Jellinek, 'love at first sight' in the grand romantic sense.

In the Stassinopoulos biography it is stated that 'men as lovers
played no role at all in her life', but on the other hand Nadia
Stancioff quotes the singer Arda Mandikian from the Athens
Opera, as saying,

Of course she had affairs! One was with the baritone Evangelias
Mangliveras, and everyone knew about it [. . .] At the time
he was already past his artistic prime but still had his loyal fans.
Perhaps it was only an insignificant affair, but he certainly took
her very seriously. Later, when he was lying sick and when

Callas had risen to world fame, he wanted to see her again. But she refused. She behaved very badly towards him but that was characteristic of her in such matters.

Début in Verona

'If you possess magnetism, then the whole world is yours'

Giovanni Battista Lamperti

The rehearsals began in July 1947 for the performances of Ponchielli's *La Gioconda* under Serafin, who in Germany is quite wrongly regarded as a routine opera Kapellmeister. Callas described him as *un vecchio lupo* – an old wolf with an infallible sense of the quality of a voice and above all of its technical skills, expressive potential and ultimately its ability to anticipate the next second of the music. Callas regarded her meeting with the conductor as 'the greatest happiness' of her early career. 'He taught me that everything one sings must have expression and deeper meaning; I drank in everything this man told me.'

Serafin had been one of the founders of the Verona Festival and conducted the very first performance there, Verdi's *Aida*. In the 1920s, when Arturo Toscanini was directing at La Scala, Serafin was working at the New York Metropolitan. Even then Serafin, who was married to the wonderful soprano Elena Rakowska, showed a special awareness for first-class voices. He had been decisive in promoting the career of Rosa Ponselle and in conducting her performances of *Norma, La Gioconda* and *La Vestale*. After her début at the Met Ponselle was told by William James Henderson that she would 'one day learn to sing'. She took eighteen months to prepare her first Norma with the constant help and advice of Serafin at her side. After Henderson had written about her Norma with enormous enthusiasm, she was recognised as *assoluta* at the Met, and she later admitted in her memoirs that

Henderson's first favourable review had been the greatest joy of
the season and of her young career. A little later Serafin also
worked with Claudia Muzio, probably the most interesting
verismo diva, whose interpretation of Violetta's 'Addio del passato' has often been compared with that of Callas. Muzio's delivery of the scene is highly expressive but very strongly influenced
by declamation. Maria Callas sees the piece more from the viewpoint of song: she moulds the words to the sound. The two
interpretations can be compared only as voices that are completely
opposite.

When Serafin first experienced the twenty-three-year-old Maria
Callas he heard, as he later put it, 'an exceptional voice. Certain
notes were not yet securely placed (especially for Italian listeners),
yet in her I immediately recognised the future great singer.' And
he was determined to smooth her path, perhaps to produce a new
Ponselle. He was her second Pygmalion after Elvira de Hidalgo.

Nicola Rossi-Lemeni has spoken in more detail about the
voice's weaknesses. His commentary is interesting for the reason
that he paints a less than glowing picture of the overwhelming
success of the five *Gioconda* performances, of which the première
took place on 2 August 1947. Rossi-Lemeni, who was on stage
with Maria Callas, is quoted by Nadia Stancioff:

> The books written about her give the impression that her career
> just took off. That's not so. Even in *Gioconda* she had no
> success, and afterwards she worked very hard to rid herself of
> the ugly sounds in her voice which sometimes seemed to come
> through a thick fog. These ugly sounds were due to a particular
> defect which we call 'the potato in the mouth' – that is to say,
> some sounds went back by themselves even if she tried to
> support them outwards. It depends on the conformation of the
> resonator [. . .] Maria worked to make her voice more pleasant
> [. . .] Maria was the hardest worker I've ever met.

The technical explanation which Rossi-Lemeni gives (as transmit-
ted by Stancioff!) is odd. It probably refers to the work needed
on the hard palate by way of forward placing and the resulting
resonance in the mask. It is worth noting that at the beginning

Maria Callas did encounter difficulties in lifting the soft palate with ease and fluency.

It is also said in a book on the American tenor Richard Tucker, that the début of Maria Callas was by no means a sensational one. James A. Drake is of the view – and gives evidence – that her début has been glorified in the light of later fame. Richard Tucker considered the singer's technique as amateur, he was far more convinced by the 'exquisite lyrical flow and flawless technique of Renata Tebaldi'. Drake quotes the critic Renato Ravazzin, who assessed the Callas *Gioconda* in *Il Gazettino* as 'dramatically gripping but spoiled by an obviously unfinished technique'.

On the other hand *Corriere della Sera* reported, as briefly quoted by David A. Lowe, that Callas and Tucker had shown themselves to be 'in excellent voice' and that they had been 'rewarded with much applause'. Again it becomes difficult, if not impossible, to separate fact from fiction. After the five performances, which she had to undertake after an accident at rehearsal in which she had sprained an ankle, Callas received no immediate invitation to return to the Verona Festival. The second opera to be performed during that season was Gounod's *Faust*. Mephistopheles was sung by Rossi-Lemeni and Marguérite by Renata Tebaldi, who a year earlier had been engaged at La Scala primarily on Toscanini's recommendation. This was the first crossing of the paths of the two divas who were later to become rivals – or perhaps they were only manipulated as such.

The sole invitation for a further engagement came from the town of Vigevano near Milan. Maria Callas was asked to repeat *Gioconda* there but declined, hoping for better offers. Her confidence, which Serafin was helping to build, suffered in consequence. An audition with Mario Labroca, artistic director of La Scala, resulted in nothing more than the usual references to certain vocal defects. There was talk of her being considered for a production of *Un Ballo in Maschera* but this was followed by two months' silence. The agents she visited in Milan were of as little help as the praise which Tullio Serafin was scattering everywhere. The explanation for these setbacks lay mostly in the strangeness of her singing (at least to audiences at that time) and in her idiosyncratic, oscillating and metallic voice. 'To listen to me was a new experience,' said Callas, 'and they did not like anything which broke with their traditions.'

For her second engagement Maria Callas had to thank the man who was decisive in building her career: Tullio Serafin. The maestro wanted to stage Wagner's *Tristan und Isolde* at the Teatro La Fenice in Venice, to be sung in Italian. She did not know the role but accepted the offer without hesitation and on Serafin's assurance that all that was needed was 'a month of study and hard work'. The première on 30 December 1947 and three further performances in January 1948 brought Callas considerable success. She was immediately engaged for five performances of Puccini's *Turandot*. These performances too, conducted by Nino Sanzogno, helped to strengthen her reputation. It was only later that Louise Caselotti said: 'I was horrified when I heard her sing Turandot. The gleaming high notes, which I had heard during our preparations for the performances planned for Chicago, now lacked freedom; they wobbled violently. Her low register was also weak. I knew that she was on the wrong track and told her so.' Maria Callas sang the role of the ice princess twenty-four times, all of them in the years 1948 and 1949 when she was still establishing herself. And it says much that she mastered the part with sovereignty, not just with the powerful summoning of will as in the complete recording in 1957.

Those performances of *Turandot* signalled the beginning of a good and great year for the singer. Suddenly she was receiving one offer after another. She sang two performances of *Turandot* in Udine in March 1948, four of Verdi's *La Forza del Destino* in Trieste, three of *Tristan und Isolde* with Max Lorenz and conducted by Serafin in Genoa; further *Turandot*s in the Roman Baths at Caracalla, in the Verona Arena and at the Carlo Felice in Genoa; four of *Aida* under Serafin at the Lirico in Turin and finally, at the end of the year, *Norma* at the Communale in Florence, again conducted by Tullio Serafin. After the Genoa performances the critic Beppe Broselli wrote in *Corriere del Popolo* of her Isolde: 'Noble and even solemn, a sublime queen and a passionate lover – her Isolde was a great interpretation. Her magnificent appearance gave the figure additional charisma and irresistible grandeur.

Yet the strongest fascination and the most moving expression came from her voice, a majestic and gleaming instrument, vibrating and warm, supple and balanced over all registers – the ideal voice for an Isolde.' This is an amazing review after what had previously been said about her voice. After further performances in Rome in 1950 she abandoned the part, saying later that neither Brünnhilde nor Isolde offered such a challenge as the role of Bellini's *Norma* which she began studying with Serafin in June 1948 and which she was to sing eighty-nine times, out of the 605 opera performances of her career.

After three performances of *Aida* at the Teatro Sociale in Rovigo in October and a single *Turandot* in Pisa in November, she gave her first two performances of *Norma* under Tullio Serafin at the Communale in Florence on 30 November and 5 December 1948. Adalgisa was sung by the mezzo-soprano Fedora Barbieri, Pollione by the tenor Mirto Picchi, Oroveso by the bass Cesare Siepi – the greatest names in Italian opera of those years. Two reviews quoted by Henry Wisneski illustrate that Maria Callas was beginning to be appreciated as a special case. Gualtiero Frangini wrote in *La Nazione*:

> Maria Callas was a new singer for us; yet right from her first appearance in the first act it was clear that we had before us a soprano of really major quality. She possesses a powerful voice with a timbre that is steady and attractive, able to be penetrating in loud passages and sweet in more delicate moments. Her technique is secure and perfectly controlled. The voice has a most unusual colour and the way in which she applies it – even if quite different from what we are used to – has an undeniable quality. Callas offered an interpretation rich in subtle and moving feminine accents. As Norma she presents, in addition to the priestess of the last act who cannot be restrained, the loving and then betrayed woman, the mother and the companion.

The critic Virgilio Doplicher emphasised that she was 'versed in the greatest demands of Italian bel canto tradition'. She had obviously profited tremendously from the collaboration with Tullio

Serafin, as Rosa Ponselle had done twenty-five years earlier.
Rémy quotes the statement which Maria Callas was to make two
decades later: 'There are only two conductors in the world: Serafin
and Giulini.' And she had worked with Victor de Sabata, Erich
Kleiber, Leonard Bernstein, Herbert von Karajan, Gianandrea
Gavazzeni, Antonino Votto, Vittorio Gui, Georges Prêtre, Nicola
Rescigno, Dimitri Mitropoulos and Fausto Cleva.

Ambizioso spirto

'The singing voice is a castle built in the air.
Imagination is its architect. Nerves carry out
the intentions, muscles perform the work.
The soul lives in it'

Giovanni Battista Lamperti

Turandot, Isolde, Leonora in *La Forza del Destino*, Aida and
Norma within one year: what courage, what energy! But Tullio
Serafin's ambition was still greater – or should one call it extreme?
Immediately after the performances of *Norma* the conductor
engaged her for a production of Wagner's *Die Walküre* at La
Fenice in January 1949. He wanted to show that the division
between lyric, dramatic and coloratura voice was a solution – or
shall we say a stopgap – to problems which the composers of the
nineteenth century had themselves created; he was convinced that
he had found in Maria Callas an interpreter who was capable of
singing with all those voices, just as Lilli Lehmann had once done.
Maria Callas accepted the challenge with a passion which one can
only describe as self-destructive.

It has been the subject of a thousand speculations as to whether
her voice would have lasted longer than the seven or eight great
years to 1957 if she had not, between 1947 and 1951, risked
hybrid parts like Turandot, Isolde, Norma, Brünnhilde, Elena and
Abigaille. Perhaps she would have been able to sing over a longer

period of time, but she would not have been Callas, not 'the only person who was worthy to be on the stage' in those years. Although Elvira de Hidalgo had advised her to start with the florid bel canto parts, she was already studying the heavy role of Brünnhilde alongside Norma in the autumn and winter of 1948.

When Maria Callas arrived in Venice, still exhausted from the *Norma* performance in Florence yet stimulated by her success, the theatre management faced a serious dilemma. The Wagner opera was scheduled to be premièred on 8 January 1949, while a première of Bellini's *I Puritani* was fixed for eleven days later. The role of Elvira, sung at its first performance by Giulia Grisi (alongside the Arturo of Giovanni Battista Rubini, who in the last act as the result of misreading the score sang a high F!), had been given to the soprano Margherita Carosio, a typical *soprano leggiero*. On the day before Maria Callas's arrival Carosio had had to cancel her rehearsals because of a heavy attack of influenza. Stassinopoulos relates that Serafin telephoned his wife Elena Rakowska in the hotel and told her of his desperate dilemma. After the telephone call Rakowska was standing near the door of the adjoining room where Maria Callas was in the habit of work-ing with Serafin outside of normal rehearsal times. She was appar-ently sight-reading Elvira's aria. 'Tullio is on his way to the hotel,' Rakowska is supposed to have said, 'Will you do me a favour? Would you sing it again for him?' Callas sang for Serafin Elvira's long aria, the only piece she knew in the entire opera. Serafin listened and said nothing. The next morning he phoned and asked her to come straight down to him. He asked her to sing the aria again, whereupon he said, 'Well, Maria, you will be singing this part within a week.'

Legend has elaborated this exchange between conductor and singer, but whatever passed between them, Callas sang Wagner's Brünnhilde on 8, 12, 14 and 16 January 1949, then Bellini's Elvira on 19, 22 and 23 January, after a week of learning the role. That she was able to *study* both parts simultaneously shows an extraordinary degree of musical ability; that she could *sing* them both borders on the miraculous, for more differing roles can scarcely be imagined: Brünnhilde's 'Hojotoho' and Elvira's 'Son vergin vezzosa' from *one* voice. Listeners recognised the battle cry from Kirsten Flagstad or Frida Leider, and the strings of coloratura from Lily Pons or Carosio.

With these performances Maria Callas placed herself in the limelight. Henry Wisneski quotes the critic Mario Nordio:

> A few days ago many people read with amazement that our wonderful Brünnhilde, Isolde and Turandot would now be singing Elvira. Yesterday everybody had the chance to experience her Elvira. Even if they noticed from the very first notes that this was not the customary light soprano, the most sceptical listeners had nonetheless to acknowledge the miracle which Maria Callas was achieving. A large part of this must be put down to her early studies with Elvira de Hidalgo. They had to acknowledge the flexibility of her fluid and beautifully surging voice and its brilliant top notes. In addition the interpretation possesses a humanity, warmth and expressiveness which we seek in vain in the fragile light sopranos who normally attempt Elvira.

Five days after the three performances of *I Puritani* she sang Brünnhilde again, this time in Palermo, followed immediately by four Turandots at the San Carlo in Naples and then Kundry in *Parsifal* in Rome, again with Serafin. Franco Zeffirelli was in Rome at the time producing Shakespeare's *As You Like It*, but he related that after attending the dress rehearsal of the Wagner opera he lost all interest in his own work; the only topic of conversation was the phenomenal new singer. He said after one performance, 'I recall clearly that my ears were tingling – the power and presence of this woman – something extraordinary had occurred.' In describing the voice the critic Adriano Bellin said: 'She triumphed victoriously over all difficulties – through the security of her vocal production, the wonderful balance of registers and fine high range.'

As she was now known outside the immediate world of opera and had become a personality of public interest in Italy, Italian radio invited her to give a concert. On 7 March 1949 she sang Isolde's Liebestod, Elvira's 'Qui la voce', Norma's 'Casta diva' and Aida's 'O patria mia'. This was the pattern, two dramatic arias contrasted with two bel canto ones, which she continued to use in later concert programmes. Except for the Aida aria, which never suited her and which she never performed to her complete satisfaction, the same programme was recorded in Turin in November 1949 under Arturo Basile. The Elvira aria in particular was a revelation, with its unbelievable *portamento* on the word 'speme' and the miraculous *rubato* effects, for in the entire history of recording one had never heard a dramatic soprano with comparable agility. In the cabaletta she sang both the diatonic and the falling chromatic scales with an instrumental perfection, concluding with an E flat *in alt* at full voice. After the concert Nazzareno de Angelis, one of the most outstanding bass voices in Italian opera alongside Tancredi Pasero and Ezio Pinza, sent a telegram: 'After this radio programme I dare to predict that the spirit of Maria Malibran will rise again in Maria Callas.' However, according to George Jellinek, de Angelis heard Callas in Rome in *I Puritani* and warned her against taking roles 'which are not your roles'.

Soon afterwards Maria Callas undertook, as Maria Meneghini Callas, her first journey to South America, to the Teatro Colón in Buenos Aires. On 21 April 1949 she had been married in the Chiesa dei Filippini in Verona, receiving from her mother, in reply to a telegram saying, 'Siamo sposati e felici', the message 'Always remember, Maria, that you belong first to the public, only then to your husband.'

Maria Meneghini Callas opened the Italian season in Buenos Aires as Turandot on 20 May 1949. Although one read in *La Pensa* that she was nervous, as the result of a slight indisposition, it must have been a memorable performance, as documented by the recording of a fragment from the second act with Mario del Monaco as her partner. Her voice cuts through the thick orchestra sound with shining intensity – with a bright ardour such as one only remembers from Eva Turner. On the rostrum was Serafin, who was greatly admired in Argentina and who had brought to South America some of the most brilliant singers of Italian opera – the veteran baritone Carlo Galeffi, Fedora Barbieri and Nicola Rossi-Lemeni. However, neither as Turandot, which she was singing for the last time, nor as Aida was Callas completely able to win over the Argentinian critics. But this did happen with her four *Norma* performances in June. She returned home and then, apart from a performance of Stradella's oratorio *San Giovanni Battista* on 18 September 1949, had almost four months clear in which to prepare her third Verdi role. At the San Carlo in Naples she was to sing Abigaille in *Nabucco* under Vittorio Gui, the part with which it is said that Verdi overtaxed, to the point of destruction, the voice of Giuseppina Strepponi – who was later to become his wife. On the opening night, 20 December, Callas was partnered by Gino Bechi, then at the height of his vocal powers and reminiscent of Titta Ruffo. In his study *Voce Parallele* Giacomo Lauri-Volpi compares Bechi with Ruffo and takes as *tertium comparationis* the concept of *suonatore*: the singer who eclipses everything with the explosive power of his sound.

If proof is needed for the assertion made by Stassinopoulos that Maria Callas intended to 'steal' the success of the première from the baritone, then it is supplied by the technically miserable recording of 20 December 1949, the singer's first complete performance to be documented; in a role which is described as hybrid because it demands a high degree of agility, the cutting power of a dramatic soprano and an enormous range. The high C, which is a note marking the transition to the very top of the third octave, and which was later often to be a tremulous note for this singer, was sung at that time without any effort, even after the chain of trills in the cabaletta following the big aria, which she also decorates in reprise. Most remarkable of all is the Act 2 duet, in which Callas enters into a duel with Bechi, winning through the sheer intensity of her singing – after her E flat *in alt* his fulminating high A seems merely loud, not of burning intensity.

With the triumphant success of these three performances there began a season in which Maria Callas staked her claim on first place among Italian sopranos. In January 1950 she sang Norma under Antonino Votto at La Fenice in Venice, early in February Aida under Alberto Erede at the Teatro Grande in Brescia, and almost immediately Isolde and Norma under Serafin in Rome. The tenor Giacomo Lauri-Volpi, who was later to partner Callas several times and who was one of the most important commentators of singing, wrote in *A viso aperto* about the second performance of *Norma* on 26 February 1950:

Norma is divine. It is a work which has inspired the depths of my heart. All those people who were amazed that the work had also been performed by Malibran, should have heard Maria Callas in order to understand how right Bellini was to entrust the opera to a more powerful voice. Voice, style, delivery, power of concentration and that vital pulse of inner meaning – all this is found to perfection in this artist of extraordinary greatness [. . .] Norma's lamenting voice in the final act touched me as the purest bliss that art can bestow.

The climax of the season, or better still the breakthrough, should have come on 2 April 1950. La Scala had asked Maria Callas to take over from an indisposed Renata Tebaldi. After the three performances both she and her husband expected an offer of a contract, but praise for her success was merely respectful and Antonio Ghiringhelli was reserved. It is possible that Maria Callas had appeared in the wrong role: as Aida. Henry Wisneski quotes a review from the *Corriere Lombardo* in which it is suggested that she had forced certain high notes.

High-flying in Mexico

'Emotion without a tone that can flow with
the breathing puts a strain on the voice'
Giovanni Battista Lamperti

After the performances at La Scala she sang two more Aidas in Naples with Tullio Serafin and then set out on her first tour to Mexico. The contract provided for performances of five operas; *Norma, Aida, Tosca, Il Trovatore,* and *La Traviata*. The engagement had come about on the recommendation of Cesare Siepi, who had said to Antonio Caraza-Campos, manager of the National Opera of Mexico: 'There is a soprano, Maria Meneghini Callas. She has sung Norma, Brünnhilde, Turandot and Elvira in *I*

Puritani; she has a fabulous range, going up to E with the sort of dramatic colouring which drives people crazy.'

Maria Callas, who had flown to Mexico via New York and had brought her mother with her, cancelled *La Traviata* immediately upon her arrival. She had not yet studied the opera and did not know that it was in the contract.

When Carlos Diaz Du-Pond, the manager's assistant, heard Callas at her first piano rehearsal with the conductor Guido Picco in the duet 'Mira, O Norma' with Giulietta Simionato, he immediately telephoned Caraza-Campos: 'Come here straight away; Callas is the finest dramatic coloratura soprano I have ever heard in my life. I heard Ponselle's Norma at the Met and also Arangi-Lombardi.' Caraza-Campos hurried along, bringing with him the score of *I Puritani*. 'He requested me to ask Maria Callas if she could sing the arias so that we could hear her E flat. To which Maria replied, 'Tell Mr Caraza-Campos that if he wants to hear my E flat then he must engage me next year for *Puritani*.'

She made her début on 23 May at the Palacio de las Bellas Artes as Norma. Giulietta Simionato was singing her first Adalgisa, Kurt Baum was Pollione and Nicola Moscona was Oroveso. Both female singers were suffering from a slight indisposition and Callas was not quite able to win the public over with her 'Casta diva'. In the first interval she said to Du-Pond: 'Carlos, I am not surprised at the cool reception; people do not like my voice on a first hearing and must get used to it.' Du-Pond explained to her that the South American public expected first and foremost effective high notes. At the end of the second act, 'Callas sang the brilliant D flat *in alt* and received an ovation for it' (As the performances were recorded, we have evidence that Callas sang a high D in the Act 2 finale). Du-Pond also reports that in the second performance she sang 'like an angel'. A critic wrote in *Excelsior* that he had left the performance blissfully happy and at the same time sad: sad because he was sure that he 'would never hear such a Norma again'.

It has often been reported that Maria Callas sang in Mexico with extreme commitment. How boundless the commitment was is shown by the recording of *Aida* on 30 May 1950 with her famous high E flat at the end of the second act. If this recording did not exist, the reports of that performance would border on the legendary.

Tension had arisen between the tenor Kurt Baum and Maria Callas during the *Norma* performances, and in the first *Aida* mounted to a sort of duel on stage. Carlos Diaz Du-Pond related in *Opera* that Antonio Caraza-Campos had invited Maria Callas and Giulietta Simionato to his home after the dress rehearsal. He there showed Callas a score which had belonged to the Mexican soprano Angela Peralta (1845–1883). Peralta had sung a high E at the end of the second act and Caraza-Campos tempted Maria Callas with the words 'Madame Callas, if you sing an E flat tomorrow, the Mexicans will go crazy.' Maria Callas refused, firstly because the note was not written and secondly because she did not wish to annoy her colleagues. Du-Pond reports that as they left Giulietta Simionato had said 'Cara per me, da il me bemolle. . . . this could lead to some fun.' At the performance on 30 May Kurt Baum, who was a typical stage tenor, annoyed his colleagues by hanging on endlessly to his high notes; one can hear in the recording how he leans on the high B at the end of his *romanza* with such strained endurance that one can almost see the whites of his eyes. Nicola Moscona went to Maria Callas's dressing room in the interval to complain. Callas turned to Du-Pond and said, 'Carlos, please go to Simionato and Robert Weede (who was singing Amonasro) and ask them if they would object to my singing a high E flat.' Now an E flat *in alt* in the Act 2 finale of *Aida* means much more than a vocal risk. This was the last time that Verdi was to compose a scene in the style of *grand opéra*, a scene of the most brilliant effect. To compete with a vast choir and full orchestra with blazing trumpets is to demand of a singer the highest possible degree of penetrative power. The sort of E flat which a *soprano leggiero* could produce would simply be drowned in the waves of sound. Maria Callas took this E flat at full pressure – in other words like a high octave. The tone cuts through the tumultuous noise of the scene – the impression is of a bolt of harsh and brilliant lightning in a stormy night; one gets the feeling that for a moment both the audience and Kurt Baum are speechless. But Maria Callas must have enjoyed the stunt. She was to repeat it a year later without the excuse of having Kurt

Baum there as a vocal blunderbuss – instead she was singing with
Mario del Monaco, who presented Radames with the emphasis
fitting for a tribune of the Roman people.

The performances have become famous for this trapeze act in
the vocal stratosphere and for the good reason, which cannot be
sufficiently emphasised, that a prima donna must take such risks
in order to get where Callas did. And yet there are better reasons
for examining her dramatic portrayal of Aida. There is not a
single studio recording where Aida's music of the first act can be
heard sung with more power of suggestion, with more life or
with more plasticity than in these Mexican performances of 1950
and 1951. If there was a 'weakness' in the performance, then it
was the C in the Nile aria. It may seem strange that a singer who
could as Norma pluck a C from the air or strike an E flat with
full attack should have had such difficulty with this C. Here it is
not an end in itself, but a transitional note, the formation of which
presents far more difficulty than an E flat at maximum tension.
But all the more convincing is Maria Callas's success in the dramatic duel with the cut-price, imprecise Radames of Kurt Baum.

The third opera in the four-week visit to Mexico was Puccini's
Tosca. The first performance had to be postponed for two days
owing to Callas's indisposition. The recording of 8 June 1950
shows that a less inspired conductor – Umberto Mugnai – and
partners whose singing was crude, particularly the tenor Mario
Filippeschi, could inhibit even Callas; compared to the grandiose
complete recording under Victor de Sabata, this performance is
low-grade and demonstrates that Callas was not a 'natural' as an
interpreter of so-called verismo music.

All the more interesting is her performance of Verdi's *Il Trovatore* on 20 June, with Giulietta Simionato, Kurt Baum and Leonard
Warren and Guido Picco as conductor. Carlo Diaz Du-Pond
wrote in *Opera* that Warren had been unwell and was therefore
unable to finish the performance; the Act 4 duet had consequently
been omitted. For the second and third performances the baritone
Ivan Petrov had been brought over from New York. However
Warren's voice can be clearly recognised in the recording.

Before singing the first Leonora of her career, Maria Callas had
turned to Tullio Serafin for his help in preparing the part. The

maestro refused to assist, saying that he was not willing to take on the preparatory work if someone else was going to conduct. It was only seven months later in Naples that she would sing Leonora under Serafin. John Ardoin's description of the Mexico performance as an 'unusual achievement' is an understatement, because after decades in which the part was given less than its due, it was Maria Callas who located it again correctly in the bel canto tradition. Yet with the clarity of her shaping and with her gift of rich coloration she transforms the devices which Verdi introduces so frequently, such as the trills on phrase endings in 'D'amor sull'ali rosee', into expressive gestures. When in Act I, after a faultlessly produced D flat *in alt* she then interpolates an E flat *in alt*, this can be taken as a concession for the South American audience which so loved these high notes. The cabaletta is a true vocal *tour de force* with powerfully executed trills, finely accented *staccati* and a further E flat, albeit this time a strained one.

At Caraza-Campos' home the singer negotiated a visit for the following year. The manager advised her to study Gilda in *Rigoletto* and Lucia di Lammermoor, but she was not to perform these roles until 1952 in Mexico, along with Elvira in *I Puritani*, Violetta in *La Traviata* and Tosca. In 1951 she repeated her triumph in *Aida* and sang her first Violetta, and though John Ardoin writes that it was 'a performance in the making', even this sketch of the role was more sharply outlined and performed with more character than the portrayals of all her rivals. Primarily she has the advantage of a vocal energy which makes her rendition of 'Sempre libera' with its many high Cs a breathtaking achievement, not to mention the concluding high E flat with a brilliance of white heat. However such notes take their toll. They burn up energy, burn up the voice. After the performances in Mexico Maria Callas was so exhausted that she had to take a break of almost three months. She sang her last performance of *Il Trovatore* on 27 June 1950, said farewell to her mother, whom she was seeing for the last time, making her a gift of a fur coat, and then departed for Madrid to meet her husband before returning to Italy to rest. Her next appearance, as Tosca, was not until 22 September. On 2 October she sang Aida in Rome, where she was preparing her first comic role: Fiorilla in Rossini's *Il Turco in Italia*.

The work was suggested by Luchino Visconti, who in conjunction with young producers and music-lovers wanted to put on
some rarely played operas at the Teatro Eliseo in Rome. Visconti
had seen Callas there the year before as Kundry. It was he who
introduced the singer to the Anfiparnasso group of artists whose
aim was to bring about a renewal of politics and art, aesthetics
and morals, in short a new model for society. Even though
Maria Callas was anything but an intellectual, she proved an ideal
medium for a man like Visconti – the 'most professional material'
with which he had ever worked. In contrast to other exponents
of so-called producers' theatre Visconti was not among those who
used the singer as a mere instrument and, as the soprano Maria
Carbone put it, 'robbed her of her whole personality'. On the
contrary, his concern was to unfold in equal measure the vocal
and acting abilities of his diva and thereby to make *opera*; his view
was that this would preclude forcing her to act in a way which
would inhibit her singing – he conceived of singing as a form of
acting. In that respect he was much closer than most practitioners
of the German school to Richard Wagner's idea of the actor-
singer. Maria Callas was to say later how surprised she had been
to find that this already renowned producer also attended the long
musical rehearsals.

This first collaboration in Rome laid the foundation for the
friendship between Maria Callas and Visconti, who promised her
that he intended to work with her again in future. The four
performances of *Il Turco in Italia* in October 1950 – with Cesare
Valletti, Sesto Bruscantini and Mariano Stabile as partners and
Gianandrea Gavazzeni as conductor – brought a triumphant success for Maria Callas. T. de Beneducci wrote in the magazine
Opera:

Maria Callas was the surprise of the evening, because she sang
a *leggiero* role with maximum lightness and in the style which
had been practised by singers at the time of the work's composition. She did not make it easy for us to believe that she can
also be the perfect interpreter both of Turandot and of Isolde.
In the first act she nonplussed everybody by singing a perfectly

tuned, gentle high E flat at the end of an effective and vocally difficult aria.

It is scarcely conceivable that, just three weeks after the fourth performance of Rossini's *opera buffa* on 29 October 1950, she sang Kundry in Wagner's *Parsifal* for Radio Italiana in Rome. This makes it easier to understand that she was considered to be a unique vocal and dramatic phenomenon. In the weeks between the two operas she was also working on another new role, which she was to sing only five times on stage and was never to record: Elisabetta in Verdi's *Don Carlo.* The performances, which were planned for Rome and Naples, had to be cancelled because of an attack of acute jaundice; this was in fact her last cancellation which was not to cause a scandal. After the two *Parsifal* performances in Rome she had to take a break of six weeks.

During the first trip to South America she had begun studying Violetta with Tullio Serafin, and it was with this role that she made her first appearance of the year, on 14 January 1951: this was the year in which Italy was commemorating the fiftieth anniversary of Verdi's death. The rehearsals had led to some minor differences with Serafin, because she was apparently no longer prepared to play the role of patient pupil to the great maestro. Yet Serafin said after the performance: 'She has had the most extraordinary success, and most people were dumbfounded by the performance.' A week after the *Traviata* performances in Florence she sang in Naples, again under Serafin, three perform-ances of *Il Trovatore* which, to quote John Ardoin, 'continued to develop more strongly what Callas had grasped only intuitively [in the Mexico performances]'. The performance, conducted in grandiose style and, in the third act, with incredible drive by Serafin, was received comparatively coolly. Discernible loud boos were to be heard amid the applause after the *stretta* of the veteran tenor Giacomo Lauri-Volpi, as can be heard in the live recording. Lauri-Volpi, whom even Arturo Toscanini had never managed to tame, wrote an open letter to the Naples newspapers, complaining about this 'dreadful indifference' towards the finer points of vocal art and expressing particular anger that the glorious singing of his young colleague had not been appreciated in a fitting way.

The *Trovatore* performances in Naples were followed by two *Norma*s in Palermo in February 1951. While she was there Callas received an emergency call from Antonio Ghiringhelli: she was again needed at La Scala to replace an ailing Renata Tebaldi. Her response, as disseminated by the media, is another part of the Callas legend. If La Scala wanted her, she is supposed to have said, then she would come as a star but not a substitute for another prima donna. She knew all too well that she could afford to wait, and she also knew that the autocratic and self-satisfied impresario would not be able to delay much longer before calling her. Each of her performances was bringing her nearer to triumph at La Scala, not least those of Verdi's *I Vespri Siciliani* at the Florence Maggio Musicale on 26 May 1951. They were conducted by Erich Kleiber, who was making his début in Italy as a conductor of opera.

7

Queen of La Scala

The Best Singer on the Italian Stage

'My God, she came on the stage and
sounded like our deepest alto, Cloë Elmo,
and before the end of the evening she took
a high E flat, and it had double the strength
of one from Toti dal Monte'

A member of the chorus recalls Maria
Callas as Elena in her La Scala debut in
I Vespri Siciliani

The performances of Verdi's *I Vespri Siciliani* at the Florence May
Festival were also part of the country-wide commemoration of
the composer who had died fifty years earlier. The part of Elena,
like that of Abigaille, is a hybrid one, demanding a *spinto* voice
of great range and, for the bolero, a fluent coloratura. It matters
little that she does not make the high E in 'Mercé, dilette amiche'
quite securely. What verve there is in the trill of the coda, what
energy in the leap to the high C.

Antonio Ghiringhelli had come to Florence for the performance. The impresario of La Scala knew that he could no longer
avoid engaging Callas and offered her the opening première of
the 1951–2 season: *Macbeth*, conducted by Victor de Sabata. The
contract also included three leading roles, thirty performances and
a salary of 300,000 lire. Although the singer was suffering from
an indispostion on the first night, both her dramatic portrayal
and her singing earned tumultuous applause. The Italian critic
Giuseppe Pugliese, one of the connoisseurs of singing, reported
in *Opera*:

I believe that at the first performance she was not in top form,
and yet her singing possessed a self-confidence and tragic bravura which was often exciting. . . . her dramatic sense was
displayed in the supple cavatina with which Elena incites the

Sicilians against the French in the first act, and the smouldering anger of 'Il vostro fato è in vostra man' had an extraordinary vitality. At this performance the voice did come in danger of losing quality when she sang at *forte* (except for a gleaming top E at the end of the bolero). But her quiet singing in the Act 2 and 4 duets was exquisite, and the long and crystal-clear chromatic scale, with which she concluded her solo in Act 4, made a brilliant effect.

Four days after the four performances of *Vespri*, on 9 June 1951, Callas sang the role of Euridice in Haydn's opera *Orfeo ed Euridice* at the Teatro della Pergola in Florence. The critic Newell Jenkins reported for *Musical America* that she had perfect mastery of the classical style but that her 'rich and beautiful voice' had been 'often uneven and tired'. One noticed that her appearances had long since attracted more than local interest; increasing attention was being given to them by the international press. After La Scala it was the Royal Opera House, Covent Garden which offered the young diva a contract. She was to sing Bellini's *Norma* in 1952. Sander Gorlinsky carried out the difficult negotiations for the contract in Verona. Her salary was to be £250, and the first person to attempt to claim her share for her part in the singer's success and wealth was her mother Evangelia. She had left her husband for a second time, had returned to Greece with her daughter Jackie and sent Maria a series of letters in which she complained bitterly about George Callas and ended up by demanding the debt of gratitude which she considered was owing from the daughter who was married to a millionaire.

In June 1951 Maria Callas travelled back to South America, this time accompanied by her husband. She had engagements in Mexico and in Brazil. In Mexico she was to meet her father, whom she had invited for the tour. She sang three performances of *Aida*, more consistent in tone and also more dramatically focused than in the previous year. A week after these and another concert, there followed, conducted by Oliviero de Fabritiis, four performances of *La Traviata* with the young Cesare Valletti as Alfredo and Giuseppe Taddei (and Morelli) as Germont père. Violetta was, like Norma, a role linked to her destiny; she had sung it only once before in Massimo and was to sing it sixty-three times in all. At this performance she was already demonstrating that Violetta can be sung by *one* voice and does not require different voices for the first and last acts. John Ardoin notes that every note of 'Sempre libera' is precisely placed. The scales are fluent and formed with the particular weight of each individual tone, the high Cs sit perfectly and the high E flat at the end is like a cry of jubilation (even if one has reservations about her conserving her voice by omitting four and a half bars before the E flat). The stature of her portrayal is only slightly lessened by the fact that she does not convey the pain of the second act or the spoken words before 'Addio del passato' with quite as much fulfilment as in the 1955 La Scala performances with Giulini.

After the triumphant Mexican performances the singer was so exhausted that she had to cancel her planned *Aida* appearances in São Paulo and Rio de Janiero; she sang Norma in São Paulo and Rio, *La Traviata* in São Paulo and Tosca in Rio. The cancellations brought the first critical comments in the press, which also made full and enjoyable use of the differences between Maria Callas and Renata Tebaldi, who were alternating as Violetta. Renata Tebaldi had recently experienced a fiasco when singing Violetta at La Scala and despite her success in Rio was irritable and oversensitive. Tension broke out after a concert in Rio's municipal theatre. Maria Callas sang 'O patria mia' and 'Sempre libera', Renata Tebaldi sang Desdemona's big scena from Act 4 of *Otello* – and Tebaldi then gave two encores. A way of thanking the audience but an affront to her colleague who had refrained from encores because it was not just *her* evening. Relations between the two divas, which had previously been good, suddenly became overcharged, and then characterised by a frostiness which was represented by the press as permanent cold war.

The tense atmosphere exploded after the first *Tosca* performance on 24 September. Stassinopoulos reports that Meneghini burst into his wife's dressing-room with rumours of an anti-Callas campaign. Soon afterwards the singer was summoned to the office of the theatre chief Barreto Pinto to be told dispassionately that because of negative reactions from the public she was released from her contract for all further performances, a dreadful affront. The singer kept her composure, reminded the impresario of his contractual commitment and forced him to agree to her singing her two scheduled appearances in *La Traviata*. Both were sold out and the singer's success was considerable. The ensuing events in the director's office are related in different versions of the same story: 'In view of the success you have enjoyed I should really not have to pay you anything', is how Pinto's words are reported by Jellinek. He is quoted differently by Stassinopoulos: 'So you want money on top of glory, eh?' The standard ending to this anecdote, and the beginning of the legend of the *diva furiosa*, is that Maria Callas, seething with anger, grabbed from the director's desk an inkstand, which she was only prevented from throwing at him by the intervention of his secretary.

It is possible that Meneghini too, who was putting his own affairs more and more in the background as he assumed the duties of his wife's manager, was getting a taste of what a diva must have: temperament. This temperament is not only an essential requirement for a singer prepared to take risks but also an inevitable prerequisite for making the headlines and becoming famous.

The Meneghinis interrupted their return flight to Italy in New York. There they met Dario Soria, director of the American branch of Cetra. They discussed a long-term recording contract. During the talks the singer behaved in a highly professional manner, not discussing money but enquiring about which works she should record and which conductors she would be working with. Three opera recordings were agreed for 1952. Then, returning to Italy, she sang two performances of *La Traviata* under Carlo Maria Giulini at the Teatro Donizetti in Bergamo and then, at the Massimo Bellini in the great Italian composer's birthplace Catania, four performances each of *Norma* and *I Puritani*. Her partners included Giulietta Simionato (Adalgisa), Gino Penno (Pollione) and Boris Christoff (Oroveso and Giorgio). The ovations must have been heard even in Milan, where she opened the La Scala season on 7 December 1951 as Elena in *I Vespri Siciliani*. It was the first of six premières in that season. The producer was Herbert Graf who had already directed the work in Florence. The set designer was Nicola Benois, son of Alexander Benois, who had prepared many productions for the Diaghilev Ballets Russes, including *Petrushka* with Nijinsky and Karsavina. After the performance Franco Abbiati wrote in *Corriere della Sera* about the 'grandiose throat' of Maria Meneghini Callas and designated the singer as 'unique' in relation to technique and all-embracing musicality. It was a wonderful début and sealed the collaboration with Victor de Sabata, under whose direction she would record Puccini's *Tosca* a little later.

After the seven performances of *I Vespri*, which were interrupted by a *Traviata* appearance in Parma on 29 December, the year 1952 began at the Communale in Florence with two performances of Bellini's *I Puritani* under Serafin and with the American tenor Eugene Conley, Carlo Tagliabue and Nicola Rossi-Lemeni. The American critic Newell Jenkins – also a trained conductor – wrote for *Musical America*:

> If this opera is to be bearable, it must be sung to perfection; however, the performance was a sensation. If one wants to write about the singing of Miss Callas, then one must reach for superlatives – for her velvet tone, her exciting phrasing, her breathtaking coloraturas, her stage presence, her majestic appearance and her fine acting. Something quite truly unusual occurred at the end of each act, which I had never experienced in any Italian opera house or concert hall since the return of Toscanini. The audience shouted, stamped with their feet and stormed to the front to call back Miss Callas for curtain after curtain. The orchestra [. . .] stood in the pit and applauded no less enthusiastically than the audience.

Five days later, Maria Callas sang the first of eight *Norma* performances at La Scala. These took place on 16, 19, 23, 27 and 29 January and 2, 7 and 10 February. It was the usual custom at that time to run performances only in the four weeks immediately following the *prima*. But Callas sang a ninth *Norma* on 14 April; the conductor was Franco Ghione, her partners were Ebe Stignani, Gino Penno and Nicola Rossi-Lemeni.

Newell Jenkins was again present. He wrote that the

performance's importance lay in the 'all-embracing artistry' of
Maria Callas, which

> electrified the public even before she had sung a single note,
> and when she started singing, each phrase came as if with no
> apparent effort; the audience knew from the first note of a
> phrase that the singer instinctively and consciously knew
> exactly where and how the phrase would end. Her notes were
> rounded and full and possessed the *legato* of a stringed instru-
> ment. Her agility was breathtaking. She does not have a light
> voice, yet she sang even the most difficult coloraturas without
> problems, and her descending *glissandi* gave the audience cold
> shivers down their backs. There was the occasional slight shrill-
> ness and sharpness on high notes, but her intonation was
> immaculate. It is to be hoped that this one slight blemish can
> be put down to tiredness [. . .]

There is unfortunately no recording extant of those *Norma* performances, which perhaps did not have the finish of later performances – of that on 7 December 1955, for example – but which
certainly possessed a savage energy.

Her next big role was Constanze in Mozart's *Die Entführung
aus dem Serail*. This role, written for the voluble throat of Mme
Cavalieri, is singers' music in the best sense and fitted like a glove
the vocal capabilities of the singer at that first performance. Maria
Callas received excellent reviews for the four performances but
in no way as enthusiastic a reception as her portrayal deserved –
with the exception of her big aria (sung in Italian as 'Tutte le
torture'), whose expressive power had scarcely ever been portrayed so evocatively. The passage work is of the highest quality,
the phrasing arches superbly, and above all the singing has a
strong pulsing quality, an inner motion. Again it is clear that the
long high C – before the coda – causes her some considerable
difficulty. And that is certainly no different in the rehearsal excerpt
from Dallas on 20 November 1957. Callas starts the aria in half
voice and then begins to sing herself in with warmth and energy.
Her first season at La Scala came to an end with the four performances of *Die Entführung aus dem Serail*, as did the Mozart chapter

in her career, a fact which must be mentioned with some regret. However, even if Maria Callas possessed the technical means for singing Mozart, as we have already explained in the chapter on her voice, she had neither the sound nor the expressive sense for that composer.

This is not, however, to perpetuate the prejudice, which was even shown by the eminent singing teacher Franziska Martienssen-Lohmann, that the Italian style of vocal acting does not suite the 'vocal atmosphere in Mozart's oeuvre'.[1] Such may be the case for the singing style which has developed from verismo music, but not necessarily for the true bel canto style – provided that the singer can find Mozart's essential tempo. Another comment made by Martienssen-Lohmann is much more important. Italian singing demands passion, both on the conscious and unconscious levels, and aims at projecting this to the listener. Italian singing takes place in a kind of measured immoderation, whereas Mozart demands abundance and moderation in equal proportion. Moderation is supplied by the dynamics of the vocal range – and by an intellectual sense of volume. But Maria Callas possessed a sense for volume which was dramatic and which tended to exaltation; she was never a lyric singer (but a nervous-dramatic one), even if she could sing lyric phrases with great charm.

By the end of her first season at La Scala Maria Callas had emerged, if not completely undisputed, at the top of the Italian diva league: Rosanna Carteri, Margherita Carosio, Clara Petrella, Giulietta Simionato and Ebe Stignani had nowhere near the charisma of the twenty-eight-year-old Greek singer. Only Renata Tebaldi remained as a significant rival because she had, at the highest level, a quite specific tone which Callas could never command: an intensely lyrical mildness. There are a whole group of *savanti* for whom a velvet and silky sound quality is as important as technical fluency and dramatic acting power. It was this acting with the voice, this acting in the singing, which Maria Callas made into a new concept which many had first to try and understand. It is what made each of her performances so gripping, what gave each of her triumphs that element of hard-won victory.

She sometimes took up works either in need of rehabilitation or needing to be put on trial for the first time. There was, for example, Rossini's *Armida*, performed a fortnight after the Scala season had closed and given at the Communale in Florence to mark the composer's 160th anniversary. It had disappeared from the repertoire, having been rejected after its première on 11 November 1817 with Isabella Colbran and probably never having had a permanent place on any theatre programme. Rossini's *Armida*, with its *expression outrée*, is a work of transition from *opera buffa* to Romanticism. Inspired not least by his relationship with Isabella Colbran, Rossini wrote 'music of passion and veiled eroticism' (Richard Osborne) which also had an extraordinary figurative brilliance. Osborne writes in his monograph on the composer: 'In *Armida* Rossini's music loses its innocence'; Stendhal spoke of a *candeur virginale*. And the work cannot be performed without a dramatic coloratura soprano of superb quality and five tenors capable of rising to tremendous heights.

Callas learned the title role within five days. Newell Jenkins, again writing for *Musical America*: 'Where else are such roulades, trills, runs and jumps, such a tempo and fireworks of this kind demanded of a singer? One can rest assured that no one but Maria Callas, indisputably the first singer on the Italian operatic stage, is mistress of this incredibly difficult part and capable of making it sound like music.' Jenkins' colleague Andrew Porter noted in *Opera*:

It is possible to feel that phrases beneath the florid passages are far too much overlaid with ornament; but it was possible to forget it when Maria Callas was singing them. This American-born Greek soprano [. . .] deserves fully the considerable reputation she has won, for she must be one of the most exciting singers on the stage today. Her presence is imperious, her coloratura not piping and pretty, but powerful and dramatic. It must be noted that a nasty edge crept into the tone from time to time; but when she sailed up a two-octave chromatic scale and cascaded down again (in 'D'amore al dolce impero', the aria from the second act), the effect was electrifying. Her brilliance continually startled and delighted throughout the opera. But whenever tenderness and sensuous charm were required, she was less moving.

The recording shows that despite the most difficult ornamentation – high D is interpolated three times – the performance of the aria comes as near to perfection as a singer can come. It must also be mentioned that she is still fresh and energetic enough at the end of the opera to set alight three brilliant E flats.

After three performances of Bellini's *I Puritani* in Rome in May 1952 alongside Giacomo Lauri-Volpi, performances which were no less succesful and which caused the critic Giorgio Vigolo to enthuse about 'four voices in her throat', Maria Callas set out for her third visit to Mexico. Her first role there was Verdi's Gilda in a production of general disappointment with Piero Campolonghi, who sang in more of a naturalistic style, and Giuseppe di Stefano, who forced his voice and, as John Ardoin describes in a fittingly pictorial way, sang his high notes not supported on his breath but more with his jaw. Solomon Kahan wrote in *Musical America* that Gilda was not an ideal role for Callas.

Now that assessment is questionable. Callas in fact took Gilda, like Lucia, away from the *soprano leggiero* and demonstrated that 'Caro nome' in particular is not a lyrical piece, but an inner drama, and it is beyond all doubt that her interpretation of the role eclipses, in broadness of perspective, that in any other of the complete recordings. For Donizetti's Lucia she achieved even more by finding a completely new dramatic concept. The part had been sung at its first performance on 26 September 1835 at the Teatro San Carlo in Naples by Fanny Tachinardi-Persiani. 'La piccola Pasta' had a fine, pure and perfectly placed voice with a range of two octaves and a fifth up to F *in alt*. Her technique was superb; despite a trill which was not perfect, Donizetti called it 'ben precisa e intonatissima'. Her tone did not have the richness of Pasta, but she compensated with her virtuosity. Thanks to her ethereal appearance she was frequently cast in the early Romantic roles, the 'amorosa angelicata'. The role of Lucia would later go to sopranos like Marcella Sembrich at the Met and Toti dal Monte at La Scala, to Adelina Patti, Nellie Melba, Luisa Tetrazzini, Amelita Galli-Curci, Maria Barrientos, Graziella Pareto and Lina Pagliughi: all with the exception of Melba, lighter sopranos.

The English critic Michael Scott wrote in *Opera News* that Maria Callas made 'something *sui generis*' out of the role of Lucia:

she gave it a tragic, perhaps also a pathological, dimension. The participants of the *Processo alla Callas* noted that her singing contained psychological perspectives which had come from the period of Freud and Kafka. This is expressed, for example, in the cries of 'Edgardo!' or the phrase 'alfin sei tua' with its dark and painful colouring. Even the first performance in Mexico offers a grandiose depiction of the role, and I do not hesitate to rate this version, as far as Callas is concerned, higher than the widely acclaimed Berlin performance under Karajan, where her voice has already lost the richness of the earlier years and in which her delivery has also lost some of its spontaneity. In the Mexican performance she sang the Mad Scene with 'astonishing tonal weight and phrasing of the greatest flexibility' (Scott) and executed the ornamented passages with a verve last heard on the legendary recording by Melba. Scott also notes that the Mexican auditorium 'itself resembled a mad scene after the E flat *in alt* – even if the note was far from free of sharpness. The ovation for the singer lasted a full twenty minutes.'

The tenth performance in Mexico was her first great Tosca, perhaps still a theatrical portrayal of the more conventional kind but a vocally impressive one nevertheless, which was electrifying in the second act and dramatically plausible in the third act. John Ardoin, who has listened to the recordings more closely than anyone else, points out that after 'Presto su! Mario', she overinterprets by prematurely recognising that Cavaradossi has really been shot. Later on, proof of the singer's sense of drama, this was to be corrected.

The reason why Maria Callas later recalled her third season in Mexico as a failure was because of the *Rigoletto* performances. On her return to Verona she swore never to sing Gilda on stage again and it is unfortunate that, apart from the studio recording with Serafin, she kept her word. Her depressive state was worsening at the time, to use the key word in the *Lucia* Mad Scene, because of the 'fantasma' of her mother.

Callas reacted irritably to her mother's demands for money: she wrote that she did not feel responsible for her sister's career and that her mother was still young enough to look around for employment. The war of letters, accusations and defamations had begun, and the next engagements were approaching. She was to open the Verona season on 19 July 1952, again with *La Gioconda*. Her ability to master completely different roles within a short period was again illustrated by her also singing Verdi's Violetta at that time. The performance of the Ponchielli opera was not an unqualified success. Claudia Cassidy of the *Chicago Tribune*, who was later to become an ardent Callas supporter, remarked that she had serious problems with her top C, and that her dramatic notes had sounded insecure and forced.

The four Verona performances of *La Traviata* in the first fortnight of August were more successful. Elisabeth Schwarzkopf heard her colleague sing Violetta and immediately resolved never again to sing the Verdi role herself. 'What is the sense,' she said 'in singing a role which has been played to perfection by another singer?' Even if this is not modesty it does show the wisdom of a diva who is aware of her own values. Schwarzkopf knew that she was as exceptional as Elvira, Marschallin and Fiordiligi as Callas was in the roles of Violetta, Norma, Tosca, or Lucia. The two sopranos became good colleagues, almost friends, perhaps precisely because there could not be any direct competition between them.

Two days after the performance of the Ponchielli opera, which she was to record for Cetra in September 1952, and after long months of negotiation, Maria Callas signed one of the most important contracts of her life: an exclusive recording contract with the British company EMI, which shortly before had reached an agreement with La Scala to record Italian operas with the ensemble of that theatre. Walter Legge described how he approached the singer in the recollections which we have already quoted. In 1947 he had been in Italy, not his usual territory, where he had discovered the still unknown Boris Christoff and had also spent a lot of time at La Scala with Herbert von Karajan. The Greek singer had come to his attention – 'at last a truly exciting Italian soprano!' – through her first Cetra recordings, 'Casta diva,' 'Qui la voce' and Isolde's Liebestod, and his interest was sharpened by the comment of one of her famous colleagues that she was 'not your type of singer'. Legge went to Rome in order to hear her as Norma; it must have been one of the performances in

February or March 1950. After the first act he telephoned his wife, Elisabeth Schwarzkopf, and asked her to come to the opera house in order to 'hear something quite exceptional'. Schwarzkopf declined because she too had no wish to miss something exceptional: the second part of a radio broadcast of a certain Maria Callas. After the performance Legge offered the singer an exclusive contract, but the negotiations 'over meals in Verona, at Biffi Scala and Gianino's seemed to be endless'. Legge recorded even the agonies he suffered carrying gigantic bouquets of flowers. Before the first EMI sessions, which took place in 1953, Callas still had to fulfil her contractual obligations to Cetra. In 1952 she recorded Ponchielli's *La Gioconda*, and Verdi's *La Traviata* a year later. By that time she had already completed her first sessions with EMI, with a producer who had the qualities of a musician and who viewed the gramophone record as an artistic document. He needed to find 'fellow perfectionists' for his work; his artists were to include Elisabeth Schwarzkopf, Herbert von Karajan, Boris Christoff, Tito Gobbi, Nicolai Gedda – and Callas.

He found her precisely at the moment when the gramophone record was taking a decisive step towards what one might call its autonomous form, becoming a *musée imaginaire* for opera. Thanks to this museum the tremendous presence of Maria Callas lives again. Such a presence in the minds of music lovers is attributable in no small way to the conditions established by the recording business in the 1950s and to the ambition of the producer Walter Legge, who was not prepared to betray his medium either to commerce or to mediocrity.

Theatre for the Imagination

'Remove your spectacles, music is only to
be listened to'

Richard Wagner

Theodor W. Adorno wrote a draft essay dated 24 March 1969

with the title 'Opera is hibernating in the long-playing record'. In it he wrote:

> It is not a rare occurrence in the history of music for technical innovations to acquire significance some considerable time after their invention. Technique in music has a double meaning. There are the actual techniques of composition and also the industrial processes which music employs in order to promote its mass dissemination. Yet these are not purely external things. Behind the technical, industrial and artistic innovations there is the same historical process, the same human strength of production; they come to one and the same thing.

Unusual optimism from the sceptical Adorno. The question is when and how technical achievements have been used for artistic purposes, or putting it another way, how a categorical aesthetic of the gramophone record was developed.

First it must be established that the long-playing record enabled entire acts to be played and that tape technique, that is working with 'takes', enabled the accidental errors of a stage performance to be eradicated; musically polished productions, free from those accidental errors, became a possibility. And Adorno emphasises in his essay a third, no less important, aspect. In his view the operas of Alban Berg were the last to be inhabited by the 'Weltgeist'. Opera had become an anachronism. It could only be saved 'by concentrating on the music as the true purpose of opera', not by the 'masquerade' of the stage. This reminds us of the philosopher Søren Kierkegaard, whose approach was not to see *Don Giovanni* on the stage but only to hear it from afar.

From this viewpoint the gramophone record could be regarded as the imaginary theatre, or as the theatre for the listener who is gifted with a sense of imagination. Walter Legge attempted to produce, by technical means, musical performances which were free from accidents, routine, exaggeration and laxity of stage performance: music theatre on an ideal stage. A glance at the discographies in *Opera on Record* reveals that various recordings with Maria Callas were the first real productions of the works in question, not to mention the live recordings of Cherubini's *Medea*,

Rossini's *Armida*, Donizetti's *Anna Bolena* and *Poliuto*, Bellini's *Il Pirata* and Verdi's *Nabucco, I Vespri Siciliani* and *Macbeth*, all of which were the first complete recordings of these operas. In the studio Callas sang the first complete recording of Bellini's *I Puritani* and the second one of *La Sonnambula*, the first of Rossini's *Il Turco in Italia* and the second of Bellini's *Norma*. What is decisive, and it applies equally to Donizetti's *Lucia di Lammermoor*, is that in these performances Walter Legge and Maria Callas were aiming at something approaching a *mise en scène*, that was however entirely acoustic: theatre for the imagination.

After Callas had completed for Cetra her first integral recording, *La Gioconda*, in September 1952, she stood on the threshold of another important début, in which she was to conquer an audience which she would not always need to conquer: the English audience. She came, she sang, she conquered, and whenever she returned she was loved for her presence.

Music, Drama and Movement

'Virtuosity is being able to perceive everything in advance and estimating what we can carry out with ease. If we can materialise what our emotions want and what our imagination envisages – at that moment we become great artists'

Giovanni Battista Lamperti

On 8 November 1952 Callas introduced herself as Norma at the Royal Opera House, Covent Garden. Ebe Stignani sang Adalgisa, Mirto Picchi was Pollione and the conductor Vittorio Gui, one of the most important in his field. Harold Rosenthal reports in his book on the Covent Garden Opera that Callas received ovations such as were otherwise given only to the prima ballerina Margot Fonteyn. Among English critics, at that time probably the most discerning of all, the voice aroused controversial discussion. 'Altogether, if as yet an imperfect vocalist,' judged Desmond Shawe-Taylor, 'she is the most interesting new singer heard in London for many years.' In *Opera*, Cecil Smith described the first of the five performances in great detail. He praised the 'fabulous *fioriture*', the faultless chromatic *glissandi* in the cadenza at the end of 'Casta diva', the effortless leap from middle F to the top G and the top D, 'stupendously held for twelve bars' in the *stretta* of the trio concluding Act 2. But there were also some critical voices. Ernest Newman spoke as *laudator temporis acti*: 'She is no Ponselle.' John Freeman, writing for *Opera News*, mentioned at the end of a generally enthusiastic review the 'covered notes in the middle voice, which gave the impression that she was singing with hot marbles in her mouth'. On the other hand Andrew Porter wrote categorically: 'Maria Meneghini Callas is the Norma of our time, just as Ponselle and Grisi were of theirs.'

Maria Callas was also having to read covert references to her uneven performance. Arianna Stassinopoulos reports that, after an *Aida* performance in the Verona Arena, one critic had written that her legs and those of the elephants on the stage were indistinguishable, and that the singer was so hurt by this impertinent remark that she still recalled, shortly before her death, the bitter tears she had wept. The continued remarks about her excessive weight made her decide to slim down; she was to achieve a sylph-like figure. Her secret model was the fairy-like Audrey Hepburn, who later recalled: 'I got to know her in Paris, because we both had the same cosmetician, Alberto de Rossi. We all met in Paris and ate together. It was an unforgettable evening. Maria explained that she wanted to lose weight and asked Alberto to correct her make-up in the way that he did for me. She took me as her model! That was an immense compliment for me. To this day I cannot really believe it.'

After the fifth *Norma* in London there were only seventeen days to go until one of the most important appearances of her entire career. November 7 is the feast day of Milan's patron saint Ambrosius, and it is the day on which La Scala opens its season. Callas was to sing the Lady in Verdi's *Macbeth*, a rarely performed work at that time. The producer was to be Carl Ebert, who had directed this Shakespearean opera in Berlin in the 1930s, and then in 1939 at Glyndebourne with Margherita Grandi, who was celebrated for the dramatic colour of her singing – her recording of the Sleepwalking Scene can certainly be compared with the one by Callas. The conductor, as the year before in *I Vespri Siciliani*, was Victor de Sabata.

The performance is preserved in a recording which is technically imperfect but generally acceptable; it has also been recorded in some excellent photographs, as shown in the evocative book by John Ardoin and Gerald Fitzgerald. Listening to the recording one can almost see the pictures, and looking at the pictures one can hear the performance. Even though the singer's appearance was still statuesque, her deportment, expression and movement are immensely suggestive, above all the look from those large penetrating eyes. To assert that she sang the role with the harsh, hollow and ugly voice which Verdi demanded is to diminish the achievement, merely to confirm a popular cliché. Callas begins the *brindisi*, for example, with the most refined elegance of bel canto, with superb tonal definition and with filigree phrasing. This is dramatically appropriate because the scene is a courtly one. Only at the moment when Macbeth, sung by Enzo Mascherini, loses his composure and cannot carry on with the charade as he sees the murdered Banquo in his mad fantasies, only then does Callas sharpen her tone so that the drinking song becomes something else: frightened, violent, hysterical. She shapes the sound as if it were gesture, her voice becomes a seismograph of what is taking place in her psyche.

The reviews which David A. Lowe quotes are somewhat contradictory. Peter Hoffer wrote in *Music and Musicians* that Callas had not been in her best voice, whereas Peter Dragadze in *Opera* had unlimited praise for her performance. Teodoro Celli, connoisseur of the first rank, explained that the role of the Lady seemed tailor-made for Callas and that the few expressions of disapproval came from people who had not expected singing with such dramatic shaping to it; he also pointed out that it was precisely those few whistles of disapproval which provoked the rest of the audience to produce a true ovation. It is an eternal loss that Maria Callas was never to portray the Lady again after those five

La Scala performances. She was to have sung the part in San Francisco – but it never happened; she was to have sung it at the Met – bitter arguments with Rudolf Bing prevented that; she should have sung it at Covent Garden but the plan came to nothing. All we have of one of the finest dramatic portrayals is the live recording from La Scala and the recording of three arias in a recital conducted by Nicola Rescigno: a lot, but not enough.

Nine days after the Verdi performances, there followed, from 26 December until early in January 1953, five performances of Ponchielli's *La Gioconda* with Giuseppe di Stefano as Enzo and with Antonino Votto conducting. She sang a sixth performance on 19 February, out of a total of twelve in that role. And yet Gioconda belongs among the roles central to her career. Not only did she sing it at her Italian début in Verona but she recorded it twice, both times with Votto. The first recording, for Cetra, created a sensation not least because people had not believed that a singer with such a dark, dramatic voice could also sing Lucia. Votto, who had been Toscanini's assistant for thirty years and had experienced Toscanini's work at La Scala, later called Callas 'the last great artist'. It was always amazing to him that despite her extreme shortsightedness and although she often stood as far as fifty metres from the conductor, she still entered precisely on the beat. Votto recalled that she was note-perfect even at rehearsals, at which she always sang at full voice much to the annoyance of her colleagues. It is interesting how Toscanini explains and justifies this: 'If one is entering a one-mile race, then one does not just run half a mile while training. Most singers are stupid and try to conserve their strength, but a rehearsal is a real hurdle.'

Votto called it insane to discuss Callas simply as a voice: 'She must be conceived in her entirety – as a unity of music, drama and movement. Someone like her is no longer to be found. She was an aesthetic phenomenon.' The performance of *La Gioconda* did not receive unmitigated praise because the voice was not in top form after the exertions of that second half of 1952. Only five days later there followed five appearances in *La Traviata* in Rome and Venice – to great acclaim in Venice, but with less success in the Italian capital.

'La voce è troppo forte' ('the voice is too strong') said those who recalled singers like dal Monte in the part. Cynthia Jolly reported in *Opera* that even the ushers took part in the vociferous discussions about her portrayal. The complaint was made that Maria Callas had seemed uninvolved and that after a brilliant first act she had sung the phrase 'Amami, Alfredo' without any great expression of pain; in the final act she had even resorted to 'histrionic means'.

Before returning to La Scala she sang her first Donizetti Lucia in Italy at the Communale in Florence on 25 and 28 January and 5 and 8 February 1953. Her first partner as Edgardo was Giacomo Lauri-Volpi, one of the young diva's early admirers. 'An unbounded triumph,' he wrote shortly after the performance. 'This young artist, who can create high tension in her listeners, has it in her to lead the operatic stage back into a new golden era.' Straight after the performances the work was recorded by EMI. Serafin conducted in place of Franco Ghione, who had led the stage performances, and the singer's partners were Giuseppe di Stefano and Tito Gobbi. Legge sent a short extract of tape to Herbert von Karajan, who immediately decided to put the opera on at La Scala with Maria Callas; this conductor always knew how to participate in the success of artists who were congenial to him. He also brought the production to Berlin and, in June 1956, to the Vienna State Opera which had re-opened only six months before. Vienna's director Karl Böhm had made headlines when he declared, after criticisms over his absences from Vienna, that he was not prepared to sacrifice his international career for the Vienna Opera, which was taken as an enormous affront. The triumphant production of Donizetti's opera was not the least of the reasons why Karajan appeared as the man who could lead the Vienna Opera back into glorious times, especially through the artistic agreement with La Scala: this was to be the upbeat for a European music market.

After the performances of *Lucia*, which were the subject of discussion all over the operatic world, Maria Callas fulfilled her final obligations of the 1952–3 season at La Scala. There were five performances of *Il Trovatore*, three in February and two at the end of March. The part of Leonora is often not included when there is discussion of the finest Callas portrayals. But John Ardoin maintains that she did more for this opera than even for *Norma*. It was known that Bellini's music made special demands on vocal technique, even though those demands were scarcely ever met. The fact that vocal portrayals of Leonora had been sloppily performed only came to light when Maria Callas started to sing the role. Her performance in Mexico had already demonstrated that Leonora's music is one of transition. Speaking in formal language, it is the transition from ornamented bel canto style to dramatic singing such as Verdi was beginning to develop in the 1850s. At her first Italian performance of the part in Naples the audience had been irritated by her elaborate singing. After the *prima* at La Scala *Oggi* wrote of her 'stupendous vocalism'. In *Opera* Peter Dragadze lauded 'her remarkable artistic intelligence, her extraordinary vocal ability and a technique which is far ahead of any other singer's'.

In March, while giving two more performances of Lucia in Genoa, she concluded her second EMI recording, Bellini's *I Puritani*. Again her partner was Giuseppe di Stefano, and Tullio Serafin conducted the La Scala orchestra, although he was not appearing in that theatre at that period.

After appearances in *Norma* in Rome and *Lucia di Lammermoor* in Catania she was again due to give new life to a museum piece at the Maggio Musicale in Florence, where she had sung Elena in Verdi's *I Vespri Siciliani* in 1951, and Rossini's Armida in 1952. For the 1953 Festival Cherubini's *Medea* was on the programme, an opera which had been premièred at the Théâtre Feydeau in Paris in 1797 but which had only reached La Scala in 1909 with Esther Mazzoleni in the title role. The reason for its then sinking back into oblivion can only be because, in the words of Robert Mann in *Musical America*, 'singers with the artistry and intelligence of a Miss Callas are so extremely rare'. Callas had only eight days in which to study the part – with Vittorio Gui.

In many respects it was to be a key role for her career. Rudolf Bing, impresario of the New York Metropolitan, attended the performance in Florence so that he could discuss a contract with the singer, but no decisions were reached. Meneghini declared to the press: 'My wife will not sing at the Met as long as Bing is in charge. And that is the Met's loss.' It was as Medea that Callas was later to enjoy one of her greatest triumphs in Dallas – inspired by feelings of revenge against Bing, with whom she had quarrelled and who had sacked her in a public slanging match. Medea was the last role which she took at La Scala in 1962 and it was also the role with which she returned to Greece in 1960. It was, in brief, a role which she could sing even with only the remnants of a voice. And it was only after the many appearances of Maria Callas in this role that singers like Rita Gorr, Leyla Gencer, Gwyneth Jones, Magda Olivero, Anja Silja, Leonie Rysanek and Sylvia Sass dared to take on a part whose first singer, Madame Scio, is supposed to have died from singing it too often.

Giuseppe Pugliese, who later took part in Italian radio's Callas debate, wrote after the first performance in Florence on 7 May 1953 that the soprano had mastered a challenge of which no other interpreter was capable. Teodoro Celli said in the *Corriere Lombardo*: 'Callas was Medea. She was astonishing. A great singer and a tragic actress of remarkable power, she endowed the enchantress with a *sinistre* vocal sound which glowed with intensity in its lower register. Yet she found heart-rending tones for the loving Medea and moving ones for the motherly Medea. In short, she went beyond the notes and discovered the monumental character of the legend.' Her success was so extraordinary that the management of La Scala called off the première of Scarlatti's *Mitridate Eupatore* which had been planned to open the 1953–4 season. The work had been chosen with a view to the other operas which Callas was to sing: there were plans for her first Lucia at La Scala (under Karajan), Gluck's *Alceste* and *Don Carlo* – Cherubini's music drama was now to replace the Scarlatti opera as opening of the season. La Scala's staff faced difficult weeks of preparation.

Before that the soprano had to fulfil further engagements in London. In June she sang three performances of *Aida* under Sir John Barbirolli and with Giulietta Simionato and Kurt Baum as partners; then followed four of Bellini's *Norma* under John Pritchard with Mirto Picchi as Pollione and Simionato as Adalgisa, and then three appearances in Verdi's *Il Trovatore* under Alberto Erede. Harold Rosenthal in his monograph on the Covent Garden Opera describes the portrayal of Aida as 'stormy and immensely dramatic', but one could also read in *The Times* that an 'excess of emotion' occasionally damaged the tone – remember our quotation of Yehudi Menuhin's statement that expression is the enemy of technique. Unlimited praise was given to her portrayals of Norma and Leonora, although the conducting of Albert Erede in the Verdi work was heavily criticised. Cecil Smith wrote in *Opera*:

> In a way I can only explain with difficulty she personified both Leonora's passionate humanity and the formality which the libretto and score employ in order to generalise her emotions. The voice – or rather its use – was a source of unending amazement. At last we could hear perfectly formed trills, scales and arpeggios which had body, the *portamenti* and extended phrases with fully supported sound and exquisite inflections. The tumultuous ovation after 'D'amor sull' ali rosee' in the last act was what Callas had earned.

Yet another reference to the extraordinary quality of this fine portrayal in the gallery of Verdi heroines sung by Callas.

There was little time for rest that summer, as Maria Callas was subjecting herself to the physical demands of a radical diet. Then in July she returned to Verona, sang four performances of *Aida* under Tullio Serafin in the Arena, Leonora in *Il Trovatore* under Francesco Molinari-Pradelli and spent the first three weeks of August recording Mascagni's *Cavalleria Rusticana* and Puccini's *Tosca*. She had only studied Santuzza, and sung it on the stage, in Athens. She would later avoid this dramatic but one-dimensional role, like many others from the verismo repertoire. And yet one never gets the impression of an interpreter merely singing from the score, as in so many modern studio recordings. Her dramatic imagination went to work at the highest level of tension even without much experience of the role on stage. It should also be noted that this recording was the only one, before the later operas recorded in Paris, that was not supervised by Walter Legge. He arrived a week after the recording of the Mascagni opera was completed, in order to supervise the production of *Tosca*.

The quality of this recording cannot be overemphasised: it marked the beginning of musical theatre produced for the

imagination or, to put it another way, the emancipation of dramatic music from the stage and its salvation by the technicians.
A comparison of the *Tosca* with the version of *La Traviata*, recorded a few weeks later by the Italian company Cetra, illustrates
how the technical imagination of the Puccini recording becomes
art: it sets the work on an aural stage, whereas the Cetra production was, by comparison, without any tension.

Maria Callas began her new season, after a long period of rest,
on 19 November at the Teatro Verdi in Trieste. She sang four
performances of *Norma*, the last of which was on 29 November,
and from there went straight on to Milan. The season opened
with Catalani's *La Wally* – and with Renata Tebaldi, for whom
Ghiringhelli had also selected Desdemona, Tosca and Tatiana in
Eugene Onegin. The fact that the two great divas would be singing
premières at La Scala within a few days of each other provided
for an atmosphere of hysterical tension. The critic Emilio Radius
wrote in *L'Europea* that the two singers wished for a public reconciliation for the higher honour of music. Callas, who we are
told read every line that was printed about her, was a member of
the audience at the première of the Catalani opera. The critic
Bruno Slavitz noted in *Musica e Dischi*: 'The rivalry which divides
the public into the admirers of a great voice (Tebaldi fans) and
the admirers of technical mastery (Callas fans), brings life to
the theatre. Fortunately rivalry and politeness go hand in hand.
Everybody was happy to see Signora Meneghini-Callas in her
box and see how she applauded warmly Renata Tebaldi's success.'

It goes without saying that there were many who regarded that
visit as calculated, even as a cynical manoeuvre before the storm
broke. Three days after that opening Callas was to sing the Cherubini opera which had only been announced at the last minute, a
decision which plunged the theatre almost into chaos. Margherita
Wallmann had to produce the work in the shortest time and
prepare sets and costumes. As set designer she was able to secure
Salvatore Fiume, who was well-known in Italy as a painter and
who, having originally been engaged for Gluck's *Alceste*, had not
made a great success of it. However, some of the wildly imaginative designs intended for Gluck's opera suited the Cherubini piece.

The scenic problems were much less serious than the fact that

La Scala had no conductor for the work. Victor de Sabata was very ill; he was never to conduct an opera again. Vittorio Gui, who had been conducting for Callas in Florence, now had other engagements to honour. The substitute came from the United States: Leonard Bernstein. In Joan Peyser's Bernstein biography, which in turn drew on Meneghini's *My Wife, Maria Callas*, it is stated that Callas told Ghiringhelli about a concert performance which she had heard on the radio. The story goes that she found the concert unusually gripping and wanted to identify the name of the conductor, which she did not know. Ghiringhelli apparently refused to consider Bernstein, who was quite unknown in Italy, but pressed by Callas he contacted the young American. Tired after a long concert tour, Bernstein had little desire to prepare a work he did not know in such a short time. He agreed only when Maria Callas spoke to him in person.

There was a curious incident at the start of rehearsals. The paper of the original 1798 score, which was sent to him, was disintegrating and giving off a dust to which the conductor developed an allergic reaction. 'He coughed and sneezed his way through all the rehearsals,' reported Margherita Wallmann. He struck up an immediate understanding with the soprano. Without a murmur she accepted the cuts he made in the score, including her own second act aria. 'She instantly recognised the dramatic rightness of this step,' he said later. 'She simply understood everything I wanted and I understood what she wanted.'

Bernstein had only five days and yet he 'worked miracles with the orchestra' (Wallmann). Maria Callas set the audience in a frenzy. 'She was the purest electricity,' said Bernstein. Wallmann recalls that at the time Callas had not yet lost much weight and that on the stage she was like a caryatid on the Acropolis. 'There was enormous power in her gestures – one felt her strength. Her physical state served her well for Medea; she gave the character something of an antique quality.' As Margherita Wallmann goes on to recall, the singer had identified perfectly with the part right from the beginning. The producer even suggested that certain sexual frustrations of a young woman who was married to an older man were being compensated for through the intensity of her work. 'Unfulfilled passions found expression in her singing.

When that ceased to be a problem for her, then she was no longer the same artist.'

The performance was an unprecedented success both for Maria Callas and Leonard Bernstein. Again it was the critic Teodoro Celli who emphasised in *Oggi* that Maria Callas had resurrected the art of Malibran in giving life to the style of the *ottocento*. Callas sang five performances of *Medea* in December 1953 and January 1954, at the same time giving some guest appearances as Leonora in *Il Trovatore* in Rome and preparing herself for her second première at La Scala. During her short Christmas holiday she was able to read the comments of Emilio Radius in *L'Europea*: 'If these were better times for music, then Maria Callas would be the most famous woman in Europe.'

Fortunately she was then still only the most famous operatic diva of the period, and her fame was further consolidated by seven performances of *Lucia di Lammermoor* under Karajan. She had first sung the part in Mexico City in 1952, and one must certainly agree with Michael Scott that she never sang the role more dramatically and more expressively than in South America. But the opportunity to really work on it in a production came only at La Scala, and so 18 January 1954 must be counted among the great days of her career. This was the time when she could still hold the E flat *in alt* for ten seconds or longer, that magical note at the highest point of her range, which she botched four years later in the Dallas performance that Zefferelli had originally produced for Joan Sutherland. So annoyed was she that, immediately the curtain had fallen, she sang the note five times over; although it came, she never again sang Lucia on stage.

Herbert von Karajan was both conductor and producer of the performances. His conception of stage design had caused La Scala's leading set designer, Nicola Benois, to withdraw from the production. His substitute, Gianni Ratto, carried out the conductor's wishes: the sets were austere and shadowy. The conductor had actually travelled to Scotland in order to get a picture of the landscape for Scott's tragic love story, and during the preparation period he demanded – and got – additional lighting rehearsals. The singer did not like the production and the stylised set, but the musical preparation with the conductor was unalloyed pleasure.

It was not only Maria Callas who said that Karajan could 'go with the voice'. This does not just mean clever accompaniment, nor just breathing with the singer, which in itself is very important, but much more a sense of timing, dynamics and phrasing which amount to more than the listing of specific technical details. However banal this may sound, it is a matter of organising time through movements which tighten and then relax. The specific understanding of movement which Callas possessed – or should one speak of an instinct, which has been guided by intelligence and artistic understanding? – was described by the Italian producer Sandro Sequi with a precision which one usually only finds in writings about singers and actors in Wagner, Brecht or Stanislavsky:

Certain artists are gifted with something special, and Callas had that kind of theatrical quality one sees today in Nureyev, Plissetskaya, Brando, Olivier. Magnani had it, too. Yet they are all quite individual, unlike each other in every respect. After watching Callas many times on stage in many roles, I realised she had a secret few theatre people know. But to explain this, I must go back a bit in my own life. As a teenager, I studied dancing with Clotilde and Alexandre Sacharoff, who were very famous in Europe during the twenties and thirties – he was a pupil of Isadora Duncan. In his lessons, Sacharoff always stressed using the brain to send tension to every muscle of the body – a tension of the mind, the intelligence, which would travel to every limb, to the fingers, the toes, the face, everywhere. But then there must be a sudden relaxation, which gives the impression of a break of energy, a kind of fall. Sacharoff would demonstrate a gesture of the most terrible intensity, then end it. The effect was extraordinary, a kind of climax, like when people die. This alternation of tension and relaxation can exert an incredible hold over the public. I believe this was the key to Callas's magnetism, why her singing and acting were so compelling. Think of the movements of her arms in the Mad Scene of Lucia. They were like the wings of a great eagle,

a marvellous bird. When they went up, and she often moved them
very slowly, they seemed heavy, not airy like a dancer's arms,
but weighted. Then, she reached the climax of a musical phrase,
her arms relaxed and flowed into the next gesture, until she reached
a new musical peak [. . .] there was a continuous line to her
singing and movements, which were really very simple.

What Sequi is describing is the secret of human gesture, singing
as emotion which has been experienced and fulfilled. Of special
importance is the conclusion drawn by Sequi, a most sensitive
and observant man. He came to the conclusion, that 'realism was
alien' to the singing and acting of Callas and that for that reason
alone she was 'the greatest of all opera singers'. Her talents were
'wasted' on verismo roles – her genius was displayed as Norma,
Sonnambula, Lucia.

The Mad Scene at the end of the opera released mad scenes in
the auditorium. 'La Scala in delirium', 'Rainfall of red carnations'
'four minutes of applause after the Mad Scene' – such were the
headlines in *La Notte*. Cynthia Jolly reported in *Opera News* that
Maria Callas received a dozen curtain calls even after the sextet.
Her Mad Scene had 'surpassed many an Ophelia in the straight
theatre. It will be difficult, very difficult, ever to hear "Spargi
d'amaro pianto" sung by another singer (however perfectly) without finding the phrase pale and insipid.' Singers of the part of
Lucia after Maria Callas have without exception been compared
unfavourably. This applies even to the Lucia of Joan Sutherland,
a Lucia of technical perfection and sensibility. With the colours
and nuances of Callas in one's ear, the less precisely articulated
singing of the Australian soprano must seem lacking in expression
and eloquence.

These La Scala triumphs were followed by three performances
each of Lucia and Medea at La Fenice in Venice and three of
Tosca in Genoa. After that preparations commenced for the first
production of Gluck's *Alceste* at La Scala (4 April 1954). George
Jellinek categorically declares that this did not reach the heights
of the previous new productions. The four performances certainly
did not cause the sensation of Medea or Lucia, because Callas did
not have the opportunity in Gluck's opera to use her talents as a

virtuoso and dramatic actress. Yet she reveals in every phrase of the performance, conducted fluently and with gentle expressivity by Carlo Maria Giulini, that she was a Gluck interpreter of the first rank. There are few recordings of 'Divinités du Styx' which approach the one sung in Italian by Callas ('Divinità infernal'), and scarcely one to surpass it. The role of Alceste is not as extrovert as Medea, Norma or Violetta and has to be sung with classical moderation. However, each phrase and legato line require maximum inner tension, and if proof were needed of the singer's unique quality it is to be found in the fact that within a few weeks she did justice to three roles which could not be more different: she was more than a diva, she was the voice of music itself.

Gerald Fitzgerald reports on the great dedication and hard work put in by Wallmann, Giulini and Callas. Giulini viewed the work as 'something holy'. He returned to the old Calzabigi text, but retained the composer's later Paris version of the music. Of Callas he said that she met every expressive demand, holding the attention of the audience even when she was not singing – another of the myriad references to the intensity which the actress Callas produced through her own inner tension. Margherita Wallmann tells how she had requested Callas to be there only for afternoon rehearsals, but when she came into the theatre in the morning, Maria Callas was already seated in the auditorium, explaining that she wanted to watch the work with the chorus so as to acquire a sense of the performance's unity.

It was only six days after the second Gluck performance that Nicola Benois, chief designer of La Scala's sets and costumes, transformed the singer into a figure from a painting by Velasquez. A wonderful change had come over Maria Callas during that 1953–4 season. She noted it in this way:

Gioconda	92 [kilos]
Aida	87
Norma	80
Medea	78
Lucia	75
Alceste	65
Elisabetta	64

Not only had she become twenty-eight kilos lighter but the change in her body had made her, according to Giulini, 'quite a different woman, for whom new expressive worlds opened. Possibilities appeared which had previously been dormant.' Was a more regal Elisabetta in Verdi's *Don Carlo* ever seen? She had studied the role four years earlier in preparation for appearances at the San Carlo and the Teatro dell'Opera in Rome, but had cancelled these because of an attack of jaundice. Her performance at La Scala, in the company of her old friend Nicola Rossi-Lemeni, Paolo Silveri as Posa and the grandiose Ebe Stignani as Eboli, was highly praised as a dramatic portrayal, but while Franco Abbiati in *Corriere della Sera* found her singing 'sweeter than usual', Riccardo Malipiero found it lacking in 'sweetness and mildness'. She never again sang the role after those five appearances in April 1954 – the second Verdi role, after Lady Macbeth, which is missing from the gramophone museum, although the incomparable recording of the great scena under Rescigno shows that she was its greatest interpreter.

'La Regina della Scala' was the title accorded to Maria Callas at the end of the season, notwithstanding the fact that Renata Tebaldi had also given some brilliant performances. Callas was admired not just as incomparable virtuosa but above all for her charisma, flamboyance and magnetism, even if a second trans-formation – into La Callas, the star – gave rise to attacks of envy and hatred.

While she was still singing Elisabetta, recording sessions had commenced on 23 April in the Metropole Cinema for Bellini's *Norma*. Serafin conducted with calm composure but never missing the tension. His way of unfolding Bellini's endless arches of melody marks him as one of the greatest Italian opera conductors – the flexibility of his accompanying figures is to be sought in vain in later recordings with conductors like James Levine or Riccardo Muti. Yet it was strange that Walter Legge's casting of the other roles did not show its usual flair: Mario Filippeschi is one of the worst of many mediocre singers of Pollione: only Giacomo Lauri-Volpi had sung 'Meco all'altar' in a way that would have made him worthy to partner Callas. Ebe Stignani

gave a competent performance as Adalgisa, but the timbre of her
voice is heavy and she sounds too old for the role.

Début in the United States

During the *Norma* sessions Maria Callas was interviewed by the
American magazine *High Fidelity*. Her USA début was approaching. Carol Fox had travelled to Europe in February and had
succeeded where Bing had failed. Maria Callas was prepared to
return to the city where her career should have begun some years
earlier with *Turandot*. Together with the young Lawrence Kelly
and the conductor Nicola Rescigno, later a regular partner for
Callas, Fox wanted to give the Lyric Opera in Chicago a new
splendour. All those taking part knew that such an attempt would
fail if the best talents were not engaged.

Rescigno performed *Don Giovanni* in February 1954 with a
superb cast: Nicola Rossi-Lemeni in the title part, Eleanor Steber
as Anna, Leopold Simoneau as Ottavio and Bidu Sayão as Zerlina.
This success encouraged Carol Fox to plan a three-week season
for the autumn and to engage for it the best stars from Europe.
Rossi-Lemeni persuaded Maria Callas to make her American
début in Chicago. She agreed, especially as the fee being offered
was generous. She was to receive 12,000 dollars for six performances; the Met's highest fee at that time was 1,000 dollars per
performance. The ensemble was no less attractive. Her partners
would be Giulietta Simionato, Ebe Stignani, Giuseppe di Stefano,
Jussi Björling, Tito Gobbi, Ettore Bastianini and Rossi-Lemeni,
with Tullio Serafin conducting.

The US visit was preceded by a busy summer of engagements.
In May she sang in two performances of Verdi's *La Forza del
Destino* in Ravenna, and she recorded that opera in August with
Tullio Serafin as conductor. Her tenor was Richard Tucker, who
had sung Enzo in her first *Gioconda* in Verona. A recording of
Leoncavallo's *Pagliacci* was made between 25 May and 17 June
1954. In July she performed in Boito's *Mefistofele* in the Verona
Arena. From 31 August until 8 September she was recording
Rossini's *Il Turco in Italia* – she was to sing the part of Fiorilla a

little later at La Scala. Shortly before travelling to the United States there were two appearances in *Lucia di Lammermoor* at the Teatro Donizetti in Bergamo. Two studio recitals were also produced. Eleven Puccini arias were recorded with Serafin between 15 and 21 September, as well as a further programme of coloratura music by Rossini, Meyerbeer, Delibes and Verdi and dramatic arias by Cilea, Catalani, Giordano and Boito. The latter recital would confirm her position as *assoluta* and demonstrate that she could perform coloratura and dramatic music with equal authority.

She had selected Norma, Violetta and Lucia for her American début. Whatever headlines may have preceded her, she amazed her colleagues and the young Nicola Rescigno with her fantastic energy at rehearsals. She followed the work of the other soloists punctiliously, also that of the chorus, and in order to get the correct balance for 'Casta diva' – Norma's entrance – she sang that immensely difficult aria nine times in rehearsal. 'She lived for opera twenty-four hours a day,' Lawrence Kelly said later.

Claudia Cassidy, the fearsome critic of the *Chicago Tribune*, set the tone of the reviews when she wrote after the *Norma* performance on 1 November 1954:

In my opinion she not only measured up to the high expectations but surpassed them. And so did Giulietta Simionato as Adalgisa, who with Callas made out of the duet 'Mira O Norma' something which we can tell our grandchildren about [. . .] If I had not seen pictures of her before the performance, I would not have recognised Maria Callas. She is as thin as a twig and beautiful within the tragic masque – with a tinge of inner serenity. She has presence and style and sings wonderfully [. . .] there is a slight unsteadiness in long-held notes. Yet to my ears her voice is now more beautiful in colour and more even over all registers than it was previously. Her range is astounding, her technique dazzling. She sang 'Casta diva' in a kind of mystical dream, like a moon goddess who has descended to earth just for a moment. When it comes to the vocal fireworks, the glitter of her attacks and the feather-light cadence of a scale – all that adds up to magnificent and beautiful singing.

Among the 3,500 spectators who cheered Maria Callas after the performance were the wonderful soprano Edith Mason, the tenor Giovanni Martinelli, the English soprano Eva Turner, the soprano Rosa Raisa – all living memories of the great times at the Lyric Opera. Irving Kolodin wrote in the *Saturday Review*:

> The sound which Miss Callas produces can best be described with the word unusual, because it relates to no conventional concept of tonal production. She follows a fundamentally instrumental concept of the human voice; and like all great instrumentalists her sole concern is with artistic ends. She is not a screamer and has no wish to decoy the public with effects. She works with – and on – the voice gradually and from outside. First she shades it down to a filigree line in 'Casta diva', then lets loose its vengeful power as she accuses the treacherous Pollione. She is acquiring even more perfect mastery of her remarkable instrument, as shown by the fact that 'Casta diva' is now better and more evenly articulated than in the gramophone recording. She sang top Cs with ease and at the end of the second act produced a towering D with absolute security. One thing seems certain: it will get a lot better before it gets worse. She impresses one as an artistic craftsman.

A good twenty years later, after the singer's death, Claudia Cassidy recalled that in Chicago Callas as Violetta had invoked memories of Claudia Muzio and Lucrezia Bori. Even though none of the performances in Chicago was recorded, it can be stated with certainty that she sang her best performances in the US at the Lyric Opera. Further appearances of this calibre were to follow in 1955. And it must also be mentioned that her first recordings for Angel, daughter company of EMI, were of decisive importance for her success. Walter Legge had, right from the start of his work with the soprano, followed the strategy of introducing the new label to the US with artists of the top rank. The recordings of *Lucia di Lammermoor, I Puritani* and *Tosca* became bestsellers and acquired for Maria Callas the image of *assoluta*.

Her début at the Lyric Opera had been used for a massive but tactful advertising campaign. 'Queen of Opera', 'La Divina': Maria Callas left the United States characterised by every conceivable superlative.

Callas and Visconti
or Art Over Art

'There is no dividing line between thought
and emotion [. . .] Nothing has less meaning than a mechanically controlled tone,
even if it is full of expression. It lacks beauty'
Giovanni Battista Lamperti

The last Lucia performance in Chicago on 17 November earned twenty-two curtain calls, after which she flew back to Milan. On 7 December she had to open the new La Scala season with Spontini's *La Vestale*. La Scala intended to present twenty-one different operas in that season, eighteen of which would be new productions. (Today's state-subsidised theatres manage seven or eight at the most.) They included Wagner performances with the best Bayreuth singers, the European première of Menotti's *The Saint of Bleecker Street* and the La Scala première of *Porgy and Bess*. Karajan was to conduct and, as a climax awaited with great longing, Toscanini had agreed to open the Piccolo Scala with Verdi's *Falstaff*. This never happened, for it was the year in which the Italian conductor finally retired. Callas was to sing in new productions of Giordano's *Andrea Chénier*, Bellini's *La Sonnambula*, Rossini's *Il Turco in Italia* and Verdi's *La Traviata*.

Working with the directors Luchino Visconti and Franco Zeffirelli, the conductors Leonard Bernstein, Gianandrea Gavazzeni, Antonino Votto and Carlo Maria Giulini made this in every respect her best season at La Scala: thirty-one performances of five stylistically and technically quite different operas and, first and foremost, the emergence of her new image. When she came to rehearsals, she was at first not recognised by some of her colleagues. She was almost as slim as Audrey Hepburn and wore carefully selected clothes from the salon of Madame Biki, grand-daughter of Puccini and Milan's leading fashion designer. Callas had lightened the colour of her russet hair so as to appear softer and milder on the stage (she later corrected this).

The new work with Luchino Visconti was a new chapter in her life. The producer, one of Italy's leading film makers, came from a distinguished Milan family and was deeply versed in his profession. Gerald Fitzgerald writes that he had grown up in 'the fourth box of the dress circle'. He had been allocated a budget of 140,000 dollars for the production of *La Vestale*, an immense sum at that time which, when it was announced, drew shudders of amazement and wonder from the press. The director noted even at the first rehearsal her 'intensity, expression, simply everything. She was a phenomenon of great magnitude. Obsessively so – a type of performer that has died out for ever.' It was during rehearsals that Maria Callas fell in love with the producer. 'It was pure imagination,' said Visconti 'but like so many Greeks, she was very possessive.' Moreover she did not like her tenor partner Franco Corelli, because he was very attractive and, according to Arianna Stassinopoulos, got from Visconti the attention which she would have liked for herself. Corelli irritated her, made her nervous and jealous. 'She was on her guard against good-looking people,' said Visconti. And she got on even less well with the baritone Enzo Sordello, with whom she was later to have a more than unpleasant encounter at the Met. Nevertheless, Visconti tolerated all her moods, anxieties and caprices because she followed his stage directions so faithfully.

Many of the gestures and poses arranged for Maria Callas and Franco Corelli were based on paintings by Canova, Ingres and David, which fitted the neoclassical style of the opera. Both producer and soprano studied the poses of Greek and French actresses. He wished to transform her into a classical actress, an actress of that great tragic style with its eloquent gestures. Like

all highly gifted actresses she could adapt without difficulty to all
these stimuli and models; on the other hand Visconti could move
the mezzo-soprano Ebe Stignani to no more than 'two standard
gestures'.

Arturo Toscanini and Victor de Sabata were in their boxes for
the première. When Maria Callas came to the footlights to a
shower of red carnations at the end of the second act, she bowed
graciously and offered a carnation to the aged Toscanini, a gesture
of respect and admiration – and of prima donna self-awareness,
which earned her still more applause from the audience.

The next 'Callas opera' that season was to have been Verdi's *Il
Trovatore*, but five days before the first performance on 8 January
1955 the tenor Mario del Monaco persuaded the director Ghiringhelli to replace it with Giordano's *Andrea Chénier*, a work
which had brought the tenor significant success at the Met just
three weeks earlier. Chénier was a role close to his heart – and to
his voice, with its top B, whereas the role of Maddalena, which
Maria Callas had to learn in five days, is not that rewarding
musically and did not lie well for her voice. Giordano's revol-
utionary piece is more the tenor's opera than the soprano's, so it
was all the more annoying when the change of programme was
ascribed to a caprice of the prima donna. In addition the singer's
voice had lost a little of its volume and its energetic attack, perhaps
because of the arduous slimming cure. The high B flat was not
quite under control, with the result that an inferno broke out after
the big aria in the third act, 'La mamma morta'. The Tebaldi
fans, and the claque which Callas had always refused to pay,
voiced a devilish demonstration; it was small consolation after the
performance when the composer's widow congratulated Callas
on her portrayal.

If one listens to the live recording today, the signs of disapproval after 'La mamma morta' seem to be simply evidence of
hostile fanaticism. Callas shades the beginning of the aria with
her own unique palette of sound, and the recording would be
worth hearing just for the way in which she dramatically emphasises the last phrase of 'l'amor'.

Visconti's explanation was that the stormy scenes were simply
caused by rival sets of fans. Ghiringhelli sought to prevent further

unrest by placing the performances of the two singers at different periods of time. But this brought little improvement, and a statement by Maria Callas, whether it was true or invented, was of even less help when it appeared in the press. 'If my dear friend Renata Tebaldi were to sing Norma or Lucia one evening and then Violetta, Gioconda or Medea, only then would we be true rivals. Failing that, it is like comparing champagne with cognac. No – with Coca-Cola.' Renata Tebaldi turned her back on La Scala shortly after that but carried on singing at the Met, and when Maria Callas returned to New York she made the discovery that the audience there, to use Fitzgerald's words, preferred Coca-Cola.

A seemingly inconsequential affair, yet it was the beginning of a chain of both minor and major disturbances. The next upset was to follow in Rome, immediately after the performances of *Andrea Chénier*. La Scala's production of *Medea* was being given in Rome, some six weeks after the season had opened with Renata Tebaldi, and it was Tebaldi's fans who disrupted Maria Callas's appearance at the première on 22 January 1955. She had already annoyed her colleagues, especially the bass Boris Christoff, by insisting on long and careful rehearsals. At the end of the evening the tall Bulgarian blocked her way when she was about to take a solo curtain call, preventing her from going out alone. Episodes like this, though mere trifles, made the headlines at the time more than her refined, 'fiery, vivid, demonic and truly stupendous characterisation of the part' (Giorgio Vigolo). Another review read: 'It is no wonder that she is so successful in portraying enchantresses (Kundry, Armida, Medea). There is something strangely magical in her voice, a kind of vocal alchemy.'

On her return to Milan from her appearances in Rome Maria Callas was completely exhausted. A boil on her neck forced her to postpone the première of Bellini's *La Sonnambula* by two weeks. This enabled the conductor, Leonard Bernstein, to have a total of eighteen rehearsals. Lawrence Kelly had arrived from Chicago to discuss the details of her second season at the Lyric Opera. Further appearances were essential after the triumphs of that first season. Perhaps in her state of exhaustion or perhaps out of caprice Maria Callas is supposed to have suggested to Kelly that he should engage Renata Tebaldi: 'Then your auditorium will have the chance to compare us and it will ensure even more success for your season.' The American had his work cut out to secure her participation. A clause of the contract contained the Lyric Opera's assurance that Maria Callas would be protected from her former agent Edward Bagarozy and any demands he might make. Nicola Rossi-Lemeni had bought his way out of the earlier contract by paying a few thousand dollars, but Maria Callas and Meneghini were of the opinion that no payment was due unless Bagarozy had performed any service. Although the Meneghinis' lawyers did not hide their reservations about her appearances, Maria Callas signed the contract.

The negotiations with Kelly took place in the Biffi-Scala restaurant, where Visconti, Bernstein and the soprano used to meet to discuss the approaching première of *La Sonnambula*. In this production Visconti presented the new Callas as a reincarnation of the legendary ballerina Maria Taglioni, a contemporary of Giuditta Pasta, whose vocal reincarnation Maria Callas was. The picture has become an icon – it shows the singer as the susceptible *femme fatale* to which she was transfigured after her death. It has nothing to do with imitation or eclecticism; rather the performance became a magnificent demonstration of art over art, giving a new reality to a work that had seemed out of date. This is another case where the photographs of the performance show what the singing, as depiction of character through sound, has made audible and visible: they convey the indescribable grace in the weightlessness of a perfectly moving ballerina. Piero Tosi recalled that the singer's waist was slimmer than Gina Lollobrigida's: 'She summoned our old wardrobe mistress, who took measurements and squeezed her into a corset. I tell you that it would have killed a film star, and Callas had to sing.' Tosi had the impression that Maria Callas, although tall and robust, suddenly appeared on the stage small and delicate – rare metamorphosis – and that she moved with light and floating steps, taking the ballerina's fifth position when standing still.

Although the idea came from Visconti it still had to be transferred into theatre and one might ask what would have happened if Joan Sutherland or Montserrat Caballé had had to carry it out.

Or if, in the second act during Amina's dream of her lover, either
of those two had been required to fall to the ground, at the
Count's touch, like Margot Fonteyn. The performance felt like a
dream made real – a dream of lost and melancholy times. It was
too an evening of theatrical magic. When in the last act Maria
Callas had to cross the bridge as the sleep-walking Amina and
reached the broken plank from which she might fall (a sigh from
the chorus), she seemed to be falling into an abyss, although she
was standing perfectly still.

Tosi had observed this at the rehearsals and wanted to find out
how she achieved it. On the first night he stood in the wings and
watched as she crossed the bridge; she slowly began to fill her
lungs with air, at the same time seeming to rise above the ground.
At the moment when she was supposed to fall she breathed out
– and seemed to fall. 'What can one say?' asked Tosi. 'She was a
magician of the theatre and knew all the tricks.' In the finale
Visconti had the superb idea of dissolving the magic which had
been evoked: at the moment of Amina's awakening with the
jubilant cabaletta 'Ah, non giunge', all the lights in the theatre
came on and Maria Callas, no longer Amina but prima donna,
stood in the centre of the stage singing with fiery and sparkling
staccati the rondo which Leonard Bernstein had ornamented – she
was drowned by applause before she had even stopped singing.
'It was magic,' said Tosi, 'she made the audience lose their minds.'

There were seven performances of *La Sonnambula* between 5
and 30 March 1955 and another three on 12, 24 and 27 April.
Between these, on 15 April she celebrated a rare triumph in a
comic role by singing Fiorilla in Rossini's *Il Turco in Italia* under
Gianandrea Gavazzeni. The producer was Franco Zeffirelli, who
was just beginning his career and who experienced no little difficulty, as Gerald Fitzgerald quotes him, in making a *comédienne*
out of the *tragédienne*. Off stage she was far from comic,[2] said
Zeffirelli, and so he had to introduce for her a little bit of
additional comedy. Knowing that she was obsessed with jewellery
and that Meneghini presented her with a new *objet de vertu* after
each première, the producer decked the Turk out with jewels and
told the soprano that Fiorilla should look in fascination at this
jewel-covered idiot and that, whenever he proffered his hand she

should stare in amazement and greed at the ring-bedecked finger. The result was a highly comic scene. But what sort of comedy was it? The comedy of emotion – or the cool distance of *commedia dell'arte*?

If the wonderful studio recording, conducted like the performances by Gianandrea Gavazzeni, can give us some idea, then Maria Callas was far more than a type from the *commedia dell'arte*; on the contrary she went with great sensitivity beyond the artifice of *opera buffa*.

Zeffirelli reports that during the rehearsal period the singer saw the film *Roman Holiday* and decided that she wanted to look as fine and delicate as the lead actress Audrey Hepburn. Beauty and jewellery, elegance and chic became an 'obsession' because she 'needed them as a weapon against an antagonistic world' (Arianna Stassinopoulos). The tenor Jon Vickers, who sang Jason with her in 1958 and 1959, always spoke of her as 'little Maria', but she never allowed the world to glimpse this little Maria. Only in her performances was she this 'little Maria', as Amina, Lucia and Violetta.

It was as Violetta in *La Traviata* that she concluded her La Scala season, her most successful of all, even if perhaps she had sung best in the 1951–2 season, when she was still able to release all her vocal and expressive energies. The production of Verdi's opera was a labour of love for Luchino Visconti, for Carlo Maria Giulini and for the singer, who said in an interview with Derek Prouse that it had taken her years to saturate Violetta's voice with sickness. 'It is all a question of breathing,' she said, 'one needs a clear throat if one is to keep up this tired-sounding speaking and singing.' Later, in a performance of the opera in London, she sang the top A at the end of 'Addio del passato' with such a fine line that the note broke for a brief moment. She explained in an interview that it was precisely this effect of dying away that she had intended – the note would have been more secure and better placed if she had used a little more pressure on her breathing, but the effect would have been ruined.

It was Visconti who was most criticised after the première on 28 May 1955. Firstly because he had transposed the action to a *fin-de-siècle* background, around 1875, so that Maria Callas could appear in costumes of that epoch; secondly because Violetta was made to throw off her shoes before 'Sempre libera'; and finally because Violetta did not die in bed but wearing her hat and coat. Thirty years ago such small departures from the composer's stage directions were viewed as sacrilege. It did not take long for the performance to enter the realm of theatre legend, first and foremost because of the evocative portrayal of Violetta. Giuseppe di Stefano was an acceptable Alfredo, Ettore Bastianini, however, an inexpressive Germont.[3] The tenor had caused difficulties at rehearsal because he was irked by Visconti's meticulous preparation, which aimed at working out exactly every gesture and every movement. He arrived late or often not at all for rehearsals and when Maria Callas was sent out by Giulini for a solo curtain at the end of the première, di Stefano took this as an excuse not only to leave the theatre but to quit the production altogether. In the three performances on 31 May and 5 and 7 June he was replaced by the efficient Giacinto Prandelli. It was not just the immediate participants who later enthused about Callas's Violetta. Nicola Benois included her, like the dancer Nijinsky, among those few artists who 'have been touched by something divine'. His designer and colleague Piero Tosi confessed to having wept during the performances; listening to the live recording with the many photographs before one can be gripping in a similar way. The singing and the countenance of the singer have the very deepest expression of suffering. Alexandre Sacharoff was astounded to find an actress of such calibre on the operatic stage; Callas reminded him of the great Sarah Bernhardt. He said that Bernhardt as Marguérite Gautier in the play had frozen in her suffering at the moment when Alfredo threw the money at her feet; Callas played the scene exactly like that.

It is difficult to explain why there were sounds of disapproval at the end of the first act in the third performance (on 5 June). 'Sempre libera' was interrupted by whistling and the singer had great difficulty in finishing the cabaletta. When she came on stage alone at the end of the act in order to defy the hostile claque she was acclaimed by the majority of the public. Yet she detected the hint of hostility. In the summer edition of La Scala's house magazine it was said that 'Callas doubtless has many enemies', and that her colleagues considered it sufficient to have a beautiful voice and to sing with one's eyes fixed on the conductor's baton as they had done half a century before. Such singers were incapable of coping with effort and sacrifice. Was it necessary to stress that Maria Callas would triumph over such attacks? And was this any comfort to the singer? 'One thing is certain: one pays a high price for separating oneself from the herd.'

Did she really separate herself? If so, it was through her professional energy at rehearsals which was misinterpreted as stubbornness; through her self-confidence when dealing with theatre directors; through the inflexibility of her requirements. Above all, and this was unpardonable, the rays of fame seemed to fall only on her and she was not clever enough to disguise her pride over those triumphs. Her colleagues considered it simply an act of provocation when she went into Ghiringhelli's proscenium box to applaud them; her applause was interpreted as calculated presumption.

Callas was now stepping on to another, much more dangerous stage where she could not act. She became a star, a world celebrity with entertainment value, a role for which it scarcely mattered if she was a singer, or at most if she cancelled or called off a performance. The furnishing of her new house in Milan's via Buonarotti, her shopping, her wardrobe, all supplied stories and mischief for the press.

Three weeks after *La Traviata*, on 29 June 1955, came another Norma for Italian radio in Rome. In July she was studying Puccini's *Madama Butterfly* in readiness for the recording with Karajan, which was made in the first week of August, and later for the three performances in Chicago. Only four days elapsed between completion of the Puccini recording and the commencement of the one for Verdi's *Aida*, between 10 and 24 August.

At these recording sessions there must have been differences between the diva and her tenor, as reported in Drake's biography of Richard Tucker. Tucker was scheduled to sing the romance 'Celeste Aida' at the second session. The first take was so perfect that Giovanni Martinelli, who was present as a guest but who did not particularly like Tucker, applauded him. After the session Tucker received a telephone call from the industrialist Frederic R.

Mann, who had travelled from Philadelphia, a man whose love of music found architectural expression in the Mann auditorium in Tel Aviv. Mann, who knew the producer Dario Soria and was friendly with Serafin and Tito Gobbi, was immediately invited by Tucker to attend one of the recording sessions. Maria Callas seemed to be nervous and tense both at the rehearsals and the first sessions, presumably because she was not in top form. In the trio after 'Celeste Aida' she kept insisting on new takes, a total of seven in fact. On the ninth day Mann came to the session, and it was Tucker's hope that they would be able to hear the major part of the Nile scene. After recording her Nile aria Callas was in a peevish mood, spoke tersely to Fedora Barbieri, sharply and brusquely to Serafin and showed annoyance with the American visitor, who presumed to call her 'Mary'. When Tucker began 'Pur ti riveggo' she walked up and down the stage until the engineers had to break off because of the noise which her heels were making. She then exclaimed, 'I would like everyone in the theatre to understand that the music of *Aida* is sacred to me.'

Her colleagues nodded with friendly approval and she continued. 'If I am to make a recording of this sacred music, then I need full co-operation in this theatre. Nobody must distract me at any time.' When Tucker asked innocently who was disturbing her, she replied in a loud voice: 'Those people up in the box. They must leave the theatre immediately.' While the horrified tenor tried to explain to his colleague who the visitors were, she threatened to leave the theatre. The Manns themselves resolved the situation by leaving silently. The Nile scene was then recorded in this tense atmosphere. The climactic phrase of the finale, 'Sacerdote, io resto a te' belongs to the tenor with its sustained top As. Callas kept complaining about the poor mixing of voices and made her colleagues perform for twelve takes.

Later in the evening Tucker spoke openly to Serafin about the diva's rude behaviour. 'Sometimes she needs tension in order to sing well,' explained Serafin, 'some singers are like that. Lauri-Volpi needed a discussion, an argument. Maria Jeritza was like that too. You should have heard the pair of them cursing each other when they were singing the Met's first *Turandot*. And that's what it is like with Callas. She must sometimes have an argument, it's in her nature.' When Tucker showed that he was not satisfied with this explanation, Serafin is supposed to have said to him: 'Don't forget, Richard, that you have a perfect technique and she knows that she doesn't have that. You sound better on the recording and that makes her jealous. Why do you think that she made you sing "Sacerdote" so many times?' The tenor had no explanation, so Serafin explained that she had wanted to tire him out. Bursting with rage, Tucker declared that by the following morning he would be singing the 'damned phrase without tiring'.

Straight after the *Aida* recording came one of *Rigoletto*, from 3 to 16 September, and with Giuseppe di Stefano as tenor. The quarrels during *La Traviata* in Milan were luckily forgotten. And a week later the La Scala company arrived in Berlin. Herbert von Karajan, just appointed chief conductor of the Berlin Philharmonic Orchestra, conducted two performances of *Lucia di Lammermoor* in the Städtische Oper. Music lovers queued two days and nights for tickets. In *Opera* Desmond Shawe-Taylor wrote:

Miss Callas, I must say, was tremendous. No more than on other occasions was she a flawless vocalist; but when singing at her best she diffused a kind of rapturous pleasure now virtually inaccessible from any other source; and even when she jolted us with one of those rough changes of register, or emitted one of her cavernous wails, or sang above pitch on a final E flat *in alt* she was always the noble, forlorn, infinitely pathetic 'mad Lucia' of nineteenth-century tradition. Nor did her performance end with the Mad Scene; through ten minutes of solo curtain calls she remained with consummate art half within the stage character, with her air of wondering simplicity, her flawless miming of unworthiness, her subtle variation in the tempo of successive appearances and in the depth of successive curtseys, and her elaborate byplay with the roses which fell from the gallery [. . .] – one of which, with such a gesture and such capital aim, she flung to the delighted flautist! Oh yes, an artist to her finger tips: the real royal thing. I dare say she will never sing any better than she does now; there is Greek resin in her voice which will never be quite strained away; she will never charm us with the full round ductile tone of Muzio or Raisa or

Ponselle. But she has sudden flights, dramatic outbursts of rocketing virtuosity, of which even those more richly endowed singers were hardly capable. Certainly at the present time she is unparalleled.

The live recording of that performance is generally considered to be the definitive Lucia portrayal of Maria Callas. She gives the entire performance a quite different tone to the one in the Serafin recording, which, as John Ardoin writes, is filled with 'brooding melancholy'. In the Berlin performance she sings almost entirely with her 'little-girl' voice, with a soaring line and her tone placed well forward. The Mad Scene is painted in pale pastel colours and dramatised with her inimitable accentuation of words – as in 'il fantasma'. In *The Callas Legacy* John Ardoin goes as far as to say that if he could possess only one Callas recording he would choose this one. David A. Lowe shares that feeling. He sees in the performance the 'climax of Maria Callas's vocal art'.

Beguiling indeed is the effect of the soaring legato of 'Regnava nel silenzio' or the opening of 'Veranno a te', sung with finest *mezza voce*. This is singing which 'goes straight to the heart', singing for ears which can love. Speaking personally, there is scarcely another Callas recording which I myself listen to with more emotion, an added reason being that the first signs of the decline of her voice are to be heard in this magnificent portrayal. It is irrelevent that she avoids the E flat *in alt* at the end of the cadenza and only sings one E flat at the end of the aria; yet it shows that she can no longer take every vocal risk. The pale timbre and the reduced dynamics are as much a result of accommodating the voice's condition as they are of interpretational intent.

If this should sound too critical, let it be stressed again: this Berlin performance of *Lucia* is one of the great moments in the singer's career, but an end can already be sensed in the consummation of that evening, even if Maria Callas was still to sing performances in which she could recall the bold vocal brilliance of the early years.

8

The Descent to Fame

'I am still trying to discover what happened
in New York – I am sorry that I could not
give you what other theatres have had from
me'

Maria Callas to Rudolf Bing

Scandal in Chicago

'In the world of music one can never have a
peaceful life'

Carlo Maria Giulini

Following four weeks' rest Maria Callas opened the second season
of the Chicago Lyric Opera on 31 October 1955. Conducted by
Nicola Rescigno, she sang Elvira in Bellini's *I Puritani*. Roger
Dettmer's paean of praise in the *Chicago American* was typical of
critical comments: 'The town, as we all know, has been Callas-
crazy for more than a year, and none has been more demented
than I. In the proper role and in good voice, I adore the woman;
I am a slave in her spell.' The other critics were equally inspired,
although Howard Talley in *Musical America* could not overlook
the fact that the interpolated top Ds in the second act were out
of focus.

Verdi's *Aida* was given with Renata Tebaldi on the second
night of the season. On 5 and 8 November there followed two
performances of *Il Trovatore*. It is a matter for great regret that,
despite rumours of its existence, there seems to be no live recording, especially as Jussi Björling was singing Manrico and two
other excellent interpreters of their roles, Ebe Stignani and the
young Ettore Bastianini, were taking part. Rudolf Bing writes in
his memoirs that the way in which Maria Callas listened to Manrico's aria 'Ah, sì ben mio' in the third act had more effect
dramatically than the tenor's singing. George Jellinek said that
vocally Björling 'was an absolutely incomparable Manrico'. And
the tenor himself said: 'Her Leonora was quite simply perfection.
I have heard many singers in the part but never a better interpretation than this.' And it must be remembered that he had sung
Manrico at the Met alongside Zinka Milanov, who is widely held
to be the ideal Leonora. Milanov certainly commanded the more
beautiful *acuti* and more softly produced *mezza voce* phrases, yet

her portrayal was not as polished musically or stylistically as that
of Callas.

Rudolf Bing had finally succeeded, just before the second performance on 8 November, in securing Callas for the Met. She
was to make her début on 29 October 1956 as Norma. The
reporter who asked about her fee – the amount of which had been
one of the points of argument – was told by the soprano that no
fee was too high for the role of Norma. Bing, charming and
cynical as he was, smoothly evaded such details. Singers at the
Met, he said, came for the sake of art and should be satisfied with
a bunch of flowers. Naturally Callas would receive a particularly
lovely bouquet.

The first big éclat in the singer's career followed a few days
later. Produced by Hizi Koyke, she had sung Puccini's Cio-Cio-
San on 11 November. In his book *The Last Prima Donnas*, Lanfranco Rasponi quotes a number of singers of the part of Cio-
Cio-San as saying that the role is a 'killer part'. The *tessitura* is
very high and above all the performer must constantly sing out
over a big orchestra in the transitional register. When Strauss said
of his Salome that he envisaged the voice of an Isolde for the
fifteen-year-old girl, this also applies to Butterfly. Putting it
simply, most of the singers who have the voice for Butterfly are
not capable of portraying a fifteen-year-old geisha with that voice.
Callas wanted to do just that – and succeeded. 'This was an
intimate Butterfly, overawed right from the beginning by the
tragedy which was to befall her. Not even the love duet had that
melodic flow which quickens the pulse. Instead, it contrasted the
man's growing ardour with the girl's repressed ecstasy,' wrote
Claudia Cassidy who, however, did not fail to add that after two
performances the portrayal still seemed to her to be at the work-
shop stage.

A third performance had not been planned. Maria Callas was
talked into it by Lawrence Kelly and Carol Fox, which was not
difficult in view of the public's glowing reception. It took place
on 17 November and was greeted with prolonged applause. After
the many solo curtain calls – a continuation of her performance
– she made for her dressing room, exhausted and 'moved to tears'
(Jellinek) by the feeling in the audience. Suddenly Marshal Stanley

Pringle and Deputy Sheriff Dan Smith burst into the room. Their
job was to hand over Eddie Bagarozy's law suit and they behaved,
in George Jellinek's words, with 'as little consideration as the *sans
culottes* during the French Revolution'. They tucked the document
into the singer's kimono.

Stassinopoulos states that when Callas had found her voice she
shouted, 'I will not be sued! I have the voice of an angel!'; the
Associated Press photo, which went round the world in the next
few days, and which did so much to devastate her image, makes
clear that Maria Callas was beside herself with rage. Jellinek infers
that this embarrassing incident would never have happened without the assistance of an anti-Callas group at the Lyric Opera.
Stassinopoulos even reports that Lawrence Kelly suspected his
colleague Carol Fox of engineering it in order to turn Callas
against him, but she goes on to declare such suppositions purely
hypothetical.

Dario Soria and Walter Legge, who had both witnessed the
grotesque incident, escorted the singer from the theatre. The next
day she flew via Montreal on to Milan, where she was due at La
Scala for the *prima* of Bellini's *Norma* under Antonino Votto, on
7 December 1955.

Callas opened the La Scala season for the fourth time just after
her thirty-second birthday. The theatre was lavishly decorated for
the occasion by Pierre Balmain and the visitors included State
President Giovanni Gronchi. Jellinek reports that observers had
detected a slight straining in her singing; Stassinopoulos mentions
noisy demonstrations by the anti-Callas faction, yet nothing is
heard of this on the live recording. It would certainly have been
surprising because she was on top form for the performance, as
the recording testifies. She had no trouble with the climactic Bs
in 'Casta diva', formed the melismas between stanzas with security and mastered the cabaletta with a verve free of any strain. An
unforgettable climax was the singing of 'Cosi trovavo del mio
cor la via', given with floating voice and a breathtaking diminuendo on 'Ah sì, fa core, abbracciami' at the top C – after which
one can actually hear the spellbound audience gasping for breath.
There is sheer frenzy at the end of the first act, where Callas
crowns the trio with a fulminating top D; anyone who at that

point or elsewhere can hear 'straining' either wants to, or has invented it in order to add to his own version of the Callas saga.

It was from this time, nevertheless, that everything which Callas did or is supposed to have done was turned into a scandal. One such instance was Mario del Monaco's report that he was suddenly kicked violently on the shins after the third act of a *Norma* performance in January 1956 and that while he was still fighting the pain, Maria Callas had acknowledged the applause by herself. A ridiculous story, but not absurd enough not to make headlines: public hunger for such vulgarity knows no limits.

If Jellinek's report is correct, Mario del Monaco had already informed Intendant Ghiringhelli at rehearsals that he would not allow solo curtain calls for any soloist. This accorded with the practice at the Metropolitan Opera. But at one of those January performances the tenor got tumultuous applause after his first act aria, which Meneghini took to be the work of a claque and lodged a complaint to that effect with Ghiringhelli. Meneghini is supposed to have gone to the leader of the claque, Ettore Parmeggiani,[1] and complained. Parmeggiani turned to del Monaco, expecting him to refute the charge. In anger del Monaco told Meneghini that he and his wife were not the owners of La Scala and that the audience would applaud those who had earned it. Again, it is difficult, if not impossible, to separate fact from fiction. Perhaps one should take episodes like this, even if fictitious, as the 'terrible truth' of life (*pace* the Prologue to *Pagliacci*), which the great operatic artists have to experience and suffer: they have a wonderful profession, but others use it for mercenary purposes alone.

It is easy to tell from the recording who the applause was intended for. Mario del Monaco sings with his customary heavy and metallic tone, lacking finer nuance or gradation, which in the duets with Callas is barely tolerable. The Bellini opera was followed by no less than seventeen performances, between January and May 1956, of Verdi's *La Traviata*, conducted by Carlo Maria Giulini and Antonino Tonini. The rising Gianni Raimondi, a tenor with a fabulous top but whose voice does not sound as good on record as it did in the theatre, replaced Giuseppe di Stefano. The Germonts included Ettore Bastianini, Aldo Protti,

Carlo Tagliabue and Anselmo Colzani. Again an incident occured which was orchestrated into a scandal by certain newspapers. At one performance a bunch of radishes was thrown on the stage in addition to the flowers. Reports state that Maria Callas received them angrily as she advanced to the orchestra pit but then picked them up – sovereign strategy – and pressed them to her bosom 'as if they were orchids' (Stassinopoulos); only in her dressing room did she burst into tears. The silly incident made headlines for several days, and the fact that the vegetables must have been imported pointed to an intrigue.

Her next role – Rosina in Rossini's *Il Barbiere di Siviglia* – was her only real failure at La Scala, where she sang twenty-three operas in all. The production was already four years old and at its première had seemed only a routine presentation. Carlo Maria Giulini, who despite his own illness had taken over from Victor de Sabata, told how he conducted with his head lowered so as not to see what was happening on the stage. Giulini is quoted by Gerald Fitzgerald as saying: 'This *Barbiere* is the worst memory of my life in the theatre. I don't feel it was a fiasco for Maria alone, but for all of us concerned with the performance. It was an artistic mistake, utterly routine, thrown together, with nothing given deep study or preparation.'

Giulini's recollections of the atmosphere surrounding the performances are still more penetrating and alarming. The audience at La Scala, complained the conductor, did not come for the experience of Callas's artistry but simply hoping for a scandal. 'In this hostile climate, most conductors, singers, choristers and orchestral players feel like gladiators in the Circus Maximus, where blood must be shed [. . .] Success at La Scala is always without joy, without love, without gratitude. The best thing a public can say to an artist is thank you. Not bravo. This already implies a judgement.' Although Maria Callas was the pride of the theatre or perhaps because she was, the public used her as a target. Giulini suggests that in a certain way she provoked such reactions, because her curtain calls showed an element of insolence. Even her greatest triumphs were struggled for and achieved in the face of adversity, so that, says Giulini, they left 'something of a bitter taste in her mouth'.

Despite Giulini's verdict, reactions to the Scala *Barbiere* were not unanimously negative. Franco Abbiati wrote in the *Corriere della Sera* of the 'surprising stylistic metamorphosis of Maria Callas' and praised a portrayal 'which almost possessed the quality of a psychoanalytical study'. Peter Hoffer noted in *Music and Musicians* that she had played Rosina 'as a coquette', and he judged her in a similar way to Giulini, that she had made Rosina into a 'sort of Carmen'. Luigi Alva, who was making his La Scala début with the role of Count Almaviva, found fault with the fact that she had used 'too much pepper' and had acted with gestures which were exaggerated; yet he stressed that she had sung brilliantly in the Lesson Scene in Act 2. Rossi-Lemeni, singing the part of Basilio, felt that his colleague was too aggressive. But Giulini, he emphasised, had conducted wonderfully, Alva had really shone and Gobbi had been incomparable.

The live recording makes it clear that Maria Callas had not worked out a detailed concept of the role and that she was often trying too hard. As Alva stressed, she really needed a producer like Visconti or the young Zeffirelli to inspire her.

The La Scala season came to a close with six performances of Giordano's *Fedora*. Victorien Sardou's play had once been a vehicle for Sarah Bernhardt, but it had died with her. Because of the historical background – the opera is set in Tsarist St Petersburg at the end of the nineteenth century – La Scala asked Nicola Benois to design the sets and Tatiana Pavlova to produce. Benois later declared that the soprano immediately grasped the elements of the Russian acting style and gave the most congenial portrayal of her role. Yet musical circles in Milan showed some annoyance. Even Teodoro Celli, a Callas admirer, considered that she had strayed onto the wrong terrain, a view which the conductor of the performances, Gianandrea Gavazzeni, emphatically rejected. His view was that no singer had ever sung Fedora with so much nuance, variety of colour and subtlety or lifted the part to such a level of theatrical art. Peter Hoffer's verdict in *Music and Musicians* that Callas had proved herself to be one of the great actresses, if not the greatest singer, is mistaken by Stassinopoulos for a reference to Callas's failing vocal powers. It is more probable that she never really felt her way into the pitfalls of verismo music, into that screaming exaltation which has been the aesthetic death of many verismo operas.

In June 1956, once the season was over, the entire La Scala company went to Vienna, where the Staatsoper had been re-inaugurated six months earlier. Callas went to sing Donizetti's Lucia under Herbert von Karajan. Jellinek mentions, and Stassino-poulos makes great play of the fact, that the soprano found that a talisman, a tiny oil painting of the madonna, was not with her when she arrived at the Hotel Sacher. It had been a present from Meneghini in 1947. A friend had to fetch it to Vienna all the way from Milan.

The Vienna Staatsoper début was like a state occasion. Theodor Körner, president of the Republic, was in the audience, which applauded for twenty minutes, and the singer's departure from the theatre had to be escorted by police in order to give her protection from the crowds. The Austrian reviews praised her ecstatically, but reading between the lines of Claudia Cassidy's report one noted that her vocal control was becoming more and more an act of will-power.

There is little of the spontaneous brilliance, the seemingly effortless incandescence, the exquisite shadow play that gave her Lyric Lucia an indelible radiance in history's hall of song. But there is superb singing of enormous skill over what I later discover to be the kind of sandpaper throat a visitor can acquire in Vienna's sudden, violent and unpredictable squalls of chilly, blowing rain. At one point in the pyrotechnics of the Mad Scene her voice just simply doesn't respond. From our high loge we can see Karajan's instant alertness, the almost pricking ears of the Scala orchestra. But Callas recovers instantly [. . .] You might not have noticed that hazardous moment at all. Just in case you did, a Callas curtain call touches a hand ever so delicately to her throat. The orchestra men are a buzz of amused admiration.

The soprano then spent the month of July on the island of Ischia in order to rest and to prepare for the new season. In August and the first weeks of September she took part in three complete opera recordings. From 3–9 August it was Leonora in *Il Trovatore* under Karajan – together with di Stefano, Barbieri and Panerai. From 20 August–4 September it was *La Bohème* under Votto, followed immediately, from 4–12 September, by *Un Ballo in Maschera*, also conducted by Votto. Di Stefano was again the tenor partner. Then, after a concert for Radio Italiana on 27 September, she set out for the United States – her Metropolitan Opera début was approaching.

Callas at the Met or the Splendid Disaster

'It was a nervous Maria Callas who took to the stage – a tremulous sound in the voice reminded one of Butterfly's entrance last November at Chicago'

Roger Dettmer, *Chicago American*

'As for her singing, Miss Callas maintained a standard that one who had heard her in Italy rather expected [. . .] It is a puzzling voice. Occasionally it gives the impression of having been formed of sheer will-power rather than natural endowments. The quality is different in the upper, middle and lower registers'

Howard Taubman, *New York Times*

'For those who have heard Miss Callas elsewhere (as well as on innumerable records) there was a basic curiosity about the marriage of the voice and the house: would they be compatible, or would there be need for a period of trial wedding? A dress rehearsal on the Saturday before left no doubt in this respect: the voice, though not a huge or weighty one, is so well supported and floated that it is audible at all times, most particularly in the piano and pianissimo effect which Miss Callas delights in giving us. So far as *Norma* is concerned, the singer refuses to force it for volume's sake alone, and it comes clearly to the ear even when she is singing out a top D at the end of the trio with Adalgisa and Pollione'

Irving Kolodin, *New York Times*

An artist must already have exceeded the limits of mere fame and entered the realms of glory before he can appear on the cover of a magazine like *Time* or *Der Spiegel*. But he must take into account that the actual story may not restrict itself to objectivity and that the journalist may attempt to describe the qualities which have contributed to the artist's fame with a damaging mixture of worldliness and ignorance. The artist becomes hero – or rather anti-hero – of a story in which statement (or news) is mixed with opinion. Hans Magnus Enzensberger writes in his essay 'The Language of *Der Spiegel*':

The story is an epic form which has degenerated; it invents action, cohesion, aesthetic continuity. To fit in with that the writer has to appear to be story-teller and all-knowing demon, from whom nothing remains hidden and who at any time can look into the heart of his hero, like Cervantes into the heart of Don Quixote. But whereas Don Quixote depends on Cervantes, a journalist has to answer to reality. Thus his behaviour is basically dishonest, his omnipresence based on presumption. He has to cheat his way through between simple correctness, which he rejects, and that higher truth of the real story which is denied him. He has to interpret, sort out, shape and arrange the facts: but he must not admit that he is doing this. He must not reveal his epic colour. It is a dubious position to be in. In order to hold it the story-writer sees himself compelled to retouch and to read between the lines. No publication has made more of an art of the technique of suggestion, penetration and innuendo than *Der Spiegel*.

The fame of Maria Callas became global, and at once irrevocably damaged, when the title story appeared in *Time* two days before her début. The subject was no longer the singer's art (which, to quote Irving Kolodin, was described with the 'vocabulary of ignorance') but the operatic monster who was a synthesis of fact and fiction, the monster mistakenly offered to the type of reader who, thinking himself enlightened, could react only negatively, with envy, spite, malicious glee and hatred. Whenever the *Time* story touches on music, vocal art or its technical details, we find no more than amateur speculation and vague generalisation.

What is one supposed to make of the following description of the voice?

> Few rate the Callas voice as opera's sweetest or most beautiful. It has its ravishing moments. In quiet passages it warms and caresses the air. In ensembles, it cuts through the other voices like the sword of Damocles, clean and strong. But after the first hour of a performance it tends to become strident and later in a hard evening begins to take on a reverberating quality, as if her mouth were full of saliva. But the special quality of the Callas voice is not tone. It is the extraordinary ability to carry, as no other, the inflections and nuances of emotion, from mordant intensity to hushed delicacy. Callas's singing always seem to have a surprise in reserve.

This is indeed the vocabulary of ignorance at its height, vague technical jargon which distorts the facts out of all recognition. All the more clear and unmistakable are the ambiguous, spiteful, and dishonourable – certainly libellous – references:

> Reared in Manhattan's Upper West Side, Maria Callas had left it a

fat, unhappy child of fourteen. She returned svelte, successful, the wife of an Italian millionaire, a diva more widely hated by her colleagues and more wildly acclaimed by her public than any other living singer [. . .] Maria Callas clawed her way to her present pre-eminence with a ruthless ferocity injecting fear into her enemies and leaving her with few professional friends [. . .] On one occasion her antagonists began to heckle just as she was reaching the high notes of her second aria in *La Traviata*. Callas pulled off her shawl [What aria can they be referring to? 'Addio del passato'? I can find no reference elsewhere to such an incident], came to the footlights and stared into the faces of her tormentors. She then sang (with bold abandon) one of the most difficult arias in all opera. Had she made a mistake, it would have been fatal, but she sang with faultless and unearthly beauty. She was called back five times by an audience moved to delirium, and five times she stood there, cold as a stone and arrogant, before turning round. At the sixth call she relented and bowed to everyone except the hecklers. She then looked at them, suddenly raising her arms in a gesture of spitting contempt [. . .] She vented her resentment on the people around her. Her first victim was another soprano, Renata Tebaldi, long-time favourite of La Scala audiences and owner of a voice of creamy softness and delicate and sensitive musicality – and a temperament to match.

There is in all these quotations relatively little that can be proved to be wrong, but still less is true or relevant or of any significance whatsoever – even if public stupidity could create a monster based on Callas's letter to her mother saying that she could throw herself out of the window if she could not put her life in order.

Rudolf Bing recalls in his memoirs, in a way which the Americans would call candid, his struggles with Maria Callas, the endless exchange of letters, the haggling over fees, his journey as a penitent to Chicago and Meneghini's business methods, which included being paid in cash like a shopkeeper and eventually getting bundles of five-dollar notes. Bing states that Callas was given treatment accorded no other artist. She was collected at the airport by the assistant manager, Francis Robinson, accompanied by a Met lawyer so as to prevent the sort of unpleasant incident that had occurred in Chicago. Bing also stressed, however, that much of her severity was compensatory and that he detected a prominent feature of her character to be a naïve 'little-girl' quality. Bing also says that it was he who fired the baritone Enzo Sordello after the performance of *Lucia di Lammermoor* in which he had held on too long to a top note – not the ominous top C specified in *Der Spiegel*.

Let us stop. The biographical thread seems to have become twisted in an inextricable knot. Very contradictory reviews of her first New York Norma . . . critical comment about the language of international magazines . . . extracts from Rudolf Bing's memoirs – where is the connection? It is certainly no longer to be found in the person of the singer. By the end of the autumn of 1956 Maria Callas was already 'in the public domain' – public property and as such a fantasy image for numerous projections which can be arranged in a story like the one in *Time* magazine. Nor was she any longer being listened to as a *singer* or judged by the facts alone. Irving Kolodin, who reviewed the soprano's Met début in the *Saturday Review*, also attacked the vocabulary of ignorance and the violations of Howard Taubman and his friends in the *New York Times*. Kolodin:

> When I read the writer's reservation that he found Callas's voice puzzling, I assumed that he was describing a singer with a small voice who is struggling with her volume in order to be heard in such a large space and who is therefore having to 'force'. Callas could scarcely be accused of being inaudible, whichever auditorium she was singing in (Chicago, the old Met, Carnegie Hall or Covent Garden).

Kolodin demonstrated that his fellow critics were incapable of differentiating between colouring the voice for dramatic effect and the use of muscular energy to enlarge the sound. He reproached them for hardly ever asking themselves really relevant questions like whether there was an excessive tensing of the neck muscles or too much tension in the lips. Was her tongue pushed down with too much force? Was the voice too deep? Too high?

Kolodin went on to quote William James Henderson's famous review of Luisa Tetrazzini's Met début, as a model of how real criticism should be 'a vocalising of a singer's performance': in other words, a song about a song, a written expression of the sound. Extracts from that review are reproduced here in order to give the reader an idea of how carefully prepared W. J. Henderson was when he attended an opera performance, how precisely he wrote about the subject – and that alone – and how uncompromising his verdict could be – harsh in a way no critic would dare to be today and too harsh for undiscriminating fans to tolerate. Henderson:

> Mme Tetrazzini has a fresh, clear voice of pure soprano quality and of sufficient range, though other roles must perhaps disclose its furthest flights above the staff. The perfectly unworn condition and youthful timbre of this voice are its largest charms, and to these must be added a splendid richness in the upper range. Indeed, the best part of the voice as heard last evening was from the G above the staff to the high C. The B flat in 'Sempre libera' was a tone of which any singer might have been proud. The high D in the same number was by no means so good, and the high E flat which the singer took in ending the scene had a head tone of thin quality and refused to stay on the pitch.
>
> In *colorature* Mme Tetrazzini quite justified much that had been written about her. She sang *staccato* with consummate ease, though not with the approved method of breathing. Her method is merely to check the flow between tones instead of lightly attacking each note separately. But the effect which she produces, that of detached notes rather than of strict *staccato*, is charming. Of her shake less can be said in praise. It was neither clear in emission nor steady, and the interval was surely at least open to question.
>
> Descending scales she sang beautifully, with perfect smoothness and clean articulation. Her transformation of the plain scale in the opening cadenza of 'Sempre libera' into a chromatic scale, though a departure from the letter of the score, was not at all

out of taste, and its execution fully sustained its right to existence.

The ascending scales in the same number were sung in a manner which would not be tolerated by any reputable teacher in a pupil of a year's standing. They began with a tremulous and throaty *voce bianca* and ended in a sweep into a full medium, with the chest resonance carried up to a preposterous height. The most notable shortcoming of Mme Tetrazzini's singing as revealed last night was her extraordinary emission of her lower medium notes. These were all sung with a pinched glottis and with a colour so pallid and a tremolo so pronounced that they were often not a bad imitation of the wailing of a cross infant. This style of tone production she carried into most of her recitative, till she seemed to be inclined to think that Violetta ought to show that fondness for 'baby talk' which is sometimes accepted as a charm among her kind.

In cantilena the new soprano fell furthest below the demands of supreme vocal art. Her *cantabile* was uneven in tone quality, the breaks between her medium and her upper notes coming out most unpleasantly and her tricks of phrasing in short and spasmodic groups, with breath taken capriciously and without consideration of either text or music, were serious blots upon her delivery. For example, in beginning 'Ah! fors' è lui', she deliberately made a phrase after the u, and, taking a leisurely breath, introduced the i as if it belonged to the next word.

The continued employment of cold colour in *cantabile* quite removed the possibility of pathos from 'Non sapete', while a pitiless description of her infantile delivery of 'Dite alle giovine' would read like cruelty.

Any listener who is capable of using his ears and who possesses vocal imagination will, if he has ever heard the voice of Tetrazzini, be able to conjure it up again when reading Henderson – and if one reads Henry F. Chorley or even Stendhal on Pasta, Grisi or Malibran, one can construct an accurate acoustical picture of the sound and style of those singers. This is because the writers had the ability to shape their language like an orchestra: they possessed not just a precise, objective vocabulary but also had at their command the required suggestive – but never arbitrary – use of metaphor.

It was Nietzsche's view that two things had to come together if an event were to have greatness: the perception of those creating it and the perception of those actively expressing it. In that sense Maria Callas's début at the Met, experienced by Rudolf Bing as 'the most exciting opening night of my tenure at the Metropolitan', was not a great event. Most of the audience, who between them had paid 75,510 dollars at the box office, had come to hear a star and not a work like *Norma*, which was quite unsuitable for such a social occasion. Kolodin notes with irony in his history of the Met that people who had paid thirty-five dollars for their stall seats knew nothing of the demands of the role of Norma, but they expected appropriate entertainment for their money.

Zinka Milanov, reigning diva of the house, made her entry to the auditorium as if it were a stage appearance, acknowledging applause as if she had sung 'Vissi d'arte'. In contrast to La Scala, the stage production was not done well enough to merit the occasion: it was an old *mise-en-scène* which Kolodin described as sloppy, which had not been appreciably improved by having been retouched. But Callas began the performance 'with a well-controlled and beautifully expressive "Casta diva",' which Kolodin considered to be the result of her strict schooling and good nerves. He admits that what the audience heard was not 'the suavest of "Casta diva"'s' but that whereas most singers would have contented themselves with a beautiful rendition of that first aria, Callas's concern was 'the creation of a character', a rounded portrayal such as the Alceste of Kirsten Flagstad or the Marschallin of Lotte Lehmann. 'Rounded musical phrases, a true musician's way of curving a melodic line, a superior vocalist's sense of dynamics and colour – all these were directed by a *tragédienne's* mind subordinated to a single overpowering purpose: that of realising what Bellini's genius had poured into his sorely tried heroine.' Even though she was vocally not on top form, Fedora Barbieri and Cesare Siepi could just about hold their own beside her, while Mario del Monaco could not even do that. Kolodin writes that the critics 'fumbled for a yardstick and came up with a rule of thumb' – 'the uncommon talent sought in vain for the uncommon appraisal that was its due'.

Kolodin himself was the only one to see the voice as 'an extension of her personality', as drama *sui generis*, and the only one also to recognise the immense discipline which Callas used to keep the drama under control. Between the third and fourth performances (10 and 22 November 1956), she sang two of *Tosca* under Dimitri Mitropoulos; her partners were Giuseppe Campora and George London. Most critics recorded that she was vocally not (any longer) the most luxuriant Tosca, but it was only Kolodin who noticed that she 'phrased her music with the instinct of an actress and acted with the instinct of a dazzling musician'. The prima donna's Met début was followed by the world star's first appearances in café society. Angel, the American off-shoot of EMI, booked the Trianon Room in the Ambassador Hotel for a large reception, to which they invited the Greek and Italian ambassadors, Marlene Dietrich, Elsa Maxwell and many other colourful specimens of society and salon fauna. Callas wore jewellery valued at a million dollars which had been loaned to her by the jeweller Harry Winston. Finally, on 25 November, she appeared, partnered by George London, on the *Ed Sullivan Show* in scenes from Act 2 of *Tosca*.

In the *Chicago Tribune* anger was vented by Claudia Cassidy over the horrific patchwork ('butchered to a jigsaw of 15 minutes'), which would confirm the worst prejudices of all those who never go to the opera, and would seem like a travesty to all those who love it. But far more attention was paid to a letter from Renata Tebaldi, which replied to one of Callas's statements in the *Time* story: 'The signora states that I have no backbone. But I do possess something important which she does not have – a heart.'

After the first performance of *Lucia di Lammermoor*, considered by many to have been the highlight of her visit, Elsa Maxwell wrote a destructive and spiteful review. A stir was also caused by the conflict with the baritone Enzo Sordello, who in the performance on 8 December held on to a top G at the end of a duet longer than prescribed, thereby giving the impression that his soprano partner did not have the reserves of breath to hold on for a correspondingly long time. Two different versions of the conflict between diva and provocateur were circulating, one of which was preferred by the press and by sections of the biographical literature. According to this, Callas reviled her partner on the stage and afterwards issued an ultimatum to the management – 'Him or me.'

Kolodin's report is less exciting. Callas complained after the performance that the tenor had intended to out-sing her. His claim that she could not sustain her tone was refuted by the conductor Fausto Cleva 'and Bing decided that Sordello's talents could be dispensed with' (Kolodin). There were no major differences in the reviews of the *Lucia* performances – a recording is available of that of 8 December. Maria Callas was not in good voice. Winthrop Sargeant heard high notes which were emitted 'like desperate screams' and yet he found the interpretation 'interesting and at times even thrilling, her coloratura extraordinarily agile and accurate, and the quality of the voice warm and expressive in *mezza voce* passages'.

Kolodin made reference to signs of vocal weariness in 'Spargi d'amore pianto' and did not hide the fact that 'she barely struck the top E flat (not in the score) before toppling over [. . .]'. Claudia Cassidy noted similar problematic sections but stressed: 'I do not know where else one could hear such exquisite coloratura, such fine-spun *fioriture* or such supple chromatic scales.' But it is noticeable that the sympathetic comments of Kolodin, Cassidy and Paul Henry Lang assume an apologetic tone; this must be an indication that at that period Callas was vocally no longer meeting all expectations. As an admirer of the soprano one might wish that the recording of that performance on 8 December did not exist – even Callas cannot bring that prosaic performance to life.

A few days before returning to Milan, Callas and Meneghini were invited to a dinner-dance at the Waldorf Astoria. The host was the Greek film magnate Spyros Skouras, and the guests included 'that barometer of the international social weather, Elsa Maxwell' (Stassinopoulos), who recalled her meeting with the singer: 'I said, "Madame Callas, I could imagine that I am the last person on earth whom you would want to meet," but Callas replied, "On the contrary, you are the first person I wanted to meet because, apart from your opinion about my voice, I see you

as a lady of honesty who is concerned with the truth." ' Elsa
Maxwell printed this reply in her next column and, having looked
into the 'beautiful sparkling and hypnotic eyes' of the singer,
praised her as 'an extraordinary personality'. From then on
Maxwell opened for her new friend all those doors behind which
the treasures of the world lay hidden. Maxwell wrote in her
autobiography: 'I have been defamed as a parasite for enjoying
the generosity of the rich, but I gave at least as much as I took.
I had imagination, they had money. It was a fair exchange of the
things which each side had in abundance.'

Although she had to appear in court in Chicago in January
1957, she wanted to spend her free time at Christmas in Milan.
On the day of her departure, 21 December, she appeared in the
New York High Court, where Bagarozy's charge had to be dealt
with. Her lawyer contested that a similar charge made by Bagarozy against Nicola Rossi-Lemeni had been settled with a payment
for 4000 dollars, and that Bagarozy's claim for 300,000 dollars
from the soprano was exorbitant. The hearing was deferred until
January. In Milan she planned the second half of the season with
her appearances at La Scala. She also accepted an invitation from
the San Francisco Opera and in a letter assured its manager, Kurt
Herbert Adler, that she would give a series of performances in
September and October 1957. For the magazine *Oggi* she revealed
her 'personal story' to the journalist Anita Pensotti. In it, her
concluding remark is significant: 'I shall soon return to La Scala
to sing in *La Sonnambula*, and finally in *Iphigénie en Tauride*. I
know that my enemies are waiting for me but I shall fight with
all my strength. I shall not disappoint my public, which loves me
and whose approval and admiration I wish to keep.'

Three days after returning to the United States she performed
at a glittering fancy-dress ball at the Waldorf Astoria in New
York. She appeared in the costume of the Egyptian empress
Hatshepshut, which rumour had it was decorated with emeralds
valued at three million dollars. She was taking these social
appearances as seriously as premières at La Scala. Elsa Maxwell
appeared as Catherine the Great.

In Chicago, when her court appearance was to take place, Callas
gave a concert on 15 January so as to make the unwelcome visit

at least tolerable. Her fee was 10,000 dollars. Claudia Cassidy's report in the *Chicago Tribune* grasps uncannily the course which the singer's career was soon to be taking:

> She began so quietly even the noisiest latecomer had to listen. From her wide choice of heroines afflicted with coloratura dementia she chose the sleepwalker of *Sonnambula*, the brooding aria with the lovely lyrical Bellini line, and she sang it superbly in its haunted world of troubled dreams. This was the Callas voice at its most magical, with the sound of the oboe in it, a dark-lustred, poignant voice, to make you believe anything it chose. Then she turned to the Shadow Song from Meyerbeer's *Dinorah*, whose heroine plays so gaily with shadows happier than reality. It was in its fey way gayer than a lark, for what lark was ever paid 10,000 dollars for a single concert. But it didn't rise to heaven's gate for the climax. It got there, but the sound was harsh and shrill. It was right then that Callas showed her mettle. She put down her bouquet, rested a foot on the podium, folded her arms, and sang 'In questa reggia' from Puccini's *Turandot*. *Turandot*, as all opera goers know, is plain dynamite. The soprano *tessitura* is mercilessly high. Callas said of it three years ago when she dropped it from her repertory, 'I am not so stupid.' But she is about to record it for Angel . . . It got them cheering, but at what cost? It meant that a superb singer, who is also an artist, and so doubly valuable, sang that cold, cruelly beautiful aria with every ounce of strength she could summon, driving it like nails into the con-sciousness of the audience. It was not beautiful, for it was forced to a degree altogether perilous to the human voice so mistreated. But it was, for sheer courage and determination, for winning at all costs, magnificent [. . .] It was a triumph for Callas, unless you value her so highly you want her restored to her incomparable best.

What harsh criticism and yet filled with admiration and love! In a few sentences Claudia Cassidy has summed up the dilemma of a singer at a cross-roads in her career, and has also, by means of criticism, demonstrated her respect, esteem and above all her

loving care. Maria Callas completed the concert with Norma's
aria, with Leonora's 'D'amor sull' ali rosee' and Lucia's Mad
Scene.

Her court appearance, the reason for her journey to Chicago
and indirectly also the reason for the concert, was short; the case
was again deferred. It was now to take place in the autumn, to
coincide with her appearances in San Francisco. She flew back to
Milan, attending the world première of Poulenc's *Dialogues des
Carmélites* on 26 January. At a reception in the composer's honour
she was dressed like a film star and was the centre of attention.
Before her La Scala appearances, which were to conclude the
1956–7 season, she journeyed to London, singing Norma there
on 2 and 6 February. Harold Rosenthal writes in his history of
Covent Garden that the management could have sold all the seats
for six performances. But Maria Callas had to be in the recording
studio between 7–14 February for the role of Rossini's Rosina,
and again from 3–9 March for Bellini's Amina.

It was at this time that the sort of artistic planning began that
was geared to making an effect. Headlines were immediately
made when there arrived at the airport not the diva of generous
proportions but a model out of *Vogue* – but these headlines
appeared *before* the performance, together with speculation as to
whether the loss of sixty kilos might have impaired her volume
and brilliance. As there is no live recording of this appearance we
cannot answer the question, and reviews of the performance are
contradictory.

Rosenthal wrote that her voice had 'in no way suffered, on the
contrary it was more unified and certainly more beautiful than
before'. The performance was 'one of the greatest triumphs of
her career', the applause more tumultuous than ever and she made
her curtain calls at the end into 'a performance in themselves'. At
the second performance on 6 February 1957 the conductor John
Pritchard had to permit an encore of the cabaletta from the duet
between Norma and Adalgisa; it was the first encore to be heard
at Covent Garden since before the war. The jubilation knew no
bounds, and a few critical undercurrents in individual reviews
were apparently overlooked. *The Times* wrote: 'It cannot be said
that the voice itself has become more beautiful [. . .] The upper

tones sometimes sounded pinched, sometimes hard and inexpressive, and the singer's sense of pitch was apt to stray in either
direction – "Casta diva" ended very sharp.'

But these reservations were only a prelude to praise of the
intensity of her pathos, her breath-control, *legato*, dramatic use of
the *fioriture* and fabulous chromatic scales. Frank Granville-Barker
noted in *Opera News* that the voice had lost some of its richness.
He also detected 'occasional shrillness and a new hard edge'.

At La Scala in March she sang six performances of *La Sonnambula* under Antonino Votto; a studio recording for EMI was made
at the same time. Claudia Cassidy confirmed that the voice was
once again in top form and she dared to prophesy: 'I am sure that
she will be a great singer for twenty years or longer.'

In the meantime Callas was preparing for the première of Donizetti's *Anna Bolena* on 14 April 1957. The work had first been
given on 26 December 1830 at the Teatro Carcano in Milan, with
Giuditta Pasta in the title role and Giovanni Battista Rubini as
Percy. The same artists brought it to London in July 1831, where,
as in Paris, it was successful enough to remain in the repertoire
for several decades (later Giulia Grisi took over from Pasta, and
Mario from Rubini). The first modern revival was in 1956 in
Bergamo, just before Visconti and Callas took it up. Gianandrea
Gavazzeni, conductor of those performances, recalled that his
important colleague Gino Marinuzzi had said the opera would
come back to life as soon as the right singer could be found for
the title role.

Visconti and Nicola Benois had designed the set only in shades
of black, grey and white. Jane Seymour (Giulietta Simionato)
wore a red costume against the dull background and Maria Callas
wore robes in many shades of blue, with majestic jewellery which
set off her eyes, the shape of her face and her stature – 'and believe
me, she had stature on the stage,' said Visconti. The robes were
inspired by Holbein's portrait of Anne Boleyn.

After the much-lauded première all theatre people agreed that
it set a new standard for productions of Romantic opera. The
applause lasted twenty-four minutes; Maria Callas was at the peak
of her La Scala career. 'An unparalleled success,' was the verdict
of Claudia Cassidy. Desmond Shawe-Taylor, the well-known

English connoisseur of singing, wrote that the work, with its anticipations of Verdi's *Macbeth*, could return to international opera houses only with Callas in the title role. Elsa Maxwell came to Milan for one of the performances, and she too had started to stage her appearances carefully, on this occasion being met at the airport. 'Ecco i due tigri' one newspaper mocked, and Maxwell complained in her column about 'the evil net of invective being woven around Maria Callas'.

And there was need for such defence. Callas cancelled an appearance at the Vienna Festival which she had at least discussed, if not formally agreed, with Karajan in the intoxication following the successful *Lucia* performances. Now Meneghini was no longer prepared to accept the fee of 1600 dollars which had been paid the previous year. Spokesmen of the Vienna Staatsoper claimed that Callas had demanded another 500 dollars, but they denied there had been a violent argument between the diva and the maestro. Embellished like a baroque aria, the little incident made the rounds not just of the world of opera. One 'report' told of an enraged Karajan tearing up the contract – which had never existed – before Callas's eyes; the story was given its own special flavour when Elsa Maxwell came forward to defend her.

La Scala was to close its season with a third Callas–Visconti collaboration – *Iphigénie en Tauride*. It was her fifth and, unfortunately, her last work with Visconti, who wanted to update the opera to the eighteenth century and to have it played on rococo sets. For the sets Benois had taken his inspiration from the architects employed by the legendary Bibiena family from the beginning of the seventeenth until the end of the eighteenth centuries; his costumes were based on paintings by Tiepolo. Both Visconti and Benois argued that the updating was justified by the music. For the first time Visconti found that the soprano only accepted his ideas with reservation; she wished to appear as an antique figure from Greek mythology – 'I am Greek'. But in the end she followed his directions, fully reliable as she was in artistic matters.

Visconti later called the production of Gluck's opera the most aesthetically positive of his collaborations with Callas. He again recalls how precisely she would realise on stage what they had worked out in the rehearsals. In one scene she had to climb a staircase and then rush down again, her long cloak blowing in the wind. At each performance she sang her top note exactly on the eighth step – movement and music were always perfectly synchronised.

Visconti was to have produced Donizetti's *Poliuto* with her at La Scala three years later. But just beforehand a play which he had produced, as well as the film *Rocco and his Brothers*, were censored, and he refused to work again for a state-subsidised theatre. Apparently Maria Callas did not want to sing the operas which he later expressed a desire to stage with her. She was afraid of Carmen, with its dance movements. Salome was not acceptable because she did not want to undress for the Dance of the Seven Veils, although Visconti had found her as 'beautiful as an odalisque' when she played Kundry in *Parsifal*. She refused the role of the Marschallin because of the German language.

The Gluck performance, Callas's twentieth production at La Scala, was a triumphant success, but it was given only fourteen times. On 21 June she was awarded the title 'Commendatore' by the Italian President Gronchi, having been recommended by the then Minister of Education, Aldo Moro. She then accepted an invitation from Elsa Maxwell to enjoy social life in Paris: visiting exclusive fashion salons, enjoying cocktails with Baroness Rothschild, tea with the Windsors and racing with Ali Khan. At the beginning of July she had two guest appearances with the ensemble of La Scala in Cologne singing Bellini's *La Sonnambula*, a performance which John Ardoin describes as more expressive and poetic than the studio one where Votto's conducting had been routine: 'Voice, intent and technique were in miraculous balance.'

Returning straight to Milan for recordings of Puccini's *Turandot* and *Manon Lescaut* she at last made it up with Tullio Serafin, who was to conduct. Although both portrayals are more subtle, more detailed and richer than those of any other singer, they reveal vocal problems at the top of the voice, especially in *Manon Lescaut*.

There were bad omens for her first visit to Greece in twelve years. Her mother Evangelia had depicted her in the worst possible light, and the opposition accused the Karamanlis government of paying fees that were insupportable in a country which was so badly off economically (she was to receive 9000 dollars for two concerts). As she was exhausted and had caught a cold, she cancelled the first of the concerts planned in the Amphitheatre of Herodes Atticus. The organisers were so apprehensive that they only announced the cancellation an hour before the concert was due to begin, which earned the singer a storm of anger. The second concert took place on 5 August under police protection, but she conquered the inimically disposed audience by sheer willpower and energy. A short holiday on Ischia failed to bring the required recovery in her health.

When she got back to Milan, her doctor Arnoldo Semeraro diagnosed nervous exhaustion. He urged her to take a four-week break. But she was due to appear with the La Scala company in Edinburgh, singing Amina in *La Sonnambula*. Meneghini was not able to convince Luigi Oldani from La Scala that she could not undertake that journey. The general secretary argued that the role was identified with Callas; the theatre could not risk travelling to the festival with another singer, although they had at their disposal a talent of first rank in the young Renata Scotto.

9

Prima Donna Without a Home

'Always fighting – the constant irritation in
my career was that I had to fight. I don't like
that. The fights and arguments, the nervous
states which they lead to are distasteful. But
if it is necessary I will fight. So far I have
always won, but never with the feeling of
inner freedom. They are hollow triumphs'

Maria Callas

'Giudici! Giudici ad Anna' or the Role of Scandal

Trouble started with *La Sonnambula* and the star role was taken by La Divina, Maria Meneghini Callas – not, however, in her most divine voice:

> The première had some uneasy moments, and by the third performance almost every sustained note around F threatened to crack and collapse. 'Ah, non credea' was a painful experience for everyone in the theatre, and yet there was engrossing art in her impersonation. After the fourth performance the diva flew back to Milan ('tired') and the role was taken over by Renata Scotto.

That was Andrew Porter's factual report in *High Fidelity*, lacking any malicious undertone, of La Scala's guest appearance in Edinburgh during the summer of 1957. Harold Rosenthal's report in *Musical America* was not appreciably different. The first performance had been weak, the second and third unbalanced, while the fourth one, which he heard, found the soprano in excellent form. Rosenthal wrote admiringly of the 'musicianship, intelligence and intensity' of the singer whose sense of duty had let her be persuaded to undertake those four performances.

An English doctor advised her to cancel after the very first performance, but she fought her way through the second evening, the success of which caused Luigi Oldani to agree to an extra, fifth, performance. On the third evening, which she survived with what remained of her almost exhausted reserves, she told La Scala's manager that she would not be singing the fifth performance. There were few who wrote so sympathetically of her departure as Albert Hutton in *Music and Musicians*: 'One was happy for her that she was able to travel back to the warm south.' But this single voice of a music critic was drowned by the screams of the scandal-mongers. The tabloids reported another Callas walkout, a chorus which the Italian papers took up when she arrived home. They said that Maria Callas had disgraced Italy's prime opera house. And even more resentment was felt for the fact that she attended a ball in Venice organised by Elsa Maxwell,

singing the blues number 'Stormy Weather' to the piano
accompaniment of the gossip goddess (Elsa Maxwell had started
out as a pianist for silent movies, later offering her services as
pianist and singer at parties). The stormy weather was followed
by a hurricane that blew straight into the singer's face when
the incomprehensibly egocentric Maxwell reported: 'I have been
offered many gifts in my life [. . .] but I never before heard of
a star cancelling an opera performance so as not to break a promise
to a friend.' It seemed that Maria Callas would not be able to
survive the ruinous consequences of such a compliment; she was
obviously not in a position to adapt her personality to public taste.
Even Antonio Ghiringhelli, intendant of La Scala, refused to make
excuses to the public for her – his greatest singer during the fifties.

From this time on every cancellation, illness or sign of weakness
became a crime. Could a singer really be ill and unable to sing if
she was to be seen at parties given by the rich or *nouveaux riches?*
When she took the advice not only of her doctor, Dr Semeraro,
but also that of a specialist and cancelled appearances planned for
San Francisco in September 1957, Kurt Adler annulled her contract, in spite of the fact that she was prepared to keep to appearances planned for the month of October. Adler even went so far
as to hand her case over to the American Guild of Musical Artists,
hoping that sanctions could be raised against the singer. Forthwith
her name became synonymous with scandal as well as *assoluta.*
Each new calumny was to surpass the last.

The éclat of 2 January 1958 made headlines normally reserved
for an event in world politics. After five performances in *Un Ballo
in Maschera*, with which she had opened La Scala's 1957–8 season,
she was due to inaugurate the season in Rome with Bellini's
Norma. On New Year's Eve she sang 'Casta diva' on television,
then went on to celebrate New Year in a Rome nightclub. Then,
thirty-six hours before the performance, she awoke voiceless,
although she had been in good voice for the dress rehearsal.
Jellinek's report states that Meneghini had great difficulty in finding a doctor on New Year's Day. Proof of genuine illness was
the fact that she immediately notified the theatre director that he
should find a substitute. But even if Patti or Pasta had been
summoned from their graves, they would not have been accepted

as substitutes. A Callas gala had been announced and the state president would be among the guests who had each paid forty dollars for a stalls seat. Even Meneghini was in the grip of his wife's fame. She should, she had to and she would sing, and indeed the following morning it seemed that the condition of her voice had improved. However after a few hours it became clear that the improvement was only short-term.

'Sediziose voci, voci di guerra avvi chi alzar s'attenta' – so begins Norma's recitative before the aria which most prima donnas would give anything to perform perfectly even once: 'Are there those who dare to raise seditious voices, warlike voices?' Maria Callas, attempting as she had to summon up her voice by dint of will power and to sing with the utmost artistry, soon heard warlike voices from the auditorium. At the end of her first scene, which she had scarcely been able to finish, the whole audience began to stir, unaware of the real tragedy taking place on stage.

She then did what she should have done thirty-six hours earlier but had not been permitted to do: she broke off the performance. All persuasion from the conductor, Gabriele Santini, the designer Margherita Wallmann and the theatre director Carlo Lantini was useless. She was in no state to go back on stage, and there was of course no understudy. The audience, including President Gronchi and his wife, had to be sent home.

The headlines were not brought about by concern for the singer but by what people assumed was an affront to the President, as if a justified cancellation became a scandal because a prominent person was in the audience. Next morning an angry crowd gathered in front of the Hotel Quirinale, where the singer was staying.

It would be difficult to establish exactly how it all happened, the scandal having in the intervening period become a tragi-comic legend. Even the reporter of the Rome *Messagero*, who was present at the performance, was unclear about precisely what shouts went round the house. Was it 'Via la Callas' – Callas must go – or 'Viva la Callas'? What is certain is that there were shouts of 'Evviva l'Italia' and 'Viva le cantanti italiane', the latter for the benefit, at the second performance, of Anita Cerquetti, a singer who was then quite justifiably to rise to fame once given this remarkable chance.

Even at that time *Opera* commented that Maria Callas, by

unseating herself in this way, was doing more for Italian opera than the chauvinists of Rome could imagine. It was astonishing that an operatic débâcle was pushing football results and political events into the background. Casual observers point out that it was immediately evident what a desolate situation faced the singer in making this appearance. The live recording shows how she was still able to focus her voice during the recitative but that soon after the finely spun opening of 'Casta diva' her soprano had hardened, taking on an acid, shrill quality. There can be no firm answer to the question as to whether she could have finished the performance or at least just recited it, as has been suggested.

Certain newspapers reacted by hurling insults. 'This second-class Greek artist,' one read in *Il Giorno*, 'Italian by marriage, Milanese only by virtue of unjustified admiration from certain sections of the Milanese public, international because of her dangerous friendship with Elsa Maxwell, has for some years been following the path of melodramatic excess. This demonstrates that Maria Meneghini Callas is an unpleasant artist who lacks the most elementary sense of discipline and acceptable behaviour.'

Such invective goes to show that a scandal embraces prejudices which are quickly converted into hatred, and that all sense of moral and critical moderation is abandoned. One cannot measure the effect of such an outburst of hatred on an artist – an artist possessing the ambition to give of her best and to strive for perfection, compromised as she may be by her own moods and stubbornness. And what the effect was on an artist who – according to Legge – had an insuperable inferiority complex. She sent the President and his wife a letter of apology. Signora Gronchi responded immediately with a telephone call expressing her understanding, but Callas's image had been reduced to tatters. The 'Callas case' was even debated in the Italian parliament. The soprano was held up as a wild circus animal – to be tamed only with chains and whip.

The story had a dramatic coda. When Maria Callas reappeared in Italy three months later on 9 April – as Anna Bolena at La Scala – when she had to make her entry before a crowd which Giulini described as thirsting for blood, when she needed a police escort to the theatre and onto the stage and the applause was intended only for her colleagues, Maria Callas defended herself in her own inimitable way. When in the opera Anna is arrested at the end of the first act, she hurls at her captors the words 'Giudici! Ad Anna! Giudici!' ('Judges! For Anna! Judges!) Callas positioned herself at the footlights for this declamatory phrase and sang it directly into the audience. And the audience yielded, shouting in jubilation, rejoicing in her courage and at the same time in its own wretchedness.

What an awful triumph! The abyss itself, already confronting the one who looked into it!

In the autumn of 1957 she had to fulfil her last contractual obligation to Cetra, the last of the three complete recordings agreed with them. Cherubini's *Medea* was recorded in September, while appearances in San Francisco immediately afterwards were cancelled. Kurt Herbert Adler, enraged by the supposed breach of contract, saw in the recording sessions proof that she could have sung. If she had taken her doctor's advice and cancelled the *Medea* recording, then she would have chalked up yet another débâcle.

Returning home to the via Buonarotti after the performance of *Anna Bolena* – which she had succeeded in making into a tribunal for her accusers – she found the doors, walls and windows smeared with dirt and excrement. When the series of performances was completed she escaped to Lake Garda for a holiday. There, in Sirmione, she started preparing herself for the last première of La Scala's season, Bellini's *Il Pirata*. The first night was on 9 May, but during rehearsals she was ignored by Ghiringhelli. Interviewed in *Life*, she declared: 'If a theatre where one is guest adds constant intrigues and unpleasantness to the tensions of a performance, then artistic work becomes impossible both physically and morally. For my own self-protection and personal dignity I had no alternative but to leave La Scala.' She left the house on 31 May 1958 after the fifth performance of the Bellini opera and her 157th appearance at La Scala. When she returned in December 1960 for five appearances in *Poliuto*, the storm which had still been rumbling in the last *Pirata* performance had subsided. In Imogene's great final scene she imagines the gallows where her lover must die: 'La . . . vedete . . . il palco funesto.'

Now *palco* is also the Italian word for a box at the theatre. Callas sang the phrase with a tone of unmistakable despisal, staring straight into the intendant's empty box. The audience realised that it was a gesture of farewell and called her back before the curtain. Ghiringhelli brought the evening to a close by having the iron safety curtain lowered, and Callas left the theatre, surrounded by a jubilant crowd. Ghiringhelli's cold comment was 'Prima donnas come and go, but La Scala remains'. Where has La Scala remained today?

'A curse on the heart that cannot be moderate' says Kleist's Penthesilea. Maria Callas could not moderate herself or lower herself to play the game that even rebellious Hollywood divas – with the exception of Bette Davis – had played. She would never have been able to play, because a performance on stage, with all the momentary risks involved, is a far greater challenge than one before the cameras. She could never conform to that story book world because she did not resemble the women on cover photographs, although her transformed beauty would have enabled her to. She was the exception, the scandal *en permanence*. Her life can be viewed as the phenomenon described by Hans Mayer. As prima donna she stood apart from the average world of art, as wife of an entrepreneur she betrayed art to society, and only after leaving the stage and being abandoned by Onassis would she be set up as an idol.

Condemned to Success

'Living dangerously is the way to harvest
the greatest enjoyment from life'
Nietzsche

'As soon as the turbulent Maria Callas appeared [. . .]' – does one need to quote any more? It was the new tone which had also infiltrated specialist magazines like *Opera News*, the tone that prevailed after one of her most splendid Verdi performances, that of 7 December 1957. Under the stage direction of Margherita Wallmann and with Gianandrea Gavazzeni conducting, she sang Amelia in *Un Ballo in Maschera* with more drama and spontaneity than in the studio recording made a year earlier. Ardoin quoted her as having said, 'On records one has to reduce everything to a minimum so as to avoid any exaggerated acoustic,' yet on stage she was able to offer striking accents without falling into histrionic exaggeration. The Act 2 love duet vibrated with tension. Callas/ Amelia's 'Ebben, sì t'amo' is an example of her most memorable sonic gestures. And yet even this performance was affected by the hostile atmosphere in La Scala.

After the disaster in Rome Maria Callas became a different woman. Arianna Stassinopoulos quotes her as saying:

> When you are young, you like to stretch your voice, you enjoy singing, you love it. It's not a question of will-power, it has nothing to do with driving ambition. You simply love your work – this beautiful, intangible thing which is called music. If you sing out of pleasure and enjoyment things come beautifully. It's like getting drunk – only from pleasure, the pleasure of doing something well. Just like an acrobat when he feels on form and feels the happiness of the public and is inspired to more and more adventurous feats of daring. The more you enjoy it, the more you feel like doing it.

Maria Callas was increasingly performing her feats in so-called gala concerts. She travelled to Chicago for one of these in January 1958. While changing planes in Paris she was pressed by journalists. When Rome was mentioned, she replied, now a virtuosa of diplomatic relations, that she had least been able to count the number of her friends there. As she left the city which *Le Figaro* described as having given her the kind of reception 'normally reserved for crowned heads of state', she was confident of having found a new haven. The concert in Chicago on 22 January was prefaced by an ovation of ten minutes' duration. Claudia Cassidy again wrote of 'her marvellous technique, a deeply probing, vividly projected sense of drama, and the widest range of any singer I have known,' and concluded with the words, 'Was everything perfection? Of course not. Great things are seldom perfect. But this was Callas at her best, except for some notes more bold than beautiful, and even those had the beauty of courage, of the indomitable will to win.'

Those words are a loving euphemism for the problems to which Roger Dettmer gave clear definition in the *Chicago American*: 'Maria Callas sounds to be in big vocal trouble – how serious only she is equipped to measure. But last night, heard for the first time in twelve months, her voice was recurrently strident, unsteady and out of tune. It seems to have aged ten years in one.' Her only salvation was her 'sheer musicality'. Soon afterwards she had to account for herself in San Francisco before the American Guild of Musical Artists. The outcome was a serious warning rather than a charge. Three days before this, she tried a new role in Ed Murrow's *Person to Person* show: she presented herself as the thinking, humorous artist so far removed from the image promoted by the press.

As a result of the Guild's decision she was able to reappear at the Met on 6 February. Her role was Verdi's Violetta, a part in which neither Tebaldi nor de los Angeles had carried much conviction. Kolodin reported 'the dramatic vocal portrayal of the season was without doubt Callas's Violetta. Cancellations and performances halted midway had thrown a shadow of uncertainty over her arrival, but she summoned her strength and pulled off the performance proudly and with ever increasing dramatic intensity.' Taubman wrote in *The Times* that she was in better voice than in the previous season. Winthrop Sargeant in the *New Yorker* described her portrayal as 'far and away the finest I have encountered at the Met or anywhere else in all the years I have been listening to opera'. He no longer considered her reedy tone to be a fault but merely a characteristic of the voice. The most accurate and illuminating report was again the one from the analytically correct Kolodin in *Saturday Review*: 'Miss Callas doesn't command the beauty of sound to be ideal in any part, but hers is the best-rounded Violetta offered here in years. For all the throaty 'covered' quality she purveys, Miss Callas makes her voice an instrument of dramatic purpose from first to last. For all its weightiness in the middle register, she sang the first act in the written key, with precision, and an emphatic top D flat. And although she could broaden her line eloquently for 'Amami, Alfredo', she could also pronounce the beautiful phrase 'Alfredo, Alfredo, di questo core' *con voce debolissima e con passione* as Verdi directed. Those who reported on the occasion without hearing the fourth act left the public uninformed of a memorable 'Addio del passato', in which the lovely half-voice effects the swells from *piano* to *pianissimo*, and the obedient delivery of the final A with *un fil di voce*, as the score requests, were sermons on the text of what operatic art is all about.' Kolodin's answer to the charge that she sometimes made ugly sounds was that if you stood before the Venus de Milo you would notice that she had no arms. Her reaction to the hysterical applause was to confess that she felt insecure and anxious: 'I feel myself condemned [both to success and to fighting]. The more renowned one is, the more responsibility one incurs and the smaller and more helpless one feels.'

Following the two performances of *La Traviata*, she sang three of *Lucia di Lammermoor* (with Bergonzi and Fernandi as Edgardo) and two of *Tosca* (under Mitropoulos and with Tucker as Cavaradossi). The Donizetti opera saw her in better form than in the previous year. The voice was 'richer and more responsive' (Kolodin), and she received eight solo curtain-calls at the end of the evening. And yet she was disappointed. Bing had not even attempted to offer her a new production, making it impossible for her to show of her best either from the musical or the dramatic viewpoint. In contrast to La Scala, where she had always been the centrepiece of an ensemble, she had in New York to play the star on shabby sets. There was not even sufficient time for thorough rehearsal with her colleagues, many of whom she had never sung with before.

It was less a matter of proving her stature as prima donna *assoluta* than of simply playing the role – as in television appearances. She was presented on a talk show by Hy Gardner, who described her in his column in the *New York Herald Tribune* as a 'warm-hearted, upright and attractive woman with both feet firmly on the ground'; she was anything but that. It was Elsa Maxwell who was pushing her more and more into her new role as a famous woman. Maxwell who was excelling herself in arranging appearances for the 'diva divina' and 'greatest prima donna in the world' at parties and in the salons of the rich and powerful, and who in the papers wrote things which could only harm the singer: 'Why must a woman capable of such noble expression in the classical arts be pursued by a fate which makes happiness an impossibility? I am convinced that this is her mother's fault.'

This was how Evangelia Callas achieved the sort of popularity which could be used by the gossip columnists, and how Hy Gardiner saw fit to ask the soprano why she did not engage a public relations officer to help improve her image. Her reply was that what she had to say could only be expressed through her singing. A clever answer admittedly, but it would have been better if the question had not been put.

Negotiations with Rudolf Bing about her next visit to the Met went off with little success. Callas insisted on singing in a new production, and manager and singer eventually agreed on Verdi's *Macbeth*. But they could not agree about other roles. Arianna Stassinopoulos even suggests that Bing offered her the Queen of Night in Mozart's *Die Zauberflöte*. Without reaching a decision – a mistake which turned out to be fatal – Callas flew to Madrid. First she gave a concert there, then took part in a gala season at the San Carlo in Lisbon, giving two performances as Violetta in *La Traviata* under Franco Ghione. One of the performances, with the young Alfredo Kraus as Alfredo, was recorded. The five La Scala performances of Bellini's *Il Pirata*, conducted by Antonino Votto and with Franco Corelli (in the role taken by Rubini) and Ettore Bastianini, scored a triumph, although the sets (Piero Zuffi) and production (Franco Enriquez) were mediocre. The Milan audience applauded for twenty-five minutes after the closing Mad Scene. The harsh and forced sound of her voice (noted by Peter Dragadze in *Musical America*) was more than compensated for by her musicality, personality and brilliant technical ability. It was the last evening in a period encompassing seven seasons, which are counted among the most glorious in La Scala's annals. Only at La Scala had Callas found the working conditions without which her genius and talent would never have developed in such richness.

And yet her meteoric course was not all sweetness and light. At La Scala she caused unrest like no other singer. She provoked jealousy and envy as well as frequent misunderstandings. Not all her colleagues were as discerning and generous as Toti dal Monte, Toscanini's Lucia in the 1920s, who came to her successor's dressing room after the Donizetti opera and declared, with tears in her eyes, that she now realised how little she herself had understood the role.

Several divas have spoken of her in critical and derogatory terms to Lanfranco Rasponi, but envy was often used to throw more light on arguments which were not entirely false. Elena Nicolai spoke of her almost 'non-existent middle range'. Hilde Konetzni invoked against Callas the example of her colleague Maria Nemeth, who never needed to change registers. Lina Pagliughi declared that although Callas had been admired by many, she had been loved by none. 'Why not? She rewarded friendliness with sharpness, and so finished up imprisoned in her expensive Paris apartment. In one respect she was lucky not to experience old age, because she was always so sarcastic and bitter while at the height of fame [. . .] what is life if one is not surrounded with human warmth?' Gina Cigna, who had recorded Bellini's Norma seventeen years before Callas did, played another diva off against Callas: 'She simply did not compare with [Claudia] Muzio. With Muzio one suffered the agonies of those heroines, never with Callas. I do not deny that she possessed *beaucoup de chien* but, my God, she sang with three voices.' Renata Tebaldi's comments were surprisingly fair and objective. Not only did she decline Callas's empty throne after her departure from La Scala – 'my return would certainly have been misinterpreted, and I only sing for artistic motives and definitely not *against* someone' – but she also stressed how her Greek colleague had 'put her stamp on an era [. . .] she insisted on singing everything and saw this through. Nowadays singers all do this, but unfortunately it does not work [. . .]' Augusta Oltrabella, an eminent verismo diva, asked, 'Why did she not stay with the coloratura repertoire? There she was simply sensational, but the other parts of her voice were manufactured.' Giulietta Simionato said:

I have admired many artists, but I don't need to mention them all. There is absolutely no doubt that Callas brought something new into our profession – a new dimension, so to speak. Maria's behaviour towards me was beyond reproach, she was always fair. When we sang *Norma* together, I always sang the C in the duet [. . .] once in an interview she expressed her surprise that the critics had not credited me for this. She was a *prima donna* through and through, she could be exceptionally difficult but also sensitive and reasonable [. . .] her interpretations I found immensely dramatic but never moving.

The verismo diva Gilda dalla Rizza went so far as to rate Simionato above Callas: 'There have been many great singers but only a handful will be remembered in the history of opera. In the group who came after me I would place Simionato at the top, not Callas. People keep stressing how Callas sang everything; she did, but how? In fact she had three voices, but it was only the coloratura voice which was really impressive and that only for a few years. On the other hand, Simionato sang everything, and with a single, wonderful voice. Her star shone because of her exceptional achievements, not because of publicity.' Mafalda Favero also expressed the opinion that Callas had 'no femininity' and that she had been 'admittedly dramatic, but never moving'.

Commentaries like this certainly reveal feelings of resentment and envy, but they also enable us to view the matter clearly. Simionato indeed sang a vast repertoire with a 'single voice' but what is 'a single voice' when considered technically and from the point of view of register? What is it when compared to the many voices which Callas used to convey colour, expression and character in all her roles? It is also true that Mafalda Favero could produce a stirring sound in verismo parts, which engaged the listener's sympathies, whereas Callas's portrayals were conceived in her head and admired as artefacts. On closer inspection the reservations of her critics serve in fact to confirm her stature.

The verismo divas take as their starting point simply their own historically conditioned ideas about vocal art. They reduce that art, as well as the shaping and the technique of a voice, to an ideal of expressiveness which is only intended for verismo opera;

they overlook the fact that opera remains artificial even when attempting to be realistic, failing to recognise that, by pushing singing closer to the emotions and effectiveness of speech, they are rendering it that much poorer and less refined. In contrast to these singers, it was the producers, conductors and designers who worked with Callas at La Scala who clearly recognised that she was a special case: not simply a '*voce isolata*' (Lauri-Volpi) but a major reformer in the art of singing.

Some years after her retirement from the stage Maria Callas gave an interview to Kenneth Harris depicting herself as victim:

> I am passionate, but about work, and about justice. I am a passionate artist and a passionate human being. [. . .] You say that many people have this or that impression of me because of what they read in some newspapers [. . .] But I do not write in the newspapers. Much of what I read about myself in the newspapers is wrong [. . .] Maybe I am Victorian. I believe in self-discipline and a degree of self-restraint [. . .] In general, I find society becoming too permissive. Today young people criticise their parents too much. Reputation is all-important in opera. My crowning year had been at La Scala in 1954. There I sang Medea, Lucia and Elizabeth de Valois. Success had not come easily or quickly. I had been singing major roles at fourteen – Tosca at fifteen – and was talked about as successful, in Italy and many other countries [. . .] In 1953, 1954, I had arrived, as they say, at the top. After that I had a great reputation. Then, immediately, the agents who wished to bring up other singers and exploit them began to try to get me down. It has not only happened to me, you understand, it is a part of the struggle for survival in the field.[1]

In that interview Maria Callas had specially grateful memories of the English public. She had enjoyed a 'love affair' with the Covent Garden audience ever since her appearances in *Norma* in 1952. When she came to London ten days after her farewell at La Scala to take part in the gala for Covent Garden's 100th anniversary, she received eight single curtain calls after 'Qui la voce' from Bellini's *I Puritani*. The management treated her not with

the diplomatic politeness aimed at satisfying the demands of vain
prima donnas but with attention and warmth. Also taking part
in the gala were Margot Fonteyn, Joan Sutherland, Blanche
Thebom and Jon Vickers, in other words more stars than there
were first-class dressing rooms. Lord Harewood, a member of
the board of directors, solved this problem by vacating his private
office to serve as dressing room for her. After the gala she was
presented to the Queen. A week later, on 17 June 1958, she sang
'Vissi d'arte' and 'Una voce poco fà' on British television.

Starting on 20 June she sang five performances of *La Traviata*
under Nicola Rescigno, her preferred conductor from the late
1950s onwards for Italian repertoire. However, the performances
ended in a 'storm of controversy' (*Opera News*). Critical reservations were focused, as increasingly happened after 1956, on the
voice's fluctuations and weaknesses. 'Some of us,' wrote Philip
Hope-Wallace, 'were only fifty-per-cent convinced. Personally I
suffered a great deal.' Most of the critics adopted a tone of wor-
shipful admiration, at the same time adopting a conspicuously
apologist tone. Peter Heyworth wrote in the *Observer*:

> And then Callas does after all sing. She may not on Friday have
> done so with beauty of tone, but in almost every other respect
> it was a performance of outstanding distinction and musicality,
> full of detail that again and again illuminated the part as though
> for the first time. Her rebuke to Germont père, 'Donna son'io,
> signore, e in mia casa', was turned with unassertive authority
> that in voice and gesture bespoke a great singing actress. But
> perhaps the most marvellous moment of the evening was the
> long sustained B flat before Violetta descends to the opening
> phrase of 'Dite alle giovine' [. . .] By some miracle Callas
> makes that note hang unsuspended in mid air; unadorned and
> unsupported she fills it with all the conflicting emotions that
> besiege her [. . .] There is no other singer in the field of Italian
> opera today who can work this sort of poetic magic. And even
> if one strikes Maria Callas on an evening on which this magic
> is only intermittent and fleeting, it remains for me a haunting
> shadow of the perfection that opera so constantly strives for
> and so rarely achieves, in which drama and music effect a

mutual reconciliation and illumination.

In a long and detailed review in *Opera*, Harold Rosenthal reported that the second act had brought operatic singing and acting at its greatest. Like Heyworth he drew attention to the soaring B flat before 'Dite alle giovine', the authority of 'Donna son'io', the terrific intensity of 'Ah! gran Dio! morir si giovine' and the almost horrific death scene, the last 'È strano!' uttered in an unearthly voice.

Reviews reveal that these performances represented the triumph of will-power and artistic sensibility over a voice that was becoming increasingly weak. Moreover, the presence of her doctor at each performance indicates the state of her body and mind. Returning to London that autumn, she made a brief television appearance on 23 September, singing 'Un bel dì' from *Madama Butterfly* and 'Casta diva' from *Norma*. She was then asked about her conception of Violetta and explained that her intention had been to free Violetta from the aura of the opera singer and instead to depict a woman dying of tuberculosis. She added that the slight break in her voice at the end of 'Addio del passato' had been deliberate. This was by no means an easy way of justifying or excusing a vocal 'fault' but an explanation from an interpreter who was suffering at the moment of singing, feeling the pain and the horror of her own downfall – perhaps the most terrible moment of her life.

Also that autumn she recorded, with Nicola Rescigno, her first Verdi recital with arias and scenes from *Macbeth, Ernani* and *Don Carlo* and another recital consisting of scenes from *Anna Bolena, Hamlet* and *Il Pirata*.

The Break With the Met

'Don't be deceived – beneath that cold, strict
and sober exterior there beats a heart of stone'
Cyril Ritchard on Rudolf Bing

After the London *Traviata*s she had had almost three months' rest, spending her holiday in Sirmione on Lake Garda. The autumn season in North America was to start in October with a concert tour. Dallas Civic Opera was putting on performances of *La Traviata* and *Medea*; Rudolf Bing wanted Callas to appear no less then twenty-six times, in *Macbeth, Tosca* and either *Lucia di Lammermoor* or *La Traviata*. The two Verdi operas would need to be sung within a short period of time and without any resting time between. This was something she could have carried off six or seven years earlier, but her voice was now no longer limitless in its flexibility nor dynamically strong enough; and her Traviata no longer possessed the vocal ardour of a *soprano d'agilità*, but was now more of a delicate, intimate portrait in pastel colours, a masterpiece of vocal economy and dramatic acting.

She travelled to New York on 7 October, with the tour beginning four days later in Birmingham, Alabama. She heard that her first appearance at the Met would be *Tosca* on 16 January 1959. The long-planned première of Verdi's *Macbeth* was fixed for 5 February. There would be two appearances in *La Traviata* on 13 and 17 February, with another *Macbeth* on 21 February.

Callas was in agreement with the operas, but not with the order in which the performances were scheduled. She feared that she would no longer be able to make such a quick change from a dramatic to a coloratura part (at least in the first act), and believed that she had the right to exercise some degree of caution. But the custom at the Met had long been different to that at La Scala, where an opera would be repeated five or six times, allowing the singers to concentrate on a role. In New York stars were simply served up to compensate for the dreariness of routine repertoire. Rudolf Bing could at that stage not change a programme which had been fixed much earlier; he simply offered the soprano Lucia in place of Violetta. This only exacerbated the situation, because the Donizetti part is even remoter in style than Violetta from Lady Macbeth. Callas had moreover already made clear the previous season that she had no wish to reappear in that shabby production of the Donizetti. She departed without coming to an agreement with Bing. The theatre was in a state of alarm.

The concert tour had been arranged by the Sol Hurok agency,

with a programme consisting of arias and scenes from Spontini's *La Vestale*, Verdi's *Macbeth*, Rossini's *Il Barbiere*, Boito's *Mefisto-fele*, Puccini's *La Bohème* (Musetta's Waltz, not one of the Mimì arias) and Thomas's *Hamlet*. It was a strategic programme. She felt it necessary to present herself in the role of *assoluta* with coloratura, dramatic and lyrical music, at these shows that were part of the razzmatazz typical of American entertainment since the days of P. T. Barnum. Jenny Lind and Adelina Patti had even been among the stars presented by the circus manager. Maria Callas was poured into the superstar mould and thereby freed from her own artistic world.

Wherever she appeared, whether in Birmingham, Atlanta, Montreal or Toronto, she received telegrams from Bing enquiring about her decision; each served to increase her nervous tension. It is doubtful whether she really enjoyed the triumphs and enthusiastic reviews after each concert – who was applauding *critically*?

She arrived in Dallas on 24 October. There was a week to rest and to prepare for the two performances of *La Traviata* and two of *Medea*, designed to attract publicity for the Civic Opera which had come into being the year before – a well-planned campaign by the young manager Lawrence Kelly, who was fully aware that he had to offer Texas a sensation which would make the oil wells bubble for art as well. A third production was to be Rossini's *L'Italiana in Algeri* with the young Teresa Berganza. Franco Zeffirelli had been engaged as producer for *La Traviata*, and the well-known director Alexis Minotis from the Greek National Theatre for *Medea* – certainly more than the Met had to offer. The other roles too were taken by first-class artists: for the Verdi there were Nicola Filacuridi and Giuseppe Taddei, leading stars of La Scala, and in *Medea* the up-and-coming Jon Vickers and Teresa Berganza.

The working atmosphere was marvellous. Maria Callas sensed the vivacity, ambition and joy of all the participants: their concern was to succeed. 'In Dallas we are making art' is what she is supposed to have said, with a critical insinuation in the Met's direction, where their season was just beginning, on 27 October, with *Tosca* and with Renata Tebaldi, Mario del Monaco and George London singing under the direction of Dimitri Mitropoulos. Bing was still waiting for her answer. Just before the Dallas première of *La Traviata* on 31 October, Callas received a congratulatory telegram which also contained the irritable and concerned (but also threatening?) question 'But why in Dallas?' He received no reply. It is not clear from the reviews whether the huge audience – the State Fair Music Hall seats 4100 – applauded the singer's fame or her art. She scored a triumph despite being apparently not on her best form.

The première of Cherubini's opera was to be on 6 November, and the day before this she received the ultimatum from Bing. The Met needed her reply the next morning – 'no later than 10 a.m.'. She was stunned and irritated by the abrupt wording of the telegram and decided that she would not yield to Bing's 'Prussian tactics'. She sang the dress rehearsal, which went on until late in the evening and then went home in a state of exhaustion. Bing's third telegram arrived the next afternoon at 2.20 p.m. – in it he announced that her contract was cancelled.

Bing, sly tactician that he was, immediately handed out a press release which could scarcely have been more cynical and infamous, however justified his decision may have been:

> I am not prepared to enter into a public argument with Mme Callas because I fully realise how much more skill and experience she has than I do in such matters.
>
> Although her artistic qualifications are the subject of violent debate between her friends and her enemies, it is well known far and wide that she has the gift of bringing her undeniable histrionic talent into her business dealings. This, together with her insistence on the right to alter or cancel a previously agreed contract, has led to the present situation. It is an experience which every opera house that has had dealings with her has had to go through. While grateful that we were able to enjoy her artistry for two seasons, the Metropolitan Opera is happy that our association is now at an end – for reasons which both the musical press and the public will appreciate.

No performance she ever gave made more of a headline than this break with the Met, which served virtually to exile her from operatic life. She was no longer allowed to sing in Milan, no longer in Vienna, no longer in San Francisco, no longer in New York. She did not even get the opportunity to try and explain or justify her conduct. Breaking her former rule never to speak before her performance, she gave lengthy interviews. 'I cannot change from one voice to another . . . my voice is not an elevator, which simply goes up and down . . . Mr. Bing is cancelling a contract for twenty-six performances just because of three *Traviata* performances . . . This could ruin my Medea [that evening]. Pray for me this evening.'

The singer's life had become a melodrama. She fired shots at the Met: 'When I think of the lousy *Traviata* performances he had me sing, without rehearsal and without knowing my partners. Do you call that art? . . . and all those performances, each with a different tenor or baritone . . . Do you call that art?' Factual discussion had become impossible. The music critic B. H. Haggin rightly pointed out that cancellations and programme changes such as those requested by Maria Callas were everyday occurrences in all leading opera houses and were usually sorted out by both parties behind the scenes. It was precisely the tone of Bing's public pronouncement which indicated that this was a trial of strength. There were few who would really have expressed gratitude, as Bing did in the Met's name, at having lost an artist like Maria Callas.

The impresario's rhetorical question as to whether the management or the stars are in charge of an opera house was dismissed as rubbish by Kolodin in his Met chronology. He maintained that Bing had not taken account of important artistic questions like the allocation of particular top notes, the transposition of arias according to the artists' wishes, or the laxity and compliance of even a conductor like Mitropoulos to the caprices of del Monaco. Kolodin admitted that Callas had been indecisive, but the issuing of an ultimatum on 6 November, the day of a performance, was a calculated affront when the performances in question were not due to take place for another three months. Kolodin's view was that Bing had taken over the star role at the singer's expense, wishing to use the occasion to launch a new diva in *Macbeth* in the person of Leonie Rysanek. The rumour still persists that Bing hired a claque to shout 'Brava, Callas!' after the German singer's brilliant solo scenes in order to raise sympathy for the substitute singer. The final outcome was that Leonie Rysanek scored a triumphant success, even if a connoisseur like Kolodin had reservations about the weakness of her lower octaves.

In response to Elsa Maxwell's pronouncement that the Met was not the focal point of the world, people with any knowledge of the operatic scene commented that Maxwell's opinion counted for absolutely nothing. Callas sang her last two performances of *La Traviata* in Dallas. The *Medea* performances were sung with such fury as could only spur her on to great achievement – and cost her the very maximum in energy. John Ardoin writes in *The Callas Legacy* that 'her vitriolic sounds are directed as much to Bing as to Jason'. In few of her later performances, if indeed in any, was she to sing with such freedom, security, concentration, spontaneity and drama – and in Jon Vickers as her tenor partner she had a true musician.

Vickers himself reported that she worked with great energy and dedication, after he had stood up to her initial attempt to test his staying power. 'She was a superb colleague. She never tried to steal anyone's thunder or to manipulate anyone. The enormous operatic revolution of the post-war era can be attributed to two artists, Wieland Wagner and Maria Callas, who put her gifts to almost masochistic use for the purpose of serving her work and bringing out the meaning of an opera.'

After the headlines 'Bing fires Callas' had appeared all over the world, it was a creature of legend, with an aura of scandal, who appeared in recitals at the Public Music House, Masonic Hall, Constitution Hall or Civic Auditorium. It helped very little that she was trying to play the new role of the charming, kind singer who was only dedicated to her art.

Bing made one final half-hearted attempt to get Callas back to the Met. He repeated his offer of the old productions of *Lucia* and *Norma*, plus *Il Barberie di Siviglia*. But these were hardly challenges of interest to Callas. She responded by suggesting *Anna Bolena*, which Bing described as 'an old bore of an opera'. This was more than a personal idiosyncrasy or an aesthetic blind spot on the part of the impresario. The Met had never been a house, neither under Bing, Johnson or even Gatti, with an aim to be the cultural centrepiece of the country, as La Scala had been under Toscanini. Bing's aim was not directed at reviving Bellini or Donizetti's operas which seemed dead, nor at presenting new works; his concern was to have long queues at the box office. When the Washington critic Paul Hume wrote that the man who fired Callas should be fired himself, the statement had about as much effect as yesterday's newspaper.

It is idle speculation to ask who was right and who was wrong in this unpleasant controversy. Maria Callas was a difficult and sometimes unreliable negotiator, not least as the result of the unbalanced management of her husband Meneghini, and she had become all the more insecure and unreliable because of the vocal problems which were increasingly evident. However, the opera world, already moving towards a market with strict and even crude economic rules, needed a new type of interpreter: the modern star with stamina, ambitious and carefree, who could read a score as if it were a cheque book.

The 'Callas scandal', seen in retrospect, turned out to be something quite different from the scandal surrounding an extremely ambivalent personality. It was the scandal of typical modern operatic life, the overshadowing of a capricious, moody and yet magnetic and brilliant interpreter by a colourful, expensive and luxurious business which would manifest itself, and still does, in festival-like performances for an audience comprising the elderly nobility and the *nouveaux riches*. A business with the all-powerful manager/impresario/conductor in the economic background and with a self-regarding public in the centre. Maria Callas was drawn into this world. She concluded her tour with concerts which culminated in dinners in New York (one of these in honour of Herbert von Karajan) or in Washington, with celebrity guests like Ali Khan or Noël Coward.

Was this compensation for a year which, artistically, had been well-nigh disastrous? It had begun in January in Rome with the broken-off *Norma*. February and March had brought all of seven evenings at the Met, plus two more in Lisbon. But she had sung ten performances at La Scala, five at Covent Garden, ending up with four in Dallas. Then there were the concerts rewarded with

10,000 dollars and shallow triumphs. It was the year in which she lost her throne at La Scala as well as the strength to combat the phantom of her fame. All that remained were Covent Garden and Paris. Her first appearance in Paris was on 19 December 1958. This was indeed in the Opéra but not in an opera performance, and before an audience including Charlie Chaplin, Brigitte Bardot, Emile de Rothschild, Juliette Gréco, the Windsors, Françoise Sagan, Jean Cocteau and Aristotle Onassis: an audience who had not particularly come to hear Callas but needed the prestige of her name to justify their attendance.

It was a gala for the Légion d'honneur under the patronage of the President, sponsored by the magazine *Marie-Claire* and directed by Luchino Visconti; it was to be followed by a dinner for 450 invited guests as homage to 'l'impèratrice du bel canto'. The soprano reported to the French that they, and only they, had really tried to understand her. The evening was relayed on television not only in France but also in England, Italy, Switzerland, Belgium, Holland, Austria, Denmark and West Germany. She sang 'Casta diva', Leonora's Act 4 aria from *Il Trovatore*, complete with the Miserere, Rosina's 'Una voce' and finally, with Albert Lance and Tito Gobbi, the second act of *Tosca*. The excerpt from *Norma* had been given only sloppy preparation, the scenes from *Il Trovatore* were acceptable and Rosina's aria demonstrated her art at its former level. The staged performance of the second act of *Tosca* – with Gobbi making his first stage appearance with her – was scarcely more than a sketch of a portrayal, although she made a considerable impression vocally. The evening's success was overwhelming; the jubilation and praise for Callas was more fanatical than after her great roles at La Scala. The Opéra's impresario A. M. Julien offered her performances of *Medea* for the 1959–60 season, and David Webster of Covent Garden was there to support her. Paris, which in the words of Everett Helm (*Saturday Review*) 'had not enjoyed such pleasure since the days of the legendary Malibran', was in due course to become Callas's chosen home.

The Voice Gives Out

'There are two sorts of bad singing – the
breathy and the guttural'

Giovanni Battista Lamperti

The year 1959 signifies the turning point in the soprano's career.
Pierre-Jean Rémy goes as far as to speak of the voice giving out
between 1959 and 1965. This is easily supported by some stat-
istics. She gave fourteen concerts in 1959, but only nine stage
performances: five of *Medea* in London, and in Dallas two each
of *Lucia di Lammermoor* and *Medea*. In 1960 she managed two
appearances in *Norma* in Epidaurus in Greece and five at La Scala
in *Poliuto*. In 1961 there were two performances of *Medea* in
Epidaurus and three in Milan. Two more of *Medea* were the only
opera appearances in 1962, and in 1963 none at all. The voice
flickered up again in 1964 with *Tosca* for six performances in
January and February in London and *Norma* eight times in Paris
in May and June. The latter were a hard struggle against both a
tired voice and a state of physical exhaustion. 1965 yielded a total
of twelve *Tosca* performances in Paris and New York and a final
one on 5 July in London. In addition to the opera appearances of
these years were the gala concerts, in which many listeners and,
it appears, several critics were hearing the singer for the first time
without confessing to themselves their annoyance that what they
were hearing did not measure up to the singer's fame.

Only the uncritical admirer can disguise the fact that she sang
for a mere twelve or thirteen years without vocal problems, not
counting those few war-time appearances. Callas thereby had one
of the shortest careers of all significant singers. Giuditta Pasta was
active for thirty-four years. Henriette Sontag also for thirty-four
years, Schröder-Devrient twenty-six, Grisi thirty-two, Rosina
Stolz seventeen, Pauline Viardot thirty-three, Patti twenty-nine,
Lilli Lehmann forty-two, Marcella Sembrich thirty-two, Ernes-
tine Schumann-Heink fifty-four, Emma Calve thirty-eight, Nellie

Melba thirty-nine, Emmy Destinn twenty-eight, Birgit Nilsson thirty-five, Rosa Ponselle eighteen – only Maria Malibran's early death at the age of twenty-eight ended her career after only eleven years. By the age of thirty-five Maria Callas was both vocally and psychologically burnt out. Only someone whose imagination can recall the ardour of the voice when young will be able to find something to admire in the cautious glow of the later performances and recordings.

While the voice itself underwent agonies and the singer's fame – fame not as an abstract greatness but as a conscious factual and admiring recognition – began to falter, so her position in the world was growing. In January 1959 Maria Callas gave concerts in the US, again arranged by Sol Hurok. Before this she appeared in an Ed Murrow show in which the other guests were the conductor Sir Thomas Beecham and the Danish musical comedian Victor Borge. It included a very thorough discussion about the relations between artist and public, the artist's responsibility, the pros and cons of studio as against live recordings, operatic life and claques. While Beecham made his pithy comments with sparkle and Borge cracked jokes, Callas made a serious, formal and 'sometimes almost ceremonial impression' (Jellinek). To conclude, the conductor suggested to the diva that she should sing the role of Deianira in Handel's *Hercules*; she would be the only one capable of doing justice to this passionate music.

On 27 January 1959 she took part in a concert performance at Carnegie Hall of Bellini's *Il Pirata*. This was presented by the American Opera Society and conducted by Nicola Rescigno. The audience comprised a body of devotees who were 'captivated by the imaginative power of her art and the strength of her characterisation' (Jellinek). Callas appeared in a formal white dress, spotlighted (in centre stage) as only Leopold Stokowski had been before her, whereas her colleagues took their positions discreetly in the background.

No member of the audience can have regretted this, for seldom had Callas sung in such mediocre artistic surroundings. The tenor Pier Mirando Ferraro and the baritone Constantino Ego were quite incapable of performing the simplest embellishments – as the live recording shows, their voices were substandard. Reports simply state that Callas was in 'good vocal form' (Jellinek), having shown plenty of self-confidence during rehearsals. Ardoin quotes a comment from Nicola Rescigno, who took a particular *stretta* passage at the end of the first act an an unusually swift tempo, compelling the singer to four bars of quick scales:

Only a machine gun could have fired so quickly, certainly not a voice. Maria looked at me a little anxiously when we got to this passage, and she failed to make it. I said that I would put the brakes on slightly when we did it again. 'No, don't do that,' she said. 'I like the tempo, it's a good idea and I don't want you to help me.' 'Good,' I replied. 'But what if you don't make it at the performance?' 'That's my problem, not yours,' she replied. Thanks to her fantastic will-power this astonishing moment came off in performance – and everything was fine.

In the *New York Times* the verdict of Howard Taubman, who had once found her voice 'puzzling' and 'the product of will-power' was as vague as ever:

Miss Callas rose to the occasion here. One barely noticed the empire-style white satin dress or the red stole which she brought into play during the performance with the skill of an artist who knows how to make an effort. Her colleagues disappeared from the stage [. . .] She stood alone in a spotlight, a slim and tense figure with an aura of theatrical magic [. . .] She sang the introductory recitative and then the aria, 'Col sorriso d'innocenza', with commanding artistic resource. She had been in good voice all evening, though her attack at the outset, probably because of tenseness, had had the impact of a buzz saw. She had sung with a grasp of the Bellini style and with enormous conviction. At times the voice had been ingratiating: at others it had had an edge. Top notes had been a gamble: either shrill or brilliantly in focus. But now at the end she did not fail. This was Maria Callas living up to her reputation. Then came the tumult and the shouting.

After such a review, using praise to say virtually nothing, and veiling criticism with politeness, note the more discriminating verdict of Irving Kolodin:

> Without a singer of Miss Callas's special endowments and acquired resources, *Il Pirata* would founder on Imogene's first entrance [. . .] it put her to the test of an unaccompanied recitative in cadenza form, followed by an aria rising to a top D. Her voice was hardly loose at this point, but all fervour and solidity. Much could be made of the extremes of range with which she coped impressively, but there was much more art and expression in her finely controlled delivery of the *legato* line and its embellishments, in her sense of the tragic accent appropriate to the words and their meaning [. . .] Throughout Act II and coming to a proper climax in the final 'Mad Scene' (which she sang alone on a darkened stage in a spotlight) Miss Callas disposed vocal powers not previously at her command in New York. The pleading 'Tu m'apriasti in cor ferita' was an example to warmly coloured *cantabile* singing [. . .] which attested to her ability to make an emotional appeal without bravura or other exhibitionistic devices.

Before her departure for Milan the 'highly valued daughter of this city, whose glorious voice and superb artistry have given joy to music lovers everywhere' was honoured by the Mayor of New York, Robert Wagner. She spent the month of February 1959 in Milan with no engagement, but was in London in March for the second studio recording of *Lucia di Lammermoor*. Demanding horrendous fees, Meneghini had negotiated a series of concerts for the coming months in Madrid, Barcelona, Hamburg, Stuttgart, Wiesbaden, Munich, Amsterdam and Brussels. In June Maria Callas reappeared on the London stage as Medea. In the recording of *Lucia*, her vocal insecurity and weakness were more pronounced than in the New York Bellini performance. Even the middle register sounded strained, the texture of the sound both rough and lacking in colour, with a dearth of top notes which could be described as confidently attacked or cleanly sustained.

10

Callas and the Consequences

'Most mimics are attracted by that which
cannot be imitated'

Marie von Ebner-Eschenbach

Artificial Singing

'We owe her a lot. She opened for us the
door to a *terra incognita*'

Montserrat Caballé on Maria Callas

It is strange and yet more than a coincidence of timing that, just
before Callas made her recording, Covent Garden put on a new
production of the Donizetti opera, directed by Franco Zeffirelli –
with the Australian soprano Joan Sutherland who had sung the
small role of Clotilde to Callas's début as Norma in 1952. Commentators ascribe the interest enjoyed by this work in London to
the influence of Maria Callas; she was the only one who had
known how to actualise Italian opera before Verdi. Sutherland's
performance – of which Maria Callas is supposed to have said,
'She has set my work back by a hundred years' – introduced a
new departure, but not a new era of singing as Callas had done.

John Steane writes in his book *The Grand Tradition – Seventy
Years of Singing on Record* that there were a considerable number
of good singers in the 1950s for Mozart, Wagner, Verdi and
Puccini, and even for Bellini and Donizetti.

I do not entirely share this view. Until well into 1950s Verdi
was mainly sung, as explained in our introductory chapter, by
interpreters who were stylistically and technically versed in
verismo opera. It was only Maria Callas who began again to
present parts like Abigaille, Leonora and Violetta in their formal
variety and who had the ability to give dramatic life to romantic
heroines in particular. But it was precisely in the operas of Donizetti and Bellini that she scarcely ever found adequate partners,
apart from the tenors Cesare Valletti and Alfredo Kraus, neither
of whom she ever sang with in the recording studio. Steane goes
on to maintain:

You have only to look at the music which Giacomelli, Riccardo
Broschi and others wrote for Farinelli and his contemporaries

to know what virtuoso singing really means and how far from
its achievements we with our present-day singers really are.
The scores of Handel's operas pay abundant testimony to the
standard of those times, and we know of course that what was
written was nothing to what would actually be performed, for
the singers would embellish freely and with a brilliance
unknown to us today.

It is not least through the efforts of Joan Sutherland that the
situation has changed considerably since the end of the 1950s.
After Callas had rehabilitated 'canary fancier's music' by singing
with dramatic gesture, new parameters of interpretation could be
found for judging coloratura music as well as that of the eighteenth century. Without the interest which Maria Callas had spar-
ked off, Joan Sutherland would probably never have been able to
immerse herself in the stylistic arsenal of bel canto and been
able to reveal a new expressive dimension, that of such music's
ingenious formal richness. An example of how much this can be
misunderstood even today is to be found in an article on the
'Donizetti Renaissance',[1] whose initiator Maria Callas is said to
be. It states that it was she who rehabilitated 'an artificial stylistic
device like coloratura as a means of dramatic and emotional
expression'. This may be well meant (in Callas's favour) but it is
basically untrue. Untrue because the words 'artificial stylistic
device' suggest that coloratura is something superficial. Maria
Callas did not reject ingenious singing as that writer suggests, but
found the way back to it. When he says later on that singers like
Sutherland, Caballé and Sills 'saw their duty in making a definite
break with the Callas tradition, which was still new, and pursuing
artificial singing instead,' then the criticism implied there is really
a form of praise. Sutherland and Caballé are not to be reproached
for singing 'artificially', but if at all because they did not imbue
many of the vocal forms with sufficient spontaneity and drama,
as Callas had demonstrated could be done; and because they did
not give the necessary weight and priority to the *words* which the
old theoreticians of bel canto had demanded.

The achievement of Joan Sutherland, and also Marilyn Horne
in particular, was that, guided by Richard Bonynge, they studied

scores and other relevant sources in order to 'draw fresh attention to the capabilities of the old singers, with particular reference to tonal range and flexibility' (John Steane).

Sutherland and Horne demonstrated this return to tradition with the programmes which they chose for their two albums *The Age of Bel Canto* and *Souvenirs of a Golden Era* (where Horne sings parts written for Malibran and Viardot). These recordings are extremely valuable examples, indeed a defence of 'artificial singing', and of the way in which such singing liberates vocal expression from that 'psychology' which tries to express itself in a state of exaltation. Through their flexibility and exemplary virtuosity Sutherland and Horne, as well as Caballé and other singers, showed themselves to be a match for the formal wealth of the language of singing. To that extent it can be said that progress is to be found in looking backwards, or as Verdi put it dialectically: 'Torniamo all 'antico – e sarà un progresso' ('Let us return to the old, and it will be progress').

Maria Callas had already finished her work when Joan Sutherland – who in the early 1950s had sung lyric and *spinto* roles – began to specialise in bel canto music seen from the point of view of its composition and of vocal technique. Callas had, as Montserrat Caballé was to say later on, opened 'the door to a *terra incognita*'. The new standards which she set are dealt with elsewhere.

In the concerts in Madrid and Barcelona in 1959, and the ones which followed in Germany, Amsterdam and Brussels, she was in very good voice. Yet the reviews quoted by David A. Lowe make it clear that the well-known weakness and insecurity – particularly on sustained notes in the higher and top registers – continued to be in evidence. Antonio Fernandez-Cid in *ABC* mentioned an 'uneven, unpleasantly hard and harsh top register' after the Madrid recital and admired 'at the next moment falling chromatic scales of textbook perfection'. The odd critical voice was raised against the false gloss of these gala concerts and the purely financial exploitation of fame. Who would have guessed that even this was both the sign of a new order and a harking back to former times. Jenny Lind, Adelina Patti, Nellie Melba and Enrico Caruso had also given concerts to make the most of their fame, whatever one may think of the cult of the singer. To dismiss it as sheer publicity–seeking and of no cultural merit is to lose sight of the worth of those concerts.

On 17 June 1959 Maria Callas returned to Covent Garden to sing the first of five performances of Cherubini's *Medea* under Nicola Rescigno; her partners were Fiorenza Cossotto and Jon Vickers. Kolodin, who had come to London for the performance, wrote in the *Saturday Review* that the period of 'relative idleness' had benefited her, the sound of the voice 'fresh, responsive and endlessly expressive'. A similar conclusion was reached by Frank Granville-Barker in *Opera News* and George Louis Mayer in the *American Record Guide*.

The Riches of This World and Their Splendour

> 'How long have you lived here? Ten years?
> Without interruption? With hardly any inter-
> ruption? *C'est étonnant!* Well, I understand.
> But I've come to abduct you, to seduce you
> into temporary inconstancy, to transport
> you through the air on my cloak and show
> you the riches of this world and their splen-
> dour, or better still set them at your feet
> [. . .] Please excuse my pompous manner
> of speech! It is really *ridiculement exagérée*,
> especially as far as splendour is concerned'
>   Thomas Mann, *Doctor Faustus*

On 21 April 1959 Maria Callas made one of her grandest appearances. It took place in Paris at Maxim's. She was celebrating her tenth wedding anniversary with Battista Meneghini, celebrating it in a style which came close to ostentation. The chroniclers report the telegrams received from all over the world, the bouquets, bunches of red roses, the number of dishes on the menu and her statement: 'I am the voice, he is the soul'. Only two months after this Onassis issued invitations to a party at the Dorchester Hotel in London after the première of Cherubini's *Medea*. It was not the usual sort of celebration which followed on from an opera performance. Mr and Mrs Aristotle Onassis had invited 5000 guests for 'the pleasure of your company'. They included Randolph Churchill and Margot Fonteyn, Cecil Beaton and John Profumo and the Meneghini-Callas couple – who all gasped at Onassis's extravagant hospitality.

The Dorchester's ballroom was decorated entirely in pink and filled with roses, also pink. With this flashy décor Onassis was meeting both the public inclinations of guests who were spiritually akin to him and seemingly the secret ones of Maria Callas, for whose benefit alone the luxury celebration had been organised. She left the party three hours after midnight and was naturally photographed being embraced by her husband and by Onassis. Onassis invited the couple to a summer cruise through the Mediterranean on the luxury yacht *Christina*. Biographers report that the singer was like a little girl who had fallen in love with a man of the world, and they wrote as if they had been eye-witnesses, had overheard the compliments and had sensed the destruction of her husband.

The last of the five *Medea* performances in London was on 30 June 1959, after which she concluded her concert tour on 11 and 14 July in Amsterdam and Brussels. For the concert in Holland she was in particularly fine form and showed exemplary musical concentration. The concert was followed by a large reception in her honour. Arianna Stassinopoulos reports that during the reception Callas asked Peter Diamand, director of the Holland Festival, if she could have a private meeting with him, and that over lunch she requested him to delay paying her her fee. She is supposed to have told Diamand, 'All my instincts tell me that there will be many changes in my life in the coming months. You will hear many rumours [. . .] please let us remain friends.' Diamand is supposed to have protested with laughter, 'Maria, che melodramma', with Callas replying, 'Not melodrama, Peter, but drama.'

Let us believe, because it fits the drama, that Meneghini went along on 22 July full of premonitions, boarded the floating palace at Monte Carlo, and that Maria Callas, with a splendid new wardrobe designed for the cruise by Madame Biki, felt like Alice in Wonderland. The guests included Sir Winston and Lady Churchill together with secretary, private doctor and the Fiat chief Umberto Agnelli with his wife. The head of the Grimaldis, Prince Rainier of Monaco, was there to say goodbye when the 1640-ton ship, loaded with Venetian and Byzantine art treasures, with an El Greco painting in the master's cabin, gold taps in the bathrooms and a mosaic swimming pool modelled on those in the palace at Knossos, set out from the harbour. The cruise has frequently been described. Jellinek reports that forty-three masseurs, cooks, servants and waiters were on board, a figure which had increased to sixty in the twenty years before Stassinopoulos related her version of the erotic odyssey. Jellinek describes the first few days of the voyage as peaceful but Stassinopoulos says that they were 'difficult' because Meneghini, having no French or English, felt isolated and sank into lethargy. Onassis was only nine years younger than the Italian but made him look like the old cuckold in *opera buffa*.

On 7 August the *Christina* weighed anchor at Mount Athos, that sacred mountain which has always been a place of pilgrimage for orthodox Greeks. On the day after their arrival the Onassis and Meneghini families were received by the Patriarch of Constantinople. With typically southern eloquence he honoured 'the greatest singer in the world' and 'the greatest sailor of modern times, the new Odysseus', and thanked them for the honours which they had brought to their homeland. Meneghini later declared that he had witnessed 'a nationalistic outburst', which had 'visibly distressed' his wife; 'She was no longer the same woman. And how could I have defended myself against the new Odysseus?' It seems that after a decade of almost single-minded concentration on her work, the singer suddenly fell into the grip of the feelings which she had hitherto only sung about. Shortly before a celebration at the Istanbul Hilton on 8 August 1959, she told her husband that she had fallen in love with Onassis and wanted to end her marriage.

On 17 August, a few days after the cruise had ended, Onassis turned up in Sirmione, leaving the Meneghinis' house three hours later in the company of Maria Callas. She went on to Milan and remained in seclusion, as friends reported, in her house in the via Buonarotti. Madame Biki told how she even avoided her closest friends and acquaintances, presumably out of shame. There then began what Rémy describes as 'the Greek chorus': the press exploited the affair. 'I had the feeling of having long been held captive in a cage,' Stassinopoulos quotes Callas as saying, 'so that on meeting Aristo I became a different woman.' It seems that her encounter caused her to be so much softer and more accessible that even a reconciliation with Ghiringhelli of La Scala now seemed possible.

For the last two years she had made all her recordings in London. Now, sessions for a new recording of Ponchielli's *La Gioconda* were to commence in Milan on 5 September. She went to the theatre alone on 2 September, where she had to be sheltered from pushy photographers, according to Peter Diamand. When asked to show his identity, Diamand pretended that he was her 'Egyptian hairdresser' and immediately found himself being quoted in a magazine as saying that when she was singing Violetta the singer's hair was smooth and soft, but that it became wild and curly when she went on stage as Medea.

On 3 September 1959 Maria Callas and Onassis were seen having supper together in Milan. Photographers immediately materialised. Pictures went round the world, and with them rumours. On 4 September reporters besieged the house in the via Buonarotti. A little later the soprano declared that the break with Meneghini was final but that it had nothing to do with the cruise on the *Christina*. 'Solicitors are at work on the matter and will issue a statement. I am now my own manager. I beg your indulgence in my present painful position [. . .] between myself and Mr Onassis there is nothing but a deep friendship, which goes back quite some time. I also have business connections with him. I have had offers from the Monte Carlo Opera, and there are also plans for films.' The same day, 8 September, Onassis was cornered by a reporter in Harry's Bar in Venice. He explained: 'Of course, how would I not have been flattered by a woman of Maria

Callas's class falling in love with me? Who would have reacted differently?'

Press reports took on a pseudo-moral tone. The rich *parvenu* from Smyrna seeking to use the fame of the great diva to put the seal on his own success; the singer with the powerful inferiority complex and her suppressed longing for love; the deceived and bitterly disappointed husband, who voiced his anger to the press with a restraint which soon gave way to anger. 'I created Callas [. . .] When I met her, she was a fat and clumsily dressed woman, as poor as a gypsy. Now I am told that I exploited her [. . .] She had nothing. Now we have to divide up our mutual possessions.'

Evangelia Callas offered her own accompaniment to all this: 'Meneghini was both father and husband to Maria. Now she no longer needs him. But Maria will never be happy; that's what my heart tells me. Women like Maria will never know true love.' Elsa Maxwell went one better: only recently a parasitical proselyte for the diva, she now took up a moral defence for Tina Onassis. Meneghini saw all the parties as 'protagonists in a drama' and he inspired *Time* magazine to a satire on the level of a schoolboy's comic. In an opera entitled *Love and Money* the list of protagonists was:

Maria Meneghini Callas, famous diva	soprano
Giovanni Meneghini, her ageing husband	bass
Elsa Maxwell, confidante	baritone
Evangelia Callas, estranged mother	contralto
Aristotle Onassis, rich ship-owner	tenor
Anthena Onassis, his beautiful young wife	mezzo-soprano

For weeks on end the singer occupied the headlines as heroine in stories which ignored her privacy and amounted to the loss of her intimacy and human dignity. And all that had happened was something quite normal – a young woman had for the first time in her life fallen passionately in love with a successful and attractive man.

11

Epilogue

'Her breach with Menghini coincided with the decline of her artistic achievements – or caused it. Her life with him had been built on community of interests, mutual respect, Spartan domestic economy, rigorous self-discipline and hard work. The sumptuous party Onassis gave for them after her first London *Medea*, and the luxury of the first Mediterranean cruise on the *Christina* as fellow guests with Sir Winston and Lady Churchill opened new vistas for Callas – and new ambitions. This suddenly appealed to her as the world she had subconsciously craved'

Walter Legge, *La Divina*

Fear of the Trapeze

'Ho dato tutto a te'
Medea

Between 5 and 10 September 1959 in Milan Maria Callas made her second recording of Ponchielli's *La Gioconda*, the tragic story of a singer. It was no longer sung with the wild flaming voice of the 1952 Cetra version but with the artistic understanding that came to her as the product of experience and the reaction to reduced vocal resources. Less can be more. John Ardoin notes that her top, which was now often subject to unsteadiness, was better controlled. The last side of the complete recording was, she told John Ardoin, one of her best recorded efforts; he quotes her as saying, 'Everything that I felt at the time can be heard there – by anyone who wants to understand.'

Immediately after the recording sessions Onassis chartered a private plane to fly her to Venice. It was the start of another cruise. Pictures taken on the voyage reveal a completely changed woman, happy and relaxed, who posed coquettishly for the cameras. From Athens she flew to Bilbao for a concert (17 September), at which she sang, with apparent indifference and lack of concentration, four arias from *Don Carlo, Ernani, Hamlet* and *Il Pirata*. This was one of her coolest receptions, and the reviews were indifferent and disappointing. On her return to Athens she described the concert as 'a silly little engagement' and resumed the cruise. George Jellinek, inspired by the mythological connotations, describes how on 22 September the *Christina* passed through the straits of Scylla and Charybdis, which held no dangers for this modern Odysseus, who held in his arms a siren he could show off to the photographers. Maria Callas explained to the press. 'There is no romance. Mr Onassis and I are good friends. I hope that you will respect our friendship.' At the same time Tina Onassis was in New York with her children, filing her divorce application.

The soprano gave a recital in London on 23 September. The programme was almost identical to the one in Bilbao, except that she replaced the *Ernani* with the sleepwalking scene from Verdi's *Macbeth*. Her lack of security was shown by her statement on arriving in London. 'Please be indulgent. I am in a delicate situation, and having to work for my living.' Jellinek reported that she was almost in top form, getting ecstatic reviews. Although another concert was scheduled for 29 September, she flew off to Milan in order to discuss with lawyers the arrangements for her divorce from Meneghini; Nicola Rescigno, her valued conductor, fell ill and would not have been able to conduct. The television concert in London was therefore postponed until 3 October, with Sir Malcolm Sargent conducting. Then she sang one concert in Berlin, although two had originally been planned. Then it was back to the United States for a concert comprising four arias – among which, as in Berlin, was Donna Anna's 'Non mi dir' from *Don Giovanni* – and two performances of *Lucia di Lammermoor* at the Dallas Civic Opera. The production had been transferred to the US from London, where Joan Sutherland had taken the title role. Before Callas could appear, she had to have a big build-up. Elsa Maxwell reported a discussion she supposedly had with Leonard Bernstein about the arrival of 'that much-heralded diva':

Bernstein: 'What do you think of her?'
Maxwell: 'I feel nothing.'
Bernstein: 'But you must have some opinion.'
Maxwell: 'Do you mean morally or musically?'
Bernstein: 'Both.'
Maxwell: 'I can only say that musically she is the greatest artist in the world.'

Speaking of morals, not of the artist herself but of those who considered themselves her guardians, let us look at two accounts of a party held on 28 October 1959 after her recital in Loew's Midland Theatre in Kansas City. This was the report of the New York *American Journal*: 'Maria Callas lived up to her reputation for being capricious. The governor of Missouri and 800 honoured guests from Kansas City's élite were left waiting.

The temperamental diva was too tired to attend a champagne party arranged in her honour. Governor James T. Blair, his wife and the wife of the Mayor of Kansas waited in vain for the great lady to appear.' But the reporter from *Time* gave the following version: 'After the thunderous applause Callas greeted Harry S. Truman with a polite "I'm honoured," paid her respects to Kansas Governor George Docking and then attended a post-concert party at the River Club, where she danced with the local millionaires and partook of caviar [. . .]'

Preparations were starting for the third season of the Dallas Civic Opera. Callas was to sing Lucia on 6 and 8 November and Medea on 19 and 21 November. Between these Teresa Berganza was to star in Rossini's *Barbiere*, but she had to cancel because she was pregnant. Lawrence Kelly asked Maria Callas if she would deputise for her young colleague, but she had to appear in court in Brescia on 14 November in connection with her divorce.

Even so it was only with difficulty that she could concentrate on her work; she could no longer summon her former energy, or at most for a few performances and only then for short stretches in those performances. It appears that the first of the Lucias, with Gianni Raimondi and Ettore Bastianini as partners, was almost a fiasco. The reviews quoted by David A. Lowe show both great enthusiasm and polite reserve. 'When she sang *mezza voce* and in the middle range', wrote John Rosenfield in the *Dallas Morning News*, 'she produced a superlative sound. One had to accept the screeched top notes . . . overall it was a better Mad Scene than that heard in New York during her time at the Met.' George Saxe's review in *Musical Courier* also revealed how an admirer of the singer could still hear the phrases, accents and nuances which only Callas commanded – and that the fulfilment of such moments was considered more important than the tremolo at the top.

This was the performance in which something terrible happened, the sort of thing that only a young singer can recover from. In the Mad Scene she attempted the top E flat but missed it. As soon as the curtain fell, she exclaimed in panic and irritation: 'I had the note, I had it. What happened? I simply don't know.' To prove to herself that nothing had happened, she repeated the E flat *in alt* five times on the way to her dressing room. Two evenings later, at the second performance, she was in better voice but decided to omit the top E flat. But any admirer, any musical listener and any sympathetic critic might ask what the importance is of a top E flat. Is it not a fetish to make reference to one spoilt top note? What is a single missed note?[1]

Unfortunately these are questions which find their place in essays on for example the 'Cult of the beautiful voice' or 'Fetishism in music and the regression of listening', but which do not help ease the mind of a singer who whenever possible goes for a top E flat, whether it is written by the composer or interpolated; or a singer who makes a display of vocal stunts or wants to surprise her audience. Certainly, a boldly attacked E flat *in alt* has no musical value of its own; but the feeling or the concern that she might no longer be able to crown a cabaletta with an E must have signified capitulation in the singer's battle for her voice. Maria Callas had never cosseted her voice or handled it with caution or circumspection, never 'played' with it in the manner of Adelina Patti, and she was never, as Patti had been, the 'consummate artist' (Verdi) in the sense of possessing a faultless tone. At an early age she had interpolated the top E at the end of Act 2 of *Aida* and taken the perilous course of demanding of her voice notes, sounds, accents, feelings and emotional states which went against the grain of what was vocally reasonable: she broke the rule that a singer should always remain within the voice's limits, always going for the vocal *tour de force* and abandoning herself to that state of intoxication which overlooks boundaries. On 9 November, when she should have sung Rossini's Rosina but was replaced by Eugenia Ratti, who had sung Oscar in the recording of *Un Ballo in Maschera*, Maria Callas flew back to Italy in order to make arrangements for her divorce. When changing planes in New York, she was questioned by reporters and surprised them with a suggestion that she might have made her peace with Rudolf Bing. But all questions about a reappearance at the Met or her relationship with Onassis were answered noncommittally.

On the morning of 14 November she appeared before Judge Cesare Andreotti in Brescia, who first listened to Battista Meneghini and then Callas. After six hours of talks she was awarded the house in Milan, her husband the villa in Sirmione.

She retained her valuable jewellery and above all the rights on her recordings. Meneghini, who had initially asked for a divorce on the grounds of his wife's misconduct, finally settled for a separation by mutual agreement. The following morning she flew back to the United States, managing to avoid the New York reporters and arriving in Dallas in time for the dress rehearsal of *Medea* and excelling herself at the performance. After a repeat performance on 21 November she flew back to Italy.

She was not to sing for the next nine months, appearing on stage only on 24 and 28 August 1960 in Epidaurus. The planned Paris appearance in *Medea* on 11 December 1959 was cancelled. The La Scala season had opened with Verdi's *Otello* with Mario del Monaco in the title role, Leonie Rysanek as Desdemona and Tito Gobbi as Iago. Renata Tebaldi returned on 9 November as Tosca after a five-year absence, with the critic of *L'Italia* writing ecstatically, 'We have never heard Tosca sung so beautifully.' It was no longer a question of a 'fight' between the two prima donnas. Maria Callas made peace not only with her rivals but also with Antonio Ghiringhelli and Rudolf Bing. She said in an interview with the critic Eugenio Gara: 'As Renata Tebaldi is returning to La Scala, the public's interest should be directed towards that important event, without direct or indirect insinuations of any kind. I myself have brought many chapters to a close this year and it is my honest wish that this particular chapter should also be closed.'

Even in interviews a new Callas was in evidence, gentle, smiling and friendly. It was reported that she wanted a child, that she had lost her pleasure in singing and that she had no more energy for disagreements of any sort. 'I have no desire to sing any more, but would like to live like an ordinary woman.' She was longing for a 'real life, a private life'. Even if the suggestion cannot be avoided that many of these public statements were part of an act which turned the enforced abandonment of her career into the fulfilment of a long-cherished wish, yet there is evidence in interviews as early as 1958 that her career and the conditions which it imposed were now an immense psychological burden. Her strength had always been in the overcoming of weakness. The first vocal crisis of threatening dimension occurred at the beginning of 1960. Her nerves were in a desolate condition, she was suffering from severe colds and inflammation of the nasal passages which caused extreme pain when she was singing. The fact was that although she did not want to sing, she needed to know that she still could. It is an open question whether she had found the real life which she longed for. She found neither the 'private life' nor even the protection which a public person needs. In an almost compulsive way she was being forced to reveal herself, not just feeling it as a need but also being compelled to. Whenever she appeared, every moment was captured by photographers. Gossip columnists pushed her into the bottom pit of social news, using to their account the book written by her mother to try to settle old debts. And it was very seldom that the question of marriage to Onassis did not come up. She no longer belonged to the world of music.

New Attacks

'It is not my voice that is sick, but my nerves'

Maria Callas

It was not until July 1960 that she made the hesitant attempt to sing again, recording arias from Rossini's *Semiramide* and Verdi's *I Vespri Siciliani* in London under the direction of Antonio Tonini. They were so unsatisfactory that she would not pass them for publication, thus making further inroads on her self confidence. Nevertheless she went on to Ostende, where a concert was scheduled. On the morning in question she awoke voiceless. Peter Diamand recalls hearing her hoarse voice on the telephone and thinking that it was that of a male acquaintance of his. The concert was cancelled, a bad omen for the two performances of *Norma* which she was scheduled to sing in Epidaurus, partly to please Onassis, at the end of August.

The couple spent the first two weeks of August in Monte Carlo. They were seen on various occasions in a night club, the

Maona, this being an anagram – MAria-ONAssis. It was there, on 10 August, that she declared her intention to marry Onassis, but the following day the shipowner dismissed this piece of flattery which amounted to a public humiliation for her. The performance of *Norma* scheduled for 22 August in Epidaurus had to be postponed because of heavy rain. Rémy observes that nobody voiced any complaint, 'whereas two years earlier they would have charged her with invoking the storm with her evil powers of magic.' The first appearance now took place on 24 August, and Callas was greeted with a thunderous ovation when she first stepped on stage. As there was no broadcast of this or the second performance, which she sang in spite of a high temperature, it is difficult to judge what condition her voice was in. The euphoric reception of public and critics cannot be entirely relied upon – her appearances were an event in themselves.

Her success in Greece did however help to boost her confidence for the coming recording sessions for her second *Norma* in Milan in September. This was to be conducted by Tullio Serafin and her colleagues were to be Franco Corelli and Christa Ludwig. It is not easy to form a judgement of this remarkable recording, which Serafin conducted with his accustomed mastery. John Ardoin speaks of an interpretation which astounds by virtue of its musical certainty and vocal control but even more he emphasises the expressiveness which transcends mere technical finish. It was another good omen for her planned return to La Scala in Donizetti's *Poliuto*. However, just as rehearsals were starting, Visconti cancelled his contract as producer. His film *Rocco and his Brothers* and the play *Araldia* had just been censored by the government. He sent the soprano a telegram, explaining his great regret at not being able to work with her again, 'because it is working with you which has given me my greatest sense of fulfilment. Although I have to ask your forgiveness, I am confident that you will understand my position and will condone my decision. As always I embrace you with all my admiration and deepest affection.'

Maria Callas's reply was that she had been counting the hours until she would work with him again but that even more she was concerned that he had been offended. Herbert Graf took the production over from Visconti – while the social side of the production was in the capable hands of Onassis and his company. Prince Rainier and Princess Grace, the Begum and Elsa Maxwell were all visitors to the theatre, which Pierre Balmain had decorated with 16,000 carnations.

Conductor Antonino Votto was of the impression that Callas's performance was 'quite excellent' notwithstanding the fact that the role of Paolina demanded none of the outbursts of a Norma or a Medea and presented none of the technical challenges of a Lucia or Amina. Franco Corelli, singing the title role, expressed a similar view to Votto's, praising her wonderful *legato* and controlled vocal production. But most of the critics were of a different opinion.

H.C. Robbins Landon wrote in *High Fidelity*: 'Callas is not what she once was. A magnificent stage presence, yes: when she appears, her personality simply singes the edges off everyone else, dramatically. She is a magnificent actress . . . But when she reached B or high C, her voice became tight, metallic, unpleasant.'

Fedele d'Amico in *Opera News*: 'Two decades of singing an extraordinarily wide repertory have left some scars on the Callas voice, particularly around her high notes, which are not always so firm or secure as before . . . Her qualities as an interpreter, however, once more reigned supreme. The force of her phrasing remains miraculous; all the coloratura was articulated expressively.'

Peter Heyworth wrote in the *New York Times*:

On the first night, she was clearly not in good voice. She is, of course, a highly wrought singer, and the feverish excitement that surrounded the evening probably took its toll, for her voice sounded strained. Her movements, gestures, and general stagecraft were, of course, as consummate as ever. What actress uses her hands as Mme Callas does? And there were moments when she achieved a poignancy that no other singer can rival.

In *Opera* Harold Rosenthal gave a thorough report of the performance. He pointed out that *Poliuto*, which Donizetti composed for the San Carlo in Naples at the instigation of Adolphe Nourrit, was primarily the tenor's opera, offering the soprano little chance to build a character study of the likes of Lucia or Anna Bolena. Callas had not been in good voice at the third performance, and although somewhat better at the fifth one, the voice had still sounded 'empty and hollow' in the first act in particular. But now and again there had been 'a few minutes of sure and exquisite singing, phrases so full of significance that little thrills would run down the spine'. His overall impression, however, was that rare one of experiencing a performance of complete artificiality: 'by Callas imitating Callas being Paolina'.

Andrew Porter attended a matinée performance and what he heard from Callas was 'fascinating, secure, fully confident of herself and radiating that confidence'. Retrospectively it seems that all concerned – performers and critics – were favourably disposed towards her, wanting above all to hear the things she did successfully. In other words, she had become a phenomenon which was beyond criticism.

Deceptive Hopes

'The strange thing about a singer's fate is
that she has to give everything for her singing – and then, in a flash, it is all over'

Lisa della Casa

Arianna Stassinopoulos writes that Callas was, after the final performance of *Poliuto*, 'physically and psychologically a wreck'. Due to insecurity, anxiety and weakness she was now singing fewer and fewer performances, with the result that the few which she ventured or forced herself to undertake became spectacular events – and this merely led to more inner tension for her. In 1964 she was to need tablets and injections just to get her on the stage for the Paris performances of *Norma*. In fact after the Milan appearances in *Poliuto* she sang only three more roles – Medea, Norma and Tosca.

But Callas continued to toy with plans. Sandor Gorlinsky, who was London-based and had become her exclusive agent after the divorce, negotiated with La Scala over the title role in Bellini's *Beatrice di Tenda* and with Dallas Civic Opera over Gluck's *Orfeo*. Callas was approached by the Monte Carlo Opera. Onassis had had film offers in mind ever since Carl Foreman – one of the guests on the *Christina* – had offered her a part in *The Guns of Navarone* alongside Gregory Peck. There was the project to play the lead in a film based on *The Prima Donna* by Hans Habes. Arianna Stassinopoulos reckons that this was just about Onassis's level, if only Callas the filmstar had really been part of his world. But now, 'mystified and confused by her art', he had started to disparage her and compromise her in public.

At the beginning of 1961 she rented an apartment in Paris at 44 avenue Foch. The French capital, where she had been received with such warmth, was to become her adopted home, a development which was also beneficial to her work. The 1960 *Norma* recording had still been supervised by Walter Legge, but starting in 1961 Michel Glotz of Pathé-Marconi, later to be Karajan's recording supervisor, became her producer. Between 28 March and 5 April he was in charge of her first French recital, which comprised arias from *Carmen, Orphée et Euridice, Roméo et Juliette, Mignon, Le Cid* and *Louise*. The conductor was Georges Prêtre, who later also conducted Callas in concerts as well as conducting her final complete opera recordings, *Carmen* and *Tosca*. Her old champion from Chicago, Roger Dettmer, considered that this recital heralded the 'supreme Carmen since the days of Calvé', the 'definitive Dalila' and the singer who 'humanised' Gluck – a paean to the 'reborn Queen' which perhaps went too far!

But audiences scarcely got a chance to see the newborn Queen. Her engagements had to fit in with her travels. On 31 May 1961, for example, she sang four arias at St James's Palace in London to the piano accompaniment of Sir Malcolm Sargent, immediately afterwards going off on another cruise. Stassinopoulos quotes Princess Grace's surprise at the end of a cruise lasting several weeks: 'You did not even practice once,' to which Callas replied, 'It's not necessary. I can do without that for a month.'

Her diary included two more appearances in Epidaurus in Cherubini's *Medea* on 6 and 13 August 1961 – two out of a total of five in the whole of 1961. She worked as if possessed for the final four days of rehearsal. The first night was to be attended by the Greek prime minister and members of the cabinet, Antonio Ghiringhelli of La Scala, where she was due to repeat the role in December, David Webster from Covent Garden and Wally Toscanini. Trudy Groth reported in *Opera News* that Callas was in better form than for any other appearance during those years. The only person to miss it was Onassis, who was reported to have gone to Alexandria 'for business reasons'. Arianna Stassinopoulos suggests that he no longer wanted to hear the congratulations heaped upon her, which certainly sounds plausible in the light of a relationship which was later to break up.

In the meantime Meneghini was attempting to 'whitewash his name' by trying to get the divorce annulled by a court. However hurtful she may have found Meneghini's reproaches, which were the outbursts of injured pride, she must have found Luchino Visconti's affirmations even more so when he said: 'I admire Callas but I do not believe that she will sing again, even once a year. She realises all too well that she was very great even two years ago and that her great time is passing. As a woman she is still young, but as a singer no longer so young. And voices change with age. In addition she is preoccupied with personal matters, and that is not good for her.'

In London she wanted to make a new recital record with arias from Rossini, Bellini and Donizetti operas. Only 'Sorgete, è in me dover' from Bellini's *Il Pirata*, accompanied by the Philharmonia Orchestra under Antonino Tonini, was partially successful. It was only published eleven years later together with Verdi arias from 1964, and it was this publication which first revealed that unpublished Callas recordings existed. Walter Legge tells how the intention had originally been to record Verdi's *La Traviata* at those sessions. When Callas called this off, probably for the simple reason that her voice was not up to it, EMI still had to make use of the orchestra, but it was an embarrassing solution which scarcely did credit to any of the participants. The recording started on 15 November and when they were over she returned to Milan to start preparing for *Medea*. This was not a new production but a revival of the one which Alexis Minotis had prepared for Dallas.

Minotis was regarded as one of the most important innovators in Greek theatre, particularly in Greek tragedy. Together with his wife Katina Paxinou he had presented works like *King Oedipus*, *Electra* and *Agamemnon* with the aim of giving new life to the expression, and even more to the gestures and poses of ancient theatre. One day during the rehearsals in Dallas he had observed Maria Callas beating her hands on the ground as Medea invoked the gods. It was a gesture which he had discussed with his wife when they had come across it in old pictorial representations. He asked Callas how she had arrived at it and her response was that it had seemed to her at that moment the most appropriate and dramatically convincing thing to do. She could never have seen these gestures, neither in her youth in Greece nor later in New York. Minotis concluded that she must have had the classical dramatic manner 'in her blood'. She had an instinct for an archetypal gesture, for a mythical pose.

In the three performances in December 1961 – and the further two on 23 May and 3 June 1962 – Callas's artistic understanding and dramatic power again drew praise and respect of both critics and colleagues. Franco Abbiati wrote in *Corriere della Sera* that discussing Callas was like walking on hot coals, because she had become too controversial a figure – the object of almost fetishistic admiration on the one hand and unmitigated despisal on the other: 'Her Medea is for us unique,' wrote Abbiati, 'on account of her psychological penetration of the character.' Yet he did not overlook the fact that her vocal resources were reduced. The same verdict is to be found in the reviews of Trudy Groth in *Opera News* ('her voice is from time to time a little weak and tremulous') and Claudio Sartori in *Opera* ('the youthful wildness and the uncurbed passion which Callas used to bring to the figure of Medea have become a little softer in the course of the years').

The live recording shows how charitably the critics were treating her. The first act sounds strained, vocally insecure and even dull. When she reached 'Deh tuoi figli' in the duet with Jason, sung by Jon Vickers, a loud, aggressive hiss was heard from the gallery.

She sang on, without seeming to have noticed, up to the point where she upbraids Jason with 'Crudel!' This was followed by two *forte* chords in the orchestra and then she again sang 'Crudel!'. The conductor Thomas Schippers said that he would remember for ever how Callas stopped singing after the first cry and then used the tension of the moment's silence to stare long and determinedly into the audience as if she were fixing each person with her stare. 'Look! This is my stage and will remain so as long as I wish. If your feeling is of hatred, then mine is even greater!' This was what Schippers 'sensed and felt'. She then sang the second 'Crudel!' directly to the silent audience and with biting sharpness. She then returned with the words 'Ho dato tutto a te' ('I have given you everything'), shaking her fist at her enemies in the gallery. Schippers said that in all his experience of the theatre he had never encountered a comparable act or similar courage, and there was nobody in that audience who dared to protest.

Arianna Stassinopoulos tells that Callas had to undergo a sinus operation on 20 December, just before the third performance of *Medea*, and was only able to sing in severe pain. She then left for Monte Carlo spending Christmas and the New Year with Onassis. He again shattered her hopes of marriage and family life. It seemed that it was around this time that she began to realise that her flight from the idealistic world of opera was into the unreal world of the glitterati, which gave her nothing. It was a world she was to leave immediately she was abandoned by Onassis.

1962 was not artistically fruitful. She sang just a few concerts and the two *Medea* performances in Milan (on 23 May and 3 June). It was remarkable that John Warrack reviewed her London recital in *Opera* so kindly:

These recitals, indeed, are perhaps Mme Callas's new visiting cards: they no lónger read, 'Prima soprano *assoluta*: all roles studied, rivals routed, managements flouted at short notice,' but indicate a gentler artist whose voice is matching the change in temperament by finding its true range on a slightly lower specific gravity. Her Cenerentola finale reflected not breathless, bubbling joy but hesitant acceptance of happiness: the scales and runs were not a burst of exuberance but a kind of elaborate vocal caress, with the notes lightly touched in a near-glissando as the voice passed easily across them. At the end, a sudden shriek of all the old sourness indicated how much care she had been exercising; just as the beautifully cradled tone of 'O mia regina' in Eboli's aria was immediately preceded by a violent low register snarl [. . .]

The Times, on the other hand, was not ashamed to point out how her voice had become 'quite ugly'. Another minus point was the concert's atmosphere, which was 'unworthy' of the singer with lighting more suited to a pop concert.

The soprano had until then sung only rarely in Germany: *Lucia* with Karajan in Berlin in 1955, *La Sonnambula* in Cologne in 1957 and two concerts in Hamburg and Stuttgart in 1959. When she came back in 1962 for a short concert tour she seemed to be almost unknown to most of the daily press writers. There are a few record reviews from this period which do justice to the Callas phenomenon but no real methodical discussion of her as an interpreter.

However, the *Süddeutsche Zeitung* of 14 March 1962 contained an illuminating article by Joachim Kaiser[4] entitled 'The fame of Callas is no coincidence':

A person who knows Callas only from the viewpoint of the magazines must consider her world fame to be the typical Western idea of millionaire's yachts, performance nerves, scandals instead of art. [. . .] But when you hear her, a better perspective is established – and you might even respect a musical public which has made Callas into their idol. The main source of admiration for her is not a perfection which disarms any resistance. In no way does she embody the American type of artist for whom nothing ever goes wrong. What stands out is her incomparable truth of expression. No other singer has this ability to make herself the recipient of lived-through emotion. The world can feel honoured that she bows before it rather than just seeking perfection.

To quote Violetta in *La Traviata*: 'È strano.' Has the world ever really bowed before the *singer* who acts and sings with such glowing accents? Surely the world depicted by Kaiser was more interested in the special monster which makes for a scandal?

Kaiser continues:

As far as the voice itself is concerned, Miss Callas has at present a top which is too sharp. She cannot in any way reach top B flat or B cleanly, the degree of wobble at the top is excessive and she does not command any facility in *parlando*. Her vocal category is almost that of lyric mezzo with contralto leanings.[3] The top was much easier for her a few years ago (the Columbia recording of *Tosca*); now she has had to start forcing [. . .][4] I make these qualifications with reluctance – and they should only be understood in conjunction with the fact that we are dealing with the most celebrated singer in the world. The middle voice is captivatingly beautiful, the coloratura is of overwhelming brilliance, the diction and nuance are splendid. But even if all these details interest the singing teachers they are not of general concern, because Callas becomes unique when we enter the realm of delivery and expression, one might say the realm of the soul. The greatness of Callas triumphs where talk about singing and mime stops.

We must again interrupt Kaiser and ask some questions. Is it only singing teachers who are interested in a captivatingly beautiful middle voice and overwhelmingly brilliant coloratura – and is it only piano teachers who are interested in a beautiful tone or perfectly formed octaves? Are beauty of tone, clean production and brilliant coloratura not prerequisites for vocal expression? In brief, is this not yet another consuming manifestation of Wagner's dictum on Schröder-Devrient? The German reviews which appeared in March 1962 gave no indication of how Maria Callas sang at her concerts.

The live recording of the Hamburg concert indicates that her singing was uneven. The elegiac aria of Chimène from *Le Cid* lacks the colours of pain, and the aria from *Ernani* is missing its cabaletta – such a virtuoso demand would probably have presented too high a hurdle. 'Nacqui all' affanno' from *La Cenerentola* is turned into a mere study, and in the Habañera from *Carmen* there are numerous memory lapses. Yet Eboli's aria is grandiose, despite the obvious struggle to get the top notes in the *stretta*.

The two *Carmen* arias were repeated at a concert in New York; this was not a Callas evening, but a gala celebrating the forty-fourth birthday of John F. Kennedy (who was also honoured by famous pop singers). The day after this concert Callas flew back to Milan for a performance of *Medea* on 23 May. The pain which she suffered was unbearable even at the rehearsals. High notes were the main cause of stabbing and incisive pain.

She ought to have cancelled. But could she cancel again, the Callas of scandals and walk-outs? Could she risk provoking another scandal? She took the risk of carrying on – and lost. On her first entry, she stood between two antique columns wrapped in a dark cloak like a messenger of terror, adopting a dominant, threatening yet secretive pose, ready to utter the words: 'Io? Medea!'

To the horror of her colleagues on the stage and the entire audience her voice broke. The rest of the performance was a superhuman struggle for her. Only a few critics were able to overlook her weakness. All that was left, according to Rémy, was the 'spirit of her voice'.

The second performance was more successful. It was – let us repeat the date, 3 June 1962 – her last appearance at La Scala. All the plans which were later discussed with the theatre foundered: performances of Meyerbeer's *Les Huguenots*, *Le Nozze di Figaro*, Monteverdi's *L'Incoronazione di Poppea* and *Tristan und Isolde*. There was also discussion of a new production of *Il Trovatore* by Visconti at Covent Garden, but this too came to nothing. Even the mere thought of going on stage, let alone the strain of lengthy rehearsals, filled her with anxiety, and yet she allowed negotiations to continue under ever-changing conditions, for they alone revived her feeling that people were still counting on her. She discussed her fee, but no sooner had her demand been met than she started discussing the tenor, the conductor and the length of rehearsals.

She made only one more appearance in 1962: she sang three arias in a BBC television concert. It was her contribution to Covent Garden's programme *Golden Hour*. She performed Elisabetta's aria from *Don Carlo* with tonal insecurity, followed by the two *Carmen* arias. Sir David Webster announced her with the words: 'If someone were to send me a telegram tomorrow and tell me the secret of how I could persuade Miss Callas to sing the role of Carmen in this house, then I would be a happy, a very happy man.' She sang the Habañera and Séguidille with more suggestive power and more subtle nuance of tone than in the EMI studio version of the opera. But this was only a small flicker of light. She was now undergoing the deepest vocal crisis of her entire career; apart from those fifteen minutes on television she did not sing at all between 3 June 1962 and 3 May 1963, and her attempts to start again were only made within the secure walls of the EMI studios and with a new repertoire: arias from French opera.

Life with Onassis, although it still gave hope of breaking free from the yoke of singing, gave no real release. He complained that she looked 'ordinary' when wearing spectacles, but she could not get on with contact lenses and made anxious attempts never to appear in front of him with her spectacles on. Even when wearing her exquisitive wardrobe with an elegance matched by few fashion models, she still felt insecure. There is a whole series of photographs of her wearing a bathing costume on board the *Christina* – but she always has the air of a woman posing in a state of anxious tension and she was always aware that her legs were on the short side. She seems insecure as she looks into the camera. Onassis, who later was to be chided by Jackie Kennedy for his ineptitude in matters of fashion, issued Madame Biki's salon with instructions for Callas's clothes. He preferred her in black, while she herself favoured red and turquoise. He sent her to Paris to have her long hair shortened by Alexander, hairdresser to the stars. She acquiesced but realised that she was becoming the plaything of his caprices. She who 'had sought the perfect relationship just as previously she had sought the perfect performance'

(Stassinopoulos) now realised that she had broken free only to find herself in another prison.

Only a few friends – like Michel Glotz of Pathé Marconi and the conductor Georges Prêtre – made real attempts to help. Between 2 and 7 May 1963 she recorded her second French aria recital, and an interview at the time testifies to her desperation: 'I need to find happiness in my music.' Or even more frightening and desperate: 'If I did not have my work, how would I fill the time between morning and evening? . . . I have no children, no family. What will I do when I no longer have a career? I can't just sit around and chat or play cards, I'm not that sort of woman.'

This was also the time when her ex-husband Meneghini, who had truly made capital out of her fame, was trying to get the divorce terms altered in his favour; and when Onassis was returning to his old habits of being seen with celebrated beauties like the Princess Radziwill. Callas therefore had to try and resume her career. Ten days after the recording sessions were over she began a second concert tour of Germany, singing in the Deutsche Oper Berlin (17 May), Düsseldorf Rheinhalle (20 May) and Stuttgart (23 May). From there she went on to London (31 May, Royal Festival Hall) and ended up in Copenhagen (9 June). The programmes consisted of 'Bel raggio' from \Semiramide, 'Casta diva' from Norma, 'Ben io t'invenni' from Nabucco, Musetta's Waltz from La Bohème, Butterfly's 'Tu, tu, piccolo iddio' and 'O mio babbino caro' from Gianni Schicchi.

Werner Oehlmann wrote a studiously polite review in the Berliner Tagesspiegel, but Harold Rosenthal, editor of Opera and long-standing Callas admirer, could no longer suppress his reservations: ' "Casta diva" was sung with an exquisite tone throughout, but the cabaletta was a mere echo of what had once been. Do you recall how crystal clear every note used to be in the descending scale?'Following the concert in Paris on 5 June Claude Rostaud wrote in Le Figaro Littéraire: 'Maria Callas belonged to the greatest delights of our time; she renewed the meaning of bel canto . . . and she created a style of dramatic and vocal interpretation which will be a landmark, and yet . . .' We need quote no more of that review – it was an epitaph. There can be nothing worse than a 'but' after an expression of admiration, a 'but' which refers to a voice which has become unsteady, insecure, trembling, unpleasant and harsh. The only thing left to praise was a festival of intelligence, charm and beauty. Yet the concert was a success: the singer was acclaimed, just as Maurice Chevalier was acclaimed when he took his place in the audience. It was like a modern television show, with famous people exchanging mutual assurances.

What had 1963 brought? Six concerts and a recital recording. But more significantly it brought ever more tortuous doubts about the waning of a career; and these doubts gained in significance from the fact that Onassis was putting new leading ladies on the stage where gala performances could be given to boost his ego. The most important of these women was Jacqueline Kennedy, who in the late summer of 1963 was guest on one of those cruises of seduction on the *Christina* – before, that is, the American president's assassination on 22 November 1963. Onassis joined the Kennedy family's guests at the funeral, from where he flew back to Paris to celebrate Maria Callas's fortieth birthday – 'the shuttle from one woman to the other had begun' (Stassinopoulos).

12

'Prima Donna, Artist, Woman'

Vissi d'arte or Torture the Heroine

'Berma's interpretation surrounded the masterpiece with a second work, brought to life
by genius. Berma could lead one to those
great visions of pain, largeness of mind and
passion which were her very own masterpieces and in which she herself could be
recognised'

Marcel Proust, *Le Côté de Guermantes*[1]

The soprano finished 1963 with recording sessions in Paris.
Accompanied by the Paris Conservatoire Orchestra conducted by
Georges Prêtre she sang 'Ocean, thou mighty monster!' from
Weber's *Oberon*, Donna Anna's 'Or sai che l'onore' and 'Non mi
dir' and Elvira's 'Mi tradi' from Mozart's *Don Giovanni* and the
Countess's first aria from *Le Nozze di Figaro*, 'Porgi amor'. She
had been working on her voice with great energy, equalising the
top which had been so unsteady during the 1963 tour, and she
summoned the courage to sing out with energy. 'She gives us,'
writes John Ardoin, 'a powerful demonstration of will-power,
technique, intellect and, in the middle register, vocal beauty.'
This was immediately followed by a Verdi recital: Desdemona's
Act 4 scene from *Otello*, arias from *Aroldo* and Eboli's 'O don
fatale' from *Don Carlo*, concluding with Elisabetta's short scena
'Non pianger'.

In January 1964 the prima donna returned to the stage, something quite unexpected by the musical world. The December
recording sessions, which she had been able to undertake without
physical pain, were balm to her wounded soul. She now confronted the uncertainty about her future with Onassis with amazing courage. She wrote to Sir David Webster that she was ready
to sing Puccini's *Tosca* at Covent Garden. The director of the
Royal Opera had had other operas in mind, Verdi's *Il Trovatore*
or *La Traviata*, but those held roles with technical problems which
she could not face at that time.

In Rodolfo Celletti's study of bel canto the writer explains how

the role of Tosca can be convincingly embodied by an actress of
only average vocal abilities. Franco Zeffirelli, who was in London
preparing a new production of *Rigoletto*, was willing to take on
another one of *Tosca* at six weeks' notice. The producer, who at
last had emerged from the shadow of Luchino Visconti, explained
that he had previously rejected all invitations to produce *Tosca*
because the right singers had never been offered. His secret hope
had been Maria Callas.

The six performances (21, 24, 27 and 30 January, 1 and 5
February), plus Act 2 for BBC television, were described as
'unforgettable' by Harold Rosenthal, who was echoed by other
critics. Reading his detailed review again after an interval of
twenty-five years, it is striking that much of it is dedicated to the
acting, the art of musical gesture and only a few lines to the
singing, which was 'better than at any time since 1957, but the
voice is so much part of the whole of a Callas performance that
one cannot really separate it from the acting. She colours her
voice much as a painter does his canvas.'

A very similar account of the performance appeared in different
words, if not from quite the same sympathetic viewpoint:

> It is the hallmark of a great artist to capitalise on his defects,
> and there is honour rather than disgrace in admitting that Maria
> Callas and Tito Gobbi played Tosca and Scarpia coolly and
> intelligently because neither has the same purely vocal gifts as
> formerly. Miss Callas dispenses with all the traditional props
> and mannerisms of the nineteenth-century diva. Dressed and
> made up to resemble Mlle Mars, the great French *tragédienne*,
> she combines the natural accents, intonations and gestures of a
> woman simply in love with the hands and arms of a great ballet
> dancer. Everything about her is expressive, even her silences,
> and the only moment of severe disappointment was her 'Vissi
> d'arte'. True, she had arrived with a heavy cold and was said
> to be singing on the first night with bronchitis and a middling
> high fever. Whatever the reason, her sustained legato singing
> was only patchily beautiful, and the excitement of her perform-
> ance lay in her *parlando* or *arioso* singing but supremely in her
> acting.

That review by Martin Cooper in *Musical America* is similar to the one by Desmond Shawe-Taylor in *Opera News*, who also found the 'astonishing intensity and subtlety of the singing actress' sufficient compensation for 'vocalising which was so faulty and at moments painful'. Zeffirelli later related that Callas only agreed to sing Puccini's tortured heroine on condition that she worked with him: 'Franco, I will do it if you help me.' His conception was of an 'exuberant, warm-hearted and rather sloppy, everyday woman, an Anna Magnani of her time. She should not be sophisticated and elegant. How I hate the grand lady who poses, the great diva who appears with four dozen roses in her arms, a cane, gloves and picture hat with feathers, immaculately dressed as if she were going to visit the Queen or even the Pope. Tosca was never like that.'

What was Tosca like? How does her vocal acting relate to the undeniable defects and weaknesses of the voice which all the critics mention? In other words – is it not a euphemism to praise the acting? Is it not an overgenerous excuse for weaknesses which would never be forgiven Montserrat Caballé or Kiri te Kanawa? In any case why was she singing so-called verismo music – which she disliked, as we have mentioned several times – while she still had the vocal and technical mastery to sing the more varied and differentiated music of Rossini, Donizetti, Bellini and Verdi?

These questions need to be examined in greater depth if we are to define precisely Maria Callas's importance for singing acting and for acting singing – and her importance for opera itself. We must also take into account the actual composition of *Tosca*, and Victorien Sardou's drama of 1887. Maurice Baring wrote of Sarah Bernhardt's portrayal that the role would not exist if anyone else were entrusted with it. The part, and Bernhardt with it, travelled the world as a theatrical masterpiece which even Proust enthused about. Puccini was another glowing admirer of the *tragédienne*, and it was he who once admitted, as a 'visual' person and a 'man of the theatre', that he 'could never write a note' without envisaging each scene clearly before him.

It was through Bernhardt's portrayal that the composer first got to know the drama of Sardou's thriller which was sensational in its sadism – Sardou himself summed up his theatrical recipe thus: 'Torture the heroine.' When Puccini came to set the text to music, he was setting not just a literary model, but also its realisation in theatrical terms. In contrast to many works of the second half of the nineteenth century, which followed the ground plan of grand opera, the plot of *Tosca* is constructed with a precision of pure mechanism. Psychological representation or development of character is not called for; it is simply a matter of stage effects which make the description 'shabby little shocker' not really so inappropriate.

Puccini removed all political references and aspects because he was interested only in 'the great pain suffered by small souls', as he put it to the poet Gabriele d'Annunzio. Puccini learned from Wagner how to combine thematic particles with the development of the plot.[1] From it he developed specific vocal gestures of pronounced illustrative energy, making the gestures – as in the first act love duet – into the actual dramatic and musical theme. When Cavaradossi is asked the question 'Non sei contento?' and in distraction absent-mindedly replies 'Tanto!', Tosca demands 'Tornalo a dir!' (Say that again!'). When she repeats 'Tanto!' with false emphasis, she says 'Lo dici male . . . lo dici male' ('You say it badly'). It is the actress, the jealous woman, criticising his bad acting. It is Julian Budden's view that Puccini altered the gestures of the original literary figure by means of the leitmotif technique.

And yet the first transformation into theatrical exaltation – or what we could call today the operatic – was brought about by Bernhardt. Apart from a silent film which she dismissed, there are only literary descriptions of her performances. But these are extraordinarily telling. They show that Bernhardt combined the high tone of classical French verse drama with the sentimental pathos of melodrama, developing out of the synthesis a stylised artistic language – a style which, since Brecht, has virtually disappeared from the theatre. Bernhardt noted this herself: 'Without being conscious of it at the time, I created my own personal technique of rendering *the resonating music of the verse, the melody of the words* as tangible as music and the melody of thought' (my italics).

The theatrical historian Jules Lemaître reported how she recited entire sentences and even longer stretches 'on a single note [!] and without variation' and certain sentences 'an octave higher'. The conductor and composer Reynaldo Hahn, who demanded from the singer a limitless range of colouring, enthused about Bernhardt's 'voice of bronze' and the 'moving notes produced from the depth of her breast'. The counterpart to the emotional musicality of speech was formed by her expressive, almost eccentric acting power. Hahn observed in the course of her performance 'terrible changes' of facial expression, and Hugues Le Roux could see the most hideous scene of torture taking place in her 'distorted features' as if in a mirror. Puccini's librettists took Bernhardt's acting as a form of stage direction and transferred it into the extensive language of the opera. An example is the pantomime with its cinematic effects after Scarpia has been stabbed. This diverges considerably from the normal course of conventional vocal aesthetics. Of the 780 bars of music which Tosca has to sing (over 250 in Act 1, over 230 in Act 2 and barely 200 in Act 3), many of these are permeated by emotional gestures, screams and cries, suggestions of meaning and indirect expression. There are scarcely any extended *cantabile* passages or endless arches of melody as in Bellini, Donizetti or Verdi, and even the 200 seconds of singing in 'Vissi d'arte' follow straight on from the exaltation of the torture scene with its top Bs and Cs at screaming pitch.

William James Henderson made a very pointed remark when he stated that many singers – and he was thinking of Emma Eames – had fallen ill with 'Toscalitis'. In other words, Tosca cannot be tackled simply. The role demands simultaneous attention to gesture, vocal shaping and modulation. No other singer has filled Tosca's sentiment and pathos with as much energy, emotion, fire, anger and desperation as Maria Callas: 'È l'Attavanti!', 'Assassino!, 'Quanto? . . . Il prezzo!', 'Muori, muori dannato' or the legendary 'E avanti a lui tremava tutta Roma'. What pathos she brings to her scarcely audible, choking sigh, after the octave fall at the end of her prayer. What a sound of pain in the phrase 'Dio mi perdona. Egli vede chi'io piango', when Tosca staggers from the church after Scarpia has sown the seeds of her doubt. Most singers take the text as a stage direction and fill their singing with sobs. But Callas *sings* with a voice itself choking with tears, a sobbing which can be heard, visualised and emotionally experienced in the sound.

With Callas's second *Tosca* recording under Georges Prêtre (1964) in our ears and looking again at Harold Rosenthal's review, it becomes clear why the English critic is less concerned with how she sang or how her top range was working than with examining in detail her vocal gestures, the melody of the words and the music resonating from the verse. In contrast to Callas's Norma, Lucia, Gilda and Violetta, this Tosca is less a vocal portrait than a theatrical portrayal. At various points in Zeffirelli's recollections of the performance the words 'real' and 'realistic' occur – and he refers to that realism, the use of gesture and expression which we are accustomed to in opera and the cinema from that period. It is a realism which dispenses with all the elements of stylisation – and mediation. There are a large number of photographs of the performances and the 1965 revival as well as the filmed version of the second act. These all bring the entire performance back to vivid life for the attentive and imaginative onlooker – each of the photographs expresses a thrilling tension.

On the morning of the third performance, 27 January 1964, Sir Neville Cardus, doyen of English music critics, published an open letter to the soprano in the *Guardian*. In it he wrote:

> Really, dear Madame Callas, your admirers are your worst enemies. They emphasise too much how your voice is better than ever before. As far as I am concerned, I almost wish that it was worse. Then at least one could hope that you might liberate yourself from those few more-or-less brainless roles in Italian opera. A high shriek can be fatal for a singer of roles like Norma, Elvira or Lucia. And yet a loud scream can be a histrionic achievement when you react with the body, the eyes and the temperament as much as with the voice, like Kundry in *Parsifal* or Elektra [. . .]. Opera for you should be the world of Wagner, Strauss, Berg and other composers who would contribute something to your intelligence, giving it something to get its teeth into [. . .]

Cardus's letter was certainly well-intended, to be taken as a compliment to an artist born to higher things – a typical critic's view. But crass nonsense of this kind is really worse than naïve idolatry. There is no need to discuss here whether some of Callas's Italian roles sounded 'brainless'; but to suggest to a singer who could only just manage Tosca under circumstances of great tension that she should be singing Kundry or Elektra or perhaps Berg's Lulu or Marie, testifies not just to thoughtlessness but to a poor understanding of the qualities and capabilities of a voice. Even the young Callas did not really have the voice for Brünnhilde, Isolde or Turandot; they are roles which she mastered by sheer will power, although she herself when asked replied, 'Not will-power, but love!'

Shortly after these London appearances she returned to the recording studios in Paris. She finished the second Verdi recital and began a third one, and also a Rossini and Donizetti record. The Verdi recordings were not brought out until eight years later; even if one can admire their great moments and discount their weaknesses, those recordings can scarcely be counted among her best.

There was an interesting incident in the studios. The soprano had become almost hysterical in her nervousness and a pause was necessary, during which Michel Glotz put on a recording of Aida's 'Ritorna vincitor' sung by Régine Crespin. Rescigno observed an immediate change in Callas. 'That is not Verdi, and it is not Aida,' she cried, 'it's like a funeral march. Come, Nicola, let's try it.' She recorded the aria in a single take – with a dramatic fire that recalled former splendours.

It seemed as if the singer might still be able to return to her true profession. But all she could summon was will-power or, to use her own word, 'love' for singing. It was enough for eight appearances in Bellini's *Norma* at the Paris Opéra, three in May and five in June 1964; after that, another six months' silence. In her adopted city, Paris, she had previously appeared in the Opéra on only one single occasion, for a gala in 1958 for the Légion d'honneur. She had lived there for six years, but it was less as a singer than as an honoured guest in salons of the wealthy and of couturiers.

In those circumstances her first Norma on 22 May 1964 can be

regarded as her proper début in Paris. The producer, as for the
London *Tosca*, was Franco Zeffirelli, and the costumes were
designed by Marcel Escoffier, with Georges Prêtre conducting.
The producer went out of his way to assist and promote her. It
was unimportant to him that the voice broke on occasional top
notes – those on the leger lines – he knew that most of the
audience would not notice unless she sang those optional notes
which would have involved transposition of tricky passages.
Many critics, and even conductors, consider this impermissible,
yet in the nineteenth century transpositions were a matter of
course, except in concerted music. No composer expected a singer
with a lower voice to sing music written for a high soprano in
the original key.

Zeffirelli went as far as suggesting that she should avoid
'unreasonable demands on her voice'. But she replied: 'Franco, I
can't do that. I will not do what Anna Moffo does in *La Traviata*.
I will not skate through the music. I have to take my chances,
even if at the risk of a disaster or even if it might mean the end
of my career. I must try to produce all the notes even if I miss
one.'

This was precisely what happened at one performance. She
missed a top C in the last act – it broke with a sound which
Zeffirelli said he had never heard in his life. The audience seemed
to groan in horror and, panic-stricken, the orchestra stopped
playing. Ignoring the cruel shouts and hissing of a few insensitive
fanatics, and horrified and annoyed with herself, she began the
scena again and reached the C. Pandemonium then broke out in
the house. There were shouts of anger and protest, which were
answered by shouts in defence of the singer. An elderly lady of
dignified appearance is reported to have snatched the spectacles off
one opponent. Stassinopoulos tells how Yves St Laurent angrily
kicked a man hurling abuse. The republican guard had to be
called to curb the arguments and attacks; meanwhile Callas was
congratulated by Princess Grace, the Chaplins, Onassis and
Rudolf Bing. Bing later said that he did not know whether he
should make any reference backstage to the disaster. 'It is like a
woman wearing a dress which is too low-cut – one does not
know whether it is more tactful to look at it or to turn one's gaze

elsewhere.' Bing looked away, and Callas made no reference to the incident.

Again, a clear picture can again be formed from the factual and critical reports. Harold Rosenthal wrote in *Opera* in August 1964 that high society would have deemed it a *faux pas* not to have been seen at the Opéra in May and June 1964. Although the Callas *Norma* was *the* event, *Don Giovanni* was playing with Nicolai Ghiaurov, Verdi's *Don Carlo* with Ghiaurov, Rita Gorr and Franco Corelli, and *Tosca* with Régine Crespin, Franco Corelli and Gabriel Bacquier.

The public could not realise that singing Norma was something quite different from acting Tosca. Nor could they be expected to accept harsh and even ugly notes above F and G, or to listen with the ears – the artistic sense and the musicality – of Andrew Porter:

> I went to the second performance to discover that hearing Callas shape Bellini's melody is still one of those revelatory experiences comparable, perhaps, to hearing Casals play Bach. Eloquent line can never have been more beautifully moulded. Callas has a superlative technique to draw a subtle, flexible line, exquisitely controlled, and ravishing in timbres ranging between soft compassion ('Oh, di qual sei tu vittima') and fierceness ('In mia man'). Only at climaxes above the stave is the line drawn with a slate pencil. The voice will not take pressure today; it could not ring out as it once did to dominate the great twin climaxes of the finale, and an attempt to throw out a bold, ferocious high C ('e di sangue scorgeran torrenti') brought momentary disaster. Yet I feel sorry for anyone who, after ninety-nine perfect notes forming one sublime phrase, then finds all spoiled by a single horrid, or fairly horrid, sound.

There was not a single critic who did not agree that 'the ugly notes were uglier than before' (Porter), but nor was there one who did not agree that 'despite her faulty technique she could still get more from the Bellini role than any other singer' (Rosenthal) and that, like no other singer, she knew how to give significance to every word, weight to every accent, form to every melody and colour to every sound. It is obvious from the reports that she could no longer, as earlier, keep at the same level for several consecutive performances and that she was now subject to considerable fluctuations of form.

Just four weeks after the last *Norma* (24 June 1964) she began recording Bizet's *Carmen* under George Prêtre with Nicolai Gedda as Done José, Andrea Guiot as Micaela and Robert Massard as Escamillo. It was her only recording of a French opera, but unfortunately it employed the standard version with recitatives by Ernest Guiraud. It was not until a decade later that Leonard Bernstein, Georg Solti and Claudio Abbado recorded the versions with spoken dialogue edited by Oeser and Dean.

This Guiraud version deprives the imaginative interpreter of the chance to give life to the character by means of nuance in the dialogue. Vocally Callas was on acceptable form even though her top was hard and the sound was under threat when she attempted any dynamic gradation.

In Paris on 3 December 1964 she began her second recording of Puccini's *Tosca*, again conducted by George Prêtre. Tito Gobbi sang the police chief Scarpia, as in the earlier version, and Carlo Bergonzi the role of the painter. This recording was intended to serve as soundtrack for the film of *Tosca* which Zeffirelli had been planning for a long time. At first the soprano hesitated to take on a new medium, and when she did at last agree it transpired that Ricordi, Puccini's publishers, had already sold the film rights to a German company. The recording was promoted in a blaze of publicity – which reflected the considerable production costs – but does not compare with the first recording. Victor de Sabata was not just the more subtle and varied conductor but also possessed more sense of the opera's theatrical drama. Many of the gestures which emerged as spontaneous in the first version, particularly the confrontation of Tosca and Scarpia in Act 2, now seem calculated, mannered and even externalised. Tito Gobbi does not completely avoid the danger of making the police chief into a B-movie villain.

The new year began with nine performances of *Tosca*. Zeffirelli's London production was transferred to the Paris Opéra with such overwhelming success that the eight performances of her contract were increased to nine. These took place between 19

February and 13 March. Immediately afterwards she flew to New York and sang two more performances of the Puccini opera, one with Franco Corelli as Cavaradossi and the other with Richard Tucker. Gobbi was again Scarpia. It was the same old production she had sung in on her last Met appearance on 5 March 1958, and it had now become even more shabby and shoddy than it had been before.

There was not a single stage or costume rehearsal, but she did not protest. Shortly before the curtain was due to rise the applause started. It was for Jacqueline Kennedy, wife of the assassinated president, making her way to her seat. When Maria Callas appeared on stage after the three cries of 'Maria' the applause reached such thunderous proportions that the performance was interrupted for several minutes. For the entire duration she did not step out of character: she did not smile, bow or express any thanks. She remained Tosca.

Stassinopoulous claims that the critics were united in praise, but that was not really the case. Certainly, Alan Rich wrote in the *New York Herald Tribune*, 'The voice I heard last night was not the voice of a woman that, in some respects, was in any sort of vocal trouble whatever. It had a creamy lightness to it which summoned up memories of her earliest recordings. She has somehow achieved this without losing her astounding ability to make the voice the servant of the drama [. . .] it was – simply as singing – one of the most remarkable achievements that I can recall.'

On the other hand Harold Schonberg wrote in the *New York Times:* 'But now we come to matters vocal, and the story is less pleasant. Miss Callas is operating these days with only the remnants of a voice. Her top, always insecure, is merely a desperate lunge at high notes. She sings almost without support, and her tones are shrill, squeezed, and off-centre.' Who is to be believed? The review by Alan Rich is vague in matters of vocal and technical considerations. But as we have live recordings of both performances it can be heard that she is in extreme difficulty in the exposed passage of Act 2, with the C emerging shrill and the climactic phrase of 'Vissi d'arte' coming to grief – Ardoin says that a squawk replaces the top B; yet the singing here is more spontaneous than in the recording with Prêtre.

All this shows that the fame had long become separated from its owner, the singer now being treated like a sacred cow. Yet news about the New York triumphs which was put into perspective in the musical press (as, for example, the report in the July issue of *Opera*, at a time when she should have long since left the operatic stage), merely served to heighten expectations in Paris.

In May she intended to sing five performances of *Norma*, starting on 14 May. On the final evening she was unable to complete the last act. She had returned in a state of complete exhaustion and was only able to get on stage with the help of various injections. In a conversation with John Ardoin (quoted by Stassinopoulos) she said, almost in tears at the thought of this and other performances which were like a crucifixion, 'Can you please go out there and tell them that I am a human being fighting with my anxiety?' At the first performance, with Giulietta Simionato as her partner, she asked the audience for their indulgence because of an indisposition. Simionato's considerate support also contributed to her getting through the first two evenings.

For the third performance Fiorenza Cossotto replaced Simionato. After the first act Maria Callas had to have medication for her high blood pressure. During the interval she lay on a couch in her dressing room, her strength all gone. Cossotto took advantage of the weakness of her colleague, who with only the remnants of a voice could still sing better and more expressively than Cossotto has ever done in her entire life. Cossotto sang out with full voice, holding all her top notes longer than Callas could.

The 29 May performance turned into a catastrophe – Zeffirelli recalls: 'Norma and Adalgisa have to sing their duet in close harmony. When Maria signalled that she needed to end a phrase Cossotto ignored her and held on to her final notes for a few seconds more. What a lack of generosity. Maria was hurt. I went backstage and swore to Cossotto that I would never work with her again. And I never did.' On 29 May Cossotto changed the duet into a duel. Callas tried to fight back but left the stage in a trance after the first scene of Act 2, and then collapsed. She was carried unconscious to her dressing room, and the performance was abandoned.

An hour later she was escorted from the theatre, whispering

apologies to the crowd of onlookers, but there was no repeat of the events in Rome. The critics were equally considerate. Jacques Bourgeois, an old admirer, remarked in the periodical *Arts* that it was admirable and an expression of 'her rare sense of professional duty' that she had sung in spite of illness; he also emphasised that her singing had shown not the slightest sign of vocal weakness. If ever there was an affirmation of Wagner's report of Wilhelmine Schröder-Devrient having no voice left and yet making beautiful use of her breathing to express a truly feminine soul, then it was supplied by these performances of *Norma*, parts of which survive in recordings.

Contrary to Zeffirelli's recollection she does sing the C at the end of the Act 1 cabaletta and an A instead of C in 'Ah' sì fa core'. But in the final scene the C emerges like lava from a volcano. And then, what *legato*, what line and siren-like *cantabile* in the middle range – bel canto in the purest, most beautiful and expressive sense. Joachim Kaiser wrote a wonderful review:

But how did she sing? [. . .] the answer is: it is part of the phenomenon and the problem of Maria Callas that this is not the question which one immediately asks when seeing and hearing her. And the answer to the question as to Callas's stature is linked precisely to what need one feels to discuss her vocal qualities. After a pause of some years, a pause which was unwise in musical terms, Miss Callas finds that singing is just one of numerous ways in which she can express herself through acting. But as her expression glows with more all-consuming intensity than anything one might encounter on today's operatic stages, she is judged either belatedly or even not at all by an entire world of music lovers, people who would normally attach great importance to perfection and would be annoyed or hiss at wrong notes where previously they had worshipped her. This amazing woman, heroine, artist strives with all her physical and vocal powers of expression to master the vocal demands of grand opera. One senses with sympathy that she is insecure, that she is dependent on chance and that she is fallible. One tries for as long as possible to give these things less importance than her unique powers of embodiment, to ignore the wrong notes and to give oneself up to the force of this Eleonora Duse born out of her time. But suddenly one realises that one is starting to deceive oneself. Yet the fascination of Callas leads a public, itself described as ferocious, to suffer with her, to accept all the evasions and all the cunning manoeuvres with a palpitating heart, not whistling but groaning when a note is fudged or simply missing. It is the groan of sympathy, as if one were witnessing a beautiful and wounded martyr throwing herself at several lions at the same time.

Kaiser then continued with detailed reference to weaknesses, to breaks in the voice and their inferences:

Her personality still continues to exercise fascination. But one is highly disturbed by the voice's insecurity and by the difference between a relatively astringent lower register, a middle voice that is quite different, a coloration facility which is still passable but a top that is now strained to excess [. . .] the Callas miracle is now almost an anti-voice miracle. [2]

After her collapse there were four weeks to recuperate on board the *Christina;* then four *Tosca* performances scheduled for London. She was due to arrive there on 28 June 1965. But her state of health did not allow the journey to England. The day before the first scheduled performance she had to telephone Webster to say that her doctor had advised her not to appear. Of course the performances, in which Renato Cioni, Tito Gobbi and George Prêtre were also taking part, were sold out; Callas fans had queued days and nights for tickets, and the last performance on 5 July was to be a royal gala.

After much discussion Callas agreed to do one performance in order to prove to the English public, which had always been loyal and fair, that she was not acting out of caprice. None the less, sections of the London press did react in great anger to her cancellation. The first three performances were sung by Marie Collier. Maria Callas arrived in London on 3 July. The *Daily Express* carried a report that a Canadian businessman in an adjoining suite at the Savoy Hotel had listened to her one night singing parts of *Tosca*. His view was that she had been in good voice. What the audience for the benefit gala on 5 July 1965 heard was a voice produced with the utmost caution. The ardour of earlier performances was virtually no longer in evidence. And yet seldom had she sung 'Vissi d'arte' with more feeling and expression than in this her very last operatic performance. The listener experienced the suffering of an entirely introverted voice, singing with almost *Lieder*-like inwardness and delicacy.

Maria Callas could scarcely have envisaged that this appearance would be her last on stage. There were plans for appearances as Norma in London and Violetta and Medea in Paris. Yet all these plans foundered, and the artist sank into a world of shadow. She spent the summer on Skorpios. She continued making plans, looking for new ways to continue her career. Her desperation was intensified as her relations with Onassis came to be more and more dictated by his moods and malice, things which only come to light when a man has lost respect for a woman. 'What are you? Nothing!', he is supposed to have said to her face. 'All you have in your throat is a whistle which no longer functions.' Onassis sometimes behaved in such an insulting manner that Zeffirelli, unsuccessfully, tried to question him over his disgraceful behaviour. Sandor Gorlinsky, Callas's London agent, was present when he screamed at her 'Hold your tongue . . . you are nothing but a night-club singer.' Gorlinsky went on to say: 'I just hoped that she would grab the nearest bottle and strike him over the head. But she just got up and left the room. She was completely under his thumb.' As Arianna Stassinopoulos reports, she was not even permitted to bring into the world the child she had long wished for – provided, that is, that this publicly spoken wish was not really the expression of anxiety in the face of continuing, or having to continue, a career of which she was no longer mistress.

Ora posso morir

'Women of particular beauty are condemned to unhappiness' writes Theodor W. Adorno in his *Minima Moralia*:[3]

Even those for whom all conditions are favourable and who are supported by their birth, wealth or talent, seem to be pursued or possessed by a pressure to destroy themselves and all the human relations which they enter into. An oracle forces them to choose between fates. Then they have to pay for the conditions with their happiness; as they can no longer love, they poison the love shown towards them and are left empty-handed. Or the privilege of beauty gives them the courage and security to renounce the agreement. They take the promised good fortune seriously and do not spare themselves, encouraged in this by everybody's suggestion that proving their own value is not a first priority.

Maria Callas had become a martyr to her career and then a martyr to longed-for and denied happiness. Her character and the ideal of feminity which formed it and which she used to project herself – both were products of masculine society. Quoting Adorno again, this society breeds in women 'their own corrective and reveals itself as a relentless master in its selectivity'. As if by the demonic singing teacher Svengali, the talent, ambition, inferiority complex and musicality of a young girl had been used by Serafin, Meneghini and Legge to create a unique artistic figure. An artistic figure who would become world famous. The reverse side of this career, this career which was at once grandiose, grotesque and – not through her own fault – dubious, made its appearance when the artist wanted to embody a different ideal of femininity: that of the beautiful, idolised woman. As she gradually started to adapt to the fashionable image of beautiful woman, and then to the image of desirable lover, she plunged into unhappiness.

The last years of Maris Callas have been the subject of endless writings. After her divorce from Meneghini she had no privacy. The intimate and personal were transformed into the 'obscene', as David A. Lowe put it: 'One reads the book with fascination,' he writes of The Woman Behind the Legend, 'but needs to take a shower afterwards.' Nadia Stancioff and Callas's sister Jackie too have written books which are mere gossip and muckraking.

The last twelve years of Maria Callas's life – from 5 July 1965, when she last appeared on the operatic stage, until 16 September

1977, when she died in Paris – have little to do with the story of the singer and her influence. They were twelve years of progressive and desperate failure. The great director Joseph Losey wanted her to play the role of an ageing actress in *Boom!*, based on a character from Tennessee Williams' *The Night of the Iguana*, a forgotten star living on her own memories and visited by an angel of death. But Maria Callas did not want to start her film career, which had been talked about ever since Carl Foreman had wanted her for *The Guns of Navarone*, by portraying an ageing actress.

Visconti wanted her to appear in a film about Puccini in which she would have played a singer resembling Maria Jeritza but the plan fell through. The only constant thing in these years was her unreliability, but it was not the unreliability of mood or caprice, rather of anxiety and insecurity. It was an unreliability which exactly corresponded to that of her voice, which, as Rémy writes, would one moment produce the most beautiful sound and the next moment the harshest scream. Until 1967 Michel Glotz was trying to get her back to the stage and recording studio, but his attempts were fruitless. Visconti was due to produce Verdi's *La Traviata* with her at the Paris Opéra; but both producer and singer proposed conditions which exceeded any affordable cost. Callas said that she asked for twenty to thirty days of orchestral and choral rehearsal, but because this was not agreed the project was abandoned.

There is no reason to doubt her, but the real reason why the project foundered was that no impresario, director or conductor could be found with the faith to do it, even with twenty or thirty days' rehearsal – it must be assumed that in 1970 there were still theatres which would have made the impossible possible in order to get a Callas performance. As late as 1968 EMI had planned a recording of *La Traviata* which had to be called off because Callas had broken some ribs in a fall – but could she really still have sung Violetta in 1968? She was keen to start again after the Onassis relationship broke up. She had even started work again with her old teacher Elvira de Hidalgo with a view to sorting out the problems and weaknesses which had forced her, not yet forty-three years old, to give up the stage.

But when in February 1969 she came back to Paris recording

studios to perform arias from *I Vespri Siciliani, Il Corsaro, I Lom-bardi* and *Attila* under the direction of Nicola Rescigno, she left out a whole series of top notes, which were intended to be inserted later. Rescigno later told how she progressed 'inch by inch', scarcely capable of singing through a few phrases, let alone an entire aria. For Rescigno it was 'nerve-racking work', because he sensed how Callas had lost all her self-confidence. The recording of a single aria emerged as a sort of patchwork, and as such the sort of manipulation of which the gramophone is repeatedly – and unjustifiably! – accused. There is absolutely no objection to a wrong note being edited out and improved upon: no objection to an important phrase being repeated again and again until the 'ideal' is reached. Even the rehearsals leading up to an actual performance are concerned with this striving for perfection. How-ever, these late recordings ultimately captured only the embers of a vocal and artistic legacy which had long since burned itself out – notwithstanding the fact that the other participants felt themselves honoured that she had not given up completely.

'If the film had been successful, it would not only have brought her back to dry land but would have meant a new start to her career,' Stassinopoulos wrote of Maria Callas's attempt at starting a new second career. Directed by Pier Paolo Pasolini she played Medea, not the Medea of Cherubini's opera but the one adapted 'for modern tastes'. However, modern times had little taste for 'classical mythology' and looked on the classical idea of tragedy as archaic. The film did not succeed, which was probably appro-priate, since it had absolutely no relevance for its time and was as out of touch as the director Pasolini's aesthetics and artistic and political morals. The film had little spoken dialogue and made little of Callas's dramatic art. It was shown in the Paris Opéra on 28 January 1970 as part of a gala which celebrated nothing but the myth of Callas. The *beau monde* attended and celebrated – but who, what and why? The film paid no homage to the singer, and if it did so to the actress, it was only as a recollection of the singer who, although repeatedly invited by Luchino Visconti, refused to appear again as an actress, as if she realised that another film would have ended the myth and finally destroyed it.

And yet, with a strangely consequential inner logic, the myth was perpetuated. In 1971 and 1972 Maria Callas gave a few master classes in the United States. The first attempt, at Philadelphia's famous Curtis Institute of Music was abandoned after the second session, because the school had not been able to offer students of sufficient aptitude to engage the singer's interest. At least that was Rémy's explanation. But what does it really mean? It was not really a question of finding her a new objective, not a question of changing from singer to teacher, but of finding a way for her to portray herself by other means, of perpetuating the myth. A few months later the experiment was repeated at the Juilliard School in New York. Some of the learning sessions were recorded, and John Ardoin also published a transcription of the master classes.[4] Conductor Nicola Rescigno writes in the preface:

> This is a book about tradition – a way of performing opera that goes beyond the printed page. It has come down to us by word of mouth and practice, often from the composer himself. For the first time, apart from Luigi Ricci's important collection of cadenzas and embellishments, this oral heritage is documented in print as practised by one of its major exponents, Maria Callas. This book is important not only because of what Callas stood for musically but because we are in danger of losing these traditions. They are still available to singers, but 'tradition' has become almost a dirty word.

What Rescigno is indirectly saying is that in her master classes Callas is not putting into practice any method or technique but attempting to give lectures about vocal acting, expression, embellishment, treatment of words and style. When reading the book, a listener who has feeling and imagination and is also familiar with the music comes to realise what endless trouble she must have taken as a singer to give not only every word its weight, but every syllable its appropriate accent and colour – we are given a microscopic view of her technique, and especially a glimpse into her extraordinary talent and artistic understanding.

We suddenly realise that even breathing is something other than an intake of air: as Rescigno says, it could be 'a sigh, a laugh, a groan or a chuckle'; we recognise that in spite of all her talent, or perhaps through it, she was not relying on her vocal capabilities but instead was working in a tireless and disciplined, even fanatical fashion; it becomes clear to us that singing is comprised of hundreds of details which have to be laboriously learned and practised incessantly, and that it is not sufficient just to sing but rather to lift those limitations which singing can impose on an actor. It is also clear from her classes how it is possible for a singer to move on stage and to co-ordinate sound and gesture.

Her master classes at the Juilliard School, which she had been invited to hold by Peter Mennin, president of that world-famous institution, took place in October and November 1971 and in February and March 1972. They were given the title 'The Lyric Tradition'. Twenty-five singers were selected from around 300 applicants. The classes covered a wide musical spectrum, ranging from Mozart arias from *Don Giovanni* ('Non mi dir'), *Così fan tutte* ('Come scoglio') and *Die Zauberflöte* (Pamina's 'Ach, ich fühls's' and the Queen of Night's arias), to Beethoven's 'Ah! perfido' and 'Abscheulicher', Cherubini's *Medea* and Spontini's *La Vestale*, from Rossini's *Il Barbiere* and *La Cenerentola* to Bellini's *Il Pirata*, *La Sonnambula*, *Norma* and *I Puritani*, from Donizetti's *Lucia*, *Anna Bolena* and *Don Pasquale* to thirteen different operas by Verdi. Arias from the French repertoire were taken from *La Damnation de Faust*, *Faust*, *Roméo et Juliette*, *Carmen*, and *Werther*. In addition there were arias from Italian opera of the turn of the century: *La Gioconda*, *Mefistofele*, *Pagliacci*, *Cavalleria Rusticana*, *Manon Lescaut*, *La Bohème*, *Tosca*, *Madama Butterfly*, *Andrea Chénier* and *Adriana Lecouvreur*.

Callas did not restrict herself to dealing with soprano arias, and even took on the impersonation of Verdi's Rigoletto – as can be heard on one of the recordings. Ardoin emphasises that she was not attempting to get young colleagues to imitate her but was concerned with giving her suggestions and advice on technique and style, and thereby on musicianship. It speaks for itself that the sessions were visited by singers like Placido Domingo, Tito Gobbi, Elisabeth Schwarzkopf and Bidu Sayão, but also by Franco Zeffirelli, the pianist Alexis Weissenberg, the actress Lilian Gish and her colleague Ben Gazzara. Callas passed on to the young singers, something of what she herself had learned from 'giants like Tullio Serafin and Victor de Sabata' (Ardoin).

It is no exaggeration when Ardoin points out that these sessions were also of compulsive interest to instrumentalists. Pianists like Vladimir Horowitz and Claudio Arrau were self-confessed lovers of singing all their lives and actually said that they had modelled their tone on the sound of the human voice and their phrasing on the breathing of the singer. It should not be overlooked that Chopin advised his pupils to attend performances by Henriette Sontag or Giuditta Pasta and to learn from these performances. One could hear Callas talking about Callas, especially with regard to the art of dramatic acting by means of singing. And there were moments, which can be heard on the recording, where Callas sang phrases and sequences in her hoarse or harshly burning voice in a way which none of the students could hope to do.

Less successful was her attempt at producing. In April 1973 she directed *I Vespri Siciliani* at the Teatro Regio in Turin, the very work in which she had made her actual début at La Scala. Her insistence on having Giuseppe di Stefano as co-director caused the conductor Gianandrea Gavezzeni to withdraw from a production which in any case received little acclaim. Franco Zeffirelli soberly stated that one can only teach and pass on what one has learned and that Callas had never learned to 'command and control the stage physically', her intuition as a performer did not extend to the planning and staging of a production.

It was however her intuition that abandoned her when in September 1973 she was persuaded by Giuseppe di Stefano, who unlike her had abused his gifts, to make a comeback. The tenor had said that his sole wish was to 'bring Maria Callas back to life, because without the stage and music she was like someone buried alive'. Caught up in a late affair with her earlier partner, she threw all caution to the winds. She abandoned herself to sing with a partner whose voice only worked at maximum tension, whereas hers needed to be reduced with utmost caution; abandoned herself to accompanied recitals where every weakness would be twice as evident; abandoned herself to a game of chance although she knew precisely that her singing had always needed the context of drama that stage and orchestra supplied. The tour was to start with a

concert in London, for which the Royal Festival Hall received
25,000 ticket orders. The BBC intended to broadcast it and EMI
to make a live recording. Three days beforehand, Maria Callas
withdrew. The official reason was trouble with her eyes. Perhaps
it was prudence.

The tour commenced in Hamburg on 25 October 1973. It was
my first meeting with the singer. It was a terrible experience,
remaining even more painfully in my memory than 16 September
1977. That was the day on which a respectful, shaken world heard
of her death.

The Janus Head

'No pain is greater than that of remembering
happiness in the midst of unhappiness'
                    Dante, *The Divine Comedy*

Maria Callas did not recognise herself in the picture which was
painted of her. It was an alien picture, distorted by gossip and
rumour, criticism and publicity, scandals and affairs, admiration
and despisal. And yet there is some foundation for all the disagreements and distortions. For Callas, both in her life and her art,
was an outsider. When she appeared on stage at the end of the
1940s and the beginning of the 1950s, she was a reincarnation of
the archetypal prima donna such as had last been a focus of
admiration, wonder and respect in Adelina Patti, Nellie Melba,
Mary Garden and Maria Jeritza. A prima donna is of necessity
an outsider. She is a person of presumptuousness and arrogance,
imagination and talent, flamboyance and discipline. If she does
not have an overwhelmingly beautiful voice and faultless technical
control, she must all the more have dramatic talent and an aura
of magnetism. She cannot live her life in a normal way; the
delights of normality are denied her. Denied by her own vanity
and pride, her self-confidence and nervous sensibility. The energy
needed for such an existence was drawn, as in the case of many

others of genius, from that energy which Voltaire describes as demonic. Other elements of her character acted as counterbalances. Maria Callas was ugly as a child, was driven by a possessed and ambitious mother, suffered terrors, especially of crowds, and it took her immense courage to overcome not just the concrete fear of obstacles and inhibitions but also deep inner anxiety. There was little, almost nothing which did not cause difficulty; nothing came easily.

After she had fought her way to the top, where she herself proudly saw her throne, she did not take on that false modesty which Goethe described as the behaviour of scoundrels. Her reactions were spontaneous, violent, aggressive, proud, lacking in caution and sometimes appeared arrogant. But when viewed closely, much of her so-called scandalous behaviour was simply the outcome of her decisiveness and uprightness, less often of impulsiveness and scarcely ever of mere caprice. Maria Callas became famous, even notorious, for her supposedly capricious cancellations. How absurd, when in fact she sang 157 performances at La Scala up to 1960, out of which only two were cancelled? When it came to signing a contract there is truth in Carol Fox's statement that she was difficult, but once an agreement had been entered into, theatres, organisers and colleagues found her to be an utterly reliable artist and an incomparably serious musician.

Walter Legge was a sometimes merciless, even terrifying, producer in the recording studio, yet he was by no means the only one to find in Maria Callas a fellow perfectionist; she was admired by the great and the giants, whether Serafin or de Sabata, Visconti or Zeffirelli, Bernstein or von Karajan. In her work she was self-critical to the point of self-annihilation, and the only arguments which she provoked, for example with Boris Christoff and Giuseppe di Stefano, came about because she wanted to rehearse for longer and with more intensity and care than those who really needed it more than she did. It was unknown for her ever to come to rehearsal unprepared; such a thing would have been a minor scandal. In her feelings and behaviour towards colleagues, friends and partners she was a fanatic. With her, said Visconti, love and hate were absolute.

She would repel those who expected friendliness and flattery.

When she was dealing in particular with the outside world and especially with journalists, this literalness emerged as a fault and lack of diplomacy. She was supercilious in answering questions to the extent of making herself too clear and inflicting injury on herself; that is, she reacted in a way journalists like, only to find herself blamed and pilloried for being so open. These are all qualities which in a politician, entrepreneur or manager would be appreciated, but not in an artist and at a time when social, aesthetic and moral ideas were being reduced to a common level. Wearing expensive jewellery, having her clothes made by the best couturiers and owning 150 pairs of shoes sufficed to place her among the salon fauna: did this suit the greatest singer in the world, the priestess of art who embodied Medea, Norma and Violetta?

She was also an outsider as artist and singer. What were her origins? What was her training? What was her pedigree? Nicola Rescigno, whom we quoted in his preface to the transcript of the masterclasses, wrote that Callas passed on the secrets of the great vocal tradition in her teaching.

That is correct, though only half the truth. Correct in as much as she passed on to her students and immortalised in her records what she had learned from Elvira de Hidalgo, Tullio Serafin and Victor de Sabata or through her study of the vocalists from Concone and Panofka. But the only ones who can be part of a tradition are those who continue the work of their colleagues and who find successors, schools and students, and it remains to be asked whether her voice fitted into any tradition: her voice as sound, as conveyor of emotion and as object of feelings.

It is strange that this singer, who did more to renew Italian opera than any other, was un-Italian through and through, by virtue of origin, musical training and the sound of her voice. By origin she was a Greek *émigrée* (and ultimately without roots in social terms), underprivileged, unattractive and inhibited, lacking opportunity but ambitious. She took advantage of the chances which came her way, allowed herself to be moulded by Serafin and Legge – and formed herself according to the image she dreamed of, that of the beautiful woman which she eventually became in the mid–1950s.

She possessed talent and ambition, a limitless ambition which was perhaps even greater than the inferiority complex mentioned by Walter Legge. At the very moment when she stopped putting achieved beauty at the service of her art – as she had done under Visconti's careful guidance – and started using it to become a star, she became one of the *beau monde*, contact with whom she sought without ever feeling ultimately at ease.

Her self-stylisation – the elaborate pose and the carefully worked gesture – was overwhelming in the theatre, where it became a combination of grandiose distancing, artistic naturalness and imagined reality. Yet the pose of the dancer Taglioni, the violent, distorted, radiant suffering of Tosca, which were as unforgettable as the snow-white mask of Greta Garbo, have an effect which is unsympathetic when encountered on the street or in magazine photographs. Pictures of Callas are pictures from two separate worlds: those of the artistic figure – beautiful, full of authority, rich in expression, tender, moving; but also pictures of the star personality – exaggerated, harsh, false, showing a façade. Adelina Patti replied to the charge that for one concert she earned more than the president of the United States by saying, 'Let him sing'. Nellie Melba was not just a guest of the English royal family, she was a guest queen and could behave like one. In daily life she could not play the prima donna.

Callas could express her individuality only by means of her voice, could emancipate and assert herself only as a star. The voice was not rooted in any tradition. She learned to sing on a desert island – and like Robinson Crusoe she learned to live and to cultivate the art of survival. She never got the opportunity to settle into an ensemble like Rosa Ponselle, who, American by birth and Italian in origin, found her way at the Met into the circle and the influence of a Caruso, Mardones or Martinelli. That was a tradition to which Elvira de Hidalgo had to introduce her. But when one hears de Hidalgo's records, one can only feel amazement, irritation and perplexity and ask what influence such a singer could have had on Maria Callas. The Spanish soprano may have instructed Callas in the formal language of singing and explained to her the need for flexibility and agility, in other words the mechanics of singing. This provided the technique that enabled the Greek girl from New York to become Maria Callas.

What happened subsequently, between 1947 and 1950, was a break with tradition, a special departure, with bel canto being given an emphasis relevant to modern emotions. André Tubeuf wrote in his essay 'Callas the stylist'[5] that she projected the immense vision of Isolde on to the mental confusion of Elvira in *I Puritani*. Until Callas's arrival the mad heroines of Bellini and Donizetti had been sung by singers such as Toti dal Monte or Lily Pons – glittering blondes. Tubeuf asks how they could possibly portray full-blooded queens like Anna Bolena or Maria Stuarda.[6]

It was decisive that Callas sang roles like La Vestale, Sonnambula or Lucia right from the beginning as if they possessed the dramatic musical and intellectual weight of a Wagner role. And it was still more important that she recreated them with an emotional energy and richness of timbre and instrumental colour which had only come into existence with Wagner's orchestra. 'She owes her musical imagination to the orchestra as it had developed by the end of the nineteenth century' (Tubeuf). The modern orchestra from Berlioz to Debussy gives orchestral timbre its individuality, as is pointed out by Pierre Boulez in the notes to his Debussy recordings. He describes traditional orchestral dress as being replaced by an orchestration of invention, and the composer's imagination as no longer being restricted by first having to write the musical text and then clothing it with miracles of instrumentation; instead not only does the orchestration reflect the musical ideas, but the style of writing actually manifests itself in the orchestration.

The orchestra's variety of differences opened up possibilities of sound for the singer's voice. Callas could sing a lyrical legato line with the binding quality of a viola, and a dramatic one with the attack of a cello. At the top of her voice she had the colours of the oboe and flute, at the bottom the dark colour of the clarinet. She could shade the sound, give it opacity, sharpness or gleaming intensity. Tubeuf goes as far as to say that Callas was a singer without roots, but that as a musician she was German. The reason for this may be the French view that it was the Germans who took out a tenure on profundity.

The question which Tubeuf does raise is how it was possible

for Maria Callas to 'dictate' a style, and how she herself represented that style. She was first of all a special case, as she came from no tradition nor did she initiate one. She entered the stage like a planet which, in the words of Teodoro Celli, had strayed into an unfamiliar galaxy, causing alarm, furore, irritation and scandal and, after her farewell, initiating a cult.

It is beyond all doubt that she owes more to the gramophone record than to all her public appearances, that is the gramophone record as theatre of the imagination and stage. It is of course a truism to state that the record gives an artist a second existence. But at least one can say that a recording career is not now possible without making wide use of its aesthetic possibilities. Under the wise guidance of Walter Legge, Callas made the gramophone record into the theatre of vocal performance. Tubeuf's view is that Callas the stage performer was only understood by a few; this is clearly untrue. As Queen of La Scala she was acclaimed by the public and admired by most of the critics, especially in Visconti's productions. But recordings enabled her to take the role of orchestra or of the voice in all its colours and nuances; to be physically present and at the same time invisible, above all to divorce herself from the ritual surrounding the Callas personality.

The record led her to cultivate minimal and infinitesimal nuances, the finest inflections of the word and utmost concentration on the music. Her recordings are that rare type which one can listen to repeatedly and yet as if hearing them for the first time. In particular they possess an emotional intensity and presence whose aura remains with one even on repeated hearings.

Her departure from the stage went almost unnoticed because of the way in which it was extended over several years. But as an artist she became more and more present, more alive and more of a threat for those who came after her. Tubeuf points out how she scarcely moved on stage and yet gave the impression of moving a great deal. The recordings emphasise this: her singing does not possess the rapid agility of Sutherland but a tense mobility such as one finds only in the greatest dancers. Its secret lies in the ability to create an interplay of movement and relaxation or, putting it another way, the architecture of time. Callas's recitatives are primarily architectural images which retain their tension on repetition by means of countless *rubato* effects.

Callas may have learned much from her teacher Elvira de Hidalgo – technique, agility and the grammar of singing, yet one is struck by the fact that there are as good as no resemblances between de Hidalgo and Callas in their recordings of the same repertoire. The only parallels between them in matters of phrasing and embellishment are to be found in Proch's variations on 'De torna, mio ben'.

The 'vecchio lupo' Serafin may have shown her in all her finesse on stage. But the teacher to whom she owed most was the producer Walter Legge. He was uncompromising in the recording studio, and had a sense for an interpreter's potential, potential which he could extend much further than most producers; he possessed the imaginative power to produce a *mise-en-scène* in acoustic terms, to handle a recording with imagination and to conjure up singing through gesture – a visual sound.

Maria Callas herself stated that the art of opera had reached its final stage. Her rediscovery of singing was and remains life-giving. Those with a vested interest in defending opera counter the diagnosis that it is in a state of crisis or in its death agonies with the argument that talk about a crisis is as old as opera itself. Perhaps this is a clever defence, but it is scarcely judicious. Opera no longer exists as a living and topical art form but as a phenomenon, less than flourishing, of the culture industry. It is of concern only to the small number of those who patronise it. However, if music theatre without a stage – the music theatre of the imagination – is worth experiencing, then Callas's recordings, the tools of memory, will give many listeners an idea of what opera was, and how it can be. It is therefore possible that Maria Callas will still be finding an audience in 400 years time, when the Furies have finally obliterated opera.

But will it be the entire Maria Callas? Does the limitation of a recording not confine our aesthetic judgement? Does it really allow a complete judgement or appraisal of an interpreter? These questions are meaningless. Even an actual performance does not permit judgement of a singer's stature because the demands of conductor, producer and partners can jeopardise as easily as they can enhance, depending on whether they demand too little or too much. Many singers live with the firm conviction that they are never in good voice on the days when they must sing, and that they never have a performance when they would like to sing. In addition it must be remembered that while the dramatic power of acting can significantly complement the vocal capability, it is scarcely compensation for its absence.

It is much more a case of the actor's expressive strength becoming the very soul of singing. As an example, interpreters like Astrid Varnay or Gerhard Stolze were so convincing as actors on stage that one would tolerate any vocal weakness, yet it becomes difficult to be so tolerant when merely listening to a recording. Those who rely on recordings, using them as the tool of memory and taking them seriously as an aesthetic medium, do not need to concern themselves with the question of singing as *acting*. There is no listener or critic today who can recall from his own experience the actress Adelina Patti or Lilli Lehmann, or the theatrical art of Maurel, Tamagno, Battistini or Caruso. We turn to the tools of memory and supplement our listening with reading written documentation and perhaps also looking at pictures, a form of reading with the imagination. Without such documents we would know nothing of the art of the castrati or the dramatic portrayals of Schröder-Devrient, Pasta or Malibran. Since the invention of the time-machine, the record, it is possible for us to carry on what Emil Berliner called a dialogue with eternity, and we can check the written descriptions with the sound recordings. There are experts in the Anglo-Saxon world who claim that they can hear the singers in question when reading the opera reviews of Henry Chorley.

That may be. At least it may be possible. The listener who has thoroughly and carefully entered into that dialogue with eternity will be able to hear all that the records have preserved when he reads the reviews of Henry Krehbiel, George Bernard Shaw, Reynaldo Hahn, William James Henderson, Desmond Shawe-Taylor and Andrew Porter. But only film and video recordings can preserve the physical gesture and the charisma of an actor. Maria Callas was not filmed very often. Admittedly there are many penetrating and accurate descriptions of her acting, especially those by Visconti, Zeffirelli, and Sequi, but these eye-witness accounts only come alive for those who hear the voice. But if one hears the acting singer as opposed to what Felsenstein describes as the singing actor, one can actually form a *picture* of her. Restricting oneself to musical, vocal and sonic acting power enables one to concentrate in a way that is rarely possible in the theatre, and certainly never so for your average festival audience. Only with concentrated listening can one appreciate those nuances and details which are frequently overlooked in the theatre.

It is no accident that the fame of Callas the singer continued to grow in proportion to her withdrawal from the stage, and also from the social stage. The fame accorded her ability and significance, a fame which for a time became distorted by her world importance as star and personality, has lived on in the recordings. We hear from Maria Callas what was heard from Schröder-Devrient, that is singing which 'makes the eye powerless' and which conjures up for the imagination's own eye 'the inner being of human gesture'. Maria Callas belongs to that very small group of acting singers whom one can actually see all the more vividly when one can only hear them. The singing was the portrayal.

13

Singing for the Imagination

'What does the man perceive who appreci-
ates the real earnestness of a melody?
Nothing that can be conveyed by hearing it
again'

Ludwig Wittgenstein
Philosophical Studies II

Maria Callas and her Records

'Culture cannot be preserved alongside the
apparatus, it can only be saved as part of it'
Arnold Gehlen
The Soul in the Technical Age

Maria Callas is one of the first artists whose career and musical
work has been comprehensively documented by the gramophone
record – or more precisely, by the possibility of sound recording.
For it is the development of the tape recorder, and later the
transistor, which we have to thank for preserving, in whatever
sound quality, the performances of numerous artists. The first
studio recordings by Maria Callas, produced by Cetra in 1949,
appeared on 78 rpm discs, but four years later the singer was one
of the protagonists of the long-playing record, whose technical
possibilities brought about a new form and a new aesthetic for
opera production.

As documented by John Ardoin's *The Callas Legacy*, the singer's
discography spans a period of twenty-four years, from short
extracts from a performance of *Turandot* in Buenos Aires to her
farewell tour in 1973–4. As far as quantity is concerned the studio
recordings are only the nucleus of that discography. Maria Callas
recorded sixteen operas in the studio including works which she
never sang on the stage like *La Bohème, Manon Lescaut, Pagliaccci*
and *Carmen*; live recordings preserve a total of thirty-four of her
forty-seven roles. In addition there are numerous recitals and live
recordings from concerts.

Because the microphones in a studio hear differently to those
in an opera house or on the radio, the live and studio recordings
have to be judged by different standards. The undiscriminating
admiration of fans, for whom, as David A. Lowe puts it, there
is no such thing as an uninteresting Callas recording, is not
reliable. Even I myself have to admit that every, or almost every,
recording is of interest, but I concede that some can only be

listened to with irritation, in pain or discomfort and that some can scarcely be tolerated. It would be foolish to deny the existence of recordings from the singer's middle period, from about 1954, which have disturbing insecurities, tremulous top notes, harsh sounds and verbal discoloration.

When Maria Callas began to record in the EMI studios in 1953, a significant portion of her career was already behind her. That had certainly not been the most important or productive artistically, but it was the period of her vocal splendour. Only between 1947 and 1952 had she been that *assoluta* with the ability to master dramatic lyric and coloratura parts. There are recordings of *Parsifal, Nabucco, I Vespri Siciliani* and *Macbeth* which are middling in recording quality, but none of *Die Walküre, Tristan und Isolde* or *Turandot*. The most painful gap in the studio discography must be that there exist no carefully produced recordings of *I Vespri Siciliani, Macbeth, Nabucco* or *Don Carlo* from the singer's early period. With a few exceptions (*Medea, Il Turco in Italia*), Maria Callas was able to record only conventional repertory in the studios, albeit singing in a way that was far from conventional: Rossini's *Barbiere*, Bellini's *Norma, Puritani* and *Sonnambula*, Donizetti's *Lucia*, Verdi's *Rigoletto, Trovatore, Traviata, Forza, Ballo* and *Aida*, Puccini's *Manon, Bohéme, Tosca, Butterfly* and *Turandot*, the one-acters of Leoncavallo and Mascagni, and Ponchielli's *La Gioconda*. She was not able to make recordings of *Die Entführung aus dem Serail*, Rossini's *Armida*, Gluck's *Alceste* and *Iphigénie en Tauride* or *Anna Bolena, Il Pirata* and *Poliuto*, operas in which she appeared between 1952 and 1960.

Is this an idle thought? Are there not enough live recordings which, as one reads everywhere, give us the sound of 'the Callas genius in a stage atmosphere'? And don't these recordings show, as is also claimed, the true Callas, the fanatical fighter who risked everything? One would not want to be without these recordings, either as an admirer of the soprano or as writer of operatic history, but that does not preclude critical listening. Many of these recordings are, because of considerable defects of not just a technical nature, highly ambivalent and problematical documents. One can reconcile oneself to the fact that certain defects are attributable to technical inadequacy: poor sound balance, serious or complete distortion, or interference from other radio programmes and drop outs. But it is worse when certain operas are pirated at too high a pitch, or with passages missing or replaced by takes sometimes extracted from commercial recordings – nor is it always pleasurable to hear Maria Callas when her vocal brilliance, not yet fully polished, is matched in ensembles or with orchestras of lesser calibre. It is different with the later live recordings from Milan, London, Berlin or Dallas, thanks to which good and even exemplary performances have been preserved. It would be wrong to play these live recordings off against the studio ones because, as Maria Callas herself emphasised, a performance has quite different rules to those of a recording. Maria Callas was a singer who could take bigger risks on stage and could extend her own limits. On the other hand certain studio recordings – like *Tosca, Lucia di Lammermoor* (1953), *Forza, Aida, Turandot, Bohème* – contain unique nuances and refinements: 'Callas has a way of pronouncing a word,' said Bachmann, and the record is the ideal medium for the art of sound play. The live versions also make clear that vocal perfection in the studio – the perfection of the *staccati*, of the rising and especially the falling scales, of the timing or pacing of phrases, of the secure control of difficult and wide intervals – was not the result of editing; on stage she would sometimes make a mistake, miss a high note or misjudge her breathing, but those were not errors of technique but simply the result of her willingness to risk everything for the sake of expression. It is worth recalling Maria Callas saying to Walter Legge that early on in her career she had sung like a 'wild cat'. An ambivalent statement, on the one hand showing pride in her energy and readiness to take risks but on the other artistic scepticism and self-criticism: the discernment that she had won the public over with means which she found questionable as an artist. It could be that she recognised the dubious nature of vocal stunts only when the time came that she no longer possessed the untamed energy of a wild cat.

However problematic some of the live recordings may be, they none the less possess significant value for the critical listener and above all the historian. They document not only the development of an individual career, with its high points and its hurdles, its dangers and catastrophes, but they also reveal a lot about performance traditions, the level of the theatre in the 1950s and the standard of ensemble. They capture not only the moments of success, when the singer excels herself, but also those exciting moments where she takes the highest and, according to Heinrich Mann, the purest artistic risk. In order to dazzle her audience the young Maria Callas would interpolate *altissimo* notes – D flat, D and E flat – which were not important but which certainly assured the tension of the performance and a place in that hall of fame reached only by those who venture everything. These recordings document the fact that she took dangerous risks. To whom did it matter that occasionally she could not muster or focus a note or conclude a phrase because of a misjudgement of breathing? The only important thing was the certainty of her commitment, her striving for the absolute.

The very young singer was already the focal point of these performances, through the energy and authority of her singing. Even when in 1950 she sang Leonora in *Il Trovatore* in Mexico City – and without the preparatory help of Tullio Serafin which she had wanted – her artistic sense still dominated the performance. Her aim to unfold the formal variety of Verdi's middle period work and to place this in the tradition of bel canto is clearly discernible. That is an achievement more deserving of admiration than the much-acclaimed interpolation of top notes in the arias of the first and last acts. As some works – *Il Trovatore, Norma, Lucia, La Traviata, Medea* – are available in three, four or more different live performances or recordings, one can also study her artistic development which almost always follows a different course to her vocal and physical developments. Sometimes one experiences those special occasions when not only was the voice still functioning but the artistic understanding was already at work: in *La Traviata* under Giulini, the La Scala *Norma* with Votto, the La Scala *Ballo* with Gavazzeni, *Anna Bolena* with Gavazzeni or the Dallas *Medea* with Nicola Rescigno.

These live recordings and most of the studio ones were still made – and this must be emphasised again – without hurrying, and against the background of a real ensemble. In the 1950s, when the voice of artistic directors like Walter Legge or John Culshaw still carried as much weight as that of the manager, the production of an opera recording was considered a challenge and not a mere contractual obligation on the part of the star. Even in the recordings where Maria Callas had partners of only average calibre – like the Pollione of Mario Filippeschi, the Arturo of Giuseppe di Stefano, the Elvino of Nicola Monti and the Calaf of Eugenio Fernandi – this scarcely affects the recording's unity or aesthetic integrity. There is no other explanation for the fact that many of her recordings are still unequalled, if not unsurpassed, after thirty years. And the recordings from the La Scala performances in particular illustrate with what dedication the de Sabatas, Bernsteins, Karajans, Gavazzenis and Viscontis made operatic theatre. Even an artistic talent like Callas's could thrive only in a certain climate and not under the bright lights of the star theatre. It would have been unlikely to unfold in that way under the conditions of the opera business of the 1960s or 1970s.

Maggie Teyte has discussed[1] how the standard of singing depends on the quality of the teacher. What must be the feeling of a teacher with strong sense of responsibility when he discovers that particularly gifted and well-trained pupils are throwing all caution to the winds and taking on roles which the teacher has warned them against? It simply is a fact that even the best technique will be endangered by the daily events in a singer's career – by indisposition, long journeys, deputising for colleagues, but also by the demands of impresarios, theatre directors and conductors, who are concerned with the success of their theatre and its performances, certainly not with the singer's success. As Lisa della Casa said: 'They take the lemon, press it – and throw it away.' Maria Callas never spared herself for the sake of success, singing in the early years many roles that were too heavy, but she achieved her reputation only by concentrating to the utmost on her role, the music and the quality of the performance and it is in that light that one should listen to her records and the live recordings of her appearances. And moreover, listen with ears open to the slow decline of her voice, and to the struggle of her art with those weaknesses of her instrument which became increasingly obvious from the mid–1950s onwards. Yet that is not to say that Maria Callas was not singing performances even in the late 1950s that were head and shoulders above those of her colleagues, rivals or supposed successors.

Ah, quale voce

The earliest available recording probably dates from 20 May 1949. It is taken from a performance of Puccini's *Turandot* led by Tullio Serafin in the Teatro Colón in Buenos Aires. Maria Callas was to sing the role for the last time in the 1949–50 season, thereby taking leave, except for five appearances in *Tristan und Isolde* in Rome in February 1950, from the heavily dramatic repertory. It was as a dramatic soprano that she viewed herself at that time. Even if she did not possess the thrustful voice of Nordica, Flagstad or Leider, she did have a dramatic gift and burning expressive energy. When Serafin had her sing Elvira in Bellini's *I Puritani* in January 1949, he was not particularly interested in developing her career, he simply needed her for the part. However, singing this part opened new perspectives for her. In December 1949 she went on to prove in Verdi's *Nabucco* that she could meet all the requirements of dramatic agility. The years 1950 and 1951 at last brought the new coloratura parts: in *Norma, Il Turco in Italia, La Traviata, I Vespri Siciliani* and again *I Puritani*. Up to 1952 – perhaps the year of the most brilliant performances of her career – Callas knew no bounds and that year was to end with her triumphant appearance as Lady Macbeth, under Victor de Sabata at La Scala.

If one is looking for evidence of Tito Gobbi's claim that the voice of the young Callas produced sounds which one experiences only once in lifetime, it is to be found in the Buenos Aires *Turandot*: 'In questa reggia'. Her partner is Mario del Monaco, who admittedly occasionally sings a little below pitch – which can be painful when the voices are in unison – but who produces a stream of sound that has astonishing fullness and a metallic brilliance. Yet Maria Callas wins with the great energy and tonal concentration of her singing, which stands up well to a comparison with the famous recording by Eva Turner. Indeed, Maria Callas can shade the beginning of the aria with more subtlety than the English singer and can colour the sound more expressively. Her phrasing is expansive, the attack is bold and the authority of her delivery impressive; the confidence with which she unfolds the tightening climactic phrases is breathtaking, and yet one does not get the impression of arbitrary and loudly powerful singing which, as Rosa Raisa once said, was, and is, so popular in South America.

Just before the appearances in Buenos Aires – *Turandot, Norma* and *Aida* – Maria Callas had sung a concert in Turin under Francisco Molinari-Pradelli which was broadcast by Italian radio. The programme consisted of Isolde's Liebestod, Aida's Nile aria, Norma's 'Casta diva' and Elvira's 'Qui la voce'. A clever self-portrait: it showed that she was an *assoluta* in the original sense, a singer of both the dramatic and coloratura repertory. Eight months later the same programme, except for the *Aida* aria, was recorded in the studio for Cetra. The three 78 rpm discs were as important for her career as the ten titles that sealed Caruso's fame in 1902. And has there ever been a more perfect début record than Callas's interpretation of 'Qui la voce'? This alone would secure the singer's posthumous fame if no other Callas recordings existed, and it would do so in testifying to her early maturity – but with a promise that the future held much more. Bellini wrote his last opera for the Paris Opéra. Giulia Grisi (1811–1869), who had sung Adalgisa at the première of *Norma*, sang Elvira in the first performance of *I Puritani* on 24 January 1835. It is clear from the writings of Gautier or Henry Chorley that Grisi was a singer who could cross vocal divisions: she mastered the coloratura style of Rossini and Donizetti yet could equally do justice to the dramatic demands of Verdi and Meyerbeer.[2] Although she is said not to have had the acting genius and vocal expressiveness of Pasta or Malibran, she was nevertheless attributed with vocal and dramatic power of some significance. It was for Malibran, who in the last act 'filled the stage with her cries of emotional derangement – unheard of on the stage of our time' (Bellini), that the composer wrote 'Son vergin vezzosa'.

This makes it clear that Elvira had been conceived by the composer as a dramatic soprano with *agilità*. But the gramophone shows that in our century the role fell to lyric coloraturas, few of whom could do justice to the cantilena 'Qui la voce' with sense, and fewer still with dramatic ardour. The English critic Richard Fairman groaned that, in order to compensate, they would perform the cabaletta in the way he described as 'empty of sense and full of notes'. These dramatically domesticated, gently pleading or meaninglessly warbled recordings by Frieda Hempel, Lily Pons, Mado Robin and others must be heard if we are to appreciate the impression Callas made in 1948: she sang music which had been misinterpreted as light and decorative with a full dark voice, expressive to the point of being archaic, and, as Bellini had demanded, with *tutta del desperazione del dolor*.

This recording already gives Callas's distinctive sound, that mixture of clarinet and oboe described by Claudia Cassidy, a sound of a colour, dark, melancholic and suffering, a sound which gave vocal form to the introverted character of this dream piece, in which the full range of colours of the voice is displayed.

There is also André Tubeuf's statement which describes the singer's vocal imagination as moulded by Wagner's orchestration. In the section 'Wortvers und Stabreim' of his main theatrical work *Oper und Drama*, Wagner explains that the vowel is nothing more than

a tone condensed: its specific manifestation is determined through its turning toward the outer surface of the feeling's 'body'; which latter displays to the 'eye' of hearing the mirrored image of the outward object that has acted on it. The object's effect on the body of feeling itself is manifested by the vowel through a direct utterance of feeling along the nearest path, thus expanding the individuality it has acquired from without into the universality of pure emotion; and this takes place in the musical tone. To that which bore the vowel, and bade it outwardly condense itself into the consonant – to that the vowel returns as a specific entity, enriched by the world outside, in order to dissolve itself in *it*, now equally enriched. This enriched, this individually established tone expanded to the universality of feeling is the redeeming 'moment' of the poet's thought; and thought, in this redemption, becomes an immediate *outpouring of the feeling* [Wagner's italics].

These aesthetic reflections might seem indulgent to some readers – those who regard themselves as modern or progressive – but they describe perfectly how Maria Callas treats the vowels of darkness and pathos of 'la voce sua soave' and how she brightens on the vowels 'voce' and 'sospir', where Ardoin and others note how she uses her 'little-girl' voice. Technically this is a matter of placing the sound immediately before the lips, but the effect cannot be grasped in technical words. It is a sound which possesses grace and refinement, a dancer's elegance, which is dematerialised and yet visible. The sound is carried by an unusual way of breathing and given life by the art of *portamento* and *rubato*. It is not the *portamento* of verismo singers, not the impure sliding onto a note, but a way of correctly supporting the tone on the breath and the simultaneous structuring of musical movement. It is a *portamento* which finds the most subtle transitions between notes, never because of a need to scoop or to seek a note by sliding. It leads to a thrilling, breathing *legato*.

The musical sense can only be grasped by illuminating the text, the words and even the individual syllables. As only the greatest rhetorician knows how, Maria Callas rests on each moment of affect and never yields to effect, concerned as she is with purely musical means – vocal colouring, the nuance of *rubato*, the inner sense of a phrase and the expressive meaning of each word. In this way she meets the most important demands of expressive singing, which Charles Gounod formulated as follows:

There are two things which are a matter of principle for enunciation. This must be clear, clean, distinct and exact, which means that there must be no insecurity as far as the enunciated words are concerned. Also, it must be expressive, which means that it must evoke in the imagination the emotional content of the enunciated words. As far as clarity, cleanness and exactness are concerned, enunciation means articulation, whose purpose is faithfully to reproduce the outward form of the words. The rest is a matter of expression. It fills words with thoughts, with sentiments and with passion. To sum up, the domains of articulation are form and the intellectual element. Articulation takes care of purity and expression takes care of eloquence.

In the case of Callas the rendition of an aria means more than the
bringing together of well-formed and melodious phrases. She
follows a plan in every recitative, in every aria and in her approach
to every role. It is a plan which progresses both dramatically and
musically.

Every artistic achievement is more than the mere sum total of
the details, and yet one has to describe the details in order to
grasp the richness of the artist's performance. Maria Callas dazzled
her listeners at the time not only with the dark fullness of her
soprano, not only with her rhetorical eloquence and not only
with her sense for *rubato* (which we otherwise only meet in Heifetz), but also with the fantastic agility of her singing. This was
an agility which went far beyond mere flexibility as it was known
in singers of earlier epochs like Luisa Tetrazzini, Frieda Hempel
or Selma Kurz. In the *Puritani* cabaletta Maria Callas sings a
diatonic scale in the first part and a chromatic one in the second
part – and sings them with precision, speed and perfect definition;
and despite the tempo one experiences those scales as if they were
pictures in quick motion, because each note is stamped with
formal perfection. John Ardoin quite rightly says that there are
few examples in the history of singing where such complete
mastery of a voice is coupled with such agility and authority of
dramatic expression. In the *Puritani* aria all is crowned with a high
E flat which in its brilliance is breathtaking and of utter ease; and
is not the most marvellous, the deepest, enchantment of singing
to be found in the effortless mastery of the greatest difficulties?

The beginning of the *Norma* aria also confirms the singer's
exceptional quality, at a time when she had only sung the role
half a dozen times. She was to sing the part a total of eighty-nine
times. These first six performances – two in Florence in 1948 and
four in Buenos Aires in June 1949 – were directed by Serafin.[3]
Callas sings the cavatina in F, in the key used by Pasta at the first
performance at La Scala in 1831, and this key suits her timbre
just as G major suits Sutherland's, which is lighter and more
silvery. Presumably the duration of the 78 rpm sides did not
permit the recitative to be recorded. The cavatina receives a consummate rendition, faultless in form, wonderfully melismatic
phrases and dynamics terraced with the utmost subtlety. In

contrast the cabaletta has more the effect of a virtuosa performance in the concert hall, and is not as eloquent as it was to become in later performances. It is abridged (by one verse) and the coda is also shortened. It ends with a C *in alt* which is not in the score.

It is not quite so easy to evaluate the recording of Isolde's Liebestod. Callas sings this in Italian, and some of the expressive vocal character, as described by Wagner, unavoidably changes with the change of text. The interpretation is not dramatic or heroic but one of emotion and pathos. The note struck is less that of a death-wish than that of the deep unhappiness which lies in recollecting past joy. This is very moving; unorthodox but very convincing, because Callas sings with a *legato* comparable to that of scarcely other singer. Perhaps the composer would have been as captivated by this as he was by Mattia Battistini's portrayal of Wolfram.

One of the most important early documents is the live recording of *Nabucco* from the Teatro San Carlo in Naples (20 December 1949), conducted by Vittorio Gui. The part of Abigaille is considered 'hybrid' (Rodolfo Celletti), because it demands both the verve of a dramatic soprano and a high degree of agility. That does not mean the mobility of a *soprano leggiero* but rather expressive coloratura. At the first performance it had been sung by Giuseppina Strepponi, who was overtaxed by the role. *Nabucco* was given at La Scala 121 times between 1842 and 1861, then disappeared from the repertory until 1912. For that first revival the title part was taken by Carlo Galeffi and Abigaille by the now unknown Cecilia Gagliardi. In Florence in 1933 and at La Scala in 1933–4 Gui conducted further performances with Galeffi and Gina Cigna, who had the strength and fullness, but no longer the agility, for the part. Tullio Serafin opened the La Scala season with *Nabucco* in 1946, with Maria Pedrini as Abigaille and Gino Bechi, who was also to partner Maria Callas in Naples, though unfortunately he was no longer up to her standard. Although his voice does not sound worn out he tends to a relentless *cantare con forza*, which damages the shape of the phrasing.

Callas gives a quite sensational performance as Abigaille: a pity that she sang the part on only three occasions. She still had the energy of ambition, already possessing the formal feeling for the

recitative 'Ben io t'invenni', one of 'the liveliest and most expressive Italian recitatives since Monteverdi'.[4] But the main characteristic of her singing was already her fully developed sense of vocal
gesture. When at the beginning she launches into 'Prode guerrier'
with 'the enforced composure of sarcasm' (Budden), or when she
pours out the rage of disappointed love into a cadenza-like and
coloratura expressive figure, and when finally in the trio's phrases
'Io t'amaro' and 'Una furia . . . à quest'amore' she expresses
love's happiness and the rage at its disappointment, we experience
acting vocalism of truly unknown intensity and suggestive power.

The voice at that time was perfectly obedient: the sustained C
in alt poses no problem, whether sung *piano* or *forte*, and the
interval jump of two octaves in the recitative before the second
act aria succeeds with instrumental precision. The rising sustained
shakes in the cabaletta, which spiral up to C, are not simply
mastered but are unfurled with effortless bravura, and she releases
expression to match the technical virtuosity. Perhaps still more
impressive is the richness of sound and colouring of her cantilena
in 'Anch'io dischiuso'. Julian Budden explains how Verdi here
follows in the steps of Donizetti in the way he unfolds the melody.
The long phrases are concluded with groups of *fioriture*, which
have to be marked as if with a silver pencil. Comparison with later
recordings with Elena Suliotis, Renata Scotto or Ghena Dimitrova
merely shows what heights were achieved by Callas. Another
great moment occurs in the third act duet between Abigaille and
Nabucco – this is Verdi's first great duet and a model for later
ones (Rigoletto–Gilda, Violetta–Germont, Aida–Amonasro).
Ardoin writes that the confrontation between Nabucco and Abigaille demands the fighting of a duel rather than the singing of a
duet. It is here that the mighty fullness of Bechi's voice explodes,
but Maria Callas holds her own in the D flat major section of the
finale with the wild energy of her attacks and her tonal focus.
She crowns the scene with an extraordinarily powerful high E
flat, a note which is usually heard only from light or high
sopranos. Bechi responds with a fulminant high A flat.

It was in the years between 1950 and 1952 that Maria Callas
established her exceptional position among the Italian sopranos
of her epoch, ascending the throne with her appearance as Lady

Macbeth at La Scala on 7 December 1952 under Victor de Sabata. The milestones on her way to fame are well documented – there are live recordings of *Norma, Tosca, Aida, La Traviata, I Puritani, I Vespri Siciliani, Il Trovatore, Rigoletto* and *Lucia di Lammermoor* which, despite their technical and sonic deficiencies, their mediocre ensembles, give an impressive demonstration of how her vocal ability was developing. The *Norma* with which she made her début in Mexico City on 23 May 1950 – under the lame direction of Guido Picco – can only be of interest to Callas fans, scarcely to admirers of the work. The singer evokes some magic moments: less in the cavatina than with the D *in alt* in the third act trio and with the nuances introduced in 'Deh! con te' and more so in 'In mia man'. She sings these with her incomparable sound figuration.

She sang Verdi's *Aida* both in 1950 and 1951, first under Picco and then under the much more flexible Oliviero de Fabritiis, and the recordings of these prove that she could also set standards in this role – the later studio version suffers somewhat from the problems with her top, which are heard not just in 'O patria mia'. Yet have there ever been more convincing portrayals of Aida than in both the Mexican performances? If we compare the versions of the music of Act I as far as 'Ritorna vincitor' with Zinka Milanov (Met, live in 1943), Herva Nelli with Toscanini, Renata Tebaldi under Erede, Milanov under Perlea, Tebaldi under Karajan or Leontyne Price under Leinsdorf or Solti, then in dramatic terms they all pale by comparison. No other Aida gives the impression in sonic terms of such agitation and torment. 'Ritorna vincitor' becomes the outburst of this tortured soul.

Singers like Elisabeth Rethberg, Rosa Ponselle, Meta Seinemeyer, or after the war Renata Tebaldi, Leontyne Price and Monserrat Caballé have perhaps sung the lyric phrases and the ending more gently and steadily, but none of them possesses such expressive vocal contrasts or such eloquence in their phrasing. Ardoin refers to the incomparable *legato* which starts with 'Numi pieta'. There is not much more to say about the Act 2 stunt of the endlessly sustained E flat *in alt*. It is sensational and, heard repeatedly, is experienced with the sort of shocked admiration that one might feel at a *salto mortale*. The third act is like a hot and

cold shower: the voice trembles with emotion at the beginning of
the Nile aria – at 'io tremo' – but at the C it is the note which is
trembling. Even then the C was a problem note when it had to
develop out of a long and sustained line. There are great moments
in the duet with Kurt Baum, whose Radames possesses much
voice but little sense of shape.

She sang Aida again a year later not only with a better conductor (de Fabritiis) but also with better male partners: Mario del
Monaco as Radames and Giuseppe Taddei as Amonasro. Her
voice is in top condition, a fact demonstrated not just by her
singing the high E flat at the end of the second act – this had
originally been intended to teach Kurt Baum a lesson. She appears
generally more radiant and more steady. The Act 3 duets which
in 1950 were not without musical weaknesses (wrong entries,
missing phrases) seem immediate and almost explosive in a way
which one would never hear in a studio recording; one has to
accept that Mario del Monaco and, surprisingly, Giuseppe Taddei
go too far and crassly over-sing.

Bel Canto and Verdi

In Mexico City in 1950 Callas sang her first Tosca – not counting
her thirteen performances in 1942 and four in 1943. It is a performance where one experiences 'a strong instinct at work' (Ardoin)
and nothing more, with her partners (particularly Mario Filippeschi) and the conductor (Umberto Mugnai) not helping to improve
the general impression.

By far her most interesting appearance of the 1950 season was
that in Verdi's *Il Trovatore* under Guido Picco, with Giulietta
Simionato, Kurt Baum and Leonard Warren as partners. It is far
from a polished performance, imprecise in ensemble and not
musically complete, and yet not without interest, indeed it is
remarkable as a portrayal of Leonora in which Maria Callas is
newly discovering Verdi singing. In the biographical section of
the book it has already been explained that she had turned to
Serafin for help in studying the part but that he had declined
because he did not wish to carry out preparatory work for another

conductor's performance. So Maria Callas had to study the part on her own, and indeed she was successful in making clear that the music was rooted in bel canto.

Leonora was at that time considered one of Zinka Milanov's party pieces, and even today she is still regarded as the ideal Leonora, in particular because of her beautifully floating *pianissimo acuti*. But in terms of musico-dramatic conception she is significantly inferior to Callas. The Yugoslav singer sang exquisitely as regards sound (and that too reveals an important technical and musical ability), but Maria Callas performed the vocal part with all the finesse of *fioritura* and trills, *thereby* depicting the character. To take an example: there exist trills at the ends of phrases in 'D'amor sull'ali rosee' and 'Vanne, sospir dolente' just as in many other parts of the role.

Yet their effect is lost when they are sung as if they were flute-like, merely decorative figures, as happens with Luisa Tetrazzini or Amelita Galli-Curci in the first aria and with Claire Dux in the second. Even Rosa Ponselle, or even an expressive singer like Claudia Muzio, do not dip the melodic line or the ornamental figures as deeply into the sound of *melancolia tinta* as Maria Callas. Putting it another way: Maria Callas has so much more to offer than notes spun out on a *fil di suono*. She does not make the part comfortable for her voice, but carries through every vocal formula and binds it into the larger shape.

This is true of the first Mexican performance (20 June 1950) even if that can rather be regarded as work in progress. After a wonderfully unfolded and expansively heightened cantilena Maria Callas sings a high D flat then C and finally, as display note, a high E flat; the effect is dissonant in two senses, both musically and atmospherically. She repeats the E flat at the end of the cabaletta, although such an interpolation is scarcely justified by the security of the performance. This is all the more regrettable because the rendition of the bravura piece is of a phenomenal overall brilliance. Not only do the trills sit perfectly and the *staccati* make their mark, but even more convincing is the expressive colouring given to the piece.

The trio at the end of Act 1 develops into a contest between three gigantic voices: Callas, Leonard Warren and Kurt Baum.

The American baritone sings with great energy and fullness of tone, Callas with brilliant tonal concentration – at the end she sails up to a D flat *in alt*. Baum follows, attempting to hold the note longer than she. He loses this duel by a fraction of a second. It must be said that later, in the third act, he does make this effect, but it is less in 'Ah sì, ben mio' than in the *stretta*, yet he never rises above singing to the gallery. But then, where today would one hear such a powerful, healthy and secure voice?

The Act 4 aria is a prime example of expressive Verdi singing, even if her high D flat at the end – as written by Verdi – does not fit in with the melancholy nature of the aria. Callas sings the note with masterful security but omits it in later performances, including the studio recording with Herbert von Karajan. There are very few successful recordings of the duet 'Mira d'acerbe', really only the one by Johanna Gadski and Pasquale Amato or the abbreviated one by Rosa Ponselle and Riccardo Stracciari, yet none has such a violent pulse as that with Maria Callas and Leonard Warren. Ardoin's notes make the point that only a perfect virtuosa, who has mastered the demands of Norma, can perform the scales and cascades in such a sovereign way and modulate the phrases with so much expression, all at a tempo of tremendous bravura. She was not to achieve this in later performances. She crowns the duet with another interpolated high C. According to Ardoin, the finale suffers from the coarse singing of the tenor Kurt Baum, who once more decides to show the gallery that there is more than one star in the firmament.

Her Leonora was repeated six months later at the San Carlo in Naples, conducted by Tullio Serafin and with Cloë Elmo, Giacomo Lauri-Volpi, Paolo Silveri and Italo Tajo as partners. Here, supported and guided by a sympathetic conductor, she demonstrates her unique qualities as a Verdi singer, just as she did in *Nabucco* under Gui. 'No other singer of our time,' wrote Conrad L. Osborne,[5] 'possesses such an alert sensitivity to the shape of Verdi's vocal gestures, and nobody can touch her in her ability to maintain a rhythm and to shape changes in rhythm without ever seeming calculated or losing spontaneity.'

Nor can one emphasise too much that these qualities can only be developed if a singer has the matching accompaniment. In

'Tacea la notte' Callas is able, thanks to Serafin, to intensify the *crescendo* to high B in a more expansive manner than she does in the Mexican performances under the rigid time-beating of Guido Picco. Whether by her own decision or on Serafin's advice she dispenses with the two high E flats of the Mexican performance, but she makes an alteration to the cadenza.[6] On the other hand she retains the high D flat in the Act 4 aria, which sits better in the voice and in the tonal shape of the aria. The filigree drawing and rich coloration of 'D'amor sull'ali rosee' is as close to perfection as one can imagine and the cadenza confirms Osborne's statement about the soprano's sense of rhythmic form. In the duet with Luna we again experience a highly dramatic virtuosa, though Paolo Silveri is not such a brilliant partner as was Leonard Warren. Lauri-Volpi, who after his *stretta* is greeted, alongside the applause, with sounds of violent disapproval, later took the Neapolitan press to task vehemently for not having recognised what in his opinion was the exceptional quality of Callas's Verdi singing.

Callas sang her next series of *Il Trovatore* at La Scala in February and March 1953 under the baton of Antonino Votto. Whereas the sound of the voice in the earlier appearances had had a darkish colour and powerful sweep, it now reflected her vocal development by taking on a more restrained tone. There are no more interpolated top notes, and the D flat at the end of 'D'amor sull'ali rosee' is also missing, but in compensation there is coloration of more refinement and more subtle verbal nuance. But one can scarcely recommend a performance in which Carlo Tagliabue as Luna is far past his vocal best and in which Gino Penno as Manrico is beyond description – as Ardoin puts it, 'One almost longs to have Baum back.'

The rumour of the existence of a live recording of *Il Trovatore* from Chicago on 8 November 1955, when Maria Callas sang with Jussi Björling and Ettore Bastianini under the direction of Nicola Rescigno, stubbornly refuses to die; to the chagrin of many, the recording of this much-lauded performance has still not surfaced. Ardoin states that it was the second performance which was taped, but that the copy was destroyed. The EMI recording under Karajan, made in August 1956, was to be Callas's farewell to the role – it was her most complete and most subtle interpretation, even if she no longer sang as generously – particularly in the high *tessitura*. When the records appeared, the critic Herbert Weinstock – one of the greatest – compared the interpretation with those of Zinka Milanov and Renata Tebaldi.[7] His view was that the Yugoslav soprano was indeed vocally ravishing but that she contributed nothing to opera as drama. He accused her of simply vocalising individual phrases for the sake of the effect which the sound made, ignoring the structure of the text; and he found it incomprehensible that conductor and producer should have approved for issue such a musico-dramatic *reductio ad absurdum*. (Milanov pursues a similar course at the end of the Nile duet in *Aida* with Jussi Björling.) Renata Tebaldi's portrayal is perhaps even worse, for she can sing neither the many scales nor the trills, and thereby ruins the vocal line.

One important advantage of the brilliantly conducted Karajan performance lies in its musical completeness. Giuseppe di Stefano (an eloquent Manrico who is, however, strained and hollow at the top of his voice) sings not only both stanzas of 'Di quella pira' but also the usual cut which the conductor opens up after the Act 4 aria. Callas sings the richly shaped cabaletta 'Tu vedrai che amore in terra' with technical brilliance and as a dramatic piece of bravura. 'I see in her the most consummate actress-singer of our time,' wrote Weinstock, and praised 'a great performance: at one and the same time serious, accurate and dazzling.' The entire ensemble is acceptable. However Nicola Zaccaria is a routine, vocally thin Ferrando (one longs for Pinza, or would be content with Giorgio Tozzi), Rolando Panerai is perhaps too light as Luna and Fedora Barbieri sounds more secure and energetic in the 1952 RCA version with Milanov and Björling.

Wagner Transformed

Back to the year 1950, from which a peformance of Wagner's *Parsifal* is preserved; Kundry was the last Wagner part of her career. It is scarcely to be believed that three weeks earlier she had been singing Fiorilla in *Il Turco in Italia*. John Ardoin's statement that the work undergoes decisive changes when translated into Italian must be firmly endorsed. Michael Scott, in his study *The Record of Singing*, praises certain early Italian Wagner interpretations – those of Fernando de Lucia, Giuseppe Borgatti and Mattia Battistini – as exemplary for their smooth production, *legato* line and elegance. There cannot be the slightest doubt that Wagner envisaged that sort of production being transferred to the sound and timbre of the German language. Even though he made particular use of alliteration in his libretti to introduce consonants which were singable, nasal or liquid, or even soft labial sounds, the melodic line is still not as easy to bind or to execute in German as it is in Italian. It is the Italian words which make Callas's Kundry sound so sensual. She has some great moments in the second act also. Did Kundry's scream – in the Klingsor scene – ever sound so musical? Or the falling eighths ('Den ich verlachte') so exact and pregnant, or 'Ich sah das Kind' so sensitive? The performance is brilliantly conducted by Vittorio Gui – Robin Holloway ranks him higher than Pierre Boulez or Georg Solti[8] – and although it must be assessed as a special case, it repays study, showing how bel canto technique gets nearer to the composer's music than the German *Sprechgesang* which degenerated, in George Bernard Shaw's description, into the Bayreuth bark. The *Sprechgesang* was to a large extent the result of the work of Julius Kniese, who worked as singing coach in Bayreuth under the aegis of Cosima Wagner. I am also convinced that the heavy, bombastic rhetoric of the second German Empire – as it is heard in actors and political speeches – was absorbed disadvantageously into Wagner singing. Is there a happy medium?

Moment of Fulfilment: Callas in Concert

Callas began 1951 with appearances in *La Traviata*, *Il Trovatore* (both under Serafin), *Norma* and *Aida*. On 12 March she made her first appearance in the series of 'Concerti Martini e Rossi'. Her programme consisted of 'Ma dall'arrido stelo' from *Un Ballo in Maschera*, the Variations by Heinrich Proch, 'Je suis Titania' from Thomas's *Mignon* and 'Leise, leise, fromme Weise' from Weber's *Der Freischütz*. This was followed on 18 February 1952 by a concert with the tenor Nicolai Filacuridi, in which she sang, under the direction of Oliviero de Fabritiis, 'Vieni! t'affretta' from *Macbeth*, the Mad Scene from *Lucia di Lammermoor*, Abigaille's big aria from *Nabucco* and the Bell Song from Delibes' *Lakmé*.

On 27 December 1954 there was a concert conducted by Alfredo Simonetto, in which Beniamino Gigli also took part, although the two stars did not sing any duets. Callas gave Constanze's aria from Mozart's *Die Entführung aus dem Serail*, Dinorah's 'Ombre légère', Louise's 'Depuis le jour' and Armida's 'D'amore al dolce imperio'. Finally, she again sang under Simonetto in 1956, performing 'Tu che invoco' from Spontini's *La Vestale*, 'Bel raggio' from Rossini's *Semiramide*, 'A vos jeux' from Thomas' *Hamlet* and 'Vieni al tempo' from *I Puritani*.

Even if one attaches no great importance to concerts like this or if one dismisses them as exhibitions for stars, they are still of distinct importance for our picture of the singer. To use the pithy expression of Will Crutchfield, they all offer 'prime Callas'.[9] And not just in the vocal sense, but also from the musical and interpretative viewpoint. Not only did Maria Callas know how to grasp the dramatic essence of a role in a single aria, but she also often sang in these early concerts with a musical concentration and technical brilliance which is only attainable on the opera stage with great difficulty. Let us give a few brief pointers. The centre-pieces of the first concert in 1951 are the Proch Variations, which were for many years inserted into the second act singing lesson in *Il Barbiere di Siviglia* as a sort of soprano party piece. It is difficult to grasp how a voice which had sung Isolde, Turandot and Kundry so recently and was now singing Violetta, Aida, Norma and Leonora, was able to master the extraordinary difficulties of the Rossini role. Ardoin describes it as 'some of the most dazzling and virtuoso singing'. The spontaneous – or seemingly spontaneous – digressions from the score, the decorations with fiendish intervals and a fantastic trill reveal an exemplary training in *bel canto* style.

The concert of 18 February 1952 is of far more importance. It is difficult to imagine that any singer could present herself and her technical and musical capabilities in a grander manner, considering that she was performing the arias from *Macbeth* and *Lucia* for the very first time (stage performances of those operas were to follow later that year). She begins with the Lady Macbeth aria (regrettably without the letter reading or the recitative), the role she was to sing at La Scala in December 1952. De Fabritiis chooses a very slow tempo which, even if not quite the *andantino* prescribed, still gives the aria weight and tension, particularly transforming the cabaletta's elements of embellished style with highly dramatic vocal gestures. In his discography in *Opera on Record* Harold Rosenthal describes the later studio recording of this piece as 'one of the greatest performances which Callas gave on record', yet this early performance, albeit not so polished, earns its place by virtue of its bold brilliance and intensity and the effortlessness of its singing.

Only Callas could have dared to follow Verdi's night piece with Donizetti's Lucia scene, and indeed perhaps only at that time in her career. She begins at 'Il dolce suono' and unfortunately omits 'Spargi d'amore' – and a new Lucia was born. Or to put it in a different way: the figure of Lucia was at last saved from the *soprano leggiero*, and this was well before the first complete performances in Mexico City. Apart from *Norma* (eighty-nine appearances) and *La Traviata* (sixty-three), Callas sang no other role as frequently as Lucia (forty-six appearances) and forty-six in *Tosca*. The Mad Scene is presented as a highly complex formal structure made up of recitative, cavatina, scena and cabaletta, in which the individual elements are loosely sprinkled with *arioso*. She was already giving detailed and 'almost scientific preparation'[10] to the scene, and nonetheless each ornament, each *acciacatura*, each trill and *gruppetto* has a spontaneous and eloquent effect. Her pacing, to use the word applied by Itzhak Perlman, is simply breathtaking, especially in the way she times the sustained notes and fast-moving scales. Callas displays what is known in the world of sport as intelligence of movement: the ability, after the highest exertion, to return slowly and with control to a position of repose, and vice versa. For example, she is able to allow a *fermata*, which many would consider too long (and often stupidly unmusical), to soar and glide over into the next phrase.

An accusation levelled in discussions of her voice – as in *Processo alla Callas* – is that she lacks tonal beauty and that her top is particularly metallic. This calls for some technical comment. A voice's sound and beauty of timbre, in particular its colour, depend upon harmonic tones which soar with absolute evenness. If a voice is absolutely pure, only the lower harmonic tones (described by H. Helmholtz as the formants) will be audible. If a voice becomes stretched and forced, then the higher and dissonant harmonies emerge: the tone becomes hard and metallic. If the harmonic tones are missing, the voice will sound flat, hollow and woolly. A long sustained note is only effective if it contains an inner flame, and that flame must be fuelled by the controlled energy of breathing. Any tension of the muscles which is not used to control a gentle emission of breath will impair the sound by disrupting the harmonic tones. And every 'beautiful' tone must equally emerge from nothing, develop without tension and then fade away into nothing. As Maria Celloni puts it, 'Chi sarà respirare, sarà cantare' ('Who can breathe, can sing').

As regards sound and beauty of timbre, on 18 February 1952 Callas sang beguilingly and with an unbelievable richness of contrast. There was hardness but no sharpness of tone in the *Macbeth* aria, no harsh colouring. It is amazing how gently, softly and carefully she begins the *Lucia* scene and how effortlessly she makes her way through the labyrinths and hurdles of this vocal course. Only at the very top – on the staccato B flats and concluding E flat – does the voice have to admit a little tension, which leads to the sound sharpening as a result of the dissonant harmonies.

In contrast to John Ardoin, I consider the interpretation of the Bell Song from *Lakmé* a brilliant achievement. It was to be assumed that Callas would not be content with just burning vocal fireworks; but is there any other way for the aria to release itself from its own vanity and lightness? She gives the piece more weight and colour than any French coloratura singer had ever done with their sounds like sour lemons; and to conclude, she manages an imposing top E.

The most important item in the concert of 27 September 1956, which she shared with the young tenor Gianni Raimondi, is the brilliantly sung scene from Thomas's *Hamlet* and her only largely successful rendition of 'Bel raggio' from *Semiramide*, with its wonderfully nuanced coloraturas of great softness and energy.

She showed herself totally a virtuosa in the concert which she gave with Beniamino Gigli in San Remo on 27 December 1957. After the slimming course (who can say because of it?), her voice had an added brightness and lightness, as well as being more even overall and technically better blended over the registers. She starts with the Constanze aria, which in 1952 she had sung four times at La Scala. As I have mentioned, in *Opera on Record* William Mann rejects her performance; this is a verdict difficult to comprehend and John Ardoin is in violent disagreement: 'The most compelling realisation of the aria extant.'[11] If there is a weak point here – the high C before the coda which is not sustained securely right to the end, and where the tone does not spin off into nothing as of its own accord – this is little compared to the many weaknesses to be found in recordings by renowned interpreters of the part. Where else, apart from in Callas, can one sense the 'forces of the words' demanded by Mozart, where else a comparable dramatic energy in the passage work? The recordings from Meyerbeer's *Dinorah* and Rossini's *Armida* can only be heard in amazement as demonstrations of expressive coloratura singing. What shading in the echo effects in the Meyerbeer, what penetration and articulated subtlety in the Rossini, whose coloraturas are delivered with an almost Verdi-like energy.

The First Important Performances

One of the most important performances of 1951 was Verdi's *I Vespri Siciliani* at the Maggio Musicale in Florence on 26 May, in which Erich Kleiber made his Italian début. This performance was such absolute confirmation of Callas's position that Antonio Ghiringhelli had to engage her for La Scala. The role of Elena could only be mastered by an *assoluta*, because, as a concession to the Paris Opéra, Verdi had written a *siciliana* of virtuoso scope for *soprano spinto* in the last act; Callas sang it eleven times, more frequently than Abigaille (three times) or Lady Macbeth (five times). The work has the reputation of being one of Verdi's least known, and this may be the reason, as Ardoin justifiably complains, why one of Callas's great expressive moments is scarcely ever mentioned. This is Elena's first act aria, where she achieves 'theatre through voice' (Ardoin). Elena, compelled to sing by an officer of the occupation, uses the opportunity to deliver a patriotic cry. 'Si, canterò,' she tells the officer, and the musical figure immediately tells us that he will not be hearing an entertaining song but an unpalatable one, political indeed. Elena calls the Sicilians to rise against the French – 'Il vostro fato è in vostra man.' The balance of the word and tone in this phrase is exemplary, and in the following allegro ('Su caraggio'), as virtuoso a conception as Lady Macbeth's first aria, we continue to experience exemplary vocal gestures, the transformation of virtuoso formulas into the language of gesture.

In the duets the level of the performance falls down because Callas again has a tenor partner who is completely inadequate, Giorgio Kokolios-Bardi.[12] But her singing of the meditative 'Arrigo, ah parli a un cor' remains unforgettable – just as the exceptional quality of her technique is made clear by a slight faultering. At the end of the scene Elena has to sing a falling chromatic scale which goes down to F sharp (below middle C). Ardoin describes how she miscalculates her breathing and is unable to complete the phrase with perfectly supported tone. But if one listens again the mishap is changed into a great moment: one realises what it means to sing such a passage and to transform it into gesture. Even more, Callas forms it in the low register, a little later singing a deep trill. Only a singer (or a clarinettist) will understand that. 'Let her sing a low scale,' said Nellie Melba bluntly when the brilliance of Luisa Tetrazzini in La Traviata was praised in her presence.

And the Siciliana, the so-called Bolero? It is a pure virtuoso piece, inserted like Oscar's 'Saper vorreste' in Ballo but nevertheless dramatically justifiable as a contrast. Callas gives it wonderful rhythmic verve, sings a marvellous trill and clean interval leaps and allows herself a little aberration when attempting the E in altissimo. The tone breaks and the situation is not entirely saved by her taking it up again.

Later in the year 1952 came the performance of Rossini's Armida in the Teatro Communale in Florence. Urged by Serafin she had learned the role within five days. It was more than just a feat of

memory, more than proof of her sovereign musicality: only a
singer who is up to all the technical demands and is in a position
to sing at sight every interval, coloratura, trill and ornament could
take up such a challenge. It is only Callas and Serafin who give
the performance its quality; certainly not the five tenors, who
were not only simply not up to it but were seriously miscast.
Coloratura singing for Francesco Albanese, Alessandro Ziliani
and Mario Filippeschi was a journey into *terra incognita*; there is a
loss of quality in the duets, of the magic of Callas's singing. That
magic is a transcendental virtuosity. Writing for Isabella Colbran,
Rossini took the *fioritura* to its limits in this work and yet the title
role is far more than a virtuoso concerto for the larynx. The
Italian critic Fedele d'Amico wrote that Rossini's coloratura can
be the expression of ecstasy and lyrical delight, of joy and anger.
But he went on to explain that it was only after hearing Callas
that he appreciated the meaning of these coloraturas over and
above their effect on the senses. They could be heard in their
most concentrated form in 'D'amor al dolce impero', which in
Callas's rendition is one of the most brilliant demonstrations
of virtuoso singing ever to have been recorded – far above any technical studies which Joan Sutherland ever mastered. What a dream
to imagine Callas in 1953 surrounded in this opera by the young
José Carreras, Rockwell Blake, Alfredo Kraus and Luciano Pavarotti.

In 1951 and 1952 Callas sang Verdi's Violetta in Mexico City,
which she had prepared for Florence under Serafin. As with
Leonora in *Il Trovatore*, she makes it clear that this is a work of
transition, combining elements of ornamented singing with the
vocal gestures of later Verdi. The 1951 performance, conducted
by Oliviero de Fabritiis, is full of promise, but the 1952 one,
under Umberto Mugnai, is a backward step. Nor is the live
recording of *I Puritani* (29 May 1952) under Guido Picco of particular interest: as always Callas has great moments (and brilliant
Ds and E flats), but the ensemble is second-rate and even Giuseppe
di Stefano does not rise above solid routine, apart from making
a terrific effort on various high notes.

The Mexico *Rigoletto* on 17 June 1952 under Mugnai can only
be described as chaotic, with a prompter taking the leading role:
he could be heard loudly throughout, although not loudly enough

to cover the Rigoletto of Piero Campolonghi. Giuseppe di Stefano is not up to the role of the Duke, which he was later to take, albeit with cuts, in the commercial recording. It is a part which calls not only for an extensive range and the ability to extend easily up to D flat and D, but also requires singing 'on the breath' in those numerous passages which lie in the so-called *passaggio* region. Tenors like Alfredo Kraus, Carlo Bergonzi and Luciano Pavarotti have stated in interviews with Helena Matheopoulos – in her book *Divo* – that they view the part of the Duke as one of Verdi's most difficult tenor roles.

Nevertheless the performance does have some interest, for Callas sings Gilda almost better than Donizetti's Lucia; it is all the more cause for regret that she sang the part only twice on stage and then on the commercial recording. She develops the role like no other singer, at first with her enchanting 'little-girl' voice, then unfolds an exemplary *legato* in the duets with Rigoletto and creates pure magic in 'Caro nome', again pacing the phrases which most singers simply chop up; how perfectly she floats the trills, with what rhythmic refinement she binds those trills into the melodic flow. The ending is a little less convincing, where instead of the long trill she goes down to E, thereby just making an effect. Then, suddenly, a completely different voice is heard in 'Tutte le feste' and in the duet 'Piangi, fanciulla', a sound which is saturated with pain and suffering. It is so hard to endure the coarse effect of her baritone partner and di Stefano's vague inton-ation in the fourth act. Yet at the end of the opera one can return to ecstasy when Callas breathes out 'Lassù in cielo' with beautifully dying tone and marvellous phrasing.

Bel Canto and Verismo

Callas's first complete studio recording took place for Cetra in September 1952. This was Ponchielli's *La Gioconda*, conducted by Antonino Votto. It is unfortunate that her only congenial partner for this opera is Fedora Barbieri, for it is a work requiring a tenor of special calibre, an exceptional dramatic baritone and a deep bass. When you hear the crude and lumpy singing of Gianni

Poggi, you can understand why Maria Callas later, when she was in a position to do so, placed the highest value on thorough ensemble work and good partners.

Perhaps a prerequisite for understanding the Callas phenomenon and her unique ability to transform herself vocally is to listen first to the *Rigoletto* recording from Mexico and then this high-tension melodrama. This is not just for her ability to sing on the one hand a light coloratura part and on the other a dramatic one with the required weight of tone; it is much more for her art in grasping at the highest level the formal languages of these two works, languages which are not just different but at completely opposite poles. Expressing the difference as simply as possible, Ponchielli's music requires full-blooded singing while Verdi's requires the art of vocal gesture. The difference is as great as between the language of French classical tragedy and a Sardou melodrama. And yet the vehement, direct and partially coarse vocal expression called for by Ponchielli must be tempered with artistic understanding; if it isn't, Gioconda's music can sound as if Anita Cerquetti were singing with Callas's voice. I am not just using background knowledge to spite another singer. Anita Cerquetti, who had to substitute for Callas as Norma in Rome in 1958, imitated specific characteristics of the Callas sound, in particular the open sounds of the lower chest register, as did Elena Suliotis and later Lucia Aliberti and Sylvia Sass, without supplementing them with any emotional inflection of their own.

To sum up, the differentiation of full, emphatic and flowing tone by means of coloration and verbal acting requires classical bel canto technique, with its artistic understanding. One element of this technique is the formation of an even and resonant tone which can be modified according to dynamics. It is something which often gave Callas special difficulty in verisimo roles, even in the early performances and recordings like the often quoted key scene of *La Gioconda*. The cry 'Ah! come t'amo' can rise softly, enraptured and suspended in a fountain of sound. Zinka Milanov, for many years 'owner' of this role at the Met, formed the phrase with unforgettable *dolcezza*, an achievement of which she was always proud. Indeed she could still make a significant impression with it in her 1958 recording, when she was long since

past her peak. The high B rests confidently on a securely supported column of air. Alan Blyth in *Opera on Record* writes of
Callas that she sounds wobbly in both of her recordings. Ardoin
puts it more euphemistically, describing her shaping of this phrase
as 'more earthbound than ethereal'. Now every voice is a law
unto itself, whether as technical artefact or as expression of a state
of mind. Sweetness of the pure and lyric variety was not at the
disposal of the Callas voice, because it was alien to her nature
which embraced sentiment but not naïvety. It goes without saying
that therein lay her ability to experience feelings and give them
expression. To my ears, putting it as subjectively as possible, it
is not just the happiness of an emotion secure in itself which
resounds in the *crescendo* and *diminuendo* on the B in 'Ah! come
t'amo', but also the knowledge that such happiness will be transi-
tory.

With the second act we step into a vocal arena in which Maria
Callas and Fedora Barbieri, an equal partner in every respect,
fight a wild vocal duel and in which Callas gives vocal shape to
hatred verging on the obsessive. When both singers end the scene
with a high B of glowing heat, the result is more than the sum
of two women struggling to express themselves. Callas's interpretation of 'Suicidio' scarcely needs any further extolling. Anyone
who knows it will be able to hear her dark deep tones vibrating
with emotions and the flaming intensity of her high phrases. Even
more remarkable is the fact that her expression is not driven to
extremes, nor affect into effect. She sings with emotion not with
rhetoric – or putting it another way, she sings a monologue not
a statement. Again and again she finds ('ultimo croce del mio
cammin') the tender sound of feeling and suffering, and perhaps
in 'come t'amo' we hear the suffering which she knew was to
come.

These expressive dimensions come even more emphatically to
the fore in the second 1959 version than in the Cetra recording,
and this is in spite of evident weakness and insecurity in the voice.
Callas's musical and artistic qualities are demonstrated by the fact
that she sings 'Suicidio' in an even more moulded and balanced
style than in the earlier version. All the more regrettable, then,
that all four of her colleagues in the other main roles sing and act

to a standard that is below average. Fiorenza Cossotto's ambition was, as in later years, to exhibit her voice rather than to develop the musical meaning; Pier Mirando Ferraro peddles the cruder effects of verismo; Piero Cappuccilli performs with a tone which is both rough and forced in volume; Ivo Vinco lacks the sonority of a real black bass.

Lady Macbeth at La Scala

For Maria Callas, 1952 ended with two particularly important appearances. She made her Covent Garden début on 8 November as Norma under Gui, and then a month later came her final breakthrough at La Scala as Lady Macbeth under de Sabata. Before the first London Norma she had already sung the part thirty-eight times, and yet 'Casta diva' has a tenseness which betrays her nervous state, and the voice seems uneasy especially on the repeated high As. Perhaps it is churlish to mention this when one hears how these notes were later to be sung by Beverley Sills or Renata Scotto, not to mention Joan Sutherland. Starting with the second act we are given singing which is exemplary in its portrayal – and sympathetic support from Gui. Also worth mentioning is the fact that the small roll of Clotilde is taken by Sutherland and, let us repeat, Callas won with her performance the love and admiration of the British public, who were to be faithful to her until the end of her career.

The most important appearance of 1952 was the La Scala *prima* of Verdi's *Macbeth* under the direction of Victor de Sabata. Apart from the performance when she stood in as Aida, she had only performed there as Elena in *I Vespri*, Norma and Constanze. *Macbeth* was her first really thoroughly prepared production, and although Enzo Mascherini in the title role was a partner of solid quality only, with a tired and coarse-grained voice, she none the less had in Victor de Sabata a sympathetic conductor and musician who challenged her talents. She went to the performance on top form, vocally secure and perfectly prepared on the musical side, and the live recording indeed conveys the tension and atmosphere of that evening. Ardoin writes that 'her voice creates scenery and

action for the mind's theatre'. However, this performance begins
in a way which is irritating and rhetorical in the bad sense. Macbeth's letter is read out not as an inner monologue, but direct to
the audience, in an extrovert manner redolent of pathos; it is not
directed towards her own soul, whose ambition only breaks out
with vehement savagery in the recitative ('Ambizioso spirto').
The heat of this recitative is taken up by de Sabata in 'Vieni!
t'affretta'. He adopts a speedier tempo than de Fabritiis did in the
concert performance of the aria but he does leave Callas sufficient
time to give nuance and shape to each vocal gesture.

The quality of her performance comes in no small measure
from the fact that dramatic accentuation never overpowers the
precise shaping of line and vocal form; what we hear is dramatised
bel canto singing, realised by means of exemplary vocal virtuosity. All other interpreters of the role lag behind Callas not
because they commanded fewer means of expression but because
they were technically and stylistically inferior to her. Karl Böhm
once described Elisabeth Höngen, who sang Lady Macbeth under
his direction, as the 'greatest *tragédienne* in the world'. The existing
recording does nothing to confirm this, because Höngen does not
have the gift of translating the richness of forms in Verdi's music
into gestures of sufficient nuance. Nor do Shirley Verrett or
Fiorenza Cossotto come near to approaching Callas in this, and
it is noteworthy that no critics commented on the forced, shrill
and hard tones of Cossotto. Even more than in its virtuosity, the
power of Callas's performance lay in the aptness with which she
filled every phrase, interjection and nuance of the dialogue with
meaning, tension and drama.

It may seem self-evident that the quality of a performance lies
in the wealth of detail which is realised. And yet how rarely does
one come across a portrayal which convinces us of the wealth of
details which are faithfully illuminated? The sound of light in the
text needs to be brought out even more in recitative and passages
of dialogue than in the aria itself. The prosodic phrasing needs to
be assimilated, the singer must not resort to vocal effect, a sense
of fantasy is required and, above all, dramatic imagination. The
second act of *Macbeth*, in which actions, like the murder, are
mirrored in the minds and fantasies of the protagonists, will only

come to dramatic life when the dialogue and recitative are so presented.

In Callas's portrayal the end of the first act becomes an intimate psychological play with infinitesimal shadings of text and colouring of tone. No less convincing is the way she forms 'La luce langue' with its alternation of expressive elements that are in turn like sceptical self-dialogue and then hysterical aggression: here a nervously suppliant 'Nuovo delitto' ('A new outrage'), there a violently decisive 'E necessario!' ('It must be!'). Just as sharply outlined are the contrasts in the drinking song, which plays on two ambivalent levels at once, one of language and one of expression: it is a *brindisi* for the guests at a ghostly party but at the same time a hidden warning for Macbeth.

Ardoin, Hamilton and other Callas writers all agree that the sleepwalking scene is less well realised. It lacks sufficient weight and dramatic contrast, beginning at a surprisingly brisk tempo; Callas's later recording of the scene with Rescigno, although vocally no longer supreme, is sung with more variety of form, due mostly to her perfect shaping of the numerous recitative-like interjections. But this is a reservation made only when hearing the live recording, and not at the time of the performance.

The Birth of the Legend or the Second Existence

'It will be like a dialogue with eternity,' was Emil Berliner's emphatic statement when over a hundred years ago he unveiled to the (learned) public his invention, the gramophone record. As far as music was concerned, the *recherche du temps perdu* had assumed a new quality. The performance of music, hitherto bound to time and space, could now be set free and perpetuated. This gave the performer something like a second existence. Caruso, who according to Fred Gaisberg 'made' the gramophone record, was the first artist whose influence was to become more and more independent of his actual physical presence and who was to live on through his recordings. Maria Callas, born fifty years after Caruso, had the opportunity to use the technical medium in a new way: she was able to rescue opera as an aesthetic and dramatic object and place it in the *musée imaginaire* (André Malraux) of the gramophone. Can one regard this as pure coincidence – on the one hand the rise of Caruso through emancipation by the gramophone, and on the other the emergence of Maria Callas and the era of the long-playing record?

There is no doubt that Walter Legge quickly saw in Maria Callas an ideal protagonist for imaginary theatre. His recollections[13] tell us how he was uncompromising in his selection of the best artists and using the recordings by these artists to promote their careers and his company's success. The recordings of *Lucia di Lammermoor, I Puritani* and Puccini's *Tosca* were to launch the Angel label in the United States with Callas as leading artist, just as the two 1954 recital LPs – one devoted to Puccini, the other to coloratura and *espressivo* arias – were intended to propagate world-wide the capabilities of Callas the *assoluta*. The fact that on record she sang arias from operas which she no longer performed on stage as well as some from ones which she had never, and would never, sing on stage, is of little importance: these are part of her second existence and do not imply that she could never, for example, have sung Mimi or Manon on stage.

That certainly applies to the Cetra *Gioconda* of 1952 and the EMI *Lucia* of 1953. Admittedly she had only performed Donizetti's heroine seven times (three in Mexico, four in Florence) before the recording, but no amount of performances could have had the effect of the tapes which Walter Legge sent to Karajan. The conductor immediately decided to put the work on at La Scala, although it would be naïve to think that Maria Callas had convinced him of the quality of the opera! Rather, Karajan recognised that the performance of any opera earns its reputation through the quality of its principals. The production at La Scala would have been impossible without the foretaste of the Serafin recording, its transfer to Berlin and Vienna would have been impossible without a try-out at La Scala, and the Met début would have been impossible without those Berlin and Vienna performances. In other words Walter Legge was acting not just as record producer but was one of the decisive architects in the Callas career – a statement which should be taken without qualification and as an expression of my admiration.

Many artists who worked with Legge report on the often painful (but always sympathetic) attention with which he observed
his artists' performances. One of his guiding principles was, 'I
believe that you can do better.' He was so confident and commanding in his aesthetic judgement that he was able to correct
even autocrats like Wilhelm Furtwängler, Karajan, Otto Klemp-
erer or Dietrich Fischer-Dieskau. And even Callas. These were
all artists who did not give in easily, or only did so to bring them
new possibilities in their work. As Adorno said, an artist's work
cannot be separated from technical progress in this age of technical
reproduction. It is rare in the cultural industry for artistic innovation and technical progress to be happily combined, and the
fact that Legge achieved this four decades ago justifies his position
as technical artist, a Svengali of the technical age.

Maria Callas had been a sensation in the operatic world for six
years when in 1953 she astonished audiences with an artistic form
that had almost sunk into oblivion. In February 1953 she recorded
Donizetti's *Lucia di Lammermoor* under Serafin, in March *I Puritani*
and in August *Tosca*, as well as *La Traviata* for Cetra (September
1953). It was these recordings which made her an object of world
attention. Between 1953 and 1960 Callas recorded each year, with
certain exceptions, at least two – sometimes even four – complete
operas, and that is not including the half-dozen recitals. Her
influence and the understanding of her aesthetic became omnipres-
ent for the general public only from the autumn of 1953 and the
early months of 1954 onwards.

It must not be forgotten that pirate records only gained wide
public in the early 1970s, in other words long after the singer's
departure from the stage. John Ardoin's *The Callas Legacy* first
appeared in 1977, the year of her death, recognising her achievement only retrospectively.

It must also be taken into account that in the case of the first
recital LPs of the early 1950s, only a few thousand copies were
produced. The public image of Callas changed around 1956, the
year of her Met début, when her voice became of less interest
than her image as a tigress.

The 1953 recordings testify to an admirable care and profession-
alism. It is not a question of *Werktreue* in the modern sense, but

of dramatic and theatrical discipline applied to the work being recorded; in formal terms, the opera was performed in accordance with current theatrical practice. As most composers, Verdi included, were practical men of the theatre who made allowance in their operas for changes to be made in performance, the practice cannot have been such a bad one.

The recording of *Lucia di Lammermoor*, with which Maria Callas put the work on the modern musical map, is certainly not as correct, complete or authentic as the version with Beverly Sills. Now, who is really interested in this correct version with Sills? Or who really delights in being able to hear the glass harmonica which Donizetti uses in the Mad Scene? Does the interest in completeness and correctness, which is of little importance in theatre practice (even for Toscanini), not really conceal an admission that the Lucia of Beverly Sills or Montserrat Caballé leaves us cold? No, it is the Callas version to which we return to get to know the opera. Better still, the Callas versions, for there are two studio and six live ones. The first studio version was the one which made Callas's portrayal into an event. Just a year after the appearances in Florence Karajan produced the opera at La Scala and then brought it to Berlin and Vienna. The fact that she also sang the role in Chicago and New York and that these appearances received almost hysterical attention, shows that not only was Lucia a central role in her repertoire but that it also became a symbol for her fame – generated by the recording.

John Ardoin has admitted that he would choose the *Lucia di Lammermoor* recorded live in Berlin as his favourite, while he declares the Florence studio recording as the most satisfying gramophone version. David A. Lowe also puts the live version, not the studio one, among Callas's greatest recordings, quoting Desmond Shawe-Taylor after the first night in Berlin: 'I would venture to say that she will never sing better.' The critic, in saying this, fully realised that in the degree of consummation achieved she was unsurpassed; he was also perhaps making reference, as mentioned earlier, to the fact that she was no longer singing with absolute security and certainly no longer with the vocal weight of earlier performances.

The prize certainly goes to the first recording under Serafin.

What is noteworthy is the change in the voice and the vocal attack. These are no longer the high notes of a 'wild cat': even the most exposed *acuti* are moulded into the line or firmly placed on a cabaletta like a crown. The greater unity and the improved evenness of the voice – the registers are better matched and yet recognisably characteristic in sound – assure the singing a wonderfully harmonic flow: 'Quando rapito' and even more the duet 'Verrano a te' possess a perfect legato, and the tone is of marvellous bitter-sweetness. Di Stefano's singing is dark in timbre, full of effect and attractive in sound, but lacks any of the polish which marks out the real romantic bel canto tenor. Pavarotti's would be the perfect type of voice for this, but even he has not etched the final scene with the elegance of Francesco Marconi or John McCormack. Di Stefano's high register seems always to be slightly veiled, as a result of his pushing the chest voice upwards.

For the Mad Scene Maria Callas reveals the meaning of the music with supreme virtuosity. As in all truly great performances time seems to stand still; the time of the action appears to become the time of reality. Just as Shakespeare can conjure up an atmosphere as in the first moments of *The Tempest* when the urgent call of 'Boatswain!' penetrates the storm, so Callas imbues her first phrases with the dark sound of melancholy, lost to the world. The legato of a brilliant violinist could not be more consummate. The phrase 'Ohimè, sorge il tremendo fantasma' is an *azione teatrale* achieved by means of sound alone and this applies no less to the sickly longing of 'Alfin sei tua'. The emotional content of the vowels pulses heavily through sound coloured with unending pain. Ardoin speaks of an agonising beauty – and to quote André Gide again, the most painful melodies are the most beautiful. Only someone who takes pleasure in sound for itself will complain about the hardness and bitterness of the odd note in the cadenza.

If we may step out of chronology for a moment, let us look at the Berlin performance conducted by Karajan. This has received such unanimous praise that it is worth quoting the critical comments of Michael Scott:[14]

By the time I saw her play the role in Dallas in 1959, she had only a thread of tone left. She had sung her first Lucias seven years earlier, and by 1955, when she assayed the role in Berlin with La Scala under Herbert von Karajan, she already sounds exhausted, the performance having an atmosphere of too diligent rehearsal. Her voice has grown wan and wavery; in the sextet she can no longer manage the repeated high A flats cleanly or firmly; and at the end of the first part of the mad scene she omits the exposed, interpolated high E flat. Karajan's conducting is unstylish, and in any event Lucia does not require a great conductor as much as a great singer. However absurd it may seem, and contrary to modern notions, all Callas's Lucia needed was someone who could follow her and keep the rest of the company together. We can hear this in the Mad Scene broadcast from Mexico City on June 14 1952, led by one Guido Picco, when she was able to undertake the music with stunning weight of tone and breadth of phrasing, executing the florid passages limpidly and fearlessly, with an accuracy that had not been approached since the days of Melba. At the end, when the performance culminates in a full-voiced high E flat, the Mexico City audience itself does a mad scene.

We should cautiously ask ourselves whether those who admire the Berlin recording are not imagining greatness in the interpretation of an interpretation; whether they are really hearing or wanting to hear an artistic struggle of wonderful musicality? If it is their imagination, it speaks for the stature and artistry of Callas that make us forget the voice.

But let us listen. 'Regnava del silenzio' flows with soft and melancholy tone but without any tonal intensity. The passages and scales in 'Quando rapito' are executed cleanly but without the fire of virtuosity. Even the magical *mezza voce* with which she begins 'Verrano a te' sounds as if she is having to adapt to a reduced vocal capability. There are grandiose moments in the duet with Rolando Panerai (Enrico), where she truly illuminates cries and moments of emotion with the colour of her singing. The Mad Scene is also painted in pastel shades – with stronger accents – at 'il fantasma' and 'Alfin sei tua'. The broad symphonic tempo adopted by the conductor may have something to do with the way in which she has to lighten her tone and not allow herself too much breath. The pacing is again wonderful, with an inner tension even in endlessly extended phrases. The repeated *staccati* B flats seem a little insecure. She omits the first E flat, and for the ending puts all her remaining energy into this obligatory bravura note.

A great performance? It is one of the grandest that she gave. Yet at the same time it is diminished as one in which the battle with her voice becomes evident. However it is certainly a great performance in the sense understood by Wagner, in which the singer handles the breath so beautifully that doubts about her voice become irrelevant.

Other *Lucia* performances are from Naples under Francesco Molinari-Pradelli, with the excellent young Gianni Raimondi, the less happy one from New York in the year of her début there, in which she was in far from secure form, another from Rome in 1957 under Tullio Serafin which is scarcely any better, and finally the second studio version, in which her partners are a contributing factor to its being far less successful than the first one.

Maria Callas's second studio recording for EMI was *I Puritani* with Giuseppe di Stefano, Rolando Panerai and Nicola Rossi-Lemeni and conducted by Serafin. This was made at the end of March 1953 but was brought out in the United States before *Lucia di Lammermoor* because Walter Legge wanted to have the recording which he considered to be the best – from the technical point of view as well – as advance publicity both for Callas and the new Angel label. Although Bellini's late work is a singers' opera *par excellence* (if one can speak of a late work from one who was consummate so early and who died so young), it did not present such a strong challenge to the soprano's theatrical imagination as the Donizetti opera, mainly because the role of Elvira is dramatically one-dimensional. Furthermore, Giuseppe di Stefano, who had been a convincing Edgardo in spite of certain reservations, was out of his depth in the part of Arturo: this possesses an extremely high *tessitura*, tailor-made as it was for the high, agile and romantic tenor voice of Rubini. It is a role which would have suited the young Nicolai Gedda, who only came to it in 1973, when he was at least ten years too late. Gedda sings Rubini's legendary F acceptably but his *portamento* approach to it is laborious and the sound of his voice is brittle and dry. Luciano Pavarotti sings the high reaches of the part in falsetto but he does possess the chest note of D flat and the right but perhaps too narrowly focused sound, as well as a *piano* which is too strained. Alfredo Kraus, like Pavarotti a romantic tenor, is technically secure but vocally brittle, not just in the recording with Muti but also a live one from 1966 conducted by Bonynge.

Di Stefano's emphatic delivery is no substitute for vocal elegance, especially as Callas sings with such polish. She illustrated how expression can be drawn solely by unfolding and colouring the line; she exhibited falling chromatic scales in the *polacca* which were of fantastic flexibility, and repeated her early masterful performance of 'Qui la voce' with a voice which was even lighter and more strongly and forwardly placed.

Tosca, or the Technical Work of Art

Those early studio recordings reveal, just as the one of Puccini's *Tosca* does with even greater perfection, the quality that was probably the singer's most significant one: her ability to illuminate the sense and feeling of a word through its sound, and to do this not only in passages of recitative or in prosodic phrases. How often, as in the case of Joan Sutherland, are the words intelligible only to someone who is already familiar with them or who is following a libretto? The listener who wants to understand finds that the words rush along like a foreign language spoken very fast. It is Maria Callas who can often articulate and declare a word or a phrase (that is, give them form and eloquence) in such a manner that even those who do not understand the language can nevertheless grasp the meaning of those words.

Artistic fluency is far more important in verismo music than in Italian classical and romantic works. Rossini, Bellini, Donizetti and even the young Verdi placed their expression to a great extent in the modulation of the sound. Even when Rossini called for a coloratura to have dramatic ardour and for a trill to be energetic, or when Donizetti or Verdi called for an accent to have power, the means of expression were still strictly musical. In verismo on the other hand, composers gave up fitting words to sound and instead transformed actual speech into musical terms. Maria Callas, with her bel canto technique, remains the supreme interpreter of verismo music because it was her aim, as far as was possible and practicable, to use vocal means to express verismo's rhetoric and its exaltation. What assisted her in this was her ability, already mentioned, to evoke in equal measure a word's shape and colour. Even when her voice became only a thin thread of sound, she still had sufficient means to play Tosca.

The recording of *Tosca*, a *technical* work of art of the highest stature, was conducted by Victor de Sabata and, as we have already put it, produced for the aural stage by Walter Legge. In it Maria Callas achieves a perfect symbiosis: that of singing which is expression alone and of expression which remains the purest song. She gives identity to elements which are not identical: expression without exaltation, sweetness without sentimentality, artistic understanding without calculation and being spontaneous without being hectic. Her portrayal is all of a piece and as such, like all great acting achievements, is more than the sum of its parts. Admittedly there are inspired details, like the sharp profile given to the three cries of 'Mario!' which portray in sound Tosca's agitation and tension, her impatience and hysteria. Callas plays out the duet with Cavaradossi with the intuition and watchfulness of jealousy; both sides of the duet are conducted on two levels of language, of understanding and of feeling. She asks – he gives an indirect reply; she stops short – he tries to placate; she hesitates – he makes for reconciliation; she is hurt – he flatters; she is coquettish – he acquiesces; she flatters – he flirts; she entices and then chides. Another detail: standing before the painting of the blonde Madonna, she utters a cry of sudden recognition that it is the Attavanti. In tears (stage direction) she asks if he loves her – but Callas does not sob. She threatens and looks again at the picture and the eyes of the supposed rival. Thereupon the painter begins his cantilena '*con grande espressione*' and '*largamente*', flatters her '*dolcissimo*', while Tosca, 'transported, her head on Cavaradossi's shoulder' (stage directions), sings '*dolce, ma sentitio ed espressivo*'. 'O come la sai bene l'arte di farti amare' ('Oh how you understand the art of flattery'). Like all the dialogue, this is from a textual point of view ambiguous. The text reads 'You are a flatterer and hypocrite', but the music says 'I want to believe you'. Callas articulates the text but at the same time adopts a tone which does not contradict but supplements it. Schnitzler said that in love there are no lies which are not immediately recognised and believed. This is what Callas sings, in a tone which we can sense and feel to convey Tosca's exhilaration, and no Tebaldi, Milanov, Price or Caballé makes it so suddenly and intoxicatingly beautiful.

A further detail: Tosca later returns to the church, still in a state of jealousy, and comes face to face with Scarpia. It is difficult to resist describing Tito Gobbi's portrayal. He was in every respect Callas's only equal partner and counterpart, although less so as a singer than as an actor. Tosca's conversation with Cavaradossi is now repeated under different circumstances: it is now the police chief who is conducting the interrogation with the incisiveness of a demagogue and criminal. Scarpia plays upon her jealousy. 'In tears' (stage direction) she leaves the church, singing, '*con grande espressione*', 'God will pardon me, for he can see how I am suffering.' Over the last phrase is the direction 'in a flood of tears'.

Does Tosca actually weep at this point? Or does she have to convey in her singing how she is weeping? In other words, should we need to experience on stage the trivial reality of sobbing, or is it rather that a musical description should bring tears to our eyes? In a normal routine or traditional performance or recording we are left with the average diva's lack of imagination. Like Renata Tebaldi. Callas does not sob. But the way and the manner in which she sings 'io piango' and transforms a tone – one tone! – with tears into the sound of pain makes her suffering clear to the listener.

She still triumphs in 'Vissi d'arte', where most Toscas are merely adequate. In the final phrases of the aria the melodic and emotional curve takes a *crescendo molto* to finish on B flat. There is a caesura, then a fresh start with A flat G, octave fall to G, and cadence. For the sake of vocal and sonic effect Montserrat Caballé manages to sing the phrase right through the caesura, that is right through the logic of text and music. Callas observes the caesura, sings the octave fall and sings a sob which is only perceived when it has finished, singing it as a spontaneous sound and not as an illustrative theatrical gesture. Previously only one singer was capable of achieving this unity of understanding and sensibility – Lotte Lehmann.

Legge tells how much time they took to master, produce and fix the shape of the last phrase of the second act. Tosca disentangles what she thinks is Cavaradossi's safe conduct pass from Scarpia's fingers, hovers over his body, takes candles from the table and sets them beside Scarpia. Then she speaks, sings, sighs the phrase 'E avanti a lui tremava tutta Roma!' This consists of eleven notes: semiquavers and dotted quavers. Its pivotal note is C sharp – a spoken phrase. It is a curious mixture of pathos, genuine and not genuine at the same time, the reason being that an actress cannot portray pathos or suffering in a concrete and real situation where the suffering is existential: she simply has to live. Callas does both: she is actress of the scene as well as its victim. But then, how many will appreciate the difference even when they have recognised it?

The Tears of Understanding

Measured against *Madama Butterfly* or *La Bohème*, not to mention *Un Ballo in Maschera* or *Otello*, Mascagni's *Cavalleria Rusticana* is a mere show-stopper, a second-rate piece. A singer who is histrionically gifted can create figures out of Tosca, Fedora and Adriana which can be enjoyed especially if one has a taste for camp. What has to be done is to sublimate an expressive mode which is partly coarse and partly anachronistic, and adopt instead a cross between naïvety and mannerism. One cannot relate to a role like Santuzza by means of a viewpoint. Starting with Gemma Bellincioni, the first singer of Santuzza, almost all Italian sopranos – and many mezzos – have recorded Santuzza, or at least 'Voi lo sapete'. The role requires little more than straight full-blooded singing.

Describing the dozen or so recordings in *Opera on Record*,

Charles Osborne uses a few adjectives which are not really adequate: 'highly effective', 'dramatic', 'moving', 'characterful'. This is not the place to criticise a criticism but rather to establish the remarkable fact that the interpretation of expressive verismo music must be described not with the vocabulary of aesthetic reflection but rather with that of emotion.

Lina Bruna Rasa (conducted by Mascagni himself), Giulietta Simionato, Renata Tebaldi and Victoria de los Angeles all sing the music with effect and drama as well as more or less beautifully. But none of these performances achieves any kind of tragic depth. Admittedly such a concept is problematical when dealing with a verismo opera. But just as Bellini's *I Puritani* deals with the 'essence of melancholy' (John Ardoin's description of Callas's portrayal), so *Cavalleria* deals with the essence of suffering. However, contrary to what Ardoin thinks I consider that the role of Santuzza is dramatically not as one-dimensional as is suggested by the sobbing and screaming.

Callas's dramatic imagination takes a course other than that of exaltation. There are only one or two instances of violent outburst – at 'l'amai' and 'io piango' – and these are precisely controlled both vocally and in the acting. And, as in the *Tosca* recording, she does not indulge in the kind of sobs which can for the most part seem silly and laughable. Particularly in the duet with Turiddu she creates rich and subtle contrasts of expression with far more subtlety than all other recorded singers of the part. She starts cool and distant, but with emotion flickering beneath the surface (as revealed in the phrase 'Battimi, insultami'). And what sublime pathos – through the deep dark tone full of pain and tears – in the phrases starting with 'No, no Turiddu' which are sung with Bellini-like bel canto. The point is that she draws expression from the shape, colour and shading of the vocal line. Her artistic intelligence is perhaps even more penetrating in the duet with Alfio in which, solely through her vocal shaping of the part, a sound is created out of tears, rhetoric and sensibility.

If we may again deviate from chronology we can look at *Cavalleria*'s twin, Leoncavallo's *Pagliacci*. Callas sang Santuzza on stage in her time in Athens, but never the role of Nedda. The opera is quite rightly considered to be the tenor's, yet this recording, brilliantly conducted by Serafin, shows that Nedda is not to be played as a mere type. She is a character, and a not entirely harmless one at that. Few other recordings or performances show so clearly that the drama has a pre-history, that Canio's jealousy is not without foundation and that it is already flickering in 'un tal gioco'. The certainty of this has to be faced in the *ballatella*. The figure of the young woman needs profile, that mixture of *joie de vivre* and frivolity which she pursues against all warnings, and which becomes the driving force of the action. The duet with Tonio has the oppressive intensity of all the dramatic duels which Callas fought with Tito Gobbi in *Tosca, Ballo*, and *Aida*. The following duet with Silvio shows again how intoxicatingly beautiful her singing can be. Not just beautiful in the sense of dramatic aptness but in the way it submerges the listener with its sound. And was Silvio ever sung more blissfully, happily and with more passion than here, by Rolando Panerai? Passion is not *expressed* by the impassioned manner of both singers, but rather it is converted into sound and shape.

Callas's portrayal in the second act demonstrates the need for Nedda to be cast with a dramatic singer. The tension of this short scene lies ultimately in the fact that Nedda has to appear and sing in the *commedia* as a type – as Colombine – but at the same time she must convey that a play is unfolding within the play, a drama of hatred. There may be vocal lightness in the magical warblings of parts of the *ballatella*, but what about the phrase 'Ebben! Se mi giudici' after Canio's outburst in the second act? Here, in a single cry, in a single wild gesture, Nedda reveals herself as a sinister figure; unlike Desdemona, she is not simply a victim but an active participant, who eventually provokes murder with her combination of hatred and pride. Nedda/Callas's 'No, per la madre', hurled at Canio/di Stefano, would drive a saint to madness.

Giuseppe di Stefano, who is enthusiastically praised by John Ardoin, sings Turiddu with more conviction and expressive tone than he does Canio, a part for which he possesses neither the dramatic tenor's weight nor the almost elegant concentration of Björling. Gobbi, who is excellent in his duet with Callas, has some difficulty with the Prologue's *tessitura* and even more with accentuated and declamatory passages such as 'de l'odio i tristi frutti'. Fortunately he omits the traditionally interpolated high note; nothing is more annoying than an effect which achieves nothing.

Medea, or the Voice of the Abyss

Even more regrettable than the recording of *Macbeth* which never took place is the fact that in September 1953 Maria Callas herself took the action which blocked the way for a recording of Verdi's *La Traviata* with the teams of Serafin/Legge or Giulini/Legge. The absence of a producer for the Cetra recording of *La Traviata* only illustrates how important, indeed indispensable, is the work of such a figure. This is not only conducted by Gabriele Santini without tension but is cast with pronounced weakness in the other main roles. Francesco Albanese as Alfredo and Ugo Savarese as Germont sing not just coarsely and roughly but without tension or imagination, so that the Act 2 duet, for example, makes no impression. Callas, although she is singing with faultless technique, does not command the energy to shape her part with the sense of purpose it had in Mexico in 1951, where at least she had a public which reacted to her. A few expressive moments of greatness, mainly in declamatory phrases or when expressing anger (Act 2 Scene 2) and the approach of death (Act 3), cannot save the performance. For Callas's special qualities can only unfold fully and completely when engaged in ensemble work; not only was the richness of her sound and expression inspired by the Wagnerian orchestra, but her artistic understanding came from the idea of opera as *Gesamtkunstwerk*. And she was only able to apply these aesthetic principles to the role of Violetta when she played it later with Visconti in Milan and with Zeffirelli in Dallas.

Quite a different kind of dramatic actress presents herself in the live recording from La Scala of Cherubini's *Medea* (10 December 1953) under the direction of Leonard Bernstein. She had first sung the role, another of those central to her career, only seven months earlier in Florence under Vittorio Gui, where her affinity with it was immediately recognisable despite the fact that she had had to learn it in a very short time. The work, composed only six years after *Die Zauberflöte*, was not successful at its première in Paris and instead found its greatest admirers in the German-speaking countries. It was Schubert's favourite opera, was highly rated by Beethoven, and Brahms saw it as a peak of dramatic music. *Medea* was, in formal terms, originally an *opéra comique* with spoken dialogue, but this was replaced by recitatives written by Franz Lachner, a friend of Schubert. The Ricordi score is based on Lachner's re-working (that also applies to the many cuts).[15]

I started out by describing the voice of Maria Callas as not just a technical artefact but as the expressive form given to a character and temperament, thereby showing that she was a singer of dark romanticism. The expressiveness of Cherubini's opera points forward, as Ulrich Schreiber has indicated with considerable penetration, to the future world of Spontini, Weber and Meyerbeer. It is an expressiveness which is extremely radical and therefore alien to the bourgeois worlds of opera and entertainment. Schreiber says: 'Don Giovanni and Medea both meet death by fire and are therefore torchbearers of downfall [. . .] Cherubini's *Medea* opened opera's gate into the nineteenth century.' The stature of Callas's interpretation lies for Schreiber in the way that she breaks the classical surface of the work and 'places it on a psychological level',[16] anticipating in Medea a figure like Wagner's Ortrud.

Apart from the admiration shown by other composers, Cherubini's opera attracted little interest after its Paris première, a situation which continued into the second half of the nineteenth century. And although it was performed at La Scala in 1909 with Mazzoleni (conducted by Vitale), it was primarily Maria Callas who brought it back to public attention. She sang the Milan revival, then performances followed in Venice, Rome, Dallas, London and, finally, in Epidaurus. There are five recordings of it from the 1950s, all with Callas, but none with other singers. Gerda Lammers sang it in Kassel in 1958 but the first other singer of international stature to perform it was Rita Gorr at the Paris Opéra in 1962. At the end of the 1960s came a recording with Gwyneth Jones, and in 1977 one with the Hungarian soprano Sylvia Sass. But the stature of the Callas versions only accentuates the monotony of the British singer and the forced sound of the Hungarian.

In spite of all its cuts the recording of the Milan performance is one of the most penetrating Callas documents. It was conducted by Leonard Bernstein, who in substituting for the indisposed Victor de Sabata amazingly made his début as operatic conductor. When John Ardoin writes that in her performance 'cool classicism turned to vibrating emotionality', he has misunderstood. What Callas distilled both from Romantic bel canto and the supposedly 'Classical' role was the expression of the soul's depths and, in the case of Cherubini's work, the archaic. It is not easy to describe or analyse her portrayal. Of course the technical artefact of singing can be described in detail and with more precision than is generally assumed (this is demonstrated by descriptions from Stendhal, Turgenev, Chorley, Burney, Hanslick, Henderson, Shawe-Taylor and Porter). But the description of expressive devices and sound figuration, which of necessity draws on metaphor, risks being imprecise and misunderstood. How does one describe hatred which has become sound by means of a figuration? What does it convey if we say that the voice of Callas/Medea is, on her first entry, hatred and only hatred? (This is not to devalue John Ardoin, who made that statement and who has been paraphrased by many other commentators.) I would like to refer to someone who was more than an eloquent connoisseur of the soul's depths and the art of dramatic acting: Richard Wagner. Just before the Paris production of *Tannhäuser*, while under great pressure of work, he wrote a letter, dated 21 February 1861, to the tenor Albert Niemann, giving what is perhaps the most penetrating description ever of what singing acting can and should be. It is at the same time an attempt to justify the crossing of a vocal barrier which brought the risk that Niemann would cry off: the tenor had plainly insisted that Wagner should delete a difficult passage. Wagner's reply:

> That it was possible for you to sing only the third act in Germany is in itself sufficient to disclose the weak point in your previous achievement. Even the most mediocre singers have known how to be relatively effective in this third act: they were able to do so as a matter of course, in much the same way that Masaniello's mad scene was effective, making every tenor seem

better than he was. I tell you, by contrast, that you can keep
the whole of this third act if you can give me a proper rendering
of the finale to the second act. It is here that the dramatic crisis
lies, and here, too, that Tannhäuser must enlist and maintain
the greatest interest: if he fails in this, the third act, however
successful, will remain a mere play for actors by which I set
no store whatsoever [. . .] Do not refer me here to the fact that
I cut the *adagio* passage for Tichatscheck: if I had had *you* then,
you may rest assured that I would not have shortened it. Nor
should you believe that I took this passage away from Tichatscheck because it might have tired his voice: on the contrary, as
far as his voice is concerned, Tichatscheck could have sung six
such passages, for the longer he had been singing, the richer
his voice became and the greater his powers of endurance [. . .]
The deficiency which ruined this important passage at the time
of the Dresden performances was as follows: a glance at the
score will show you that the entire ensemble of minstrels continues to sing at the same time as Tannhäuser himself; their
voices cover his to the extent that Tannhäuser's solo gives the
impression of being simply an inner part which might, however, have stood out if Tichatscheck had been capable of
expressing any real sense of tragic pain: but we know that this
was precisely where his weak point lay. The inspired idea of
omitting the ensemble and having Tannhäuser sing on his own
did not occur to me at the time . . . Well, you have doubtless
realized how important this passage is, and know not only how
effective it can be in itself but also how important it is for our
interest in Tannhäuser. You are concerned only for your voice,
and your anxiety is increased by the belief that Tichatscheck
himself had not been able to sing this passage. It was to refute
this belief and to restore your confidence that I have just
recounted this entire incident all over again, and repeated the
reason why I cut it on that occasion . . .

You should therefore abandon this fear of yours . . . Do not
think about the third act: this is not a problem for you. Think
only of this finale to the second act and throw yourself into it
body and soul, as though you did not have another note to
sing after this finale. The gain will then be certain: at the most

crucial point in the opera – where everything has reached the highest pitch of intensity, and the slightest sound will be picked up with breathless suspense – here it is that the course of the *entire evening* will be decided! Believe *me* and trust in me just this *once*! You shall never hear from me again as long as you live!! – If you produce this 'pitié pour moi' as I have already heard you sing it on repeated occasions and as I know you can, and if you produce it, moreover, in such a way that everyone's hair stands on end and their hearts tremble, *everything*, but *everything* will have been achieved, the immediate effect will be immeasurable [. . .]

It was the energy, concentration and willingness to make sacrifices that Wagner demanded from Niemann that Callas brought to the *Medea* production in Milan – and also to the later productions, especially the Dallas one, where her 'vitriolic sounds' (Ardoin) were also directed at Rudolf Bing, who had not only just fired her but also publicly defamed her. Callas's portrayal resounds with the darkest, most violent colours. Nor does the voice fail her at those moments when the utmost is demanded, something which means a lot more than the fact that the high C at the end of Act 2 is attacked with bold precision.

Everything hinted at in the first long recitative before 'Dei tuoi figli' (sung with pain-filled softness), a recitative which is saturated in all dark emotions, everything is heightened in the duet with Jason at the end of Act 1 into raving of extreme, but never externalised, wildness. That she can still surpass this by expressive means in the third act when invoking the gods and in the double murder, places her portrayal as one of the unique artistic achievements in the interpretative history of opera.

What a chance missed! One sighs with regret when encountering the live recording of Gluck's *Alceste* from La Scala in 1954 under Giulini. If it were possible for any singer, then Callas should have achieved the symbiosis of declamatory delivery and eloquent line; this is illustrated all too clearly by the performance, particularly by the exemplary rendition of 'Divinités du Styx'. But she sings the work in a form which approaches a mutilation, and furthermore the sound quality is quite off-putting. This is a Callas performance which fails to do justice to the work.

In August 1954 came her first Verdi recording – *La Forza del Destino* – for EMI under the direction of Walter Legge,[17] who in a reminiscence which is not entirely free of malice tell us that the voice was so tremulous at the top during these sessions that he told the soprano that a sea-sickness tablet would have to be given away with every set of records. It is surely rather spiteful of him to have related with enjoyment that Callas was shown by Elisabeth Schwarzkopf in a restaurant how to sing top Bs; if intended as an advertisement for his wife, it was in bad taste. Callas *was* having trouble with the highest register at this time. Some top Bs are neither perfectly focused nor held securely, and the notes lack above all a decisive quality: they do not end in themselves. To quote the singing teacher Lamperti, a note must be self-beginning, self-prolonging and self-ending.

We do not know the reason for this insecurity, and are not concerned with making excuses. To say that a few wobbly notes do not matter is out of place in a critical assessment (even if one can and will accept it in a spontaneous discussion). The expressive quality of Callas's mid–1950s recordings would not have suffered if the high register had been more constant or if the top notes had been more 'beautiful'. The singer, but not the singing, can be excused for the insecure notes.

Leonora in *La Forza del Destino* has to do more than sing 'La Vergine' or dazzle with a brilliant top B flat at the end of 'Pace, pace'. If those are what you want to hear you should listen to recordings by the young Renata Tebaldi (preferably the live one under Mitropoulos) or by Zinka Milanov in her prime. If you wish, these two can be used to argue against the Callas recording. Yet why does Lord Harewood not consider Tebaldi a 'central Verdi singer'? And is Milanov an all-round Verdi singer if she does not perform Violetta and if her *Trovatore* Leonora is not masterly in all respects? Can a soprano be an all-round Verdi interpreter if she does not attempt, in the already quoted dictum of Reynaldo Hahn, to produce that combination and indissoluble unity of sound and thought? Hahn held the view that admitting surrender to pure tonal beauty was a 'weakness' or sign of 'a

morbid and inert state of mind'. Is this in contradiction of Stendhal's statement that one can be transported to the angels by a
voice? Not at all. But it happens when word and sense are supplemented through the sound with intensity, emotion and poetry.

'Me, pellegrina ed orfana, lungi del patrio nido' – these words
of Leonora's are, as text, nothing more than a statement. Only
Maria Callas sings as if they encapsulate the entire approaching
drama, using a tone of pain which almost smothers the voice.
The duet which follows shortly with Alvaro becomes a dialogue
not of happy release but the expression of conflicting minds.
Ardoin points out how Serafin gives the scene a broad frame.
More than that, he gives it the greatest intensity by means of a
slow and meditative beat, which covers more tension than Riccardo Muti's polished orchestral excitement. Nor does 'Madre,
pietosa vergine' sound like the prayer of a placid and beautiful
soul. Leonora's 'Son giunta' explodes into the orchestra's *tutti*
outburst, which is then followed by a song which seems an echo
of Schubert's 'Gretchen am Spinnrade', the song which years
earlier Verdi had set in Italian.[18] The scene should be sung 'come
un lamento' and the *tremolo* movements in the orchestra must also
tremble in the voice. No other singer fills the recitative with so
much tension as Callas: she puts even more expressive light into
the vowels, calling to mind the incomparable *chiaroscuro* one sees
in paintings of the high Renaissance. The high point is the phrase
'Deh! Non m'abbandonar' – no, it is the tiny pause before 'Deh,'
a deathly pause which is filled with a sigh, not the routine verismo
sigh but that despairing intake of breath which frees the suffocated
mind. If you want, you can hear the effort involved from time
to time in the three repetitions of the phrase: the first time she
sings 'Deh! Non m'abbandonar', it is with *mezzo voce* and the
tone is not quite securely placed on the breath. But what other
singer has made the powerfully expressive details of this prayer
so full of emotion? Lord Harewood writes of Rossi-Lemeni's
Padre Guardiano that like most others in the role he phrases with
more weight than finesse – and it is with him that Callas has to
sing the following duet. Yet when he greets her 'fidente alla croce'
(with the sign of the cross), he proves himself an inspired partner.

Wherever and whenever this recording is discussed it is the

arias which take central position. But to experience Callas the actress one must also listen to another part: 'Più tranquilla l'alma sento'. Ardoin makes a wonderful observation when he says that she sings these phrases 'as much on the rhythm of notes as on the notes themselves'. The act closes with 'La vergine', preceded by the bass solo 'Il santo nome di Dio'. There is a legendary recording of this with Rosa Ponselle and Ezio Pinza, which possesses marvellous tonal concentration and sounds as if it is truly felt. But we must remember that aesthetic phenomenon which is typical of the gramophone record: when comparing individual scenes or arias divorced from their dramatic context, it is easy to give preference to the one which may be vocally 'better' or 'more beautiful' – in other words to avoid the question of whether a dramatic concept can be drawn from the excerpted recording. Callas's 'La vergine' brings the act to a moving conclusion: she begins the prayer with her 'smallest', most tender voice, the one which in another coloration would be called her 'little-girl' voice but which here is all suffering and self-sacrifice. In keeping with that is the shaping of 'Pace, pace' as an outward cry (Ardoin) instead of as an inner reflection.

The recording, which is so splendidly conducted by Tullio Serafin, does have a big weakness in the totally worn-out singing of Carlo Tagliabue. It can only be viewed as a blunder that Walter Legge engaged this singer. At the time of the recording Tagliabue was fifty-six years old. In Italy he was considered the last really great Verdi baritone and was rated above Gobbi. Giacomo Lauri-Volpi affirms his stature in his book *Voci parallele*. However, Richard Tucker's Alvaro is not entirely without problems either. The American tenor brings to his part an athletic energy and a beautiful command of phrasing but permeates his singing with unnecessary effects which verge on the comic: sobs and sighs which, rather than adding expression to the delivery, put the eloquence of the musical line strongly in jeopardy. It is no excuse, but rather an explanation, to say that Tucker, who at the time appeared almost exclusively at the Met, was following the kind of singing which had been imported with great success by Italians (above all by Mario del Monaco).

Rosina, Fiorilla or a Vocal Witticism

Nothing needs less justification than entertainment. This was said by Brecht, who, however, certainly made a mistake in considering that entertainment was *not* distraction or diversion. Rossini's *Il Turco in Italia* is by no means one of his most ambitious works, but senseless German depth goes too far in suggesting that Rossini lacked ambition. Of course it goes without saying that a light touch is more difficult to realise in the theatre and that the comic meets more resistance than the tragic or the sublime. *Il Turco in Italia*, which in thematic terms is really a kind of paraphrase of the more seriously laid out and systematically developed *L'Italiana in Algeri*, is nothing more than a *divertissement*, a pretty little comedy with a store of figures from the *commedia dell'arte*. Personally I can only agree with Ardoin's praise for this recording, which is conducted in inspired fashion by Gianandrea Gavazzeni. Callas's name does not come to mind so easily in comic roles, as in the way that one associates the name of the Spanish mezzo Conchita Supervia with certain Rossini roles.

But here again we have to challenge the misconceived judgement that Callas's Rosina was not 'funny' and that, particularly in the La Scala performance under Carlo Maria Giulini, she gave the impression of a Carmen in disguise. What really happened was that most critics were used to a certain vocal *type* in the role and therefore were irritated when confronted with a *character*. The type they expected was the agile mezzo or the brilliant *leggiero*, singers for Epicureans: the voices of nightingales with the brains of a peacock (Newman). Does Giulietta Simionato have comedy in the part of Rosina? No, she sounds like Azucena (Osborne). Does Victoria de los Angeles have comedy? No, she sounds like a sensitive madonna. Does the twittering Rosina of Roberta Peters have any effect at all? And what of Teresa Berganza, from whose throat fine roulades issue like pearls and yet who as a character is like a chubby baroque statue? Most painful of all, how can one view the qualities of Beverly Sills as *comédienne*? Her performance runs like an unintentional parody – and has anyone thought to mention that she produces more shrill and harsh notes than in all of Callas's later and weaker performances? Callas as *comédienne* is what we witness in both her Rossini opera performances, the transformation of a type employing vocal formulae to create a character which expresses itself in gesture. Admittedly it leads to certain exaggerations in the performance conducted by Giulini, which seeks a deeper dramatic meaning where merely the play of artifice would suffice.

It is this artifice that gives us Callas as Fiorilla, and she further succeeds with her sensitivity, in breaking out of the really quite stereotyped plot and its standardised *buffa* passages. A fine example is the duet between Fiorilla and her husband Geronio,[19] 'Per piacere alla signora'. It is a typical *buffa* situation, in which the little enchantress puts a ring through her husband's nose and makes him perform like a dancing bear. She plays on two levels of language and meaning. Fiorilla first adopts a tone of teasing anger, but just at the moment when the husband reveals that he is truly hurt, this has its effect on her. The pearly quick-silver voice becomes softer and utters sounds of genuine feeling, causing Geronio to start purring. This is where the purely playful and non-committal tone of *buffa* changes into the sensitive expression of comedy and where humanity threatens to come into play with a man's feelings. One is happy to report that Franco Calabrese really possesses *vis comica* and proves himself an excellent partner, although the voice itself sounds rough and colourless. Vocal finesse is not the suit of Nicola Rossi-Lemeni, who plays the 'bel turco'; Richard Osborne may be correct in assuming that Filippo Galli sang the divisions with more speed and suavity. But Rossi-Lemeni has presence as well as that grave humour which gives the foil to Fiorilla's double game. Their duets together are full of delightful nuance and verbal inflection. Throughout the entire recording, and even in interpolations at the top, Callas's voice has the delicacy of a figurine in its light and silvery grace.

The commercial version of *Il Barbiere di Siviglia*, recorded twelve months after the ambiguous performances at La Scala, was produced in London in the second week of February 1957 under the excellent musical direction of Alceo Galliera (for the record, only surpassed in grace and smile by the Glyndebourne production with the Royal Philharmonic Orchestra under Vittorio Gui). Orchestral playing and ensemble work are subtle and

precise. Galliera presents the work as a classical comedy and not
as a farce, without the crude acting of vocal gags or jokes from
the lower level of humour. Take the scene where Almaviva bursts
into Bartolo's house disguised as a soldier. The intention is that
he should be arrested, but the officer summoned to help is only
concerned about the peace being disturbed. Callas then comes in
with 'fredda ed immobile', and just as in *Medea* her voice became
an expression of hatred it here becomes one of banter, with the
phrases of the *stretta* finale hidden in the partial accelerations of a
Rossini crescendo.

The Mozart scholar Ernst Lert has stated in his observations
on history of style that *opera seria* gives the soul a lyric portrayal
but that French opera has its characters declaim; further, that the
Singspiel lets German souls express themselves in song, whereas
opera buffa portrays the emotions 'rhythmically and in their external movement'. A telling description, but one that does not do
full justice to Rossini. With Rossini people often speak of the
paucity of the 'melodic framework' as if it were conceivable that
this composer's melody was mere decoration. The inner nature
of Rossini's music lies rather, as Carl Dahlhaus puts it, in the
'element of embellishment'.[20] Precisely because the substance of
the melody is underdeveloped, 'the tightly outlined rhythmic
stamp becomes the musical centre; and precisely because the
themes are restricted to motif-like figures which present themselves energetically without appearing to have special significance,
the technique of unrelenting and almost obsessive repetition,
which yet avoids monotony, can create a flush of turbulence.'

Galliera never runs the risk of driving the 'obsessive repetition'
into a metric monotony, as does Claudio Abbado – who, according to Osborne, is 'relying overmuch on speed and polish to
generate comic tension'. Galliera has that rhythmic pacing which
fits the vocal movement like a glove. This is as important for
accompanying *fioriture* as it is on phrases which need to be acted
in the voice. The elaborate shapes of *canto fiorito* – the embellishments – need to be translated into live gesture. This cannot be
done with *buffa* mechanisms, for Rossini's song needs convincing
mimicry.

Rosina, once a party-piece of Malibran, is not well served by a high soprano. Some of these – Amelita Galli-Curci, Lina Pagliughi, Gianna d'Angelo – have performed the role well enough, but their type of sound is not suited to its expressive character.

If, for example, Amina in *La Sonnambula* is an unsuspecting innocent, Rosina (and Gilda for that matter) are innocents who are consciously aware, however much their expectations may be clothed in playful artifice. 'Una voce poco fà' is magical and at the same time coloured with menace. Callas's Rosina is not to be trifled with. There can be few other recordings of this 'bravura scene' in which the *fioritura* is fitted rhythmically into the vocal flow with such perfect evenness. And what fine pointing of the text by means of accentuation and coloration in the duet 'Dunque io son' with Tito Gobbi. John Ardoin says of Gobbi that he is one of the few interpreters of the part in this century who did not have to fake it by technical means. But let us not praise him too much, for it is in this very same duet that Gobbi sings his passage work in half voice – not such a convincing solution (compared, for example, to hearing it sung by Thomas Allen, not to mention Titta Ruffo). Gobbi makes much of verbal play and wit, and Callas peppers the scene with her own cheeky nuances. Luigi Alva as Almaviva offers a solid standard performance, and that is all that one expects from a *tenorino*. On the other hand we have heard far better singers in the bass roles than Nicola Zaccaria (Basilio) and far more precise ones than Fritz Ollendorff.

A few years after Callas's death Pathé-Marconi, the French branch of EMI, published a boxed set of all her studio recital recordings. This comprises eleven records, discussion of which in their entirety would be too much even for this singer, who was done no favours by the publication of certain later recordings. Yet it is not just the earliest recitals that deserve mention. Walter Legge viewed the two aria collections recorded in the third week of September 1954 as her international visiting cards.

Critical reservations have often been raised about recital recordings by stars, especially tenors, suggesting that the singer is more important than the music (albeit taken out of its context). But the recitals are an indispensable part of our recollection of Maria Callas; and who does not harbour regret that there are no such recordings covering the years 1947–51? (The Cetra 78s are very important, but there are not enough of them.)

The climax of the Puccini recital is Turandot's aria, which Callas sings with great bravura. Not only does the voice ride the orchestra with composure, concentration and glimmering brilliance, but her delivery has a rare degree of penetration by means of the very telling articulation. Callas does more than sing the fearsome leaps; she brings meaning and emotional weight to the text. This applies too to the arias and scenes from *Manon Lescaut, La Bohème, Madama Butterfly, Suor Angelica* and *Gianni Schicchi*. But even more admirable than the elegance and tension of the melodic delivery is the play of colours on the one hand and the weight given on the other to small phrases and vocal gestures; Callas gives each character its individuality by means of her vocal colouring alone. Ardoin points out that each aria or scene is given more vivid form in the complete recordings. This is typical of Callas; she was a dramatic actress and not a purveyor of beautiful moments. And one can overlook a few of the high notes in this recital where one would need to take one of Legge's seasickness pills. *Suor Angelica* especially exceeds the boundary of what Edward Greenfield calls wobble tolerance.

The second disc is a collection of florid arias and others from repertoire of the turn of the century for which the description of verismo is not really adequate. The choice of programme was obviously intended to give Callas's versatility opportunity for impressive display. The outstanding item is Margherita's 'L'altra notte' from Boito's *Mefistofele*, which no other recorded soprano has rivalled and which combines line and setting in a wonderful way. Callas does have considerable competition in the arias from *Adriana Lecouvreur* (Cilea) and *La Wally* (Catalani), and that is from Magda Olivero, but certainly none in 'La mamma morta', however far back one goes. This is because of 'verbal potency, mastery of vocal colour and inflection' (William Mann). The only other singers to display comparable musical eloquence are Claudia Muzio and Lotte Lehmann.

The other side of the LP gives us Rosina's aria from Rossini's *Barbiere*, with more embellishment than in the complete recording with Galliera, but not with more expression. The *fioritura* is not integrated into the whole with such a consequential sense of rhythm, but none the less it is an interpretation which dwarfs most others. As for the *Lakmé* aria, one should go back to the live version, but the one from *Dinorah* – with its splendid echo effects – is a masterpiece of virtuoso singing. Equally brilliant is the Bolero from Verdi's *I Vespri Siciliani*: here the dynamic and rhythmic shadings and nuances, which make this warhorse into a piece of expression, are more impressive than the boldly pitched top E.

In 1955 Callas recorded 'Dei tuoi figli' from *Medea*, together with scenes from Bellini's *La Sonnambula* and Spontini's *La Vestale*. She did not allow the Amina aria to be issued, and it was only published after her death, leaving both critics and fans to puzzle over what her dissatisfaction with it might have been. Most artists would have been content to sing Bellini like this once in their lives. She sings Medea's music with more expression in the stage performances, but the Spontini scenes are best described as grandiose.

Lady Macbeth, or the Infernal Voice

Callas's first studio recording in 1958 was the Verdi recital conducted by Nicola Rescigno, her friend in the later years of her career. It is a painful reminder that she never recorded commercially the complete roles of Lady Macbeth, Abigaille in *Nabucco* and Elisabetta in *Don Carlo*. Although the voice had become lighter and slimmer, it still paints with the dark colours of an Umbrian master. Even if the individual performances are not free of acidity, she realises the unity of line, expressive word power and colour differentiation more fully than any other Verdi soprano – and that includes Rosa Ponselle, Claudia Muzio, Margherita Grandi, Elisabeth Rethberg and Leontyne Price.

The recital begins with the definitive interpretation of Lady Macbeth's first aria. In contrast to the La Scala performance, she now finds the right sound for the letter-reading. At La Scala she had read it to the audience, not to herself, with heavy accentuation. She reads, even when loudly, like someone who does not want to believe what they read, and yet desperately wants to at the same time. The energy of attack on 'ambizioso spirto' knows no bounds, and the delivery of the aria becomes highly charged as vocal forms are transformed into white hot *espressivo*. The *andantino* passage starting at 'Che tardi? Accete', which works its way up into a *furioso* and almost exceeds the limits of what can be sung, is not just mastered by the soprano but performed as if nothing more were to follow (compare Wagner's letter to Niemann!); but what does follow is the cabaletta and the eruption 'Ministri infernali' with embellishment on the phrase's last syllable which is shaped with as much delicacy as a bel canto figure, and with the heat of expressionist speech. Following this is the great scena 'La luce langue' from the second act, composed eighteen years after the première when Verdi was revising the work: the bravura piece ('Trionfai') was replaced by the scene which uses words as gestures and an orchestral coloration of startling originality, which has also to be taken up by the voice. Her singing of 'Nuovo delitto!' (A new crime!) and 'è necessario' far exceeds the bounds of mere dynamic contrast – there a whisper, here a penetrating scream: it is unreasonable political ambition expressed in sound.

Julian Budden considers that the 'gran scena del sonnambulismo' is a unique high-point in Italian opera. The orchestration is especially select -- muffled strings, with clarinet and cor anglais to accompany the *obbligati* and an absence of any brighter woodwind – and exactly matches the language of the vocal gestures. The first part has to be sung at a constant 'sotto voce', with individual phrases in 'voce spiegata'; this part is placed almost entirely in the voice's lower register. In spite of the clean articulation one gets an impression of 'unending, uninterrupted but never repetitive melody' (Budden), rising on a *fil di voce* to a concluding D flat *in altissimo* – and on heights of expression which cause a shudder. We experience in Callas's interpretation 'one of the most descriptive moments of singing ever captured on record' (John Ardoin). One cannot cease to be amazed, even on repeated hearings, by the plenitude of detail in sound and gesture. The sound fades away to a strangulated sigh on the words 'No, mai pulire io non saprò' (I know not how I will ever clean my hands), while the phrase

'Araba intera romanda si piccol man' – emphasis on the first two words, cold desperation on the others – is a masterpiece of declamatory contrasts. Only Verdi himself could have imagined it like this.

The highlight of the second side is Elisabetta's aria from *Don Carlo*, but this is not to undervalue the scenes from *Nabucco* and *Ernani*. Has any singer ever given the cry 'Ernani' more movingly, or with more tenderness and emotion? Only this architect of song, who knew how to build a scene written with such complexity, how to fill it with tension and depict it with such contrasts. It commands nothing but admiration and amazement. Callas's interpretation towers above all other recordings, even the one so highly praised by Lord Harewood, by Meta Seinemeyer, one of the rare singers to possess an 'orphic' tone. Seinemeyer grips us because the sound of the voice is permeated with the suffering of one destined to die, while Callas convinces us with the heroic stress used to portray a figure at once royal and vulnerable, sublime and sensitive. The *arioso* passages are sung with majestic emphasis, while those of recitative and inner monologue are declaimed with gripping inwardness. In order to appreciate the stature of this recital one should perhaps first read those letters of Verdi where he deals with vocal expression, with words as setting the scene, and with the dialecticism of the aesthetically beautiful and the ugly. Read first, and then listen to the record, which illuminates and puts into practice the composer's ideas: ideas which are themselves guiding principles for the art of vocal expression.

Romantic Heroines, or Voices of Madness

'This is perhaps the best of all Callas's solo records.' This statement from *Opera* referred not to the Verdi recital but to the one made immediately after it and containing the long final scene from Donizetti's *Anna Bolena*, Ophélie's Mad Scene from Thomas's *Hamlet* and Imogene's scene from Bellini's *I Pirata*. It was the soprano's wish to make complete recordings of these Donizetti and Bellini works, but by 1958–9 work in the recording studio had become difficult both for and with her. Ardoin quotes the conductor Nicola Rescigno's recollection of the recording of the Donizetti. He was working with the first horn of the Philharmonia Orchestra on the long solo with which he has to introduce the cavatina. Callas came along and listened intently, then sang the horn line for him, which led on to a discussion about the music and how a melody by Donizetti differed from one by Bellini, also how a trill should be started and how it should be concluded. In this way, they discussed the nuances surrounding the musical material, the execution of which assures the stature of a performance.

The scene from *Anna Bolena* is by no means as celebrated as the more vocally distinguished Mad Scene from *Lucia di Lammermoor*, yet it is, in Callas's version, one of the great moments of dramatic singing. In contrast to the secularised saint (for Lucia is none other than a stigmatised Virgin), the Tudor Queen does not give herself up to elaborate ornamentation. The vocal line is to a certain extent reduced to the essentials of strict and heavy pathos. Callas interprets it with a dark, weighty and richly expressive tone and with maximum authority. On the phrase 'Al dolce giudami', Richard Fairman describes how 'the veiled tone has an expression which gives the feeling that a distant voice is rising from the depths of Anna's soul'. In the cabaletta she finally sings again with the carefree verve of her early years, secure and energetic and lacking the dreaded sharpness which was so much in evidence on the Verdi recital.

The Ophélie aria from *Hamlet* by Thomas is also a mad scene, and it may have been vocalised with more technical efficiency by this or that soprano from the first two decades of the century; yet who performed it with more meaning and variety of shape? Thomas composed the part for a light high soprano with perfect command of coloratura, for the Swedish singer Christine Nilsson, who was a considerable rival to Patti. But there is more to this role than mere agility: without inflections of pathos and careful vocal colouring, 'à vos jeux, mes amis' loses its effect. A major section of the opening is composed as recitative, leaving the performer to decide on a tempo for her speech-singing in accordance with her own sense of the momentum. Yet the declamation is

precisely measured by the composer. Speaking to the peasants
Ophélie adopts the naïve accents of a child ('mes amis' and 'de
grâce'). On the second phrase – 'nul n'a suivi' – she shades the
tone as if whispering a secret. For the *andantino* she initiates a
passage of graceful singing which completely lacks self-conscious-
ness – the voice is simultaneously infused with the imagined trill
of a bird, in the conclusion ('plânait dans l'air') finally conveying
enjoyment of its own sound. There follows a masterpiece of vocal
structure, the section in which Ophélie's thoughts centre round
Hamlet ('Hamlet est mon époux'), where she conjures up happiness and yet gives expression to her helplessness. Here we have
pianissimo shading, carefully and precisely weighed *ritardandi* –
sound-speech of the greatest intensity and expressiveness. Then a
contrasting episode, a section resembling a waltz . . . then a trill
on F . . . which brings us to the end of the dance episode. 'Et
maintenant, écoutez ma chanson,' demands Ophélie, intoning
one of those indomitably sad songs, peaceful, slow and full of
melancholy. Thoughts of death, sung in one breath on a long
four-bar phrase. The care with which Callas has studied the piece,
as well as the shaping of its text, is shown by the fact that she
correctly articulates 'la Willis'.[21] Great tension is given to the
following two phrases by the weight placed on the *fermate* – and
'd'un bonheur si doux' is a figure of the sweetest sadness. For the
scene's conclusion the girl's madness explodes in a state of cohe-
sive power. The deliriously high coloratura phrases, strung
together and at the same time separate, can only be sung by a
virtuosa of the front rank and acted by a *tragédienne*. They are
expressions of laughter, violent exclamations, rapid falls into nonsense, sensitive emotions but all integrated into the forms of florid
singing. As always, Callas places her voice with exactitude: it is
as forward as it can be, with the sound held in extreme concentration, slender and finely spun. In contrast to most coloratura
sopranos, the parts are related by means of her exemplary *legato*
and she demonstrates that if one can really sing, there is no need
for the vocal shape given by the Italian language. One must
also mention that the trills are not always executed with perfect
evenness and that notes in the upper region occasionally take on
an acid quality.

The closing scene from *Il Pirata*[22] also justifies the opinion that this was her best recital record so far. The contrasts between recitative and *arioso* passages, between vivid word-setting ('La . . . vedete . . . in palco funesto') and brilliantly elaborated coloratura in the cabaletta, are only achieved by a vocal actress of the highest stature.

Late Recitals, or the Luck of Sadness

We must remember that 1958 had begun for Maria Callas with the *Norma* walkout in Rome and was to end with her being fired from the Met by Rudolf Bing in November. She did not make a single complete opera recording that year, while on stage she made less than thirty appearances. Her state of mind is revealed in the statement that she felt she was 'wasting her energy' and 'squandering her young life for the sake of fame'. After the remakes of *Lucia* and *La Gioconda* (1959) and *Norma* (1960), she performed her first French opera recital in Paris in 1961 with Georges Prêtre, followed by a second one in 1963.

These two LPs are highly rated by the singer's admirers, even the critical ones, on account of their many great moments and a pathos and sensitivity which allows the listener to overlook the actual state of the voice. It is not just a matter of an 'acquired taste' which can actually enjoy the sharpness and bitterness, but of listening with love. But in saying that one's criteria for making an aesthetic judgement become shaky. It is an unusual situation: I can only say personally that, when listening, I get a feeling that combines admiration and sadness. The sadness is for the actual condition of the voice, the clouded timbre, the hollowness in the middle range which echoes as in a bottle, the top notes strenuously attacked and then cracked (even a B flat is produced with great effort), and the poorly supported high *piani*. It is not a simple matter to listen through all this, and one cannot avoid the issue by saying that the success of the whole is more important than an individual perfect tone, or that the dramatic impression is more important than vocal perfection.

What endows some late Callas recordings, particularly these

two French recitals, with their outstanding quality is the fact that on a different level, that of vocal technique, they do possess an *intended* consummation. The weakness of individual notes or insufficiencies in the sound do not prevent her from producing singing which is faultless from the point of view of musical technique. For example, Orphée's lament is not just sung with deep pathos but its phrases are shaped as a sculptor would shape the details of his work; Dalila sings not just with a silkiness which is 'sexy' but she also spins the long phrases with an exemplary *legato*; Carmen's vocal gestures are not just carried out but they acquire unusual rhythmical point and verbal nuance; and even Juliette's 'Je veux vivre' from Gounod's *Roméo et Juliette*, where the sound of certain passages may be out of control, acquires conviction from the way in which the tempo of certain phrases is given expressive nuance, and from a diction which is both faultless and eloquent. 'Can one detect a beat on certain high notes?' asks Richard Law in his discography of the opera,[23] to which he replies: 'Now, I should be critical, but I simply cannot do that.' Who could be, when they hear how the outburst of *joie de vivre*, composed as musical gesture at the beginning of the waltz, is realised to perfection? More brilliant and effortless recordings certainly exist – but are there any of greater intensity? Or any with finer pacing of the *accelerandi* and *ritardandi*? The same applies to Titania's polonaise from Thomas's *Mignon*. This is the opera's showpiece and once enjoyed immense popularity; it was sung in the first decades of the century by Italian divas like Amelita Galli-Curci and Luisa Tetrazzini, later by Toti dal Monte, Margherita Carosio and Lina Pagliughi, also by Maria Barrientos, Irene Abendroth, Hedwig Francillo-Kauffmann, Margarethe Siems and even Lillian Nordica, not forgetting the Russian prima donnas. These include Antonia Neshdanova, magnificent by any standards, singing with absolute effortlessness and yet taking the trouble to create, phrase by phrase and garland by garland, the sound of a life which is happy within itself.

Might one ask what Callas could find in a piece like this? The answer is much: verbal filigree, rhythmic nuance and femininity. However, it would be difficult to put the recording among her most important, as certainly applies to Chimène's lament 'Pleurez, mes yeux' from Massenet's *Le Cid*. Considering its purely vocal demands the aria can be performed by a lyric soprano with good volume, provided that singer has a truly dramatic sense. Grace Bumbry's version demonstrates that it is not sufficient simply to possess the tonal weight of a great mezzo. The aria has to begin 'slowly, and with pain and sadness' (composer's instruction). The first phrase is 'De cet affreux combat je sors l'âme brisée' ('After this terrible combat I remain here with my heart broken'). Massenet does not allow for any form of recitation, so Callas lingers for a moment on 'sors' and lets 'brisée' soar, so that one can hear Chimène's suffering in the sound. The phrase 'soupirer sans contrainte' is given in one breath, emphatic and at the same time resigned. The lament calls for *piano* and *legatissimo* with tonal production which is soft and elegiac, although every vowel is accented with maximum feeling, more from coloration than from dynamic emphasis. Take the stress given to 'mes yeux', the sonorous vocalising of the liquid sound on 'triste', the unendingly subtle extension of the (unpronounced) 'ée' in 'rosée', the energetic accentuation of 'c'est de bientôt mourir', in which every syllable is given its correct dynamic accent; take the intensification of emphasis in the lament on death, the magnificent pathos, spread out expansively, of 'tu ne saurais jamais conduire qu'aux chemins glorieux', and finally an ending which is soft, suspended and choking with tears: a monumental interpretation, one of Callas's most unforgettable. On the other hand the recording of 'Depuis le jour' from *Louise* suffers from the vocal unsteadiness already mentioned: the top of the voice simply slips out of control in many phrases.

These problems are intensified in the second recital, recorded at the beginning of May 1963. Maria Callas sang only a few concerts that year, attempting to regain her vocal form after a large number of illnesses affecting her neck. But the first aria, 'O malheureuse Iphigène' straightaway exposes her voice in notes which she can scarcely reach any more: the sound is hoarsely clouded and the singing resembles the desperate efforts of an athlete who is losing the strength to lift his body up for a final time to avoid falling down. And then, the wonder and the riddle of Callas, there comes Marguerite's 'D'amour l'ardente flamme' from Berlioz's *La Damnation de Faust*. There are a few strained high notes, yet her feeling and musical sense of phrasing and gradation, of the inner movement within each single word, bear witness to a vocal and musical genius. David Cairns, the recognised connoisseur of this work, puts the recording above all others for its dramatic penetration (and that includes Suzanne Danco, Janet Baker, Edith Mathis, Josephine Veasey, Yvonne Minton, Frederica von Stade, Shirley Verrett and Leontyne Price). Another high point is Charlotte's letter scene from Massenet's *Werther*.

A recital was made in December 1963 and January 1964 comprising Beethoven's 'Ah! perfido', Donna Anna's 'Or sai che l'onore' and 'Non mi dir' and Elvira's 'Mi tradi', 'Porgi amor' from *Le Nozze di Figaro* and 'Ocean, thou mighty monster!' from Weber's *Oberon*. One can agree with John Ardoin, who, listening chronologically, reports that the voice now sounds better, steadier, and fuller; one can, indeed must, listen to the recitative of 'Ah! perfido', the energy of that first exclamation, the declamatory emphasis; one must succumb to the sensitive phrasing of a loving ego and simply put aside all other recordings of the piece; one can be amazed by the Weber aria with its brilliant unity of *espressivo* and *seria*, swallowing a few sour notes on the way. At the same time, however, one cannot but register discomfort at the way the voice itself is suffering agonies. These are particularly noticeable in 'Non mì dir', where a once brilliant virtuosa can be heard engaged in hopeless struggle with the florid passages.

A second Verdi recital was made at about this time, with arias from operas which Callas had not sung on stage (except for *Don Carlo*). Again, great moments go hand in hand with painful ones. She shapes Desdemona's scena as 'mistress of mood' (Ardoin) and with more subtlety than most interpreters. The name 'Barbara' can scarcely have ever been pronounced with more feeling, the cries of 'salce' are sound pictures of melancholy, anguish and anxiety while the sense of rising fear gives the performance its inner pulse which accelerates step by step. The concluding A flat is sung, as tradition has it, on a *fil di voce*, but weakness can be detected in the tonal support (forgive me, John Ardoin). The top notes in the Eboli aria (C and B flat) are also struggled for, whereas the aria is delivered with such penetration and passion and with such differentiation in the lyrical phrases ('O mia regina') as is scarcely heard from any other singer. Again, I am disturbed by the hollow sounds 'sung in a bottle', and again, I am not.

But that disturbance cannot be denied in the Donizetti and Rossini recital (also 1963–4) and the Verdi programme recorded in February and April 1964 but not published until 1978. The discrepancy between her intentions and what is possible is particularly wide in the Donizetti and Rossini arias: 'Nacqui all'affanno' from *La Cenerentola* must shimmer and sparkle, but this version lacks cohesion, charm, tone and lustre. There are a few phrases in the Verdi recital which Callas and only Callas could sing and dramatic situations are still conveyed: this is a lot, but not enough. To have published the 1969 recordings from *Vespri, Il Corsaro, I Lombardi* and *Attila* – which Rescigno relates were produced 'inch by inch' or, to be honest, pieced together with remnants of a voice which has lost all beauty – is to have damaged Callas's reputation; or was it carried out on the premise that in studying a great person we must see everything and hide nothing?

Triumphs

The year 1954 (where we broke off with the complete recording of *La Forza del Destino*) ended for Maria Callas with a production of Spontini's *La Vestale*, which Ardoin describes as a 'junior' Norma. The live recording is little more than a stroke of the brush in one picture of the soprano, and the same applies to the production of Giordano's *Andrea Chénier*. This opera belongs to the tenor, in this case Mario del Monaco, who spent the entire performance duelling with Maria Callas – and who is granted the honour never to have been addressed in song so inwardly and tenderly as by Maria Callas with her cries of 'Andrea! Andrea! Rividerlo!'.

Artur Rubinstein once said that the dividing line between sweetness and sentimentality need never be drawn, only that one must never cross it. And what goes for Chopin the *bel canto* piano composer, whose *fioriture* are formed like those of Bellini, applies also to the role of Amina in *La Sonnambula*. It was with this role that Callas's image changed – not just in her stage performance but in the public picture. Visconti presented her as a Taglioni *reincarnata*, as gracious ballerina, and the singer forthwith took the form of a beautiful swan.

I cannot avoid pointing out again the discrepancy between stage and private photographs from this period. The stage photos seem genuine or inward and have expression or pathos – according to the role being portrayed – while the private pictures seem artificial and engineered, showing Callas in the role of diva, playing a part for the public, and, in particular, for that fatal world of woman cultivated by the tabloids.

The spectrum of expression which Maria Callas found for this supposedly naïve figure is perhaps made clear if one first listens to the recording made by Lina Pagliughi, a mere sketch lacking any musical or dramatic intent. Callas performed Amina twenty-two times and we have a studio recording (1957) in addition to live versions from Milan (1955) and from Cologne and Edinburgh (1957). John Ardoin describes the Cologne appearance (4 July 1957) as a 'mystic night in her career where voice, intent and technique were in miraculous balance', and David A. Lowe agrees with him. Such is Callas's stature that one cannot disagree with this appraisal, and yet one might rate other performances higher. As I hear it, the La Scala version under Leonard Bernstein possesses more light and exuberance, and the figure who emerges radiates us with 'her wide-open eyes and the sound of open vowels' (R. Fairman).

Visconti's production inhabited that magical world of art over art, and Maria Callas worked the same captivating magic with her voice: she sings this naïve girl with a high degree of artistry, transforming consciousness back into nature. A puppet theatre – the highest charm, that is an artificial one. It was said of Malibran that her portrayal possessed 'a vehemence too nearly trenched on frenzy to be true', and it is such exalted cries of joy and trouble that resound from the Callas performance. Her very first phrases show her voice to be in fantastic form. It is free of all those dramatic and demonic roles, all those dark colours and sorrows; it sounds bright, light, soft and yet delicate and melancholy. Amina appears with the little-girl voice and begins 'Come per me sereno', the song of a lyrical soul with long soaring phrases, inwardly sweet like a viola d'amore and rich in verbal inflection; all is pervaded by the smile of a Raphael angel who suddenly, in the coda, begins a brilliant dance.

The magic continues in the duet with Cesare Valletti, who sings with the elegance of a true *tenore di grazia*. Ardoin mentions that he omits certain top Cs, but this is *quantité négligeable* compared to his meltingly soft and elegiacally intoned cantilena. There is also an extraordinary flexibility in the duet 'Son geloso del zefiro', with an admirable spontaneity on the *fioritura* reminiscent of Fernando de Lucia. We hear the cry of pain at the end of the second act when Amina watches in desperation as her happiness disappears. Callas rises to the E flat *in altissimo* and holds it for four full bars.

John Ardoin accords Callas the highest praise for her singing in the final act. As far as the pointing of words is concerned, even the finest actor could not speak the recitative in a better fashion, yet at the same time all this pointing is further intensified by the musical colouring. The aria ('Ah! non credea') unfolds like pure vocalism brought to life by the finest colouring. The sound of the voice has the warm glow of gentle candlelight yet without so much as a flicker. Faultless *legato* with a complete welding together of vowels and consonants. Then there emerge the fireworks of the cabaletta, and suddenly every note is sparkling, the voice gleaming in brightest light. Leonard Bernstein added some bold ornamentation to the second verse, entrusting the singer with a salvo of *staccati*, which act as a challenge; some of them misfire, whereas with Tetrazzini they would have been better targeted and yet only have emerged as *staccati* and not as cries of bliss. And that is what it is all about.

Ten weeks after the performances of *La Sonnambula* came the production of Verdi's *La Traviata* under Carlo Maria Giulini at La Scala. Ardoin sees in this performance the decisive step towards the consummate portrayal which finally came about in the London appearance on 20 June 1958 under Rescigno. Even Michael Scott, who felt that the 1955 Lucia was vocally somewhat reduced (and criticised it as such), argues that Callas as Violetta was able to conceal her declining vocal energy with her febrile acting. For example, she sang the top A at the end of 'Addio del passato' in London with such a finely spun tone that it eventually broke. The soprano insisted in an interview that this break in the voice was intentional for expressive reasons. That may be, although one may also doubt it: what was intended was the reduction in the tone until it was deathly silent, but not the actual break in the voice. She could have given the tone more breath support in order to keep it secure, but a securely produced tone would never have had a comparable effect.

But we are anticipating. The Milan performance, although perhaps a little mannered in the last act, gives the opera an extra dimension of sublimity and pathos. Lord Harewood calls it the high water mark of her career.[24] This is strongly confirmed by the recollections of the other participants (primarily Visconti and Giulini). Callas proves herself to be the only 'complete' Violetta of the post-war era. Those few singers who could perform the brilliant music of the first act did not have at their disposal the expressive means for the second, and *vice versa*. And most of them should not have been singing Violetta in the first place (Renata Tebaldi, Antonietta Stella, Beverly Sills!). The high point of the first act is the *brindisi*, whose lilt belies the fact that Violetta is no longer at the centre of the life pulsating around her. Realisation does not always meet intent in 'È strano – Ah! fors'è lui' and 'Sempre libera'; the repeated high Cs flicker like a faintly stretched metal band, and the top E flat trembles. And yet this is sensed not as a deficiency but as a momentary weakness – what gymnast would have landed securely after this triple somersault?

The second act would have transported us to Verdi's seventh heaven if only Callas had not been partnered by Ettore Bastianini, a singer who might have become one of the finest Verdi baritones of the century. He possessed, as few others did, not just a vibrant voice with a light extension at the top but also a dark, indeed black, lower register. What he did not have were dramatic imagination or the ambition to assume something more than just a costume when he went on stage. The monotonous sound with which he responds to the outbursts, lamenting, weeping and sighing of the suffering madonna – which is what Callas makes of Violetta in the second act – reveals the mentality of a singer

who sings beautifully but with no imagination. The scandalous
way in which Alfredo insults Violetta in the second scene of Act
2 has never hit me in the way it does in this version. And even
if in the final act there are a few mannered exaggerations, comparable to the exaltations in the action of a Greta Garbo, one can
listen, once one has heard her, only to Callas in the sounds of
suffering and the fearful cries of death.

   La Traviata was only one of the great performances in that
memorable year, while two others confirm her unique stature as
Norma. The first is from Rome, and is a concert performance
conducted by Tullio Serafin on 29 June (note that the recitative
to 'Casta diva' is borrowed from the EMI recording!). The second
is the *prima* from La Scala on 7 December 1955 under Antonino
Votto. John Ardoin deals with it respectfully without giving it
special emphasis; but is there a performance which overall is more
successful? It possesses the energy of the early years together with
the finesse of the experienced artist. The voice has security right
from the first recitative. The cantilena of 'Casta diva' flows forward, the melismas curling like the waters of a pool when rippled
by a gentle breeze and shimmering as if in moonlight, the top
notes, like the B flat, repose on the breath and respirate with
marvellous *diminuendo*, and the scales of the cabaletta do not just
flow but are also integrated energetically (Norma is no Amina).
The duets with Giulietta Simionato are exemplary, and the phrase
'Ah si, fa core, abbracciami' is a real high point, with Callas
taking a top C with perfect attack and then letting it die out on
a *diminuendo* – the audience holds its own breath, takes a breath
as the note ends and then breathes again before releasing an audible
sigh and shouts of jubilation: at the end of the act there is also
excitement of frenetic proportions with a perfectly placed top D.
In the second act duet – 'Mira, O Norma' – Callas and Simionato
do not quite reach that perfect blend achieved on the legendary
recording with Rosa Ponselle and Marion Telva. The final scene
again confronts us with the avenging angel, demanding 'sangue
romano', savouring her triumph over Pollione ('In mia man alfin
tu sei') and shooting out the bravura passages like tongues of
flame.

   The summer months of August and September were spent in

the recording studios, producing *Madama Butterfly* under Karajan and then *Aida* and *Rigoletto* under Serafin. Although she had sung Butterfly on stage in Chicago, the role did suit her dramatic imagination and her range of sensitivity. Ardoin describes how she brings to the role Amina's innocence, Gilda's metamorphosis and disappointment, and Violetta's passion. The part has indeed received several brilliant recorded performances (Renata Tebaldi, Victoria de los Angeles, Leontyne Price and Mirella Freni) but rarely dramatic ones as from Renata Scotto. Butterfly's entrance of course needs no acting, but must be sung and crowned with a top D flat, a note which for Callas at that time depended on her disposition. On the day on which this was recorded she was obviously not on top form. Everybody knows what we mean, those acid and shrill tones. But then she goes on to develop Butterfly's drama with her voice, as innocence flowers into passion in the love duet, as the drama of expectation develops ('Un bel dì') and as the last act brings its sounds of desolation. To cast Pinkerton with Nicolai Gedda (then still a lyric lightweight) has the special advantage that this Pinkerton has all the thoughtless stress of a youth who fails to recognise, in his intoxication, what he is doing. The subsidiary roles are all taken idiomatically, a fact which counts for more than having individual vocal characteristics.

In his *Aida* discography[25] John Steane writes that if someone wants to learn something about the Callas genius he should simply lower his stylus anywhere in this set, provided it is not on the climactic note of 'O patria mia'. What a marvellous way of putting it! It treats the weakness in the way it deserves. Yes, of course Milanov, Tebaldi, Price and Caballé have risen on more beautiful Cs . . . but elsewhere those singers, except for Leontyne Price, are 'skating on the Nile', a description used of Emma Eames. The performance, conducted by Serafin with more reliability than sense of structure or effect, has other weaknesses: in the great dramatic crowd scenes Callas is no longer the radiantly dominant centrepiece, particularly at the end of the second act which she had dominated in Mexico. But there is a unique sense of climax in the Aida–Amonasro duet at the beginning of Act 3.

The king's rage and the daughter's supplication are, once heard, unforgettable.

Verdi himself described *Rigoletto* as a long series of duets, and full advantage is taken of them by Callas and Gobbi, if not by Callas and di Stefano. There is one reservation here. Gobbi is in my opinion an overrated singer, or rather an overrated vocalist. But he was such a splendid actor (who could conjure up a *suggestion diabolique* with a single colour) that one seldom needed to draw attention, for example as Rigoletto, to his difficulties with high *mezza voce* phrases – of which there are more than a few. Nevertheless, there are few interpreters who have brought more expression to the scene with the courtiers before Rigoletto's invective (the aria itself is better sung by De Luca, Warren or Merrill). In short, Gobbi was an important interpreter of the role if not its best singer. Callas was both: almost the perfect Gilda in acting terms and one of the best vocally. Her recording of 'Caro nome', imbued by her with more perfect rhythmic movement than by any other soprano I have heard, has the immeasurable advantage of not ending *altissimo*: it concludes with an enraptured trill. But in order to see in Gilda more than an *ingénue* one must hear the dramatic scenes which unfold in the ensembles of the last act.

Her first important studio work in 1956 was Verdi's *Il Trovatore*, conducted by Herbert von Karajan and with a cast of di Stefano, Barbieri and Panerai, her colleagues in almost all the great La Scala performances in those years. Most of them are also heard in the recording of Puccini's *La Bohème*, a version which is not generally included in the list of ideal recordings (these include ones by Toscanini, Beecham, Karajan and, aside from minor reservations, Serafin). But our aural memory is not always reliable, indeed can be deceptive. Listening again, Callas is admittedly not the most moving Mimì – if one is expecting, that is, a *femme fragile* – but rather one experiences in her portrayal a *femme fatale*, spiritually akin to Violetta.

As in no other performance, Callas's portrayal for once helps us to understand Rodolfo's dismissal of Mimì as a way of freeing himself from his consumptive macho jealousy. From no other performance can one recall so many acting/singing gestures. Although the recording is conducted only routinely by Antonino

Votto, the ensemble makes its mark: admittedly Giuseppe di Stefano does not sing with the elegant line, certainly not the expansive phrasing, of a Jussi Björling, but he does give more detail, life and charm, almost approaching the excellent Carlo Bergonzi and the endlessly fine differentiation of Nicolai Gedda. Rolando Panerai keeps a high standard, but Anna Moffo as Musetta sings not just with dullness but also with laxity and a lack of rhythmic tension.

La Bohème was scarcely finished when sessions for Verdi's *Un Ballo in Maschera* started on 4 September 1956, again conducted by Votto. Here it is the conductor's dramatically clipped manner which gives cause for regret. The live recording from La Scala on 7 December 1957 (an almost identical cast has Bastianini instead of Gobbi) is comparatively volcanic in its energy and has a musical finish to match: the conductor is Gianandrea Gavazzeni. It is Maria Callas's Amelia which gives the Votto recording its stature, and Amelia is a part which could have been made to measure for the emotions and dramatic imagination of Callas. Although one cannot ignore the fact that she is unable to crown the climactic phrase of her big aria with a secure C, who can overlook the way in which she concludes the aria with the phrase 'O signor, m'aita'. This vocal monologue is one of Verdi's most penetrating dramatic inventions, and needs to be acted and sung in equal measure. Callas acts the initial *allegro agitato* with an expression of nervous anxiety and tension. She has the dark mezzo colour for the phrases which lie lowest ('t'annienta'), the colourless tone for 'm'affisa' and 'terribile sta' and sufficient breath to unfold the broad spans of the slowly intensifying final phrases starting with 'miserere'. We hear her eloquent and penetrating singing in the duet with Riccardo: phrases like 'Ah! deh soccorri' or 'Ma, tu nobile me difendi dal mio cor' or the outbursts of 'Ebben, sí t'amo' after a slow and frightening delay, remain in the memory as moments of suffered happiness.

Less successful is the rendition of 'Morrò, ma prima in grazia', the reason being that this aria, like the Nile aria in *Aida*, is too one-dimensional and too much a piece of lyrical singing. On the other hand the confrontation with Tito Gobbi's Renato is dramatic acting of the calibre of the *Aida* duet. As Riccardo, di

Stefano sings with his customary ardour – and his customary
laxity, as well as open notes which are far too crude. Gobbi again
proves himself to be a marvellous actor and exemplary partner in
duets, but not a superb Verdi stylist.

Wrested Triumphs

In October and November 1956 Callas made her début at the
New York Met as Norma, Tosca and Lucia. Her success was,
viewed strictly, only one of respect. If one takes the evidence of
the *Lucia* broadcast (8 December 1956) as indicative of the voice's
condition in the other performances, then one can understand
why the reviews were euphemistic. If the nerves are on edge the
vocal chords will flicker, and this *Lucia* recording should be heard
only by those who are interested in the darker sides of a singer's
career. The year 1957 was to yield the studio versions of *Il Barbiere
di Siviglia, La Sonnambula, Turandot* and *Manon Lescaut* as well as
broadcasts of *Anna Bolena* and *Iphigénie en Tauride* from La Scala,
La Sonnambula from Edinburgh and Cologne, *Un Ballo in Maschera* from La Scala and, last but not least, the Ricordi studio recording of *Medea*.

In comparison to the La Scala version conducted by Bernstein
the studio *Sonnambula* is more straightforward and restrained. It
lacks the extremes of expression which Bernstein and Callas had
explored together. It has brilliance but no magic, and the brilliance
all comes from Maria Callas who combines text, musical line,
fioriture and sound to produce much more than a finely drawn
portrait. One can scarcely improve on Ardoin's description that
not only does she present Rosina as a loser and Amina as shy,
altering the voice in order to fit the character, but also makes it
plain that joy and happiness are different things for Rosina and
Amina. To put it briefly, her singing is an exploration of the
mind.

The Cologne *Sonnambula* on 4 July 1957 – from the opening
week of the new opera house – is described by David A. Lowe
as one of the last Callas performances in which everything was
successful. It was this success which Ardoin felt was a justification

for the existence of pirate recordings which might in other respects be questionable. For the picture of Callas would be incomplete without the Berlin *Lucia*, the Cologne *Sonnambula* and the Dallas *Medea*.

My view is that one can look at the Cologne performances under Votto in two ways. Lowe holds that 'In earlier portrayals of Amina, both in the studio and on stage, Callas's voice sometimes acquires a steely quality very much at odds with Amina's personality. In the Cologne performances, however, Callas approaches many of the high-lying passages softly and almost cooingly. The *fioriture* thus seems more like fine embroidery than prima-donna razzle-dazzle.'[26]

The other view puts forward the reservation that microphones in a studio have quite a different way of hearing to those in an opera house, the latter picking up the singer from a much greater distance. The studio microphone is a means of acoustical close-up and therefore produces the essence of a voice with much greater clarity. But this is only a technical reservation. One cannot deny that Callas *had* to approach high passages with greater caution and to sing with reduced tone and an especially light touch. Even more than in the Berlin *Lucia*, the voice sounds 'wan and wavery', as Scott puts it. But that cannot detract from the beautiful rendition of the cabaletta 'sovra il sen la man mi posa' or the well placed top E flat at the end of that cabaletta. Callas is Callas precisely because of her ability to develop strength out of weakness. For example, she employed the reduction of volume to intensify her *legato*, concentrating on those expressive moments which are gentle and restrained rather than those which are brilliant. Her portrayal has many moments of subtlety and intimacy, but in order to understand this as a progression, indeed a progression through reduction, one must also have heard the Milan performance.

The royal heroines of opera disappeared from the stage with the operatic revolution of the 1880s. Mythological figures from *opera seria*, as well as these royal heroines, no longer touched the hearts of a public which had become political in a nationalistic sense and whose sensibilities had become private. In spite of any public setting they might have, the dramatic line of many great operas was characterised, when viewed according to genre, by a political conflict which was merely a foil for a private (love) story. Donizetti's Tudor queens, in *Anna Bolena, Maria Stuarda* and *Roberto Devereux*, had been ignored in the twentieth century, even by La Scala. When Maria Callas first sang Anna in Milan in 1957, it was the first performance there for 114 years. The very first revival had been in 1956 in Bergamo, the composer's birthplace. In *Opera on Record*, Richard Fairman draws attention to the remarkable fact that there is no aural history for the presentation of these works and especially of the leading female roles. And yet we can thank the gramophone for giving a precise picture of how Mozart, Wagner, Rossini, Bellini and above all the composers around the turn of the century had been sung.

Our picture of Donizetti as musical dramatist was formed, as Fairman puts it, in the post-Callas era. The production of *Anna Bolena* by Visconti, conducted by Gavazzeni, is important for other reasons. It marks a high point in the singer's career, even if this must be taken in an ambivalent sense, as Carlo Maria Giulini pointed out. It was a triumph which she had to fight for, especially in the 1958 revival after the scandals in Edinburgh and Rome. Like Norma and Amina, Donizetti's Anna was a role written for Pasta, whom contemporary reports describe as giving the sense on stage of being both majestic and reserved. Her style was chaste and expressive,[27] and Chorley and Stendhal report how she eschewed any elaborate embellishments. Thus we can deduce that it was the romantic vocal *tragédiennes* who were first reponsible for giving bel canto a psychological basis, an achievement formerly attributed to Verdi.

Callas sang twelve performances of the work. Her portrayal had a depth and a sharpness right from the start, as if she had been as familiar with the role as with Violetta or Norma. And indeed she was familiar with it in a certain sense, because her early portrayals of 'wounded characters' (Ardoin), had already sharpened her sensibility. Just as Pasta, as reported by Chorley, could arouse the audience to a frenzy simply with her utterance of the word 'Sorgi', so Callas can make the listener tremble with 'Tu, mia rivale' or 'Va, infelice', not to mention her fury at 'Giudici! Giudici ad Anna!' So secure and self-confident is she here that she sets light to the notes *in alt*, a C and a D in the first act, as if with a firebrand. The final act is built up with remarkable density: every detail of language, drama and colouring is an integral part of the portrayal, and even the passage-work and coloratura are essential parts of the music's expression.

Shortly before recording Puccini's *Turandot* (9–17 July 1957), Callas had sung Gluck's Iphigénie at La Scala, Lucia in Rome and Amina in Cologne, in the latter, as we have said, singing with a tone which was subdued, a tone not only suited to the role but also dictated by the condition of her voice. That she could *then* sing Turandot is a miracle; or an achievement of energy such as only Callas could pull off. The challenge and excessive demands which this made on her voice are clearly audible. She sounds so stretched that the listener is in constant fear that she will crack. But (and as almost always with Callas it is a 'but' which forgives, justifies or admires) there are 'wonderful compensations' (Ardoin): majestic declamation, iridescent sounds and an unchallenged intensity in the duets. While most Turandots are content to make a silver trumpet of the voice, which they then use to override the orchestra (and not so many can even do that), Callas demonstrates that the 'ice princess' is a vulnerable being.

The casting of Liù is highly interesting here, for it seems that in ancient times the Tartars must have found their slave girls in the Marschallin von Werdenberg's salon. Elisabeth Schwarzkopf sings the part captivatingly but with artifice. As Calaf, Eugenio Fernandi offers little charisma or princely charm, although the voice is powerful and robust. The ensemble work of La Scala's singers (especially Mario Bornello, Renato Ercolani and Piero de Palma) is of exemplary quality; it is after all the *comprimarii* who give a performance its dramatic cohesion.

Tullio Serafin, who conducted that recording, was also in charge of *Manon Lescaut* immediately afterwards, although this was not published until three years later because of the alarming problems which Callas was having, particularly when having to sustain high-lying phrases or to sing *mezza voce*. The self-ending tones, those final notes which fade out gently, are only produced with the greatest effort. Even the B flat in 'In quelle trine morbide' is a note that both trembles and makes us tremble. Then after all

the critical reservations there is the big 'but', which Edward
Greenfield sums up in a single sentence: 'As to the portrayals of
the heroine in the complete sets, there is no doubt that Maria
Callas's is by far the most vivid.'[28] It is not necessary to draw
attention to the vocal weaknesses (which even the impartial and
untrained listener will be aware of), or to praise the numerous
dramatic nuances (which the connoisseur will not miss). Of much
more importance is the fact that she develops a voice from the
'character to be portrayed', as Wagner would have said. The voice
of Manon and not of Mimì or Tosca. In this respect she even
surpasses Licia Albanese, whose name was closely linked with the
role. (There have always been parts which were the possession of
particular singers.) Passages which Callas did not master with the
utmost security are not necessarily sung better or more securely
by Albanese; the latter's voice had a touch of graininess and
hoarseness. It possessed its own strong character and could be
feverishly intensive, but her singing does not have Callas's technical finish. If only Callas had had Albanese's partner Jussi Björling,
rather than Giuseppe di Stefano, for Björling sings more spon-
taneously here than in any other of his roles.

The live recording of a concert from Athens on 5 August 1957
needs no special mention. The vocal problems which also affected
the *Sonnambula* in Edinburgh are all too evident (I have not been
able to hear the latter and am therefore guided by the comments
of John Ardoin). Although by this time vocally and physically
exhausted, she managed a contractual recording of Cherubini's
Medea with Serafin, a role which cannot be undertaken in a state
of exhaustion, let alone in the way Callas was later to present it
in Dallas and London. For this reason I pass it by.

All the more interesting, therefore, is the recording of a
rehearsal for a concert in Dallas on 20 November 1957, which is
one of the few documents we have of Callas at work. The voice
sounds refreshed after a longish period of rest, an impression
strengthened by the fact that at first she does not sing with full
voice, thus avoiding all the difficulties which the tension of an
actual performance can present. It is a fact that singers can perform
better and more beautifully not just because the worry of a performance is absent, but also because they can sing more softly

and with restrained caution, in other words, they can keep within their vocal limits. Although they may only be sketches, these performances of 'Martern aller Arten' from *Die Entführung aus dem Serail*, 'Qui la voce' from *I Puritani* and 'Ah! fors'è lui' from *La Traviata* (transposed down an octave), all take us to the heart of the music. The fascination of this document is enhanced by the fact that the soprano's security, both technically and musically, can be discerned as she works.

1957 ended with the La Scala opening of Verdi's *Un Ballo in Maschera*, in which Callas gave her portrayal a broader framework and sharper contours, not to mention greater eloquence, than the one she had presented in the studio recording. The fine condition of her voice is demonstrated by 'three of the most beautiful top Cs she had ever sung' (Lord Harewood in his discography). The Act 3 aria has particularly more intensity and inner cohesion than in the studio version. The great duet in Act 2 is marvellous in both versions, finer in verbal nuance in the studio but with more ardour and intensity on stage, where Giuseppe di Stefano's voice also sounds fresher. Ettore Bastianini is a Renato of vocal mastery (with far more beauty in the tone), but Gobbi comes into his own in the dialogue. Which version should one choose? – both.

Addio del passato

'Fame is very dangerous, because I know that I cannot always sing top notes in the way expected of me. I carry out my work with as much seriousness as possible, but I am a human being. With fame comes anxiety. It is the applause that intimidates me'

Maria Callas

When the *Norma* performance was broken off in Rome, Callas

had to go through purgatory, and there are a thousand reasons to believe that she never really recovered. The recording shows that she was not able to use the voice with maximum security, but I do not feel that it really reveals the true extent of her exhaustion. It is impossible to judge whether she could have carried on. As far as the two live recordings of *La Traviata* are concerned, the London one (under Rescigno) is distinctly preferable to that from Lisbon (under Ghione and with the young Alfredo Kraus); many consider the former to be the portrayal strongest in expression if not flawless vocally, and it has the advantage of a Germont of great musical and dramatic conviction in Mario Zanasi, whose voice sometimes takes on an almost tenor-like timbre. Cesare Valletti is also outstanding as Alfredo, singing Verdi's music with the elegance of a golden age tenor like Anselmi, de Lucia or Bonci.

The new season began, after the Verdi recital recordings in September 1958, with the second great scandal, the break with the Metropolitan Opera. Much has been made of how the public humiliation through Bing fuelled the fiery anger which permeates the Dallas performance of Cherubini's *Medea*.

The performance itself has also been examined in detail. Callas is in good form and one notes extreme concentration, as well as the fact that she is finely partnered by Jon Vickers and the young Teresa Berganza. Viewed in its entirety the performance is more compact and better balanced musically than the one from La Scala. The London version, which was to follow in 1959, need not detain us, and Ardoin describes it as a 'pale imitation'. Nor do I view the performance of Bellini's *Il Pirata* as one of Callas's great evenings, even if there are moments of great fury in the finale. As far as the 1959 studio remakes are concerned – Donizetti's *Lucia di Lammermoor* and Ponchielli's *La Gioconda* – the verismo piece is here more interesting than the romantic one. Listening to the Donizetti one feels like a Callas admirer who is having to defend her out of a sense of duty (as also the short-breathed and dull singing of Ferruccio Tagliavini), whereas in the case of Ponchielli's crowdpuller one listens with sympathy as private feelings are voiced – Callas said as much herself. All in all, a painful experience.

Regarding the second studio recording of *Norma*, Callas admirers like Ardoin and Porter are in agreement that, although the voice is no longer as secure and vehement in its upper reaches as was formerly the case, yet the well-honed portrayal has taken on even more finesse and expression. As a result of careful reductions of volume, the middle register in particular has a sound of iridescent beauty which can be described as mesmerising. Porter does list a whole series of notes which lose their effect through wobble, and yet he repeats: 'Callas gives an interpretation of Norma in both her recordings which Sutherland, Caballé and Sills, the heroines of later versions, cannot begin to approach' (Andrew Porter in his discography).

Returning to La Scala on 7 December 1960 after a two-year absence, she was no longer queen of the house. She sang Paolina in Donizetti's *Poliuto*, which is a tenor's opera. Franco Corelli carried off the evening's triumph. It was only in the last act that she was able to give a hint of her former acting intensity and vocal brilliance. In 1961 she made her farewell to La Scala and to Italy with three appearances in *Medea*, and the live recording, conducted by Thomas Schippers, shows that it was not a triumphant farewell. All we have from 1962 are a few live concert recordings – she did not sing much that year; these are discussed in *The Callas Legacy*. There Ardoin carries out his mission, that of herald with a strong sense of duty, to back up his defence. We have already considered the studio recitals from 1962 and 1964.

The Callas *Carmen* was announced at the end of 1964 in a great wave of publicity. It was strongly criticised by Rodney Milnes in *Opera on Record*. He felt that the portrayal lacks charm (but so does the character in Merimée's novel), and that the voice is not sufficiently weighty in its lower register. Additionally, he considered her French to be 'individual'. What he meant was that it is not idiomatic. But this has less to do with the ability to pronounce correctly than with vocal problems. Callas has to accommodate many vowels to the condition of her voice and to give them a guttural colouring. Ardoin describes the recording as an achievement which demands admiration but I consider that a sympathetic statement in her defence. The many telling details, worked out and put into practice on a musical level, do not add up to a unity. It all strikes me as artificial. It is not even, like the *Tosca* recording, a work of art on the technical level, merely a work of art robbed of its aura, partly through Georges Prêtre's externalised and gaudy conducting of an editorially dubious score.

The same conductor is no more successful in Puccini's *Tosca*, which in this version really is little more than the 'shabby little shocker'. It would be wrong to say that Maria Callas and Tito Gobbi adapt themselves to a conciliatory style. Because both are experiencing the same embarrassing reduction in their vocal means, they have to resort to precisely the histrionic gestures and rhetorical exaggerations from which Callas had, in earlier recordings and performances, liberated verismo music. Carlo Bergonzi is admittedly a model of vocal elegance, but he cannot approach the sensual empathy of the young Giuseppe di Stefano.

There are live recordings of *Tosca* and *Norma* from 1965, the final year of her career. But these cannot be judged by the standards which one will have learned after studying Maria Callas. One can only listen to them in sadness and amazement. One would not want to play them to anyone as an introduction to Callas, or to those who already admire her. This is no way to show love, but if one is mourning her, one can mourn best alone. Individual phrases and expressions of suffering recall the great performances. As Pauline Viardot tearfully explained, when she heard Pasta in her sad comeback: 'It is like the Last Supper of da Vinci in Milan – a wreck of a picture, but the picture is the greatest picture in the world.'

Notes

1 MARIA AND MEGAERA

1. Ingeborg Bachmann, 'Hommage à Maria Callas'.
2. Hans Magnus Enzensberger, 'The Language of *Der Spiegel*'.
3. George London, *Opera Annual*, 1959.

2 THE ONE AND ONLY

1. Lanfranco Rasponi, *The Last Prima Donna*.
2. A reaction as described by Theodor W. Adorno in 'On the Fetish-character in Music and the Regression of Listening' (1938).
3. Cf. Lilli Lehmann, *Meine Gesangskunst*; Frida Leider, *Das war mein Teil*.
4. Opera at the turn of the century was no longer concerned, as was *opera seria*, with abstract virtues or the transfiguration of a ruler, nor was it concerned, as was Romantic opera, with the polarisation of good and evil or with moral problems, but with sensual and physical passion – the central theme of Puccini's works is romanticised eroticism.
5. Rodolfo Celletti, *History of Belcanto*.
6. Concert pitch is normally fixed at a'=440. Many orchestras play at a'=447, which can be a dangerous risk for singers in parts requiring a high *tessitura*.
7. Cf. Ethan Mordden, *Demented: The World of the Opera Diva*.

3 THE PARADOX OF EXPRESSION

1. One of the biggest dangers for the female voice is the upward forcing of the chest voice. Nellie Melba made it a cardinal rule that the high F should be the upper limit for the chest voice. The chest register should be confined to the lower voice, while the main register should be achieved only with the middle voice at full tone. If the voice is constantly pressed or crudely forced above to E, it will suffer from too much use of the chest. Such a use gradually increases in heaviness,

producing flat, distorted vowel sounds which are too open and bring about a loss of agility when rising to the top. It cannot be pointed out too emphatically that a distorted vowel can completely alter the meaning and emotional content of a word. Compare, for example, the German words *Seele* and *Säle*.

4 MARIA CALLAS AND THE OPERA WORLD OF THE 1950s

1. No one recognised this more quickly than W. J. Henderson. After Titta Ruffo had made his Met début on 19 November 1912 and caused a furore with the powerful tone of his singing, the critic put out a polemical article with the title 'Get-Rich-Quick Singing'. Henderson's complaint was that the golden age of singing – that of the 1890s – was being brought to a close by the production of such a powerful tone. He wrote that this tone was not even necessary. There had been no seats in the Met where one could not hear 'the *moderato* of a Sembrich or the finely spun *mezza voce* of a Bonci'. But it took time, according to Henderson, to achieve that level of mastery. Singers who were now using the examples of Caruso and Ruffo to give priority to increasing their volume were simply pushing their voices towards an early decline.

2. Ardoin and Fitzgerald's *Callas* contains this and the following descriptions of *La Traviata* of 28 May 1955, by Giulini, Visconti, Piero Tosi and Sandro Sequi.

3. While in Paris in 1852 Verdi had seen one of the first performances of *La Dame aux camélias* by Alexandre Dumas *fils*, the dramatisation of an 1848 novel of the same name based on a true story. Its theme is the liaison with a celebrated courtesan who was the focal point of the artistic and intellectual circle frequented by, among others, Liszt and some well-known literary figures and lovers of noble birth. The young woman in question died of tuberculosis in 1847, shortly after her twenty-third birthday.

4. 'Non mì dir' is one of Donna Anna's arias in Mozart's *Don Giovanni*. This recording was withheld from publication for many years, but can now be heard in the EMI CD

anthologies 'Les Introuvables du chant Mozartien' and 'Callas at Juilliard'.

5. Walter Legge's 'La Divina – Callas Remembered' first appeared in *Opera News* in November 1977, shortly after the singer's death, and later in his recollections *On and off the Record*, edited by Elisabeth Schwarzkopf.

7 QUEEN OF LA SCALA

1. Cf. *Ein Leben für die Sängerin*, ed. Gloede and Grünhagen, in particular the chapter entitled 'Mozart und die Sänger', p. 278 ff.
2. See Ardoin and Fitzgerald, *Callas*.
3. Bastianini possessed one of the most beautiful Italian baritone voices of the post-war era, with an attractive dark colouring which pointed to his origins as a bass. However, he did not command the art of what Verdi called '*miniare*', of coloring the voice.

8 THE DESCENT TO FAME

1. Ettore Parmeggiani was born in Rimini in 1895 and made his début at La Scala in 1927 as Max in Weber's *Der Freischütz*, continuing to sing there until 1937 mainly from the German dramatic repertory, especially Wagner.

9 PRIMA DONNA WITHOUT A HOME

1. Quoted in Hans Mayer, *Outsiders*.

10 CALLAS AND THE CONSEQUENCES

1. *Fono-Forum*, January 1990.
2. *Observer*, 8 and 15 February 1970.

11 EPILOGUE

1. Singers such as Rosa Ponselle, Claudia Muzio, Renata Tebaldi and Victoria de los Angeles went through similar agonies after botching top notes – for example, the high C in Verdi's

'O patria mia' (*Aida*) – and in consequence avoided certain roles.

2. Reprinted in Joachim Kaiser, *Erlebte Musik*, see pp. 635 ff.
3. A problematical statement. The lyric mezzo possesses a voice which is quite short and restricted in its range. Even if Callas fell into this category, she was a *mezzo acuto*, a mezzo with extended top. She certainly had a rich chest voice in her early years, but she never had sufficient power to produce sustained notes within the true contralto range.
4. The range for Puccini's Tosca only goes up to C and cannot therefore be considered the true test for a soprano's security at the top. The concept of 'forcing' is only tenuously linked to a voice's 'top'; what 'forcing' really means is the application of pressure to force an increase in volume.

12 PRIMA DONNA, ARTIST, WOMAN

1. See Julian Budden's article '*Tosca*, Puccini and Sardou', written for the programme book of Karajan's 1988 Salzburg Easter Festival production of the opera.
2. Joachim Kaiser, *Erlebte Musik*, see note 2 of chapter 11.
3. Theodor W. Adorno, *Minima Moralia*: 'L'inutile beauté'.
4. John Ardoin, *Callas at Juilliard*.
5. Many of this French writer's thoughts and aesthetic assessments coincide with my own; however, they were reached quite independently.
6. Tubeuf does not recognise that casting the roles of Elvira or Lucia with singers like Toti dal Monte and Lily Pons was the twentieth century's way out of problems which the nineteenth century had posed; and that up to the time of Lilli Lehmann and Lillian Nordica dramatic sopranos had also undertaken florid music.

13 SINGING FOR THE IMAGINATION

1. Gary O'Connor, *The Pursuit of Perfection: A Life of Maggie Teyte* London 1979.
2. Cf. the contribution of Elizabeth Forbes to *The New Grove Dictionary of Music and Musicians*, vol 7, p. 737.

3. John Ardoin says that she had sung only two performances of the role before making the Cetra recording. However, the records were not actually made until 8–10 November 1949.

4. Julian Budden, *The Operas of Verdi*, vol 1, p. 102.

5. Quotation taken from David Hamilton, 'The Recordings of Maria Callas' in *High Fidelity*, March 1974, p. 44.

6. These details are supplied by John Ardoin.

7. Herbert Weinstock, 'Maria, Renata, Zinka . . . and Leonora' in *Saturday Review*, 13 April 1957.

8. *Opera on Record* ed. Alan Blyth, vol 1, p. 442.

9. Will Crutchfield, 'Martini & Rossi's Vintage Voices' in *High Fidelity*, April 1984. But this is much more than just 'prime Callas'. These concerts presented not just stars who were established and well represented on recordings, like di Stefano, Ferruccio Tagliavini, Tito Gobbi, Renata Tebaldi, Mario del Monaco, Ebe Stignani, Carlo Bergonzi, Franco Corelli, Fiorenza Cossotto and Giulietta Simionato but also singers like Margherita Carosio, Rosanna Carteri, Gertrud Grob-Prandl, Gianni Raimondi, Agostino Lazzari, Anita Cerquetti, Alda Noni, Luigi Infantino, Ivo Vinco, Magda Olivero, Giacinto Prandelli and Pia Tassinari. The concerts are a good barometer for Italian singing standards in the 1950s – standards that have done nothing but sink since the 1970s.

10. Rolando Manicini in his notes for 'Maria Callas: Un mito, una carriera', Foyer LP – set FO 1007.

11. John Ardoin, *The Callas Legacy*, p. 92.

12. This opera is so little known that little thought had been given to its casting. The role of Arrigo is a long and fatiguing one – particularly as a result of its high *tessitura*. It can only be attempted by a tenor with the agility of the Duke of Mantua in *Rigoletto* combined with the brilliance of, for example, Raoul in Meyerbeer's *Les Huguenots*. When Riccardo Muti opened La Scala's 1989–90 season with *I Vespri Siciliani*, he expressed the opinion that the part of Arrigo (then taken by Chris Merritt) was even more difficult than the role of Arnoldo in Rossini's *Guillaume Tell*.

13.　Walter Legge and Elisabeth Schwarzkopf, *On and Off the Record*.

14.　Michael Scott, 'A Connoisseur's Callas' in *Opera News*, September 1987.

15.　For the extent of the historical influence of *Medea*, cf. Ulrich Schreiber, *Opernführer für Fortgeschrittene*, Kassel 1988, p. 524.

16.　In his discography Ulrich Schreiber deals with the studio recording conducted by Serafin, which is by no means complete but is not so heavily cut as Bernstein's La Scala version; those cuts cannot be explained, let alone justified, by claiming that they make the opera more effective in the theatre.

17.　Cf. *Opera on Record*, vol. 1, discography of *La Forza del Destino*, p. 279.

18.　Cf. Julian Budden, *The Operas of Verdi*, vol 2, p. 464.

19.　*Opera on Record*: discographies of *L'Italiana in Algeri* and *Il Turco in Italia*.

20.　Carl Dahlhaus, *Realism in Nineteenth-Century Music*.

21.　Martial Singher draws attention to these details in *An interpretative guide to operatic arias: a handbook for singers, coaches, teachers and students*, Pennsylvania State University Press, 1983, p. 241.

22.　The Act 1 scena 'Sorgete – lo sognai ferito esangue', which was included in a later CD issue, was recorded in 1961. The conductor was Antonino Tonini, a conducting assistant from La Scala. These sessions were originally intended for Verdi's *La Traviata*, but the project had to be postponed due to the soprano's condition. A programme of arias was designed at least partially to recoup costs.

23.　*Opera on Record*, vol 2, discography of *Roméo et Juliette*, p. 202.

24.　Lord Harewood, 'The Art of Maria Callas' in *Recorded Sound*, journal of the British Institute of Recorded Sound, October 1979 (no. 76), p. 95.

25.　*Opera on Record*, vol 1, p. 307.

26.　David A. Lowe, *Callas – As They Saw Her*, p. 241.

27.　Cf. R. Fairman, *Opera on Record*, vol 3, p. 52.

28.　Cf. *Opera on Record*, vol 3, p. 213.

Glossary

accelerando	getting gradually quicker
acciaccatura	ornamental or grace note of the shortest possible length of time
acuti	high notes
allegro	quick, lively, bright
in alt	for example, E *in alt* is the E above the C above middle C
altissimo	E *altissimo* is the E above E *in alt*
andante	moving along, flowing
andantino	a little faster than *andante*
appoggiatura	leaning note, or grace note, which takes a prescribed part of the time of the supporting note
aria d'urlo	an aria sung with a scream or a shriek, as in verismo singing
arioso	a recitative of the more melodic kind
assoluta	absolute, free, alone; used here of the prima donna
ballatella	little ballad
bel canto	an imprecise term for the traditional Italian art of singing in which beautiful tone, fine *legato* and impeccable technique are emphasised
bolero	Spanish dance in triple time with accompaniment of voices and castanets, sometimes with tambourine and guitar
brindisi	drinking song, as in Alfredo and Violetta's 'Libiamo' from *La Traviata*
cabaletta	final, rousing section of elaborate operatic duet or aria
caesura	a pause or interruption of the musical beat

cantabile	singingly, with the melody smoothly performed and well brought out
cantilena	part of a vocal composition containing the main tune, or the flowing, melodious part
canto fiorito	ornamented singing, as perfected by castrati (male sopranos) in the seventeenth and eighteenth centuries and adapted for the 'coloratura' soprano. This singing is distinguished by light, agile runs and leaps and *fioriture*, elaborate ornamentation decorating the main line of the melody
cavatina	song-like air forming part of a long scene
coloratura	from the German *Koloratur*, a general term for a soprano voice using all kinds of ornamentation. See *canto fiorito*
crescendo	getting louder
diminuendo	getting softer
divertissement	entertainment of dances and songs introduced into a ballet or opera
espressivo	a loose term for expressive singing
fermata	pause on a held note
sul fiato	sung on the breath, i.e. without a break
fil di sono, fil di voce	drawing out of the voice, holding of a long note with no dynamic change
fioritura	ornamental figure, as in *canto fiorito*
forte	strong, i.e. loud
con forza	with force
glissando	sliding the voice or instrument up or down through a series of notes
gruppetto	one of the myriad ornaments of baroque composition, the most common of which is the alternation of the main note with two subsidiary notes, those immediately above and below

largamente	slow and dignified, used of performance rather than tempo
legatissimo	very slowly and smoothly
legato	bound together: with no perceptible pause between notes, smoothly
in maschera	in the mask: projecting the voice into the head cavities to produce a reverberating quality
melancolia tinta	melancholy timbre, a special quality of the *soprano sfogato*
mezzoforte	half-loud
mezzo-soprano	in Italy the mezzo-soprano has a slightly lower vocal range than the soprano, and the tone is of a darker quality. In Germany it is a more distinctly different voice, with a lower range still
mezza voce	singing at half voice, with consequently muted expression
miniare	to illuminate with great finesse: Verdi's word for a singer's colouring of the voice
obbligato	indispensable: adjective attached to the name of an instrument where its musical part is important, special or unusual in effect
opera buffa	opera with a comic subject, with characters drawn from everyday life
opera seria	serious opera: as in the seventeenth and eighteenth centuries, becoming increasingly formal and complex, often with mythological stories
opéra comique	French term from the seventeenth century for pieces by Molière and Lully, that changed its meaning over time, coming to refer to opera retaining spoken words, and was performed at the Paris Opéra

Comique after dialogue had been banned at the Opéra

parlando	musical directive for the voice to approximate to speech as closely as possible
passagio	passage-work, a section of music affording opportunity for brilliant display by the soloist
pianissimo	very, very softly
piano	softly
portamento	the smooth carriage of the voice from one note to another
prima	première
prima donna	first lady, leading female singer in opera
ritardando	holding back, i.e. gradually diminishing the speed
romanza	aria of the simpler kind, generally amorous or soliloquising
roulade	long vocal run, consisting of short notes
rubato	robbed time: a feature of performance in which strict time is for a while disregarded – what is 'robbed' from some note or notes being paid back later
salto mortale	(vocal) somersault
siciliana	pastoral song, dance or piece popular in the eighteenth century, in compound duple or quadruple time and with a swaying rhythm, often in a minor key
solfeggio	performing with particular attention to notation; the grammar of *canto fiorito*
soprano d'agilità	female soprano voice excelling in high notes and virtuosic floridity
soprano leggiero	soprano of ornamented singing, but without inner dramatic sense
soprano sfogato	Maria Malibran and Guiditti Pasta were the supreme *soprani sfogati* of the nineteenth

century, contraltos who extended their range by rigorous training into the soprano, thereby also extending the emotional force of their singing. What the voice gained in expressiveness, it was said to lose in purity, a criticism frequently levelled at Maria Callas

soprano spinto   used also of the tenor voice, '*spinto*' implies a voice that has been pushed into more forceful singing, as for the role of Madama Butterfly

staccato   detached method of playing or singing notes so that they are shortened; the mood may be sharp or soft

stretta   passage at the end of an act in which the tempo is accelerated to make a climax

tenore di grazia   Italian tenor voice of grace and charm, as required for the role of, for example, Nemorino in *L'Elisir d'amore*

tenorino   a lightweight tenor voice

tessitura   the average range of notes encompassed by a voice

tremolo   shaking or trembling between two notes or on the same note as opposed to *vibrato* which involves an alteration of pitch

verismo   term describing the realistic or naturalistic school of Italian opera that flourished briefly in the late nineteenth and early twentieth centuries

virtuoso/a   performer of exceptional skill, with special reference to technical ability

vis comica   comic perception and energy

voce bianca   a voice without colour

voce isolata   an individual voice, one that stands out

voce soffocata   a strangulated or stifled voice

Discography

The discography does not claim to be a complete listing of every version of a Callas recording which has ever been published, but a list of what is currently available.

Many of the live opera recordings are already obtainable in as many as five or six different CD editions, but again mention is only made of the versions which appear to be most readily available at the present time. In the few cases of complete live operas not yet available on CD, mention is made of the last available LP edition.

Although the EMI complete operas still appear to be obtainable on both CD and LP formats, only the CD catalogue numbers are given here. However, the EMI operatic recitals are listed under separate LP and CD headings, as in most cases the CD version takes into account a longer playing time by including extra items. Our aim here has been to make clear which arias are contained on which CD.

A complete discography of live Callas anthologies would scarcely be possible because rarely a month goes by without the appearance of some collection containing arias or scenes from versions already available in their complete form. We have therefore concentrated here on those with material taken from Callas concerts as opposed to stage performances. The LP editions are not listed, now being mainly out of print; for details about them reference should be made to John Ardoin's *The Callas Legacy*, revised edition 1982 and now available in paperback.

Complete Operas (and Extended Scenes)

BELLINI

Norma
Mexico 1950/Melodram 26018
London 1952/Melodram 26025/Verona 27018/Legato 130
Trieste 1953/Myto 91340 (Scenes only)
EMI 1954/EMI CDS 747 3048
Rome 1955/Cetra CDC 4
Milan 1955/Hunt 517
Rome 1958/Melodram 16000 (Act 1 only)
EMI 1960/EMI CMS 763 0002
Paris 1965/Legendary 1009 (Scenes only)

Il Pirata
New York 1959/Melodram 26013/Hunt 531

I Puritani
Mexico 1952/Melodram 26027
EMI 1953/EMI CDC 747 3088

La Sonnambula
Milan 1955/Myto 89006
EMI 1957/EMI CDS 747 3788
Cologne 1957/Melodram 26003 Verona 27904/Hunt 503
Edinburgh 1957/Virtuoso 269 7252

BIZET

Carmen
EMI 1964/EMI CDS 754 3682

CHERUBINI
Medea
Florence 1953/Hunt 516
Milan 1953/Melodram 26022/Cetra CDE 1019
Ricordi 1957/Cetra DOCL 201/EMI CMS 763 6252
Dallas 1958/Melodram 26018

London 1959/Melodram 26005
Milan 1961/Hunt 34028

DONIZETTI

Anna Bolena
Milan 1957/Melodram 26110/Hunt 518

Lucia di Lammermoor
Mexico 1952/Myto 91340
EMI 1953/EMI CMS 769 9802
Milan 1954/Legato 831 (heavily cut)
Berlin 1955/EMI CMS 763 6312 (also published in many other
    editions)
New York 1956/Raritas (OPR) 412 (LP only)
Rome 1957/Melodram 26014/Hunt 34022
EMI 1959/EMI CDS 747 4408

Poliuto
Milan 1960/Melodram 26006

GIORDANO

Andrea Chénier
Milan 1955/Melodram 26002

GLUCK

Alceste
Milan 1954/Melodram 26026

Iphigénie en Tauride
Milan 1957/Melodram 26014

LEONCAVALLO

I Pagliacci
EMI 1954/EMI CDS 747 9818

MASCAGNI

Cavalleria Rusticana
EMI 1953/EMI CDS 747 9818

PONCHIELLI

La Gioconda
Cetra 1952/Cetra CDC 9
EMI 1959/EMI CDS 749 5182

PUCCINI

La Bohème
EMI 1956/EMI CDS 747 4758

Madama Butterfly
EMI 1955/EMI CDS 747 9598

Manon Lescaut
EMI 1957/EMI CDS 747 3938

Tosca
Mexico 1950/HRE 211 (LP only)
Rio 1951/Voce 34 (LP-scenes only)
Mexico 1952/Melodram 26028
EMI 1953/EMI CDS 747 1758
New York 1956/Melodram 26011/36513 (Act 2 scenes only)
Paris 1958/Laudis 16010/Rodolphe 32495 (Act 2 only)
London 1964/Melodram 26011/Virtuoso 269 7242/Verona 27027
EMI 1964/EMI CMS 769 9742
Paris 1965/Melodram 480 (LP only)
New York 1965/Melodram 26030 (with Franco Corelli)
New York 1965/HRE 306 (LP only – with Richard Tucker)
London 1965/Voce 13 (LP only – abridged)

Turandot
EMI 1957/EMI CDS 747 9718

ROSSINI

Armida
Florence 1952/Melodram 26024

Il Barbiere di Siviglia
Milan 1956/Melodram 26020
EMI 1957/EMI CDS 747 6348

Il Turco in Italia
EMI 1954/EMI CDS 749 0578

SPONTINI

La Vestale
Milan 1954/Melodram 26008/GOP 54

VERDI

Aida
Mexico 1950/Melodram 26009
Mexico 1951/Melodram 26016/Legato 508/Virtuoso 269 9222/
   Cetra CDE 1026
London 1953/Melodram 36513 (Act 3 only)
EMI 1955/EMI CDS 749 0308

Un Ballo in Maschera
EMI 1956/EMI CDS 747 4988
Milan 1957/Hunt 519/Virtuoso 269 7412

La Forza del Destino
EMI 1954/EMI CDS 747 5818

Macbeth
Milan 1952/Nuova Era 2209/Hunt 34027/Movimento Musica
051 022/Legendary 1003

Nabucco
Naples 1949/Melodram 26029/Legendary 1005

Rigoletto
Mexico 1952/Melodram 26023/Legendary 1006
EMI 1955/EMI CDS 747 4698

La Traviata
Mexico 1951/Melodram 26019
Mexico 1952/Melodram 26021/Rodolphe 324 3132
Cetra 1953/Cetra CDC 2
Milan 1955/Hunt 501/EMI CMS 763 6282
Milan 1956/Myto 89003
Lisbon 1958/EMI CDS 749 1878
London 1958/Melodram 26007/Virtuoso 269 7292/Verona 27054

Il Trovatore
Mexico 1950/Melodram 26017
Naples 1951/Melodram 26001
Milan 1953/Legendary 1007/Myto 90213
EMI 1956/EMI CDS 749 3472

I Vespri Siciliani
Florence 1951/Melodram 36020/Legendary 1008

WAGNER

Parsifal
Rome 1950/Melodram 36041

EMI Recitals 1954–1969

LP versions
1. Puccini recital 1954 (Manon Lescaut/Bohème/Butterfly/Suor Angelica/Gianni Schicchi/Turandot)
2. Lyric and coloratura arias 1954 (Adriana Lecouvreur/Andrea Chénier/La Wally/Mefistofele/Il Barbiere di Siviglia/Dinorah/Lakmé/I Vespri Siciliani)
3. Bellini/Cherubini/Spontini recital 1955/1958/1961 (La Sonnambula/Medea/La Vestale/Il Pirata)
4. Mad scenes 1959 (Anna Bolena/Hamlet/Il Pirata)
5. Verdi arias 1959 (Macbeth/Nabucco/Don Carlo)
6. French arias 1961 (Orfeo/Alceste/Carmen/Samson et Dalila/Roméo et Juliette/Manon/Le Cid/Louise)

7. French arias 1963 (Iphigénie en Tauride/La Damnation de Faust/Les Pêcheurs de Perles/Manon/Werther/Faust)
8. Verdi arias 1963/64 (Otello/Aroldo/Don Carlo)
9. Beethoven/Weber/Mozart 1963 (Ah perfido/Oberon/Don Giovanni/Le Nozze di Figaro)
10. Rossini/Donizetti recital 1963/64 (La Cenerentola/Guglielmo Tell/Semiramide/La Figlia del Reggimento/L'Elisir/Lucrezia Borgia)
11. Bellini/Verdi recital 1964/69 (Il Pirata/Attila/I Vespri Siciliani/Il Corsaro/Il Trovatore/Un ballo in maschera/Aida)
   These 11 LPs also available as a set (EMI 165 54178–88)

CD versions
1. Puccini recital 1954 + Sonnambula arias 1955/EMI CDC 747 9662
2. Lyric & coloratura arias 1954 + Medea/Vestale arias 1955/ EMI CDC 747 2822
3. Mad scenes 1959 + Donizetti arias 1964/EMI CDC 747 2832
4. Verdi arias + Aida/Ballo/Lombardi/Vespri arias 1964/EMI CDC 747 7302
5. Verdi arias 1963/64 + Corsaro/Attila/Trovatore/Ballo 1964/ EMI CDC 747 9432
6. French arias 1961/63 (except Faust/Werther)/EMI CDC 749 0592
7. Mozart/Weber/Rossini arias 1963 + Faust/Werther 1963/ EMI CDC 749 0052

Beethoven's 'Ah! perfido', which is missing from the above CD compilations, is included as a fill-up on the EMI CD issue of Cherubini Medea (CMS 763 6252)

Maria Callas at Juilliard: the masterclasses/EMI CDS 749 6002 includes various excerpts from the EMI complete operas and recitals + 1953 unpublished version of 'Non mi dir' (Don Giovanni)

Live Recitals etc.

Callas Rarities
Ah perfido/Don Giovanni/Entführung/Oberon/Armida/Lucrezia
Borgia/Don Carlo/Vespri Siciliani/Trovatore/Lombardi/Aida
(with Franco Corelli)
EMI CDC 754 4372

Maria Callas: the unknown recordings
Tristan (Athens 1957)/Don Carlo/Il Pirata (Amsterdam 1959) +
EMI recordings: La Cenerentola/Guglielmo Tell/Semiramide/
Lombardi/Vespri Siciliani/Attila 1960–1969
EMI CDC 749 4282

Cetra recordings 1949 and the RAI concerts 1952–1956
Norma/Puritani/Tristan/Macbeth/Lucia/Nabucco/Lakmé/
Entführung/Louise/Armida/Dinorah/Vestale/Semiramide/
Hamlet
Cetra CDC 5/Verona 27067/Rodolphe 32484–7

Les inédits de Maria Callas
Turandot extract (Buenos Aires 1949) + selections from various
Mexico performances 1950–1952.
Rodolphe

The Dallas rehearsals 1957
Traviata/Puritani/Macbeth/Anna Bolena/Entführung
Legato 131/Verona 28007–9

The Hamburg concerts 1959/1962
Vestale/Macbeth/Don Carlo/Il Pirata/Le Cid/Carmen/Ernani
Hunt 34010/Movimento Musica 51023/Frequenz CMH 1

The Paris concert 1958
Norma/Il Trovatore/Il Barbiere di Siviglia/Tosca Act 2
Rodolphe 32495/Laudis 16010 (also available on EMI video)

The Paris concert 1963
Semiramide/La Cenerentola/Manon/Werther/Nabucco/La
Bohème/Madama Butterfly/Gianni Schicchi
Melodram 16502 (CD booklet incorrectly attributes the concert
to Amsterdam 1959)

New York recital with Giuseppe di Stefano 1974
Don Carlo/La Gioconda/Carmen/Manon/Werther/Cavalleria
Rusticana/L'Elisir/Gianni Schicchi
Legato 137

Maria Callas 2
This 3-CD compilation contains certain items not available else-
where on CD:
Aida Act 3 London 1953/London concert 1962 (Le Cid/La
Cenerentola/Anna Bolena/Macbeth/Oberon)/Norma duet Buenos
Aires 1949/Athens concert 1957 (Tristan/Hamlet/La Forza del
destino)/Paris recital 1965 (Manon/La Sonnambula/Gianni Sch-
icchi)
Melodram 36513

The David Frost interview 1970
Verona 28007–9 (set also includes Dallas rehearsal + duets with
di Stefano)

John Hunt
June 1992

Bibliography

Notes on the Literature about Maria Callas

There is a saying by Goethe: 'If you want me to show you the surroundings, then you must first climb onto the roof.' This suggests that an artist's biography cannot be written from too close a proximity – or at least only with difficulty. It makes the book which George Jellinek wrote as early as 1960, entitled *Callas: Portrait of a Prima Donna*, all the more commendable. This is the work of a writer who maintains a distance from the object of his admiration and love. The author avoids getting entangled in the gossip which was flourishing at that time; he writes about the artist with the cooled ardour of emotions which are under control – the biography was published again in 1978 and remains one of the few standard books about the singer. This also applies to the factual, lapidary and critical biography published in 1978 by Pierre-Jean Rémy, a prime aim of which is to penetrate the thorny undergrowth of anecdotes, rumours and tales of scandal. However, the assessments of Callas's singing which it offers are rather generalised and are not verified by any analysis of the recordings. This was to be the achievement of John Ardoin, who uniquely demonstrated, in his 1982 book *The Callas Legacy*, how the medium of the gramophone record – to which the musical artist owes his second existence – can be taken seriously. Although Ardoin has glowing admiration for, and indeed was a friend of the soprano, he never loses his critical distance. The basis of his study was laid as early as 1974 in a biography, undertaken in conjunction with Gerald Fitzgerald, where Ardoin starts with an excellent and historically comprehensive essay explaining Callas's position in the tradition of singing and acutely summing up her individual achievement. The second part of the book is a documentation, with pictures and interviews, of her most important performances (particularly at La Scala), containing many excellent photographs and commentaries from conductors, producers and colleagues with whom Callas worked. A similar plan is adopted by the visually attractive 1975 book by Henry Wisneski, but its text does not compare to Ardoin's. A picture biography of even greater richness is the one published in Paris in 1979 by Sergio Segalini, entitled *Callas: Les Images d'une voix*. Collections of important documentary value are those by David A. Lowe (*Callas – As They Saw Her*) and Martin Monestier (*Le Livre du souvenir*). Lowe's book is a comprehensive collection of critical comments and essays on Maria Callas, and contains part of the English translation of the Callas Debate (*Processo alla Callas*).

The biography by Arianna Stassinopoulos, which claims to give us *The Woman Behind the Legend*, is highly ambivalent; it leans heavily on the opinions of Jellinek, Rémy, Ardoin and many other important critics, which Stassinopoulos uses simply to justify discussion of the episodes of Callas's private life which she has researched in such detail. This is a writer who deserves the epithet coined by Helmut Schmidt, that of the 'indiscreet gossip-monger'. One reads the book with a mixture of fascination and disgust. As for the revelations and apologies of Evangelia Callas, Jackie Callas, Giovanni Battista Meneghini and Nadia Stancioff, one can only conclude that the reader will claim compensation.

Publishers' note: Where possible the British editions have been cited for books which the author evidently consulted in American or original language editions.

Books about Maria Callas

Ardoin, John: *The Callas Legacy*, London 1982
Ardoin, John: *Callas at Juilliard, The Master Classes*, London 1988
Ardoin, John & Fitzgerald, Gerald: *Callas*, London 1974
Callas, Evangelia: *My Daughter, Maria Callas*, New York 1960
Callas, Jackie: *Sisters*, London 1989
Dufresne, Claude: *La Callas*, Paris 1990
Galatopoulos, Stelios: *Callas: La Divina*, London 1966
Jellinek, George: *Callas: Portrait of a Prima Donna*, New York 1960 (2nd edition 1978)

Linakis, Stephen: *Diva: Life and Death of Maria Callas*, London 1981

Lorcey, Jacques: *Maria Callas: D'Art et d'amour*, Paris 1983

Lowe, David A.: *Callas – As They Saw Her*, London 1987

Meneghini, Giovanni Battista: *My Wife Maria Callas*, London 1982

Monestier, Martin: *Maria Callas – Le Livre du souvenir*, Paris 1985

Reiss, Jeanine: *La Callas*, Paris 1991

Rémy, Pierre-Jean: *Maria Callas – A Tribute*, London 1978

Scott, Michael: *Maria Meneghini Callas*, London 1991

Stassinopoulos, Arianna: *Maria Callas: The Woman Behind the Legend*, London 1981

Stancioff, Nadia: *Maria: Callas Remembered*, New York 1987

Wisneski, Henry: *Maria Callas: The Art Behind the Legend*, New York 1975

Selected Essays and Articles about Maria Callas

Only extensive articles possessing biographical and critical importance are listed: quotations from them are incorporated in the main body of the book. It was not possible to mention all the many hundreds of reviews which were read, consulted, accepted or rejected. The main periodicals in which these were found are *Gramophone*, London; *Music and Musicians*, London; *Hifi-Stereophonie*, Karlsruhe: *Fono-Forum*, Bielefeld/Munich, *Opernwelt*, Hanover; *Opera News*, New York; *High Fidelity*, New York.

'Callas Remembered', *Opera*, November 1977. Recollections, tributes and commentaries by Tito Gobbi, Carlo Maria Giulini, Lord Harewood, Rolf Liebermann, Sir John Tooley, Margherita Wallmann

'Maria Callas – The Prima Donna', *Time* 44/1956

'Maria Callas – Die Primadonna', *Der Spiegel*, 13 February 1957

'The Callas Debate', *Opera*, September and October 1970 (English version of '*Processo alla Callas*', *Radiocorriere TV*, 30 November 1969, see also Lowe, David A. *Callas – As They Saw Her*)

Bachmann, Ingeborg: 'Hommage à Maria Callas', *Die Wahrheit ist den Menschen zumutbar*, Essay, Reden, Kleinere Schriften, Sevie Piper no. 218

Ardoin, John: 'The Kelly Years', *Opera News*, November 1974

Ardoin, John: 'The Callas Legacy Updated', *Opera News*, August 1978

Barnes, Clive: 'Callas – The Unique', *Music and Musicians*, January 1964

Cassidy, Claudia: 'Splendor in the Night – Callas Remembered', *Opera News*, November 1977

Celli, Teodoro: 'A Song from Another Century', *Opera Annual* January, 1959

Christiansen, Rupert: 'Callas. A polemic', *Opera*

Crutchfield, Will: 'Martini & Rossi's Vintage Voices', *High Fidelity*, April 1984

Culshaw, John: 'Callas – A Personal Footnote', *High Fidelity*

Du-Pond, Carlos Diaz: 'Callas in Mexico', *Opera*, April 1973

Hamilton, David: 'The Recordings of Maria Callas', *High Fidelity*, March 1974

Hamilton, David 'Who speaks for Callas?', *High Fidelity*, January 1979

Harewood, Earl of: 'The Art of Maria Callas', *Recorded Sound*, October 1979

Heinsen, Gerd: 'Aufgelegt. Maria Callas auf CD – Erbe und Distanz', *Orpheus*, October 1987

Legge, Walter: 'La Divina – Callas Remembered', *Opera News*, November 1977

Leibowitz, René: 'Le Secret de la Callas', *Les Temps Modernes*, ed. Jean-Paul Sartre, no. 161 1958/9

London, George: 'The Prima Donnas I have Sung Against', *Opera Annual* 1959

Luten, C. J.: 'Callas on Compact Disc', *Opera News*, August 1988

Schonberg, Harold C.: 'Callas at the Met', *Show*, May 1965

Scott, Michael: 'A Connoisseur's Callas', *Opera News*, September 1987

Schröter, Werner: 'Der Herztod der Primadonna', *Der Spiegel* 40/1977

Tosi, Pier Francesco: 'Opinioni d'cantori antichi e moderni', translated as 'Observations on the Florid Song, or, Sentiments on the Ancient and Modern Singers' (1726), Reprint William Reeves, London 1967

Voigt, Thomas: 'Demonstrations konkurrenzloser Vielsteitigkeit – Compact-Disc-Ausgaben zum 10, Todestag von Maria Callas', *Fono-Forum*, September 1987

Weinstock, Herbert: 'Maria, Renata, Zinka . . . and Leonora', *The Saturday Review*, 13 April 1957

Winterhoff, Hans-Jürgen: 'Maria Callas – Die wichtigsten Einspielungen', *Fono-Forum*, January 1979

General Literature

Adorno, Theodor W.: 'Die Oper überwintert auf der Langspielplatte', *Der Spiegel*, 24 March 1969

Adorno: *Minima Moralia*, London 1979

Adorno: *Musikalische Schriften Gesammelte Schriften*, Frankfurt 1978 and 1982

Barthes, Roland: *Mythologies*, London 1972

Benjamin, Walter: 'The Work of Art in the Age of Mechanical Production', *Illuminations*, New York 1991

Bing, Rudolf: *5000 Nights at the Opera*, New York 1972

Blaukopf, Kurt: *Musik im Wandel der Gesellschaft*, Munich 1984

Bloch, Ernst: *Essays on the Philosophy of Music*, Cambridge UK 1985

Bonynge, Richard: 'Bonynge on Bel Canto', *Opera News* 1976

Bovenschen, Silvia: *Die imaginierte Weiblichkeit. Exemplarische Untersuchungen zu kulturgeschichlichen und literarischen Präsentationsformen des Weiblichen*, Frankfurt am Main 1979

Budden, Julian: *The Operas of Verdi*, Oxford 1992

Burney, Charles: *Musical Tours of Europe*, London 1973

Carner, Mosco: *Puccini: A Critical Biography*, London 1976

Celletti, Rodolfo: *Le Grandi Voci*, Dizinario Critico-Biografico dei Cantanti, Rome 1964

Celletti, Rodolfo: *History of Bel Canto*, Oxford 1991

Chorley, Henry F.: *Thirty Years' Musical Recollections*, New York 1926

Clément, Cathérine: *Opera, or the Undoing of Women*, London 1989

Crutchfield, Will: 'Authenticity in Verdi: the Recorded Legacy', *Opera*, August 1985

Dahlhaus, Carl: *Realism in Nineteenth-Century Music*, Cambridge UK 1985

Diderot, Denis: *Paradox sur le comédien*, Paris 1981

Drake, James A.: *Richard Tucker*, New York 1984

Einstein, Alfred: *Greatness in Music*, London 1977

Enzensberger, Hans Magnus: *Einzelheiten I. Bewusstseins-Industrie*, Frankfurt am Main 1971

Enzensberger: *Mediocrity and Delusion*, London 1992

Gehlen, Arnold: *Die Seele im technischen Zeitalter*, Hamburg 1957

Gobbi, Tito: *My Life*, New York 1980

Gollancz, Victor: *Journey Towards Music: A Memoir*, New York 1965

Grove, George: *The New Grove Dictionary of Music and Musicians*, ed. Stanley Sadie, London 1980

Habermann, Günter: *Stimme und Sprache. Eine Einführung in ihre Funktion und Hygiene*, Munich 1978

Hahn, Reynaldo: *On Singers and Singing*, London 1990

Henderson, William James: *The Art of Singing*, New York 1938

Horowitz, Joseph: *Understanding Toscanini*, London 1987

Kaiser, Joachim: *Erlebte Musik*, Hamburg 1977

Kesting, Jürgen: *Die grossen Sänger*, 3 vols, Düsseldorf 1986

Kellogg, Clara Louise: *Memoirs of an American Prima Donna*, New York, 1978

Kolodin, Irving: *The Metropolitan Opera 1883–1966*, New York 1966

Kolodin: *The Opera Omnibus*, New York 1976

Lamperti, Giovanni Battista: *Vocal Wisdom*, New York 1957

Lauri-Volpi, Giacomo: *Voci Parallele*, Bologna 1977

Legge, Walter and Schwarzkopf, Elisabeth: *On and Off the Record*, London 1982

Martienssen-Lohmann, Franziska: *Der Wissende Sänger. Ein Gesangslexikon in Skizzen*, Zürich/Freiburg 1956

Martinelli, Giovanni: 'Singing Verdi', *Recorded Sound*, Summer 1962

Mayer, Hans: *Outsiders: A Study in Life and Letters*, Cambridge Mass. 1982

Mellers, Wilfrid: *Masks of Orpheus*, London 1987

Mellers, Wilfrid: *Music in the Making*, London 1980

Mordden, Ethan: *Demented: The World of the Opera Diva*, New York/Toronto 1984

Opera on Record: ed. Alan Blyth, London 1979, 1983, 1984

Pleasants, Henry: *The Great Singers*, New York 1981

Praz, Mario: *Romantic Agony*, Oxford 1970

Pugliese, Giuseppe: 'Verdi and Toscanini', *Opera*, July/August 1976

Rasponi, Lanfranco: *The Last Prima Donnas*, New York 1982

Rosen, David and Porter, Andrew (eds): *Verdi's* Macbeth – *a Source Book*, Cambridge UK 1984

Rosenberg, Wolf: *Die Krise der Gesangskunst*, Karlsruhe 1968

Rosenthal, Harold: *Two Centuries of Opera at Covent Garden*, London 1958

Sachs, Harvey: *Reflections on Toscanini*, London 1992

Saint-Saëns, Charles Camille: *Musical Memoirs*, Boston 1919

Sontag, Susan: *Against Interpretation*, London 1991

Schreiber, Ulrich: *Opernführer für Fortgeschrittene*, Kassel 1988

Steane, John: *The Grand Tradition: Seventy Years of Singing on Record*, London 1974

Stendhal: *Life of Rossini*, London 1970

Verdi, Giuseppe: *Letters*, London 1971

Wagner, Richard: *Stories and Essays*, London 1973

Wagner: *Briefe*. Ausgewählt, eingeleitet und kommentiert von Hanjo Kesting, Munich 1983

Weaver, William: 'Tullio Serafin', *Opera*, April 1968

Index

Opera houses are listed under their cities, e.g. Milan, La Scala